Eyewitness Accounts of the American Revolution

The Siege of Charleston

Capts. Johann Ewald, Johann Hinrichs, and Maj. Gen. Johann Christoph von Huyn

Translated and edited by Bernard A. Uhlendorf

The New York Times & Arno Press

THE SIEGE OF CHARLESTON

PLATE I

VIEW OF CHARLESTON IN 1776
Insert of Des Barres' map of Charleston harbor in the *Atlantic Neptune*

THE SIEGE OF CHARLESTON

With an Account of the Province of South Carolina:
Diaries and Letters of Hessian Officers
From the von Jungkenn Papers in the
William L. Clements Library

TRANSLATED AND EDITED

BY

BERNHARD A. UHLENDORF

ANN ARBOR
UNIVERSITY OF MICHIGAN PRESS
1938

PRINTED IN THE UNITED STATES OF AMERICA
BY THE CAYUGA PRESS · ITHACA · NEW YORK

TO THE MEMORY OF
WILLIAM LAWRENCE CLEMENTS

PREFACE

THE present volume contains all the primary sources relating to the siege of Charleston in the von Jungkenn Papers. The German text follows the original as closely as is typographically possible, except that periods or commas are occasionally substituted for dashes which quite definitely stand for periods or commas, while a few superfluous dashes are omitted.

The translation is as literal as can be, consistently with intelligibility and the broader aim of rendering both the sense and the spirit of the original. Proper names, which frequently appear in various guises, have been given correct forms whenever these could be positively ascertained. In all other instances the forms given in the manuscript have been questioned in the translation. The spelling of place names has been modernized, though eighteenth-century names no longer in use have been kept.

It is hoped that the notes will serve the needs of the historian and the layman as well. No attempt has been made to annotate the parts of the diaries dealing with the history of the Carolinas and Georgia, although they have been carefully checked against accounts available at the time of the Revolution.

It is a pleasure to acknowledge my indebtedness to Dr. William Warner Bishop, Librarian, Dr. Randolph G. Adams, Director of the Clements Library, and Professors Norman L. Willey, Hereward T. Price, Verner W. Crane, and Lieutenant Colonel F. C. Rogers, University of Michigan; to Miss Edna Vosper, of the National Archives; to Colonel Oliver L.

Spaulding, Jr., of the Army War College; to the editor of the University of Michigan Publications, Dr. Eugene S. Mc-Cartney, and to Miss Grace Potter, assistant editor. They have all given generously of their time.

B. A. U.

UNIVERSITY OF MICHIGAN

CONTENTS

ILLUSTRATIONS

(All illustrations are from originals in the William L. Clements Library.)

PLATES

MAPS

INTRODUCTION

INTRODUCTION

THE following letters and diaries are among the von Jungkenn Papers acquired by the William L. Clements Library in 1932. Until its acquisition by the Library this collection had remained in the possession of the family at Schloss Hüffe, Kreis Minden, Westphalia. It consists almost entirely of the letters and dispatches sent to Baron von Jungkenn (Minister of State for Hesse-Cassel, 1780–89) by the Hessian officers serving with the British in America during the Revolution. The collection begins with the first embarkation at Bremerhaven and continues until the final return to Germany in 1784. By far the greater part of the correspondence is of a semiofficial nature and is, therefore, free of the cold and formal tone of army paper work.

Since the Hessian officers had no great patriotic motives in subjugating the "rebels," their letters are less biased than those of the men with whom or under whom they fought. Their descriptions of the new country and its people are interesting and enlightening, and their remarks about the social and economic conditions frequently very discerning. Not a few of them envied the inhabitants of the New World and were in sympathy with their cause. Of the 16,992 men sent by Hesse-Cassel, 6,500 did not return. Many of these had deserted; many others received permission to remain in the country at the close of the war. Johnson contends that when Charleston was evacuated not a Hessian soldier went back save under compulsion.[1] They had learned to love the land and its people (by whom, as a rule, they were better liked than

[1] William Johnson, *Sketches of the Life and Correspondence of Nathanael Greene* (Charleston, 1822), II, 368.

the British)[1] and saw that they could live in much greater comfort among the Americans than they could in the Fatherland under petty princes.

*

*   *

Friedrich Christian Arnold, Baron von Jungkenn, Münzer von Mohrenstamm, the youngest son of the Colgenstein branch of the Jungkenn family, a very old family of the lesser German nobility, was born May 1, 1732, at Colgenstein.[2] At an early age Friedrich entered a Prussian infantry regiment commanded by one of his cousins, and was made an ensign at the age of twenty-one. In 1757 he became a second lieutenant in the regiment of the hereditary prince of Hesse-Cassel, who was then Prussian commandant of Wesel. Under Prince Friedrich he served in the campaigns of 1758, participating in the siege of Olmütz and in several minor battles in Bohemia and Silesia. Having the Prince for a patron prepared his way for a brilliant career. When in 1760 Prince Friedrich became Landgrave of Hesse-Cassel, von Jungkenn left the Prussian service and was commissioned captain in the First Hessian Guards, acting at the same time as third adjutant general to His Most Serene Highness. The following year he became a major, in 1764 a lieutenant colonel, and in 1766 a colonel. When the Landgrave was bargaining for terms with the agent of George III, whose aunt was Prince Friedrich's first wife, von Jungkenn, we find, was still with the regimental rank of colonel, though he held at the same time the court position of chamberlain. It is not surprising, therefore,

---

[1] Cf. Letter of George Washington, Feb. 5, 1777: "One thing I must remark in favor of the Hessians, and that is, that our people who have been prisoners generally agree that they received much kinder treatment from them than from the British officers and soldiers." See *The Writings of George Washington* (Bicentennial ed., Washington, 1931—), VII, 108.

[2] Fritz Herrmann, *Die Familie Jungkenn. . . . Als Manuscript gedruckt* (Oppenheim a. Rh., 1931).

that some of the higher officers address him as an equal, in
intimate terms. The year after the first Hessians arrived in
America von Jungkenn became a major general, and in 1779
he received a seat and the right to vote in the council of the
Landgrave. In 1780 he was made minister of state, succeeding
Baron Martin Ernst von Schlieffen, and the following year
was commissioned lieutenant general. In the little principality
of Hesse-Cassel the duties of a minister of war were performed
by the minister of state. Consequently, recommendations for
military advancement passed through von Jungkenn's hands.
How much the Landgrave valued his services as military
leader may be seen in a remark quoted by Mr. Herrmann:[1]
"If von Jungkenn should leave us—*alors adieu nos manoeuvres*."
After he had asked three times in vain to be permitted to retire, von Jungkenn's resignation was finally accepted in 1789,
whereupon he withdrew to Hüffe, a château which he had
acquired. He died there November 11, 1806.

That von Jungkenn was generally esteemed may be seen
from a contemporary account attributed to Friedrich Justin-
ian Günderode: "The youngest in years among the ministers
is General Jungkenn-Münzer—a most industrious worker,
which is proved by the fact that he conscientiously super-
intends the various departments entrusted to him, of which
the military is the most important. . . . He is highly esteemed,
is beloved by the Landgrave, the court, and the military, and
it is justly said of him that he willingly serves all those who
turn to him for help."[2]

*

* *

The first diary published here is not signed and might
have remained anonymous did not the diary of Captain von
Hinrichs furnish undeniable proof that it was written by

[1] *Ibid.*, p. 77.

[2] Quoted by Herrmann, *op. cit.*, p. 77, note 3, from *Briefe eines Reisenden
über den gegenwärtigen Zustand von Cassel* (1781), p. 206.

Johann Ewald, like Hinrichs a captain in the Jäger Corps. It will be seen from the facsimiles in this volume that it is not written in Ewald's own neat hand, as is the long journal-like letter preceding the diary.

Von Ewald's biography may be found in the *Allgemeine deutsche Biographie*[1] and in the *Dansk biografisk Lexikon*, which, however, is not necessarily an indication that he was a better officer than were the other men of whom this introduction treats. His being included may, perhaps, be attributed to the fact that Ewald wrote a number of books and treatises. He was born in Cassel in 1744. At the age of sixteen he entered the military service and took part in the last campaigns of the Seven Years' War. He lost his left eye in a duel in 1770. He studied military engineering at the Collegium Carolinum in Cassel under Jakob Mauvillon (1743–94), a well-known writer on economic theory and military science. (It is very probable that Captain Hinrichs, too, had studied under Mauvillon.) Upon publication of his booklet on military tactics[2] Ewald was made a captain of the Leibjäger. He sailed for America with the second contingent of Hessians, commanding the Second Company of jägers, and arrived at New Rochelle on October 22, 1776. The next day he was engaged by a force of enemy riflemen, and henceforth we find him and a little group of his devoted men always at some outpost reconnoitring and skirmishing. For his valor during the battle of Brandywine, where he and his jägers served with the advanced corps under Lord Cornwallis, the Landgrave rewarded him and Captain von Wreden with the *croix de l'ordre de la vertu militaire*, a great honor, for, according to Lowell,[3]

---

[1] Based on a biography by his son, Karl von Ewald, Copenhagen, 1838.

[2] *Gedanken eines hessischen Offiziers über das, was man bei Führung eines Detachements im Felde zu thun hat* (1774).

[3] Edward J. Lowell, *The Hessians and the Other German Auxiliaries of Great Britain in the Revolutionary War* (New York, 1884), p. 199.

this was the first time that officers of the rank of captain were thus distinguished. That his services were valued by Sir William Howe may be seen from a letter of appreciation the latter sent to him prior to leaving for England in 1778.[1] At the capitulation of Yorktown he was taken prisoner and paroled to Long Island, where he almost died of dysentery.

Upon his arrival in Cassel in May, 1784, he was promised a promotion as soon as a vacancy should occur. After waiting for four years in vain he entered the Danish service as a lieutenant colonel and commander of a jäger corps, which he was to reorganize along the lines of the famous Hessian corps that he had built up in America. Since he was elevated to the Danish nobility it may be assumed that his services were appreciated. In 1795 he became a colonel and in 1802 a major general. As the commander of a corps stationed in southern Holstein to uphold the neutrality of Denmark, he skirmished with the French under Murat and Soult. In 1807 he partook in the assault on Stralsund, whereupon he was made a lieutenant general. Though his body of troops was incorporated in the Eleventh French Army Corps when Napoleon set out for Russia, he and his command remained in Holstein. He died in 1813, after a brief illness. Von Liliencron speaks of him as a man of "keen intellect, great courage, and with a thoroughly honest, strictly military character."[2]

Besides the treatise mentioned above he published in 1785 his *Abhandlungen über den kleinen Krieg*, with a dedication to Frederick the Great. In this booklet he crystallized his experiences in the American Revolution, especially what he had learned about the use of infantry. Five years later appeared his *Abhandlungen vom Dienst der leichten Truppen* and

[1] Max von Eelking, *Die deutschen Hülfstruppen im nordamerikanischen Befreiungskrieg, 1776–1783* (Hannover, 1863), II, 8.

[2] *Allgemeine deutsche Biographie*, VI, 44. Von Liliencron's father was von Ewald's adjutant and constant companion from 1803 to 1813.

in 1794 the *Gespräche eines Husarencorporals, eines Jägers und leichten Soldaten*. His best-known work, a veritable source book for American Revolutionary history, appeared in three parts (1798, 1800, and 1803) under the title *Belehrungen über den Krieg, besonders über den kleinen Krieg, durch Beispiele grosser Helden und kluger und tapferer Männer*. Finally, in 1802, appeared his book entitled *Vom Dienst im Felde, für Unteroffiziere der Infanterie.* . . . . In addition to these published works there is in the von Jungkenn Papers a short unpublished tract: *Abhandlungen von dem was ein Officer von der Reuterey im Felde zu wissen nöthig hat.*

Captain von Ewald may not have had so many interests as Captain von Hinrichs had, but he was an excellent soldier and perhaps shows more critical acumen in his remarks.

*

*   *

Of Johann Hinrichs (or von Hinrichs), the author of the second and longest of the diaries published here, we know very little. He called himself an engineer.[1] When he arrived in America with the first contingent of Hessians, he was a lieutenant in the Jäger Corps, and early in 1778 was commissioned a captain. Von Eelking[2] gives the following biographical note: "Wounded several times, most severely after the occupation of New York, when a bullet penetrated his breast. In 1784 he was transferred to the infantry, but soon thereafter he entered the Prussian service. He was elevated to the nobility and advanced to the rank of lieutenant general. Died in 1834."

Further information must be gathered from his letters and diaries.[3] Apparently he joined the army to see America. He

---

[1] Cf. Introduction, p. 6.

[2] *Op. cit.*, II, 265–266.

[3] In addition to those published here see: "Abstracts from the Letter-Book of Captain Johann Hinrichs of the Hessian Jäger Corps, 1778–1780,"

wrote to Professor Schlözer in Göttingen in the fall of 1776:
"I should not be able to fulfill it yet [my promise to write to
you], if I were not spending a few weeks by myself as convalescent here in a most attractive region, back from the
noise of war, and as convalescent doing those things for
which, as you know, I became a soldier."

In his letters he appears hopeful and enthusiastic, intelli-
gent, honest, and frank. He was interested in everything, had
an astonishing insight into English, French, and American
politics and spoke discerningly of economic conditions in the
colonies. His education must have been good, for he knew
Latin and French as well as ancient and modern history. He
read books about America and came to the conclusion that
but few of the authors "have seen the shell, none the kernel."
He studied maps of the continent, and finding some to be inaccurate took pains to correct the mistakes. Wherever he
went he made sketches and drew maps and plans, not only for
himself, but also for his fellow officers and superiors. In one
letter he speaks of a large number of plans he was drawing for
Captain von Wreden, and in another of having to "perform
some extraordinary duty for Gen. Erskine . . . prior to his
return to England"—probably more sketches and plans.

Furthermore, he seems to have recorded his impressions
wherever he was. Thus he wrote to his brother: "I would
fain write you more from here [near Philadelphia], but of the
war I do not like to write, and of the country—well, I have
sent away all my manuscripts with the baggage which has
been put aboard of the ships this fortnight." Perhaps some

by Julius F. Sachse, in the *Pennsylvania Magazine of History and Biography*,
22 (1898), 137–170, and Hinrichs' letters in A. L. Schlözer's *Briefwechsel
meist historischen Inhalts* (Göttingen, 1780–82), which are translated in Roy
W. Pettengill's *Letters from America, 1776–1779* (Boston, 1924), pp. 172–190.
Though both Sachse's and Pettengill's translations are very literal, they
will be followed here nevertheless.

·day these memoranda, maps, and drawings will come to light and find their way to America. He also mentions writing several treatises and essays. "I am busy now," he says, "with a little essay, which is to contain the parts most necessary to the conduct of a war in one's own country, as applied to America . . . in which essay I am going to show what parts thereof America can draw from out herself, and what must be drawn from abroad." Later he records that this treatise is almost finished and that "according to its contents it is both political and military." Other essays dealt with the characteristics of the inhabitants of Pennsylvania, the contemporary state of learning in America, and the origin and progress of the war. Nor do these indicate all his interests. In the same letter in which he tells his brother that he is working on three of these treatises, he continues: "During my leisure hours I have composed quite a number of pieces:—English airs, marches and recitatives. This is my favorite recreation and I succeed fairly well therein. I now have a handsome piano."

He was engaged, moreover, in collecting objects to enrich the cabinet of a certain "celebrated Dr. Dolten," but lamented the fact that his baggage had been lost the previous winter and with it a lot of birds, "artistically and scientifically preserved." He also complained that someone had stolen the Indian hunting implements he had collected.

It seems that at one time Captain Hinrichs considered remaining in America, and, when his brother-in-law asked him about it, replied (Aug. 16, 1778): "That I should now leave the army is impossible. (1) Gratitude toward my master obliges me to stay. (2) It were frivolity since I have chosen this my calling and besides have been so fortunate that in less than two years I have been promoted to captain. . . . Moreover, (3) a French war is brewing now in which experienced officers of light troops will be wanted, and then, (4) circum-

stances in America are of such a nature that I know of no
employment which I might choose, unless I became a rebel.
Even though such were possible, I could not resolve leaving
the army. In consequence of these commotions all is in such
a chaotic condition that an agreeable life cannot be thought
of before the expiration of at least twenty years. The richest
loyalist runs the risk of becoming a beggar in case of a dis-
astrous issue. Unless something extraordinary should come
to pass, I shall assuredly not attempt it.''

Hinrichs participated in many battles and minor actions,
generally commanding the left wing of the Jäger Corps. He
was wounded several times and also suffered from a severe
attack of dysentery, from which he recovered but slowly.
Before Charleston he was almost constantly exposed to heavy
fire, usually in the most advanced trench. "If possible," he
wrote to Herr H . . . , Counselor of the Court, "conceal
from my mother the fact that I am now serving in front of
Charleston, until you hear of its capture, for there will be
some stubborn fighting." To his brother he wrote somewhat
later: "All that we have had to undergo in America hitherto
is nothing in comparison with the present. . . . Bullets are
whizzing around us thicker every day, thicker than the
powder and puff balls [do] around a coquette [when] at her
toilette [while] preparing herself for fresh conquests!"

As an officer Hinrichs seems to have been beloved by his
troops and respected by his superiors, who, he naïvely tells
us, always asked his advice, which, however, may have been
a matter of routine, since he was a staff officer. Once he was
detailed to carry dispatches through the enemy's lines, an
indication that his English must have been good. It was on
this occasion that he spent the night with Colonel Armand,
a French major of dragoons and commander of a battalion of
rebel volunteers.

The material for his journals was jotted down at odd

moments, for, as he tells us, he was usually out on duty with a patrol. After the siege of Charleston he engaged two scribes, one of whom, no doubt, wrote the clean copy of parts two to five of his diary.

*

*   *

The third diary was written by Johann Christoph von Huyn, major general in the infantry and commander of the Garnisons Regiment von Huyn. On the Charleston expedition he was in command of a brigade made up of his own and the Sixty-third and Sixty-fourth British Regiments. After the siege, though his regiment remained at Charleston, he returned to New York, suffering from consumption, and died there on July 25, 1780, in his sixtieth year.[1]

Of Major Philipp von Wurmb we know nothing except the little given by von Eelking.[2] When von Wurmb came to America he was serving with the infantry. In 1778 he was transferred to the Jäger Corps, but after the war he resumed his duties with the infantry. In 1806 he held the rank of major general and headed the Regiment von Wurmb. He died in 1808, having previously retired from active service. During the siege of Charleston he commanded a jäger detachment of two hundred and fifty men.

Even less is known of Wilhelm von Wilmowsky. He probably was the Captain von Wilmowsky of von Lengerke's Grenadier Battalion, who was detailed to staff duty as a major of brigade.[3]

*

*   *

Since the two longest diaries were written by captains in the Jäger Corps, a few remarks about this corps may not be

---

[1] Gaine's *New York Gazette*, July 31, 1780.   [2] *Op. cit.*, II, 264.
[3] J. G. Rosengarten's appendix to the English translation of von Eelking's work (cited p. 7, note 1), pp. 285, 290.

amiss. The name *Jäger* indicates that the men were generally recruited among the hunters, game wardens, and foresters, who were always expert marksmen. The English and the French called them "chasseurs," and sometimes the Germans too.[1] They were light troops, both foot and horse, and carried rifles. During several campaigns of the Revolutionary War some hundred were mounted. They wore green coats with crimson trim and were therefore called *Grünröcke*, "green-coats," by the British and the Americans.

One company came to America with Lieutenant General von Heister in August, 1776; a second, with Lieutenant General von Knyphausen in October of the same year. They were found so useful that, by special treaty with the Land-grave in December, 1777, the Hesse-Cassel jäger establishment was raised from the original 260 to 1,067. There were to be five companies, one of them mounted. "This augmentation," specifies the treaty,[2] "shall be composed only of experienced chasseurs, all well-trained marksmen; and if it is not possible to find the number demanded, of these skilful marksmen, His Majesty will content himself with a less number, rather than accept of men not having the dexterity requisite." His Majesty had to be content with a smaller force, for it is unlikely that the total ever exceeded seven hundred effective men.

In the summer of 1777 the entire Corps, consisting of Hesse-Cassel, Hesse-Hanau, and Anspach jägers, about six hundred in all, was put under the command of Lieutenant Colonel Ludwig Johann Anton von Wurmb. The jägers

---

[1] In addition to the jägers in this famous corps there were jägers or chasseurs serving with individual regiments. For the Charleston expedition 120 (200?) of these regimental chasseurs were formed into a company and put under Captain Hanger. His company should not be confused with the Jäger Corps (cf. von Huyn's diary and von Wurmb's letter).

[2] Almon's *Parliamentary Register*, Ser. 1, VI, 152–153.

generally operated in detachments rather than as a corps. These detachments were employed to great advantage in scouting and patrol duties, in guarding the general's staff when it went forth to reconnoitre and in covering headquarters. In column formation they usually formed the vanguard, and in a regular siege they occupied the front trenches, for their accurate fire was very effective in the enemy's embrasures. That the British were fully aware of what the jägers accomplished before Charleston may be seen in the following remarks of Captain Hinrichs to his brother: "Laughing eyes now beam upon us, and an incessant cheer is our reward, whenever a Briton sees the greencoats. . . . How gratifying are the expressions of gratitude when we feel that we have deserved them!" Similarly, he wrote to Herr H . . . , Counselor of the Court: "The English now praise us and everyone shouts 'hurrah!' when they see a jäger."

The journals of the two jäger captains are of special interest because the diarists usually served on opposite wings in the most advanced works. Thus their accounts supplement each other ideally. Besides, both observers were able to record with a good deal of accuracy what the enemy were doing. That the daily entries do not always agree on details is not at all surprising, for frequently the men had to wait some time for an opportunity to write. The fulness of Captain Hinrichs' diary may be accounted for in part by the fact that he was under instructions to keep the official journal of the Jäger Corps on this expedition.

The diary of Major General von Huyn in turn supplements the narratives of the two jäger captains, for von Huyn usually operated in a different sector of the front, the greater part of the time not on the Neck of Charleston but on the other side of the Ashley River.

The manuscripts were by no means difficult to transcribe. They are in a remarkable state of preservation, written on excellent (mostly gilt-edged) paper and with a good nut-gall ink that has browned but little.

It is obvious that the writers and copyists of these diaries came from the western part of central Germany and spoke the dialect of that region. This is particularly noticeable in their spelling of foreign names. The sentence structure is at times extremely complicated and the spelling in general, as might be expected, very irregular, for there was no standardized German orthography in the eighteenth century.

Captain von Ewald's diary, containing thirty rather small quarto pages, is a finely written copy, from what must have been a well-written original. The scribe wrote so small a hand that it is about equal to twelve-point type.

The diary of Captain Hinrichs is written on fifty folio pages and one hundred and twenty-nine quarto pages. The first part, which covers the voyage from New York to the North Edisto, was sent to Baron von Jungkenn on the day of landing. It must have been copied from a carefully written original, for there are no corrections whatever. It is in a very even, though somewhat extreme, eighteenth-century clerk's hand. The remaining four parts seem to have been written in the present form after von Hinrichs' return to the North. The copy before the scribe must have been less perfect, for there are some corrections by Hinrichs. At times the copyist seems to have been unable to figure out the words and so left blanks, which Hinrichs has filled in. Moreover, a few proper names have been inserted by an English hand. Thus we have on one page the name "Savage" neatly written in by this English hand while every other time it appears as "Savitsh." The last four parts are uniformly well written; the hand is beautiful, perhaps a schoolmaster's rather than a professional scribe's. It is impossible to determine the sources of Hin-

richs' historical digressions in the first part and in the Appendix, for his statements and misstatements may be found in many of the eighteenth-century writers on the Carolinas and Georgia. He obviously used English sources, which is borne out by the facts that the words "property and jurisdiction" occur twice after the German equivalents and that the marginal headings in the Appendix are given in English.

The diary of Major General von Huyn, written on eleven folio pages, probably was dictated to a scribe, who, apparently, was less well educated than the other copyists.

Ewald himself wrote a very neat, legible hand and, furthermore, left such beautiful margins that they seem almost a bit too luxurious for wartime. Hinrichs' hand is good and distinct, but rather ordinary. The letters of Major von Wurmb and of Wilhelm von Wilmowsky were written by the officers themselves. They show that both men were lacking in formal education.

*

*   *

When, in December, 1779, Sir Henry Clinton embarked for Charleston, the war had been in progress nearly five years without decided advantage to either side. The British held New York, and their operations in the North were confined to its environs. New England, the central provinces, and the Carolinas were in the possession of the Americans; but the strategic importance of their large holdings was minimized by the British occupation of Georgia, which had been overrun by Campbell and Prevost in the fall of 1778. The success in Georgia naturally encouraged further efforts in the South, and further efforts in the South required a seaport and a base from which to invade the Carolinas and, eventually, Virginia. Charleston was the largest seaport and most important city in the South and the most desirable base for operations in the Carolinas.

LETTER OF CAPTAIN JOHANN EWALD

RIGHT HONORABLE BARON,
ESPECIALLY HIGH AND MIGHTY GENERAL:—

Humbly I inform your Excellency that on the *19th of December* last year a corps of 7,000 men, consisting of all the grenadiers, light infantry, five English regiments, and several light corps, as well as 250 jägers under Major von Wurmb embarked at New York with his Excellency General Clinton and Lord Cornwallis. On the *23rd* the fleet left the wharf at New York. An exceptionally heavy flow of ice drove the ship on board of which were myself, Lieutenant von Wintzingerode, and fifty jägers upon reefs along the coast of Long Island, where she ran aground. However, the boats of the men-of-war immediately came to our assistance, and the detachment was distributed over other vessels in the best way possible. On the *26th*, Admiral Arbuthnot and his men-of-war having joined the transports at Sandy Hook on the same day, the fleet departed from the Hook in the following formation:

	Perseus frigate, 20 guns	
	Europe, 64 guns,	
	the Admiral's ship	
Roebuck, 44 guns	Principal Agent	*Romulus*, 44 guns
The transports with		Those with the
the English grenadiers		English light infantry
	2nd Agent	
Hessian generals'	Hessian	English generals'
ship	troops	ship

Robust. 74. C.		Defiance à 64. C.
Ordonnance	3te Agent	Ingenieurs
Schiff	Engl: Regtr.	
Renown	Provisions Schiffe.	Raisonnable
50. C	Provincial Corps	à 50. Canons
	4te Agent	
	Russell à 74 Canons.	

Der Lauff der Flotte wurde gegen Suden gewendet; wo man leicht vermuhten konnte, dass der Besuch auf Charlestown gemüntzet seye, um, wenn man von diesem Platz Meister ist, der Handell derer Sudlichen Provintzen mit denen Frantzosen unterbrochen ist, mit welchen Producten dieser Länder, die Rebellen jederzeit das nöhtige zu dem hiesigen Krieg an Franckreich bezahlt haben. Den 28^t fielen harte Stürme ein, welche die Flotte so zerstreüete, dass man oft in einigen Tagen nicht über 10 bis 20 Schiffe zehlen konnte, ohnerachtet solche aus 100 und etliche Seegell bestande. Diese Stürmische Witterung hielte bis den 20^t Ianuar: an, wodurch die Flotte bis in den 28 Grad Nord Breite und in die Länge bis in gleiche Linie mit denen Bermudas getrieben wurde, und wobey der Admiral genöhtigt war, Trouppen von verschiedenen Schiffen, welche durch den beständigen Sturm so hart beschädigt, in hoher See zu debarquiren und solche auf andere Fahrzeüge an Bord zu setzen. Die Flotte versam̄lete sich nach und nach, dass wir dann ohngeachtet d: 2^t Februar: in die Mündung das Savannah Flusses mit 62 Fahrzeügen glücklich einlieffen und bey Tybee Anckerten, wo wir auch den grösten Theil derer verschlagenen Schiffe schon vor Ancker fanden. Diejenigen Fahrzeüge, welche Pferde der Cavallerie und Artillerie an Bord hatten, waren genöhtigt den grösten Theil derer selben über Bord zu werffen, welches hier in diesen Ländern, wo die Plantachen sehr zerstreüet liegen, ein unersetzlicher Verlust ist. Dieses mag auch wohl die Ursache seyn, dass wir so weit aufs neüe in See gegangen synd, um so nahe wie möglich bey

Robust, 74 guns		*Defiance*, 64 guns
Ordnance	3rd Agent	Engineers
ship	English regiments	
Renown,	Provision ships	*Raisonnable*,
50 guns	Provincial corps	50 guns
	4th Agent	
	Russell, 74 guns	

The fleet directed its course southward, and we could well surmise that we were to pay a visit to Charleston. Once we are masters of it, the trade of the southern provinces with France will be interrupted, for it is with the products of these provinces that the rebels have been paying France for the necessities of this war. On the *28th* severe storms set in which scattered the fleet so widely that frequently we could not count over ten to twenty ships for several days, notwithstanding the fact that it numbered some hundred sail. The stormy weather continued till the *20th of January*, driving the fleet as far as the twenty-eighth degree north latitude and the longitude of the Bermudas. While on the open sea the Admiral was compelled several times to take troops from ships that had been badly damaged by constant storms and put them on board other vessels. Gradually the fleet assembled again. In spite of great adversity sixty-two vessels ran safely into the mouth of the Savannah River on the *2nd of February* and anchored at Tybee, where we found the greater number of the scattered ships already at anchor. The transports carrying the horses of the cavalry and artillery had been obliged to throw most of the horses overboard, an irreparable loss in these provinces where the plantations are far apart. Lack of horses probably was the reason for our putting to sea again in order that we might land as near as possible to Charleston.[1]

[1] The North Edisto had previously been agreed upon as the place of debarkation. See Arbuthnot's dispatch to the Lords Commissioners of the Admiralty, printed in various places, e.g. *Keith Papers*, I, 139–142 (*Publ. of the Navy Record Soc.*, Vol. 62).

Charlestown zu landen. *Den 9ᵗ* des Morgends verliess die Flotte, welche aus 35 Seegell bestand, den Ancker platz Tybee und nahmen den Cours Nord Ost und lieffen d: 11ᵗ gegen Mittag über die Bar, welche oft nur 14 fuss wasser hat, in die Mündung des Nord Edisto Fluss ein, wo wir Nachmittags nach 2 Uhr Ancker warffen. Die Mündung dieses Flusses bildet sich bey nahe in einen gantzen Zirckell, in welcher nur der Eingang vor zwey Schiffe bleibt. Die Uffer von diesem Fluss synd niedrig, sandigt und sumpficht. Wir erhielten so gleich die Befehle, fertig zu seyn, um zu debarquiren und auf zwey Tage Saltz Provision mit zu nehmen. Wir haben uns noch jederzeit mit der Hoffnung geschmeichelt, dass die, durch den Sturm, von der Flotte abgekoͤmene Schiffe, sich wieder einfinden würden, welche noch aus 6 Seegell, welche Truppen und Artillerie, an Bord haben, bestehen, unter welchem sich eines mit 19 Hessische und mit 11 Anspachische Jäger, benebst 100 Hessische Chasseurs befinden. Die Officiers der Marine vermuhten, da noch das Kriegs Schiff Defiance fehlet, dass solche unter dessen Bedeckung nach die Bermudas oder Westindien, da solche vieleicht durch den Sturm zu hart beschädigt wären, geseegelt seyen. Uberhaupt diejenige Truppen, welche noch fehlen, können sich auf 7 bis 800 Mann belauffen. *Den 12ᵗ* verliess die Flotte, welche aus 62 Seegell bestand, indem heüt verschiedene Fahrzeüge zur Flotte ankamen, ihren Ancker Grund, und wählte nicht weit von ersteren, einen andern, worauf die gantze Armee so gleich nach dem gegebenen Signal auf Simsons Eyland (die aüsserste Spitze von Iohns Eyland wozu auch dieses gerechnet wird) debarquirte. Gegen Mittag war die gantze Armee, (ausser allem Geschütz und der Bagage) an Land, worauf so gleich marschirt und bey Simson Plantache gegen Abend posten gefasst wurde. Den 13ᵗ und 14ᵗ

---

[1] The latter is the ill-fated transport *Anna*, which was taken in tow by the *Renown* soon after sailing from New York. It had on board, under the

On the morning of the *9th* the fleet, consisting of thirty-five sail, left its place of anchorage at Tybee. Our course was northeast, and toward noon of the *11th* we crossed the Bar, which often has only fourteen feet of water, and put into the mouth of the North Edisto River, where we cast anchor a little after two o'clock. The mouth of this river forms almost a complete circle, leaving an inlet wide enough for only two ships. The banks of the river are low, sandy, and marshy. We immediately received orders to be ready to disembark and to take along two days' salt provisions. We have all this time been flattering ourselves with the hope that the ships which were separated from the fleet in the storm would join us again. Six sail with troops and artillery on board are still missing, one of them with nineteen Hessian jägers, eleven Anspach jägers, and one hundred Hessian chasseurs.[1] Since the *Defiance* man-of-war is also missing, the officers of the navy suppose that the missing ships have gone to the Bermudas or the West Indies under her convoy, as it is likely they suffered considerable damage in the storm. The troops still missing number perhaps 700 to 800 men. On the *12th* the fleet, consisting of sixty-two sail, some craft having joined us today, left its place of anchorage for another one near by, after which the entire army, at a given signal, disembarked on Simmons Island (the extreme point of Johns Island, of which it is a part). By noon the whole army (except artillery and baggage) had landed, whereupon we set out to march, taking post at Simmons' plantation toward evening. On the *13th* and *14th* all the light troops were advanced as far as the

---

command of Captain the Hon. George Hanger, later Lord Coleraine, a company of jägers (chasseurs) drawn from the several German regiments (see p. 13, note 1). Eventually the cable snapped, and the *Anna* drifted to England, as we hear at the very end of Hinrichs' diary (cf. Lowell, *op. cit.*, pp. 243–244, and von Eelking, *op. cit.*, II, 63–64, where a gruesome story is told about the fate of the crew and the soldiers).

musten die saṁtlichen leichten Truppen biss an das rechte Uffer des Stono flusses vorrücken, um von denen Uberfahrten Besitz zu nehmen. Die leichte Infant: bey Fennings und Chesum Hauss, und das 33ᵗ regt: benebst dem Detachement Jäger unter dem Major v.Wurmb bey Stono Ferry, wo wir, bey dem recognosciren des Generalitat, mit dem gewesenen Pulawskischen Corps, ohne Blutvergiessen, eine viertel stunde Scharmutzirten. *Den 16ᵗ* passirte die leichte Infant: den Stono fluss, welchen die feinde verliessen, bey White Hauss und das 33ᵗ regt: benebst denen Jägers, zu Stono Ferry, wo das 7ᵗ und 23ᵗ regt: zu uns stiess und der hl. General Lesle diesse drey Brigaden, nachdem von denen alten Redouten Position gefast wurde, commandirte. Die Armee war in dieser Zeit biss Gibsons Hauss an den Stono fluss vorgerückt. *Den 27ᵗ* gieng die leichte Infanterie vom Iohns Eyland auf Iames Eyland bey Fennigs Hauss über, welchen die Armee den 28ᵗ folgte. An eben diesem Tag marschirte das Webstersche Corps, (da der h: Oberst Webster den hl: General Lesle hier ablösete) zurück nach Iohns Eyland, und wurden nur ein Capit: und 100 Mann in erwehnten alten redouten zu Stono Ferry zurückgelassen. Da das Geschütz und Munition durch Hülffe kleiner fahrzeüge über 30 Engl: Meilen weit den Stono fluss aufwärts muss geführt werden; so gieng dieses sehr langsam zu. Da wir aber nunmehro von Iames Eyland Meister synd und zwey 40 Canonen Schiffe unter einem heftigen feüer von denen feindlichen Fahrzeügen, (welche aus 6 Fregatten und 10 Galleeren bestehen und Sulivanns Eyland, welches sehr gut befestigt, so wie auch Charlestown von der wasser Seite decken) die Bar von Charlestown passirt haben; so hoffe ich, dass bald zum Hauptwerck wird geschritten werden. Nach der Land Seite soll die Stadt sehr gut bevestigt seyn und die rebellen haben ein tieffes Canal zur Vereinigung des Ashley und Cooper flusses gezogen. Die Garnisoll [*sic*] soll 3 bis 4,000 Mann starck seyn, und der General Lincoln stehet mit einem

right bank of the Stono River to occupy the ferries, the light infantry moving to Fenwick's and Chisholm's houses, and the 33rd Regiment and the detachment of jägers under Major von Wurmb to Stono Ferry. While covering the General's staff on an excursion of reconnoissance we skirmished for a quarter of an hour with Pulaski's Corps without bloodshed. On the *16th* the light infantry crossed the Stono at White's house [1] (the enemy abandoning the river), and the 33rd Regiment and the jägers at Stono Ferry, where the 7th and 23rd Regiments joined us. After occupying the old redoubts, the Honorable General Leslie took command of these three brigades. The army had in the meantime advanced to Gibbes' house on the Stono River. On the *27th* the light infantry crossed at Fenwick's house from Johns Island to James Island, the rest of the army following on the *28th*. On the same day Webster's corps (Colonel Webster had relieved General Leslie as commander) withdrew to Johns Island, leaving only a captain with a hundred men in the old redoubts at Stono Ferry. Since artillery and munitions have to be brought up the Stono River by means of small vessels for a distance of more than thirty English miles, considerable time was consumed. Now that we are masters of James Island, and two 40-gun ships have crossed the Bar of Charleston under a heavy fire from the enemy's vessels (six frigates and ten galleys covering both Sullivan Island, which is strongly fortified, and Charleston on the water side), I hope that we shall soon proceed to our principal task. On the land side the city is said to be very well fortified. The rebels have dug a deep canal uniting the Ashley with the Cooper River. The garrison is said to be 3,000 to 4,000 men strong, and General Lincoln with an observation corps is posted behind the swamps of

[1] White's house is probably the same as the Abraham Watt house mentioned by Hinrichs, p. 187.

Observations Corps hinter denen Morästen von Poan Poan, 16 Engl: Meilen von Charlestown. Die Feinde reden von einer Vertheidigung biss auf das äüsserste; allein ich vermuhte, da es oben offen ist, dass sie anders Sinnes werden werden.

Derjenige Theil, welchen ich bisshero von Sud Carolina gesehen habe; könte nicht rühmen. Das Land ist Marsch Grund, gantz eben und mit morastigen flüssen sehr durchschnitten, in welchen man Crocodills von sechszehn fuss; so bald es etwas wärmer wird, findet so wie die unwegsahmen Gehöltze voll von Wölffen und verschiedenen Arten vergifteter Schlangen, synd. Die Plantachen liegen 5 bis 6 Meilen aus einander und Indigo, Baumwolle und Reiss synd die Producte derer selben. Die Eigenthümer dererselben synd sämtlich nach der Stadt geflüchtet. Ich werde nicht ermangeln von der ferneren Eroberung der Stadt, Eüer Hochwohlgebohrnen schuldigste Nachricht zu geben, wobey ich aber zugleich unterthänigst um Verzeihung bitte, wenn ich solches nicht mit der gehörigen Nettigkeit, da es an allem fehlt, im stande zu thun bin.

Ich befehle mich zu Eüer Hochwohlgebohrnen ferneren gnädigen Andencken und Wohlgewogenheit und beharre in tiefster Erfurcht.

Euer Hochwohlgebohrner Frey Herrn
unterthänigster
J Ewald

Iohns Eyland
am Stono fluss bey
William Archel plantache
d: 29ᵗ Februar.
1780.

Ponpon,[1] sixteen English miles from Charleston. The enemy are speaking of defending the city to the last extremity. However, since it is open on top, I suppose they will change their minds.

I cannot say very much in favor of the part of Carolina that I have seen so far. It is marshland, very level, and cut up by swampy rivers, in which, as soon as it turns a little warmer, may be seen crocodiles sixteen feet long. The impassable woods are full of wolves and several species of venomous snakes. The plantations are situated five to six miles apart. They produce indigo, cotton, and rice. The owners have all fled to the city. I shall not fail to give your Lordship further news concerning the reduction of the city, at the same time humbly asking your forgiveness if I am unable to do this with proper neatness, since we are lacking in everything.

I commend myself to your Lordship's further kind remembrance and benevolence and remain in deepest reverence,

Right Honorable Lord,
your humble
J. Ewald

Johns Island
on the Stono River
William Archel's plantation[2]
February 29
1780

[1] It was not General Lincoln but General Moultrie who commanded this outpost. Lincoln had his headquarters in the city.

[2] The editor has been unable to identify this plantation. Though it might have belonged to William Ashley, it certainly is not the plantation where he lived.

KURTZE BESCHREIBUNG
der
EXPEDITION NACH CHARTESTOWN [*sic*]
und derselben Belagerung,
vom 28ten Mart:
bis zum 19ten Iunij 1780. als der erfolgten
DEBARQUIRUNG
auf
STATEN–EILAND.

Mart:
28ten Da heute Abends der General Patterson mit seinem Corps, sich mit der Armée bey Trydons-Hauss vereinigte, und eine Anzahl Flatt-boats benebst 2. bewafneten, durch Stono-Inlet bis in die Mündung des Wappau-Criques angeken [= angekommen] war, so erhielte die ganze Armée den Befehl sich auf den ersten Wink marchfertig zu halten.

29ten Mit Anbruch des Tages legten sich beyde bewafnete Boats benebst einer Anzahl Flatt- und Wahl boats längst dem rechten Ufer des Ashley-Flusses bey Trydons Hauss, um die Truppen einzunehmen, in die gehörige Ordnung. Die Armée brach sogleich auf, und bestieg nach 6 Uhr in folgender Ordnung die ihr angewiesene Boots, wobey Capit: Tomkin, das Embarquement und Capt: Elphingston die Landung führte: 1) leichte Infant: 2. Bataill: unter Gen. Leslie. 2) Detachement Iäger unter dem Major v: Wurmb, 3) Hessische Grenad: 4. Bataill: Gener: Cospoth, 4) 2 Bataill: Engl: Grenads. 5) das 7te und 23te Regt, Obrist Clarck, 6) das 33te und 1^t Regt, Colon: Webster, 7) 1. Esquad: von 7-Dragon: Regt. Alles unter Comãndo des Lord Cornwallis.

SHORT DESCRIPTION
OF THE
EXPEDITION TO CHARLESTON
AND THE SIEGE OF THE CITY
MARCH 28 TO JUNE 19, 1780
AND THE SUBSEQUENT
DISEMBARKATION
ON
STATEN ISLAND

Since General Paterson with his corps had joined the army March 28 at Drayton's house this evening and a number of flatboats and two armed ships had arrived by way of Stono Inlet at the mouth of the Wappoo Creek, the entire army received orders to be ready to march at a moment's notice.

At daybreak the two armed ships and a number of flat- 29 boats and whaleboats drew up along the right bank of the Ashley River near Drayton's house to take in the troops in their proper order. The army broke camp, and at six o'clock the troops boarded the boats in the following order: (1) two battalions of light infantry under General Leslie; (2) the jäger detachment under Major von Wurmb; (3) four battalions of Hessian grenadiers, General Kospoth; (4) two battalions of English grenadiers; (5) the 7th and 23rd Regiments, Colonel Clarke; (6) the 33rd and 1st[1] Regiments, Colonel Webster; (7) one troop of the 7th Dragoon Regiment—all of these under the command of Lord Cornwallis. Captain

[1] Should read "71st," an error of the copyist, no doubt.

Um 7 Uhr stiessen die Flatt-boats ab, und um 8 Uhr bestiegen schon, die leichte Infant: und Iäger das linke Ufer des Flusses bey Benjamin Fullers Hauss 1½ Meile höher als Trydons Hauss, wo der Fluss einen doppelten Bogen macht, und wo das Ufer fest und erhaben liegt. Welche Gegend der Nuck genennet wird, und 14. Meilen von Charlestown entfernet ist. Wir wurden einen Trupp feindl: Dragoner gewahr, mit welchem ich da mich der Major Wurmb mit 20 Jägern eine halbe Meile vorwärts detachiret, um auf einer Anhöhe Posto zu fassen, charmutzierte, worauf sich selbige zurük zogen. Gegen Mittag hatte die gantze Armée den Fluss passirt, und war in der Form eines halben Mondes aufmarchirt, jedoch ohne Geschütz und Equipage, ausser denen 4. leichten Feld-Stüken der leichten Infanterie.—Um Mittag sezte sich die Armée in March, gerade nach der grossen Strasse, wo solche, nachdem man 8. Meilen marchiret, eine Meile auf den Höhen von dem Quater-Hauss, 6 Meilen von der Stadt, ein Lager bezoge, welches die Form eines 3-Eks hatte, von welchem die Passis der Ashley Fluss war. Wir trafen auf unsern March, wo die Iäger die Avant-Garde der Armée machten, nur eine kleine feindl: Partey an, welche aber imer ausser dem Büchssen-Schuss der Iäger blieb. Der General Pattersohn hatte unterdessen, mit seinem Corps welches durch das Haynisch: Regt verstärkt worden, auf Iaimes Eiland, in dem Retranchement bey Hutsons Hauss, und in den Redouten auf Feñings-Point, und bey Leñings Hauss, Posto gefast, um die Comunication zwischen der Armée, und den Transport-Schiffen, so im Stono Fluss lagen, zu deken. Die Nacht war gantz ruhig, und wir hörten und sahen nichts vom Feinde. Während dieser Landung hatte Colonel Tarlton, mit 200 Pferden, eine Partey gegen Dorchester gemacht, um Vieh und Gefangne zu holen, allein der Obriste Wassington hatte sich auf erhaltene Nachricht

[1] Captain Tonken (called Tomkin by Ewald, and Tomkins by Hinrichs) is Captain Thomas Tonken, who was one of the four agents for transports

Tonken[1] superintended the embarkation, Captain Elphinstone
the landing.

At seven o'clock the flatboats put off, and at eight o'clock
the light infantry and the jägers landed on the left bank of
the river at Benjamin Fuller's house, one and one-half miles
above Drayton's house, where the river makes a double bend
and the bank is firm and high. This part is called the Neck
and is fourteen miles from Charleston. Major von Wurmb
detached me with twenty jägers to take post on some rising
ground half a mile in advance, where I saw a troop of dragoons. I engaged them and they withdrew. By noon the entire
army had crossed the river and taken post in the shape of a
crescent, but without guns and equipage except the four light
fieldpieces of the light infantry. At noon the army set out to
march along the highway. After eight miles they went into
camp on the heights one mile from the Quarter-House and six
miles from the city. The encampment was in the form of a
triangle, with the Ashley River as the base. On our march,
during which the jägers formed the vanguard, we encountered
only one small hostile party, which, however, did not come
within range of our rifles. In the meantime General Paterson
and his corps, reinforced by Huyn's Regiment, had proceeded
to James Island and taken post in the trenches at Hutson's
house, and in the redoubts on Fenwick's Point and at
Linning's house, in order to cover the communication between
the army and the transports which lay in the Stono River.
The night was very quiet, and we saw and heard nothing of
the enemy. While we were landing, Colonel Tarleton with
two hundred horse advanced toward Dorchester to bring in
livestock and prisoners. But Colonel Washington, having

under Admiral Arbuthnot, perhaps the "principal agent" mentioned in
Ewald's letter, p. 21 (*Keith Papers*, I, 145, 175).

von unserer Bewegung über den Ashley Fluss bey Paquens bridge retriret.

Den 30ᵗᵉⁿ
Mart

In der vergangenen Nacht hatte man die Hessischen Regts Stüke, 2. 12 ttor und 2. 6 ttor benebst der Bagage der Armée bey Ashley-Ferry übergesezt, welche des Morgens zur Armée kañen. Gegen 9. Uhr Morgens sezte sich die gantze Armée in March. Die Iäger machten die Avant-Garde, welcher die Engl: und Hessischen Grenadiers, und die übrigen folgten. Die Armée marchirte die grosse Strasse, wo der General en Chef auf dem Gouverneurs Hausse 4. Meilen von Charlestown die Ufer des Cooper-Flusses recognoscirte, wobey ich selbigen mit 12. Iägern dekte. Wir hatten kaum das Gouverneurs Hauss eine Meile zurük gelegt, so stiess die Avant-Garde unter dem Capit: v: Bodungen auf eine feindliche Partey von 300 Mann, welche aus der Stadt gekoñen waren, uns zu recognosciren. Der General en Chef, welcher mit seinem gantzen Gefolge, der Avant-Garde folgte, wurde so warm empfangen, dass nahe bey selbigen der ObristLt: Earl Cadmus hart verwundet ward. Der Major v: Wurmb unterstützte sogleich mit den übrigen Iägern die Avant-Garde, wodurch wir die Feinde in eine 2 Engl: Meilen von ihren Werken entfernte, an der Strasse gelegene kleine Flesche zurük trieben. Die Gegend macht hier ein Defilée wodurch ein Morast gehet, und beyde Höhen trennt. Der Befehl des coñandirenden Generals war diesseits des Defilées halt zu machen, weil man dachte, diese Partey währender Nacht zu coupiren. Zu welchem Ende eine Compag: leichter Infant: zu Unterstützung der Iäger vorrükte. Wir charmutzirten einige Stunden mit dem Feind, welcher, nachdem er einige Scheuren im Felde verbrannt hatte, sich retirirte. Capit: v: Bodungen besezte sogleich die Flesche mit der Avant-Garde. Kaum aber erhielt der Major v Wurmb den Befehl diesen Posten nicht zu behaupten, so näherte sich ein feindliches Coñando mit 2

received intelligence of our movements, had withdrawn across the Ashley River near Bacon's bridge.

Last night the Hessian regimental pieces, two 12-pounders, March 30 and two 6-pounders, as well as the baggage of the army, were brought over at Ashley Ferry and in the morning conveyed into camp. Toward nine o'clock the entire army set out to march along the highway. The jägers made up the vanguard and were followed by the English and Hessian grenadiers and the rest of the troops. From the Governor's house, four miles from Charleston, the Commanding General reconnoitred the banks of the Cooper River. I with twelve jägers formed his guard. We had hardly advanced one mile beyond the Governor's house when the vanguard under Captain von Bodungen encountered an enemy party of three hundred men who had come from the city to reconnoitre. The Commanding General, who with his entire suite was following the vanguard, got such a warm reception that Lieutenant Colonel the Earl of Caithness, who was very close to him, was severely wounded. Major von Wurmb with the rest of the jägers immediately supported the vanguard and forced the enemy to retire into a small flèche situated on the highway two miles from their works. The country here forms a defile which is traversed by a swamp that intersects the higher ground. Hoping to cut off this party during the night, the Commanding General gave orders to halt this side of the defile. A company of light infantry advanced to the support of the jägers. For several hours we skirmished with the enemy, who retired after burning a few barns in the fields. Captain von Bodungen with the vanguard immediately occupied the flèche. Just after Major von Wurmb had received orders not to maintain this post and Captain von Bodungen and Lieuten-

Feld-Stüken, welches die Flesche, nachdem sich Capt: v:
Bodungen und Lieut: Schæfer als Iäger Offrs gehalten hatten,
wieder einnahm, bey Erblikung unserer Stüke auf der grossen
Strasse aber, solche gleich wieder verliess. Wir hatten 1. ver-
missten, 1. hart, und 1. leicht verwundeten Iäger. Ich vermuthe,
dass die Rebellen, uns durch diesen Streich, unter ihre Canons
loken wollten. Unser General war über das gantze, was die
Jäger heute gethan hatten, sehr zufrieden. Gegen Abend
wurden die Iäger, durch die leichte Infant: abgelösst, welche
ihren Posten in dieser Gegend hielten. Die Armée lagerte sich
bey dem Gouvern: Hausse, so dass der rechte Flügel nicht
weit von dem Ashley Fluss, und der linke nahe an den
Cooper-Fluss zu stehen kam. Die Iäger erhielten ihren Posten
bey Gibsons Hauss, wo ich mein Piquet in einem der ange-
nehmsten Lust-Gärten von der Welt erhielte. Das Detachement hatte den rechten Flügel an Gibsons-Crique gestützt,
und allinirte mit der leichten Infanterie. Eine halbe Meile von
diesem Hausse, nach dem linken-Ufer des Ashley Flusses, ist
eine Ferry, wo durch Hülfe einiger Criques man bis eine
Viertelmeile nach dieser Plantage kom̃en kann. Der Colon:
Webster, stand mit dem 33ten und 71te Regt: zwischen dem
Gouverneur und dem Quater Hauss, und dekte den Rüken
der Armée.

Mart: Diese Nacht war sehr ruhig, ohngeachtet die feindl: Vorpo-
31.   sten, nur 600 Schritte von den unsrigen standen, welche sich
aber mit Tages Anbruch retirirten. Gegen 9 Uhr Morgens
muste ich, damit die Generalitæt recognosciren konnte, mit
dem Piquet, durch das vor Gibsons Hauss gelegene Holz, und
Morast längst dem linken Ufer des Ashley-Flusses vorrüken.
Jch poussirte meine Partey glüklich, bis and die Däm̃e über
den Blak-Crique welche unter den feindl: Canonen liegen,
wobey der Feind mich mit 3 Stük-Schüssen beehrte. Das
Piquet wurde in das Holz bey Gibsons Neger Häussern
placirt. Heute wurde ich gewahr, dass der Major Montcrief

ant Schaefer of the Jägers had therefore deserted it, an enemy detachment approached with two fieldpieces and reoccupied the flèche. However, at the sight of our pieces on the highway they immediately withdrew from it. We had one jäger missing, one severely wounded, and one slightly wounded.[1] The rebels presumably executed this move to lure us within range of their guns. Our general was very much pleased with all the jägers did this day. Toward evening the jägers were relieved by the light infantry which had been stationed near by. The army encamped near the Governor's house, with the right wing not far from the Ashley River and the left wing near the Cooper. The jägers were posted at Gibbes' house, where I did picket duty in one of the most beautiful pleasure gardens of the world. The right wing of our detachment rested upon Gibbes' Creek and was in a line with the light infantry. Half a mile from the house there is a ferry on the Ashley River from which, making use of several creeks, one can get by boat to within a quarter of a mile of this plantation. Colonel Webster with the 33rd and 71st Regiments was stationed between the Governor's and the Quarter-House, covering the rear of the army.

This night was very quiet, in spite of the fact that our March 31 advance posts were only six hundred paces from the enemy outposts. At daybreak the hostile pickets withdrew. Toward nine o'clock in the morning I was ordered to advance with my picket through the wood in front of Gibbes' house and through the swamp on the left bank of the Ashley River, so that the General's staff could reconnoitre. I pushed my party without mishap as far as the dams across Black Creek, which are within range of the enemy's cannon, and was honored with three shots. The picket was posted in the wood close to Gibbes' Negro houses. Today I found out that Major Moncrieff, who had already been here during the expedition

[1] For a detailed statement of the fatalities on the American side see p. 51.

welcher schon bey der Expedition des Gen: Prevot hier gewesen, sich sehr geirret hatte. Denn hätte dieser gestern den Anschlag gegeben, während dem Charmützel, eine Partey über Gibsons Hauss zu schiken, so konnte man die Rebellen, die sich soweit vom ihren Linien entfernet hatten coupiren, oder wenigsten Flanquiren. So viel ich sehen konnte, so waren die feindl: Werke in Form eines halben Mondes erbauet, und zählte 57. Embrassures. Die Front ist durch einen droknen Graben und Verhak gedekt, vor welchem in einer Entfernung von 50 Schritten ein Canal mit noch einem Verhak befindlich ist. Hinter diesen Werken sahe ich ein höheres von 2 Bastionen, und 1. Courtine hervor ragen, wo sich auf den beyden Fassen 3 Embrassuren presentiren. Dieses Werk soll auch einen breiten drokenen Graben haben, und wird das alte Königswerk genennt.

April D. 1te   Seit gestern und heute, hat man sich beschäftiget, schwer Geschütz, Munition, Schanzzeug, Schanz-Körbe, Faschinen und Provision von Lennings-Crique nach Gibsons Ferry über den Ashley Fluss anhero zu führen, auch ist die Gegend von Gibsons Hauss zum Parc und Depot der Belagerung, und das Treibhaus zum Laboratorio gewählet worden. Der Ingenieur Montcrief hat heute in der Nachbarschaft, alle die von Holz aufgerichtete Häusser abbrechen lassen, aus welchen derselbe eine Art Mantelets, 6 Fuss hoch und 14 Fuss lang mit 3 Füssen, von Bretern und Balken verfertigen lässt, aus welchen man die innere Seite der Batterien, und Redouten, so wie auch die Baken der Embrassuren erbauen kann. 18 Mann werden zu Tragung auf jedes gerechnet. Hierdurch werden Stroh-Seile und Faschinen ersparet; Wie sie der Ingenieur sezt, so ist auch gleich die Form der Batterie oder Redoute fertig, und die Arbeiter dürfen nur die Erde aus dem Graben gegen solche werfen. Diese Erfindung, macht seinem Erfinder Ehre, vornemlich sind sie hier in dem sandigen Boden sehr nützlich. In vergangener Nacht, hatte Maj: Montcrief die feindl:

of General Prevost, had made a grave mistake. For had he yesterday suggested that a party be sent by way of Gibbes' house during the skirmishing, the rebels who had proceeded so far beyond their lines could have been cut off or at least flanked. So far as I could make out, the enemy's works were built in the form of a crescent and numbered fifty-seven embrasures. The front is covered by a dry ditch and an abatis, fifty feet in front of which is a wet ditch with another abatis. Behind these works I saw a higher one consisting of two bastions and a curtain, the two faces of which presented three embrasures each. This work, called the old royal work, is said to have a broad dry ditch also.

Yesterday as well as today we have been engaged in bring- April 1 ing heavy pieces, munitions, entrenching tools, gabions, fascines, and provisions from Linning's Creek over the Ashley River to Gibbes' Ferry. The country around Gibbes' house has been made a park and depot for the siege, and the greenhouse a laboratory. Major Moncrieff of the Engineers had all the wooden houses in the neighborhood torn down today. From the boards and beams of these he had his men make mantelets[1] to be used in building the inner side of the batteries and redoubts and also the cheeks of the embrasures. These mantelets are six feet high and fourteen long and have three legs. It takes eighteen men to carry one of them. They are a great saving in straw ropes and fascines. Just as soon as the engineers set them down the form of the battery or redoubt is finished and the workmen need only throw the earth from the trenches against it. This invention does honor to the inventor. They are especially useful here in this sandy soil. Last night Major Moncrieff reconnoitred the enemy's works,

---

[1] Captain Hinrichs says that the mantelets had been made in New York and were merely assembled here (p. 231). Cf. letter of Sir A. S. Hamond to Captain Elphinstone, March 26, 1780 (five days before Hinrichs' entry): "The *Fame* with the Engineers' timber is on her way" (*Keith Papers*, I, 154).

Werke recognosciret, und sich bis an die feindl: Graben
geschlichen, demohngeachtet in der Weite oder Anlage, weil
er die Belagerung zu sehr auf die leichte Schulder nimt, wie
die Folge gelehret hat, sehr geirret.

April
2ten

Gestern Abend wurden 1500 Arbeiter von der Armée comandiret, zu deren Bedekung der Obriste Abercramby mit der
leichten Infanterie, und der Obristlt: Webster, und v Linsing
mit 500 Mann zur Reserve dienten. Der Place d'armes vor die
Bedekung und Arbeiter, wurde auf der grossen Strasse von
Dorchester nach Charlestown bestimt, wo sie der Weg nach
Gibsons Hauss durchschneidet. Es wurden 3 Redouten in der
Entfernung auf 600 Schritte von denen feindl: Werken angelegt. Allein in der Folge wird man sehen, dass solche beynahe
100 Yard weiter von dem Feind entfernet waren. Die gantze
Arbeit bestand, aus einer Redoute zur rechten 40 Yards,
ohngefehr 200 Schritte von dieser zur linken war eine Redoute
von eben solcher Grösse, und in einer etwas grösseren Entfernung eine von 80 Yards angelegt. Zur Comunication, oder
besser zu sagen zur 1ten Paralelle diente ein Feldgraben 3 Fuss
tief, welchen die Rebellen zuzuwerffen, vergessen hatten. Der
Umfang der gantzen Arbeit wird ohngefehr 600 Yards
ausmachen. Die Rebellen thaten die gantze Nacht hindurch
ohngefehr 12 Stük-Schüsse. Man beschäftigte sich den gantzen
Tag über, um das Nothwendige von jenem Ufer des Ashley-
Flusses anhero zu bringen, welches sehr langsam von statten
gehet, indem das schwere Geschütz, Munition und Provision
von dem rechten bis zum linken Ufer des Flusses durch Boats,
und von Gibsons-Ferry bis zur Niederlage durch Negers mit
vieler Beschwerlichkeit muste geführet werden. Gegen 12
Uhr Mittags, waren doch schon 5.24 ttor, und 2.6 zöllige
Mörser im Parc. Man arbeitete stark an Mantelets à la
Montcrief, um in künftiger Nacht die 1te Paralelle in Stand
zu bringen. Das schwere Geschütz zu dieser Belagerung,
wurde von dem Kriegs Schif Reasonabel pr 54 Canonen, unter

creeping right up to their ditches. Nevertheless, he was greatly mistaken either in their extent or in their layout, as was subsequently seen. He is taking the siege too lightly.

Yesterday evening one thousand five hundred workmen April 2 were detailed from the army. They were covered by Colonel Abercrombie with the light infantry and by Lieutenant Colonels Webster and von Linsing with five hundred as a reserve. The *place d'armes* for the guard and the working parties was to be on the highway from Dorchester to Charleston, where the road to Gibbes' house intersects it. Three redoubts were raised at a distance of six hundred paces from the enemy's works. But, as will appear later, they were almost a hundred yards farther than they thought. Our whole work consisted of a redoubt of forty yards at the right, another of the same size approximately two hundred paces to the left of it, and, at a somewhat greater distance, one of eighty yards. A ditch three feet deep, which the rebels had neglected to fill up, served as a communication, or rather as the first parallel. The entire work stretched over approximately six hundred yards. The rebels fired about twelve cannon shots during the whole night. The day was taken up in bringing over necessities from the other bank of the Ashley River, a tedious process indeed, since the heavy pieces, ammunition, and provisions had to be brought in boats from the right to the left bank of the river and thence with great difficulty by Negroes from Gibbes' Ferry to the depot. Nevertheless, by noon five 24-pounders and two 6-inch mortars were in the park. We worked hard making mantelets à la Moncrieff in order to finish the first parallel during the coming night. The heavy artillery for the siege was brought from the warship *Raisonnable*, 54 guns, under the superintendence of the ship's commander, Captain Evans, for we were so unfortu-

Aufsicht des Schifs Comman: Capit: Evens anhero gebracht, weil wir durch einen Unglüks-Fall, Artillerie und Canoniers verlohren hatten.—Gegen Abend wurde das Iäger Piquet wieder nach Gibsons Hauss zurükgezogen.

April 3ten In der vergangenen Nacht wurde die angefangene Paralelle und Redoute verbessert, wobey die Feinde auf die Arbeiter eine kleine Anzahl Stük-Schüsse thaten. Man war beständig beschäftiget Geschüz etc etc über den Ashley Fluss nach dem Parc zu führen, und man arbeitete fleissig an Mantelets. Die Feinde warffen heute etlich und dreyssig 6. zöllige Bomben nach unserer Paralelle, wodurch 2. Hessische Grenad: verwundet wurden.

4ten In der vergangenen Nacht, wurden 2. neue Redouten, jede in Form eines halben Mondes angelegt, eine zur rechten, nahe an dem Ashley-Fluss, ohngefehr vor 200. Mann, und die andere zur linken auf einer kleinen Anhöhe, nahe an dem rechten Ufer des Cooper Flusses, vor 9. schwere Stüke. Sie waren beyde ohngefehr 100 Schritte den feindlichen Werken näher. Die Feinde wurden nichts davon gewahr, und richteten ihre Schüsse, nur auf die Paralelle. Da man sich eines feindlichen Ausfalles vermuthete, so wurde der Major v: Wurmb 2. Stunden vor Tage, mit 160 Jägern befehliget, die Besatzung dieser 2. Redouten zu verstärken. Der Major muste mit 100 Mann in die zur rechten, und ich mit 60. Mann, nach der zur linken rüken. Da die leztere zu frey, ohne Communication lag, so wurden 2 Hessische Feld-Stüke in dieselbe geführt, welche aber verborgen gehalten wurden. Der Tag war kaum angebrochen, so machten die Feinde ein heftiges Geschütz Feuer von ihren sämtlichen Batterien auf solche, so dass wir schon gegen 8 Uhr 200 Schüsse gezählet hatten. Gegen halb 9. Uhr, sezten sich die beyden feindl: Fregatten Queen of France und Boston erstere von 36. lezte von 26. Canonen, welche in dem

[1] See p. 51, where Ewald expresses his joy that Captain Collins has arrived with eighty English artillerymen, rescued from a foundering ship.

nate as to lose our artillery and gunners.[1] Toward evening
the jäger picket was withdrawn to Gibbes' house.

Last night the parallel and the redoubts were improved, April 3
the enemy firing only a few cannon shots at the working
party. We were still engaged in bringing guns, etc., etc., over
the Ashley River into the park, and worked hard making
mantelets. The enemy threw some thirty 6-inch shells at our
parallel, wounding two Hessian grenadiers.

Last night two new crescent-shaped redoubts were raised, 4
one for about two hundred men on the right near the Ashley
River and the other for nine heavy pieces on the left on some
rising ground close to the right bank of the Cooper River.
Both were about a hundred paces nearer the enemy's works.
The enemy were not aware of what was going on and directed
their shot only at the parallel. Since we expected them to
make a sortie,[2] Major von Wurmb was ordered two hours
before daybreak to reinforce the parties of these two redoubts
with 160 jägers. The Major with 100 men occupied the one
on the right and I with 60 men that on the left. The latter
lying too open and without communication, two Hessian
fieldpieces were brought into it, but these were kept con-
cealed. Day had hardly dawned when the enemy opened upon
these redoubts a violent cannonade from all their batteries,
so that by eight o'clock we had already counted two hundred
shots. Toward half-past eight the two enemy frigates, the
Queen of France and the *Boston*,[3] the former a 36-gun, the latter
a 26-gun ship, which lay at anchor in the Cooper River

---

[2] McIntosh says: "A sortie, to be commanded by Gen. Scott, Col. Clark,
Lt. Col. Laurens, etc., was intended, but was not put into execution"
(W. G. Simms, *South Carolina in the Revolutionary War*. . . . [Charleston, 1853],
p. 109). Also, Moses Young (*ibid.*, p. 110) speaks of an intended sally of
500 men.

[3] McIntosh and Gervais speak of the second vessel as the *Ranger* (*ibid.*,
pp. 109, 110).

Cooper Fluss an der Stadt vor Anker lagen, unter Seegel, legten sich auf die Flanque unserer Redoute, und beehrten mich mit 10 bis 12. ihrer Laagen. Der Major Montcrief, welcher sich fürchten muste, dass dieses Werk, in welchem sich die Leute noch nicht verbergen konnten, möchte in Stüken geschossen werden, eilte 2. 24 ttor und eine Haubitze, welche er bey die Brandeweinbrennerey, 400 Schritte hinter die Redoute placirte, denenselben entgegen zu setzen, welche sie nöthigten nach ihrer Station zurüke zu gehen. Gegen 6. Uhr Abends legte sich ein feindlicher Skoner an diesen Platz, und gab der Redoute im Rüken 8 Stük-Schüsse, worauf dieser 3 Meilen höher in den Cooper-Fluss seegelte, und sich dem Gouverneur Hausse gegen über vor Anker legte. Das feindl: Geschütz Feuer hielt den ganzen Tag an, wobey die Feinde gegen Abend 20 Bomben spielten, wovon eine, neben die 2. Munitions-Kästen, unserer 3 ttor, zu der Zeit, als der Gen: en Chef und Lord Cornwallis in der Redoute waren, doch unschädlich fielen. Diesem heftigen Geschütz Feuer aber ohngeachtet, kamen nur 2. Schüsse in die Brustwehr. Es wurde ein Soldat von dem 33 ten Regt: getödtet, 1. hart und 2 Hessische Grenadiers leicht verwundet. Das unangenehmste des gantzen war die unerträgliche Sonnen-Hitze, und die Menge deren Sand-Fliegen deren Stich sehr empfindlich ist. Es waren schon über 20 schwere Stüke, 2. 6 zöllige Haubitzen, und etliche Mörser seit gestern in das Depot geführt.

April:
5ten

In der vergangenen Nacht wurden die neuen angelegten Werke verbessert, wobey die Feinde die gantze Nacht die Arbeiter beschossen, welche aus 500 Mann, und die Bedekung aus 1500 M. bestanden. Es wurde hiervon 1. Engl: Offr: und 2. Grenadiers hart blessirt. Das feindl: Geschütz-Feuer hielt den gantzen Tag an, und gegen Abend wurde solches auf unsere Arbeiter verdoppelt. Nach 7 Uhr früh fing die Batterie bey der Brandeweinsbrennerey zu spielen an, um den Cooper Fluss nach seinem rechten Ufer zu, rein zu halten, damit sich

against the city, got under sail, came to the flank of our redoubt, and honored me with ten to twelve broadsides. Major Moncrieff, who must have feared that this work, in which the men could not yet conceal themselves,[1] might be shot to pieces, hastened to face the ships with two 24-pounders and one howitzer, which he placed close to the distillery, four hundred paces behind the redoubt, thus forcing the ships to return to their station. Toward six in the evening an enemy schooner came to the same place and fired eight shots at the rear of the redoubt, then proceeded three miles farther up the Cooper River and anchored opposite the Governor's house. The enemy kept up their cannonading the entire day. Toward evening they also threw twenty shells, one of which, without doing damage, struck beside the two ammunition boxes of our 3-pounders at a time when the Commanding General and Lord Cornwallis were in the redoubt. But in spite of their furious fire only two shots came over the parapet. One soldier of the 33rd Regiment was killed, one man severely wounded, and two Hessian grenadiers slightly. The most unpleasant thing of all was the unbearable heat and the great number of sand flies, the bites of which are very painful. Since yesterday more than twenty heavy pieces, two 6-inch howitzers, and several mortars have been brought into the depot.

Last night the newly raised works were improved. The April 5 working party was fired upon throughout the entire night. It consisted of five hundred men, who were covered by fifteen hundred. An English officer and two grenadiers were severely wounded. The enemy's gunfire continued the whole day, becoming doubly severe toward evening, when it was directed against our working parties. After seven o'clock in the morning the battery near the distillery began to play in order to keep the enemy craft from approaching the

[1] See, however, p. 237.

nicht etwa ein feindl: Fahrzeug diesem Ufer nähern möchte.
Gegen 8 Uhr liess der General en Chef die beyden Batterien,
welche auf Fennings-Point, und bey Lennings-Hauss, auf dem
rechten Ufer des Ashley Flusses angeleget waren, über 2
Stunden nach der Stadt spielen, welches die Einwohner in
solches Schreken sezte, dass man das Geschrey in dem Lager
vernehmen konnte. Zu gleicher Zeit hatten sich die beyden
Ruder-Galeeren, welche am Tage in der Mündung des Wappao
Criques bey Fennings-Point liegen, der Stadt von dieser Seite
ebenfalls genähert, welche mit ihren Stangen-Kugeln ein
entsetzliches Gerassel in denen Häussern machten. Die feindl:
Batterien verhielten sich während diesem unvermutheten
Feuer gantz stille. Diesem Abend veränderte das Detachement
der Jäger das Lager; Wir rükten in das Holtz, nahe an das
linke Ufer des Ashley-Flusses, so dass wir Gibsons Hauss 200
Schritte im Rüken behielten. Zugleicher Zeit schlugen auch
200 Matrosen unter Comando des Capit: Evens, benebst
5. Officiers von der Marine ihr Lager hinter uns auf, welche
bestimt sind, das schwere vom Kriegs Schif Reasonable und
Europa genommene Geschütz, (welche Schiffe im Port-Royal
Fluss liegen) zu bedienen.

April:
6ten
    In der vergangenen Nacht hat man 1. Batterie von 9.24
ttorn zwischen der Redoute No: 1. und 2. in der 1ten Paralelle angelegt, diese soll vor die Matrosen bestimt seyn. Die
Feinde thaten seit dem Schreken in der vergangenen Nacht,
bis heute Mittag 4 Uhr nicht einen Stük-Schuss. Man arbeitete den gantzen Tag über an denen Plat Forms in denen
Redouten und der Batterie, auch führte man 7.24 ttor und
1.13 zölligen Mörser halben Weg nach der ersten Paralelle.
Man suchte auch ein grosses Flattboat auf Waltzen zu Land,
von dem Ashley-Fluss nach dem Cooper-Fluss zu schleppen,
welches mit 2.6 ttorn soll besetzet werden, um diejenigen
Boats aufzufangen, welche währender Nacht von der Stadt

right side of the Cooper River. Toward eight o'clock the
Commanding General gave orders that the two batteries on
Fenwick's Point and at Linning's house on the right bank
of the Ashley River should play upon the city for over two
hours. This alarmed the inhabitants of the city so much that
their shouting could be heard in the camp. At the same time
the two row-galleys which during the day were stationed in
the mouth of the Wappoo Creek at Fenwick's Point approached the city. Their crossbar shot made a terrific clatter
on the houses. The enemy's batteries were silent during this
unexpected fire. In the evening the jäger detachment changed
camps. We moved into the woods close to the left bank of
the Ashley River, so that we had Gibbes' house two hundred
paces behind us. At the same time two hundred sailors under
the command of Captain Evans and five [junior] officers of
the navy made their camp behind us. They are to serve the
heavy pieces of artillery removed from the warships *Raisonnable* and *Europe*, which are at present stationed in Port Royal
River.

Last night a battery of nine 24-pounders was raised in April 6
the first parallel between redoubts Nos. 1 and 2. It is to be
manned by sailors. After being terrified last night, the enemy
did not fire another gun till four o'clock this afternoon. We
were engaged the entire day in constructing platforms in the
redoubts and the battery. We also took seven 24-pounders
and a 13-inch mortar halfway to the first parallel and tried
to haul a large flatboat on rollers from the Ashley to the
Cooper River. It is to have two 6-pounders and will attempt
to capture the boats which pass during the night from the
city to the left bank of the Cooper River. Toward four in the
afternoon the enemy's batteries opened a brisk fire upon our

nach dem linken Ufer des Cooper-Flusses gehen. Gegen 4.
Uhr Nachmittage feuerten die feindlichen Batterien heftig auf
unsere Werke, welches bis in die Nacht dauerte. Heute stiess
auch die Legion von dem Pattersohnschen Corps von jenem
Ufer des Ashley Flusses zu der Websterischen Brigade.

April: In der vergangenen Nacht wurde an denen noch unvoll-
7ten kommenen Werken gearbeitet, und eine Communications-Linie
von 150 Schritt, zwischen No. 5. et 6. verfertiget. Man war
beschäftiget schwer Geschütz nach der Redoute No. 6. zu
bringen, allein da man versäumet hatte, die Wege, welche
über Morastige Oerter, nach dieser Redoute lauffen, wohl zu
untersuchen, und solche mit Faschienen und Horden gangbar
zu machen, so blieben etliche 24 ttor steken, und es konnte
nur ein Stüke nach erwahnder Redoute geführet werden. Das
feindliche Stük und Mörser Feuer, war die gantze Nacht
hindurch sehr anhaltend, welches aber unsere Galeeren und
die beyden Batterien am Ashley Fluss sehr wohl beantworteten. Nachmittage kam ein Uiberläufer aus der Stadt
bey uns an, welcher meldete, dass die Feinde bereit wären,
einen Ausfall gegen Anbruch des Tages zu wagen. Die leichte
Infanterie und das 33te Regt:. wurde sogleich befehliget die
Trancheen zu verstärken, und im Fall solches wahr sey, sich
mit denen Feinden zu vermischen, und so in die Stadt zu
dringen. Zu ihrem Kentzeichen hatten diese weisse Tücher
um ihre Köpfe gebunden. Die feindlichen Batterien feuerten
heute sehr heftig, welches von der Batterie bey der Brande-
weins-Brennerey beantwortet wurde. Gegen 1. Uhr passirten
11. Skoners und Chalouppen mit Truppen beladen den Cooper
Fluss nach der Stadt, welches, wie wir erfahren, ein Succurs
vom General Wassington seyn soll. Nach allen Betracht der
Fahrzeuge, können es nicht über 600 Mann gewesen seyn.—
Hier kann man sehen, was aus einem kleinen Versehen in dem
Kriege, entstehen kann. Wenn der Zufall mit denen bösen
Wegen gleich in Obacht genommen worden wäre, so würde

works and kept it up into the night. Today the Legion came over from Paterson's corps, stationed on the other bank of the Ashley River, to join the brigade which was under Webster's command.

Last night we resumed construction of the unfinished April 7 works and also threw up a line of communication one hundred and fifty paces long between Nos. 5 and 6. We were engaged in taking heavy pieces to redoubt No. 6, but since we neglected to examine carefully the roads, which in some places lead through marshy ground, and to make them passable with fascines and hurdles, several 24-pounders were mired; we succeeded in bringing but one piece into the redoubt. The enemy's guns and mortars continued to fire briskly the whole night, but they were well answered by our galleys and the two batteries on the Ashley River. In the afternoon a deserter arrived from the city who informed us that the enemy intended to make a sortie shortly before daybreak. The light infantry and the 33rd Regiment were immediately ordered to strengthen the trenches and, should this information be correct, mingle with the enemy and so attempt to get into the city. White rags tied around their heads served as distinguishing marks. The enemy's batteries fired very briskly today, but their fire was answered by the battery at the distillery. Toward one o'clock eleven schooners and sloops loaded with troops passed down the Cooper River to the city. These troops, we found out, were sent as reinforcements by General Washington. Considering the size of the craft there cannot have been more than six hundred men. This shows what may happen in war just because of a little oversight. Had the bad roads been attended to immediately, several pieces could have been mounted in redoubt No. 6, and the ships would have paid dearly for their passage. The

die Redoute No 6. mit einigen Stüken montiret gewesen seyn, welche diesen Fahrzeugen die Passage sehr übel bezahlen konnte. Die Feinde machten ein grosses Freuden-Geschrey, und liessen sämtliche Gloken bis in die späte Nacht spielen, wobey solche nach unserer Paralelle ein artiges Feuer machten. Jedoch kam zu unserer Freude der Hauptmann Collins mit 80 Englischen Artilleristen hier an, welcher von der Flotte verschlagen, und in dem Augenblike, da sein Schif sinken wollte, von einem Englischen Corsaren gerettet, und nach denen Bermudas geführt worden, und von daher nach Stono Inlet kam.

April: 8ten In der vergangenen Nacht, wurde eine Redoute in der Form eines halben Mondes vor 6. schwere Stüke denen feindl: Werken 200 Schritte näher erbauet, auf welches die Feinde ein beständiges Feuer machten. Man führte zugleich 4. 24 ttor nach No: 6. und das bewafnete Boat wurde flot gemacht. Jn der vergangenen Nacht nahm auch die leichte Infant: einen doppelten Posten vor dem feindlichen Verhak weg, wodurch wir sicher erfuhren, dass die Feinde bey dem ersten Charmützel mit den Iägern, 1. Capit: 1. Lieut: 1. Sergt: und 7. Gemeine an Todten, und 1. General-Adjut: vom Gen: Lincoln nebst 30 Gemeinen an Verwundeten erlitten hätten, welches die Ursache gewesen wäre, dass solche dem Iäger, welchem wir vermisst, kein Quartier gegeben hätten. Man beschäftiget sich noch beständig, Geschüz Munition u.d.g. anhero zu schaffen.—Gegen 4. Uhr sahen wir ein sehr reitzendes Schauspiel. Die Flotte unter dem Admiral Arbuthnot, passirte den Canal unter dem Geschütze des Fort Multric [sic], welches mit 20 schweren Canonen besetzet war. Der

---

[1] See Archibald Robertson's *Diaries and Sketches in America*, ed. by H. M. Leydenberg (New York, 1930), p. 219: "By the Rebel Accounts they had this Day 3 Officers and 40 men Killed and Wounded." Captain Hinrichs' figures are practically the same as those given by Ewald and Robertson. On the other hand, McIntosh (Simms, *op. cit.*, pp. 104-105) says: "Our loss Capt. Bowman killed, Major Hyrne and seven privates wounded." This is

enemy cheered a great deal and rang their bells until late into the night, firing all the while at our parallel. However, to our great joy Captain Collins arrived with eighty English artillerymen. Their ship had been separated from the fleet, and just as she was about to sink, the men were rescued by an English privateer and taken to the Bermudas, whence they came to Stono Inlet.

Last night we built two hundred paces closer to the April 8 enemy's works a crescent-shaped redoubt for six heavy pieces, upon which the enemy fired continuously. At the same time four 24-pounders were taken to No. 6; the armed brig was floated, and the light infantry captured a double post in front of the enemy's abatis. From these men we ascertained that during the first engagement with the jägers the enemy lost one captain, one lieutenant, one sergeant, and seven rank and file killed and one adjutant to General Lincoln and thirty rank and file wounded,[1] which, they said, was the reason they gave no quarter to the jäger we had missed. We were still engaged in bringing up artillery, ammunition, etc. Toward four o'clock we witnessed an entertaining spectacle. Under the command of Admiral Arbuthnot the fleet passed through the channel under the fire of Fort Moultrie, in which were mounted twenty heavy pieces.[2] The Admiral was on the

the commonly accepted number of losses on the American side. Captain Bowman was adjutant to General James Hogan of the North Carolina Brigade and Major Hyrne, deputy adjutant general for the Southern Department.

[2] Historians are bewildered by the fact that the various accounts, especially the official reports, do not agree on the date when the ships passed Fort Moultrie. Both Lincoln and Clinton give the 8th, while Arbuthnot gives the 9th. Ewald, Hinrichs, and von Huyn, as well as Lieutenant Colonel Robertson, say it was the 8th. Arbuthnot must have erred. W. G. Perrin, the editor of Volume I of the *Keith Papers*, states in a footnote to Arbuthnot's report (p. 140): "Nautical time; really p.m. on the 8th." This is a mistake, for according to astronomical time, used by seamen until 1925, the day began twelve hours later, not earlier.

Admiral befand sich auf dem Roebuck, auf welchem die
Fregatte Richmond folgte, welche das gröste Feuer aushielten.
Leztere verlohr ihre Mäste. Inzwischen passirte die Flotte
glüklich in Zeit von 2. Stunden das Fort, und legte sich
zwischen der Insul Sulivan und der Stadt gegen Abend vor
Anker. Das gantze bestund aus 14. Seegeln. Das bewafnete
Transport Schif New-Vigilante seegelte auf den Sand, welches,
nachdem die Equipage gerettet, in Brand gesetzt wurde. Die
Rebellen wurden auf dieses Schreken gantz stille, indem sie
diese Passage vor impassable hielten. Der Verlust der Englischen Flotte bestand aus 7 Todten und 20. hart verwundeten.
——Es ist bey allen Belagerungen in der Welt gebräuchlich,
dass man den Parc, so sehr mit doppelten Schildwachten
bewahret, besonders den Ort in welchem das Pulver auf-
bewahret wird, und wo man laboriret, dass sich kein Mensch,
er mag seyn wer er will, wenn er nichts in demselben zu thun
hat, bis auf 300 Schritte nähern darf, damit nicht etwa das
Pulver Magazin durch ein vom Feinde bestochenen, in die
Luft gesprengt, der Vorrath von Arbeitszeug und Faschienen
angezündet, oder wohl gar die Canons vernagelt werden.
Allein bey dieser Nation ist alles dieses nicht gewöhnlich,
man liess jederman, ja sogar die Deserteurs in diesem Orte
herumlaufen;
    Während der vergangenen Nacht und bis heute den Tag
über, haben die Rebellen nicht über 20. Schüsse auf unsere
Linie gethan, und in der Stadt ist man beschäftiget, Menschen,
Vieh und Güter aus derselben nach dem linken Ufer des
Cooper-Flusses zu schaffen. Gegen Abend wurde das 2te
bewafnete Boat Flott gemacht.—Da man iezt die feindl:
Werke näher betrachten kann, so ging ich aus dieser Ursache
nach unserer Paralelle, wo ich fand, dass die beyden Ba-

    [1] Robert Beatson (*Naval and Military Memoirs*, Vol. V) and, unfortu-
nately, also W. L. Clowes (*Royal Navy*, Vol. IV) tell of the *Roebuck* being
fired on after she had come to anchor, every shot going through her sides,

Roebuck, which was followed by the frigate *Richmond*. These ships withstood the heaviest fire, the latter losing her masts. Within two hours the fleet safely passed the fort and anchored toward evening between Sullivan Island and the city.[1] The entire fleet consisted of fourteen sail.[2] The armed transport *New Vigilant*[3] ran aground on a sandbank and was set on fire after the equipage had been saved. The rebels, having considered this place impassable, were so dumfounded that they ceased firing. The losses of the English fleet were seven killed and twenty severely wounded.—Everywhere it is customary during sieges to guard with double sentry the park, the laboratory, and especially the place where the powder is stored, so that no one who has no business there can approach within three hundred paces; otherwise, the powder magazine might be blown up by someone bribed by the enemy, the stores of tools and fascines set on fire, and even the guns spiked. However, with this nation all this is not customary. Anyone was permitted to go about in this place, even deserters.

During the past night and through this day the enemy [April 9] fired only twenty shots at our line. In the city they are busy taking people, livestock, and goods over to the left bank of the Cooper River. Toward evening the second armed boat was floated. Since the enemy's works can now be inspected

and laud her commander for deceiving the enemy by not taking notice of it. This is not borne out by any of the present accounts and seems sheer fabrication.

[2] There were eight ships of the navy, which passed in the following order: *Roebuck* (44; since February increased to 50), *Richmond* (32), *Romulus* (44), *Blonde* (32), *Virginia* (32), *Raleigh* (32), *Sandwich* (armed ship), *Renown* (50). The rest of the fourteen vessels (if Ewald's number is correct) must have been transports loaded with supplies.

[3] It was the *Aeolus* (*Eolus*), a storeship. Some accounts, both contemporary and modern, call her *Acetus*, and even *Acteus*, the latter, no doubt, being simply a typographical error.

stionen, welche die Flanque deken, und durch die darhinter
liegenden gedekt, detachirte Werke sind. Besonders fand ich
die linke, da dieses Werk ein wenig zu weit ablieget, und
durch eine gegen über liegende kleine Höhe comandiret wird,
als den schwächesten Theil. Der mitlere Theil der Werke
bestehet aus einer Linie en Redans, deren Flanquen-Feuer
allein auf den Graben gerichtet ist, allein die Front auf eine
kurtze Weite bestreicht: welches vermuthlich der feindl: Ingenieur aus der Ursache gethan hat, weil er eher einen Sturm,
als eine feindliche Belagerung vorgestellet hat, welches nun-
mehr den Feind nöthiget, dass solcher die Embrassures täglich ändern muss.

April: Da in der vergangenen Nacht eine Batterie von 6. Canonen
10ten 300 Schritt vor die Paralelle zwischen No: 4 und No: 5 vor-
geleget worden, so wurde ich nebst dem Lieut: v: Winsingrode 40. Jägern, und 1. Capit: mit 50 Grenadiers comandirt,
dieses neu angefangene Werk eine Stunde vor Tage zu besetzen, und im Fall eines feindl: Ausfalles, so lange als
möglich zu behaupten. Jch vermuthete dieses auch, da der
Feind sich die gantze Nacht hindurch stille gehalten hatte;
Allein er liess es bey 280 Canon-Schüssen, und 10 Bomben
bewenden. Hätte der Feind einen Ausfall gethan so würde
er ein gutes Spiel gehabt haben, weil der Graben nicht
einmal halb fertig war, mithin ich mich darinne nicht deken
konnte, sondern genöthiget war $\frac{2}{3}$ des Comando in den halb
tiefen Graben, der über dieses voll Wasser war, zu legen.
In No: 1. wurde 1. M. von der leichten Infant: getödtet, auch
legten sich die beyden feindl: Fregatten wieder bey die Stadt.
Gegen 6. Uhr Abends liess unser comandirende General
durch den Major Crasby die Stadt auffodern, welcher mit der
Antwort zurüke kam, dass General Lincoln Willens sey, sich
so lange als möglich zu halten, wozu ihm Pflicht und Befehl
vom Congress anhielte. Es wurde heute Abend das 3te bewafnete Boat in den Cooper-River gebracht.

at closer range, I went to our parallel and learned that the two bastions which cover their flank and are covered by others behind are detached works. I also ascertained that the left one is especially weak, since it is a little too far advanced and is commanded by some rising ground across from it. The center part of the works consists of a line of redans, only the flanking fire of which can be directed at our trench, while they can rake our front but a short distance. No doubt this was done by the enemy's engineers because they expected an assault rather than a siege. It compels them to make daily changes in the embrasures.

Last night a battery of six guns was advanced three hundred paces in front of the parallel, between Nos. 4 and 5. With Lieutenant von Winsingrode and forty jägers, as well as a captain with fifty grenadiers, I was ordered to occupy this new work one hour before daybreak and hold it as long as possible in case the enemy should make a sortie. Since they had remained quiet throughout the entire night, I really expected a sortie. However, they were content to fire 280 shots and throw 10 shells. Had they made a sally, they would have had little difficulty, for the trench was not even half finished. Consequently it gave no cover and made it necessary to post two thirds of the command in a ditch that was only half its supposed depth and, moreover, was full of water. In No. 1 a light infantryman was killed. The two enemy frigates also came up to the city again. Toward six o'clock in the evening our Commanding General sent Major Crosbie to the city with a summons; but he returned with the answer that General Lincoln intended to maintain himself as long as possible, being bound by duty and the orders of Congress. This evening the third armed boat was brought into the Cooper River.

April 10

April: So bald der Mond untergegangen war, so wurde an der neu
11ten angefangenen Batterie, und an einer Coñunications-Linie
von der 1ten Paralelle bis zu dieser gearbeitet, und Geschütz
nach unseren Werken geführt, welches ohne Geräusch nicht
vor sich gehen konnte, vornemlich da man an den Plat Forms
arbeitete. Dahero feuerten die Feinde stark mit Canonen und
spielten viele Bomben, welches bis 5 Uhr diesen Morgen
dauerte. Am Tage übrigens feuerten die Feinde wenig, und
warfen nur 16 Bomben, welches von unserer Batterie auf
Feñings-Point beantwortet wurde. Die bewafneten Boats
waren in vergangener Nacht zum erstenmahl ausgelauffen,
um einen feindl: Skoner, der in der Mitte des Cooper Flusses
lag, zu erhaschen. Allein da vieles Volk auf dem Verdek und
munter war, so hielten sie vor gut sich zurük zu ziehen.

12ten In der vergangenen Nacht wurde an einem demi place d'armes
von 200 Schritten zu beyden Seiten der vorgelegten Batterie
gearbeitet, wobey die Feinde vor Mitternacht heftig auf die
Arbeiter feuerten. Capit: Hinrichs muste dieses mit 30 Jägern
besetzen. Den Tag über thaten die Feinde wenig Stük-Schüsse,
und spielten nur einige Bomben ohne Wirkung. Gegen 4.
Uhr Nachmittags passirte eine Fregatte und 3 bewafnete
Brigantinen das Fort Multric unter dem heftigsten feindlichen
Geschütz Feuer ohne einen Schuss zu thun, und vereinigten
sich glüklich mit unserer Flotte. Es kañen auch heute 2.
Deputirte von Nord Carolina in dem Haupt-Quartier an,
welche sich erboten, so bald sie in ihrer Gegend durch die
Königl: Macht geschützet würden, 400 Mann in Wafen zu
stellen. Der Obriste Webster marchirte heute mit dem 33ten
Regt und der Legion den Weg gegen Dorchester und der
Major Ferguson mit seinem Corps die Strasse, längst dem
rechten Ufer des Ashley Flusses. Man vermuthet, dass dieses
Corps den Cooper Fluss passiren wird, um denen Rebellen die
Coñunication von dieser Seite abzuschneiden, und solche zu
nöthigen, die Werke auf Lambergs Point zu verlassen.

As soon as the moon was down, work was resumed on the unfinished battery and on a line of communication between the first parallel and this battery. Also, artillery was taken to our works, which could not be done without noise, especially since we were working on the platforms. Hence the enemy fired briskly and played many shells, keeping up their fire until five o'clock this morning. During the day, however, they fired but little and threw only sixteen shells, to which our battery on Fenwick's Point responded. The armed boats set sail for the first time last night to capture a hostile schooner stationed in the middle of the Cooper River. But since many persons were on deck, and all wide awake, their commanders thought best to retire. April 11

Last night work was begun on a demiparallel, two hundred paces long, on both sides of the advanced battery. The working party was subjected to a violent fire up to midnight. Captain Hinrichs was ordered to occupy it with thirty jägers. During the day the enemy cannonaded and bombarded us but little and without effect. Toward four o'clock in the afternoon a frigate and three armed brigantines passed Fort Moultrie under the most severe fire and safely joined our fleet without firing a single shot. Two deputies from North Carolina arrived at headquarters today and promised to put four hundred men under arms as soon as their district should be protected by the royal forces. Colonel Webster, with the 33rd Regiment and the Legion, started out on the highway to Dorchester, and Major Ferguson with his corps on the road along the right bank of the Ashley River. It is expected that this corps will cross the Cooper River in order to cut off the rebels' line of communication from that side and in order to compel them to abandon their works on Lempriere's Point. 12

April
13ten

Da unsere Batterien mit 21. 24 ttorn, 2. 12 ttorn 2. Haubitzen, und 1. Mörser montirt, so beschäftigte man sich gestern am Tage, als auch in der vergangenen Nacht Munition nach denen Magazins zu bringen, und 1. Mörser Batterie in dem demi place d'armes zur linken der vorgelegten Batterie anzulegen, während dessen die Rebellen jede halbe Stunde etliche Stük-Schüsse auf unsere Arbeiter thaten, wodurch 1. Hessischer Grenadier getödtet wurde. Diesen Morgen halb 10 Uhr, wurden unsere Batterien geöfnet, und feuerten mit so glüklichen Erfolg, dass verschiedene feindl: Stüke, durch die ersten 20 Schüsse demontiret wurden. Man warf auch von No: 6. etliche Carcasses nach denen feindlichen Werken, welche von ohngefehr in die Stadt fielen, wodurch etliche Gebäude zur rechten der Stadt in den Brand geriethen. Das Canonen Feuer war zu beyden Seiten heftig, und hielte den gantzen Tag an, wir verloren dadurch 2. Matrosen und 1 Artilleristen 1 L. Infant: und 2 Matros: wurden verwundet. Gegen Abend passirte das 64te Regt: den Achley Fluss, und folgte dem Websterisch: Corps. Capit: v: Bodungen besezte heute den demi place d'armes.

14^t

In der vergangenen Nacht, war das feindliche Geschütz Feuer nicht stark; allein das unsrige desto heftiger, und man hatte sowohl von der rechten der 1ten Paralelle linker Hand von No 2. als auch von dem demi place d'armes aus ohngefehr 130 G. lang nach Art der doppelten Sappe approchirt, ohne von dem Feind viel gehindert zu werden. Ich besezte heute vor Anbruch des Tages mit 60 Jagern die Approche zur linken, wo ich den gantzen Tag mit den feindl: Büchssen Schützen in Feuer lag. Das feindl: Canonen Feuer war nicht stark, und der Feind spielte nur etliche Bomben. Unsere Batterien thaten alle Stunden 3. Schüsse, allein man warf über 40 Bomben und Haubitzen Granaden. Das 23te Regt: ist heute ebenfalls dem Obristen Webster gefolgt, welches bestim̃et ist, den Pass bey Strawberg zu occupiren, und den Rüken dieses Corps zu deken.

Yesterday, during the day as well as during the night, we were engaged in bringing munitions to the magazines, for we now had mounted in our batteries twenty-one 24-pounders, two 12-pounders, two howitzers, and one mortar. We also raised a mortar battery in the demiparallel at the left of the advanced battery. Every half hour the rebels fired several gunshots at our workmen, killing one Hessian grenadier. This morning at half-past nine we opened with our batteries and fired with such good results that we dismounted several pieces with the first twenty shots. From No. 6 we threw several hot shots at the enemy's works; they accidentally fell into the city and set fire to a few buildings on the right section. The firing was fierce on both sides and continued throughout the day. We had two sailors and one artilleryman killed and one light infantryman and two sailors wounded. Toward evening the 64th Regiment crossed the Ashley River and followed the corps under Webster's command. Captain von Bodungen occupied the demiparallel today.

Last night the enemy's gunfire was moderate, while ours was very brisk. Without much interference from them we approached about one hundred and thirty paces from the right wing of the first parallel, on the left of No. 2, and also from the demiparallel, the approaches being built much like double saps. Before daybreak I occupied the approach on the left with sixty jägers and exchanged rifle fire with the enemy all day long. The enemy's gunfire was not severe, and they played only a few shells. Our batteries fired three shots every hour, but our mortars and howitzers threw over forty shells. The 23rd Regiment also followed Colonel Webster today. They are to occupy the pass at Strawberry and cover the rear of the corps.

April: Man eröfnete in der vergangenen Nacht die 2te Paralelle,
15. wobey die Feinde die gantze Nacht mit Trauben-Schüssen und
kleinem Gewehr auf die Arbeiter feuerten, von unsern
Batterien geschahen jede halbe Stunde etliche Schüsse, und
etwa 12. Bomben wurden geworfen. Capit: Hinrichs muste
mit 60 Jägern nach den Flanquen der 2ten Paralelle rüken; 2
Mann von der leichten Infanterie wurden verwundet. Die
feindl: Batterien feuerten den gantzen Tag über stark, und
unsere wenig. Die feindliche Galeeren, welche neben Lambergs
Point lagen, legten sich heute neben das Gouverneurs Hauss,
und beschossen das Grenadier Lager. Es wurde sogleich eine
Batterie von 2. 24 ttorn an diesem Orte errichtet, worauf die
Galeeren sich wieder nach ihrer alten Station zogen.—Heute
wurde auch bekañt gemacht, dass der Obriste Tarlton gestern Morgen, mit seiner Cavallerie, den Obristen Wassington bey Baken-bridge, überfallen, über 30 Dragoner niedergehauen, (unter welchen der 3te Comandeur des Pulavsky-
schen Corps, Major Vernier war) etlich und 60 Dragoner
gefangen, und auf 400 Pferde nebst der Equipage erbeutet
habe.

16ten Man hatte angefangen in der vergangenen Nacht, an zwey
Orten aus der 2ten Paralelle zu approchiren. Die Feinde
feuerten wenig. Capit: v: Bodungen muste diese frische
Arbeit besetzen, und war den gantzen Tag mit dem Feind
engagiret, der in vergangener Nacht eine Contre-Approche
für seine Schützen, zwischen seinen ersten und 2ten Verhake
gemacht hatte. Ein M. von der leichten Infant: wurde getödtet. Die Feinde schossen heute meistens Trauben, welche
unsere Bomben-Batterien, die durch etlich und zwanzig Royals und Coehorns waren verstärket worden, beantworteten. Heute wurde die neue Batterie von 4. 24 ttorn, welche
der Admiral auf Iaimes Eiland an dem rechten Ufer des Wappau-Criques angeleget hatte, eröfnet.

17ten Man verbesserte und verlängerte die Approchen, wobey die

Last night the second parallel was finished, the enemy April 15 firing grapeshot and musketry at the working party all night. Our batteries fired a few shots every half hour and also threw about twelve shells. Captain Hinrichs was ordered to go with sixty jägers to the flanks of the second parallel. Two men of the light infantry were wounded. The enemy's batteries fired briskly the whole day, while ours fired but little. Their galleys that had been lying at Lempriere's Point came close to the Governor's house today and cannonaded the encampment of the grenadiers. A battery of two 24-pounders was immediately erected at this place, whereupon the galleys withdrew to their former station.—Today we were informed that yesterday morning Colonel Tarleton with his cavalry surprised Colonel Washington at Biggins bridge, that they cut down more than thirty dragoons (among them Major Vernier, the third commander of Pulaski's Corps), that they made prisoners of some sixty dragoons, and that they captured about four hundred horses with their equipage.[1]

We began last night to build two approaches from the 16 second parallel. The enemy fired but little. Captain von Bodungen occupied these approaches and was engaged with the enemy the entire day. During the night they had made a counterapproach for their musketry, between their first and second abatis. One man of the light infantry was killed. The enemy fired mostly grapeshot today. They were answered by our bomb batteries, which had been reinforced by some twenty royals and coehorns. We also opened a new battery of four 24-pounders that the Admiral had thrown up on James Island on the right bank of the Wappoo Creek.

We strengthened and extended the approaches. The 17

[1] This encounter took place at Moncks Corner, not far from Biggins bridge. Here General Huger was posted with his cavalry.

gantze Nacht hindurch mit kleinem Gewehr und Trauben auf die Arbeiter gefeuert wurde, wodurch 5. Hessische Grenadiers verwundet sind. Ich besezte diese Approchen mit 60. Iägern, und da der Graben seine gehörige Tiefe noch nicht auch keine Traversen hatte, so wurde ich den gantzen Tag von beyden Seiten und im Rüken, von dem feindl: Geschütz-Feuer enfiliret, wobey der Feind beständig aus 2.6. ttorn zu meiner rechten mit gehaktem Eisen und Glass schoss. Unsere Batterien warfen aber doch kaum 10. Bomben. Ich liess solches melden, und die Batterien fingen sich endlich an zu regen. Es wurde 1. Jäger, und 1. Mann von der leichten Infanterie durch eine Stük-Kugel in Laufgraben verwundet, und ich hätte gewiss viele Leute verlohren, wenn ich nicht gleich, sobald ich sahe, dass ich konnte enfiliret werden, an 5 traversen arbeiten liess

Aprl: Man hatte in der vergangenen Nacht angefangen, ohngefehr 18. 300 Schritte von der 2ten Paralelle auf beyden Flanquen deren Approchen einen demi place d'armes zu machen, wobey die Feinde beständig mit Trauben und kleinen Gewehr feuerten, von unserer Seite wurden nicht über 30 Bomben geworfen. Capit: Hinrichs muste heute mit 60 Jägern, diese neue Arbeit besetzen, und wurde eben so warm, wie ich gestern gehalten. 1 L. Infant. wurde durch eine Stük-Kugel getödtet 1. und 1. Engl: Canonier hart verwundet.

19ten Man hatte in der vergangenen Nacht an der völligen Comŭnication der 2ten Paralelle gearbeitet, wo bey die Feinde die gantze Nacht hindurch ein heftiges Cartetschen und klein Feuer machten, wodurch 2. Hessische Grenadiers verwundet wurden. Man brachte auch die kleinen Mörser nach dem demi place d'armes und 2ten Paralelle, welche heute viele Grenaden und Bomben nach denen feindlichen Werken mit bester Wirkung spielten. Capit: v: Bodungen muste heute die demi place d'armes besetzen. Nachmittage erhielten wir auch die

enemy fired upon our workmen all night with small arms
and grapeshot, wounding five Hessian grenadiers. I occupied
the approaches with sixty jägers. Since the ditch was not
yet of proper depth and had no traverses, I was exposed the
entire day to enfilading gunfire from both sides as well as
from the rear. Two enemy 6-pounders at my right kept up
a continuous fire of scrap iron and glass. In spite of the heavy
fire our batteries threw at the most ten shells. I made a report
concerning this, whereupon our batteries began to be more
active. One jäger and one man of the light infantry were
wounded by a gunshot while in the trench. I should certainly
have lost many men had I not begun work on five traverses
when I saw that I could be enfiladed.

Last night we began to construct from the approaches on April 18
both sides demiparallels three hundred paces in front of the
second parallel. The enemy kept up a steady fire of grapeshot
and musketry, while our side threw no more than about thirty
shells. Captain Hinrichs was ordered to occupy the new works
with sixty jägers. He was kept just as warm as I was yesterday. One light infantryman was killed by gunfire; another,
as well as an English gunner, was severely wounded.

During the past night we were engaged in completing the 19
communication of the second parallel, the enemy keeping up
a severe fire of canister shot and musketry, wounding two
Hessian grenadiers. Some small mortars were brought to the
demiparallel and the second parallel and during the day they
threw many shells and bombs upon the enemy's works with
the best effect. Captain von Bodungen occupied the demiparallels. In the afternoon we received the good news that a
fleet of twenty-four sail has arrived here from New York in
eleven days, that it has on board reinforcements consisting of

angenehme Nachricht, dass eine Flotte von 24. Seegeln von
York aus in 11. Tägen anhero geseegelt, welche 2,600 M.
Truppen, Artillerie, Munition und Provision zu unserer
Verstärkung am Bord haben soll, und zu Stono Inlet ein-
gelauffen sey. Dieses Corps soll bestehen: aus dem 42ten
Regt, dem Braunischen Corps, den Volontairs von Irrland,
Queens-Rangers, und dem Hessischen Regt: von Ditforth.
Heute kam auch ein Chef der Niederen Creck Indianer im
Haupt-Quartier an, um die Gewissheit zu erfahren, ob es an
dem sey, so wie die Rebellen dieser Nation weiss gemacht,
um solche von der Engl: Partey abzuziehen, dass unsere
Armee vor Charlestown in solchen üblen Umständen sey dass
wir niemals diese Stadt erobern könnten. Er hatte einen 78
jähr: Schottisch: Obristen Makendoslw [sic] als Begleiter
bey sich, welcher in der lezten Rebellion in seinem Vaterlande
von der Partey des Pretendenden war, und in der Schlacht
von Culotten den linken Flügel comandiret. Dieser Greiss,
welcher seit 1748 unter dieser Nation gewohnet, war noch
so rüstig als ein Mann von 30. Jahren, und in diesem Kriege
einer der treuesten Unterthanen seines Königes. Der Nahme
des Indianers, war König Iacob. Er wurde zur Uiberzeügung
durch das gantze Lager, und in die Trancheen geführt. Er
war ein grosser Krieger unter seiner Nation, redete etwas englisch und war in seinem Thun ein sehr manierlicher Mann.

Aprl: In der vergangenen Nacht, wurde zur linken approchirt,
20^t welches ein heftiges Geschütz-Feuer und viele Bomben nach
sich zog, wodurch 2 Engl: Soldaten getödtet, und 5 verwundet wurden. Unsere Batterien spielten die gantze Nacht
hindurch Bomben, und die auf Fennings-Point feuerten beständig nach der Stadt. Jch muste heute mit 60. Iägern die
neue Arbeit besetzen, und lag wie gewöhnlich den gantzen
Tag in dem kleinen Gewehr Feuer. Die Jäger feuerten heute
so gut, dass ich das Feuer von 2 Embrassures zur rechten der
feindlichen Werke den gantzen Tag über aufhielte. Unsere

2,600 troops, artillery, ammunition, and stores, and that it has run into Stono Inlet. This corps is said to be made up of the 42nd Regiment, Brown's Corps, the Volunteers of Ireland, the Queen's Rangers, and the Hessian Regiment von Dittfurth. Today a chief of the Lower Creek Indians arrived at headquarters to see for himself whether our army before Charleston was really in such shape that we would never be able to reduce the city, as the rebels had tried to tell this nation in order to disaffect it. As a companion he had with him a seventy-eight-year-old Scotsman, Colonel McIntosh, who during the last rebellion at home was with the party of the Pretender and had commanded the left wing in the battle of Culloden.[1] This old man, who has lived among this nation since 1748, was as robust as a man of thirty and has been during the war one of the most faithful subjects of his king. The name of the Indian was King Jacob. To convince him of the falsehood of what he had heard, he was led through the whole camp and into the trenches. He is a great warrior among his nation, speaks some English, and is well mannered.

Last night we advanced the approach on the left, which April 20 brought us severe gunfire and many shells. Two English soldiers were killed and five wounded. Our batteries played bombs the whole night, and those on Fenwick's Point kept up a constant cannonade upon the city. I was ordered to occupy the new work with sixty men and, as usual, was under small-arms fire the entire day. The jägers' rifle fire was so effective today that I silenced the fire of two embrasures on the right of the enemy's works for the whole day. Our

[1] Captain (not Colonel) William McIntosh was Indian agent for the Southern Department. He was the son of Captain John McIntosh, whose family had lived in Georgia for some time. The McIntoshes played important rôles in the rebellion of 1715 and that of 1745, but the McIntosh mentioned here did not fight in the interest of the Stuarts (E. J. Harden, *Life of George M. Troup* [Savannah, 1859], pp. 7-8).

Batterien feuerten heute sehr viel, besonders wurden unsere
Bomben so gut gespielet, dass 2. kleine Pulver Magazine der
Feinde in der 1ten und 2ten Bastion in die Luft gesprenget
wurden. Ein Iäger wurde heute mit einer Stük-Kugel getöd-
tet. Die von York neulich angekom̄ene Truppen, sind heute
auf Iaimes Eiland bey Hamiltons-Landungs-Plaz debarquiret
worden.

Aprl: Man approchirte in der vergangenen Nacht, und legte in der
21ten 2ten Paralelle gerade auf der grossen Strasse eine Batterie vor
3. 6. ttor an; Der Feind machte die Nacht ein starkes Ge-
schütz und Musqueten Feuer auf unsere Arbeiter, welches mit
vielen Bomben beantwortet wurde. Capit: Hinrichs muste
heute diese neue Arbeit besetzen. Nachmittage schikten die
Rebellen einen Offr: aus der Stadt, um zu capitulieren. Da
solche aber freyen Abzug begehreten, so wurde wieder abgebrochen, und man fing gegen Abend über 2. Stunden das
heftigste Geschütz-Feuer an.

22.ten Man hatte in der vergangenen Nacht rechts und links denen Approchen, 2. demi place d'armes, jeden ohngefehr 150
Schritte lang, angelegt, bey welcher Arbeit die Feinde ein beständiges Feuer unterhielten. Capit: v: Bodungen besezte heute
die neue Arbeit, und lag den gantzen Tag über in kleinem
Gewehr Feuer, wodurch 1. Iäger erschossen wurde.

23.ten Man hatte in der vergangenen Nacht so weit approchiret,
dass man mit einem Stein in das feindl: Verhak werfen konnte,
wobey von beyden Seiten die Batterien die gantze Nacht
hindurch spielten, wodurch 1. Engländer getödtet, und 5.
verwundet wurden. Ich besezte heute diese neue Arbeit, wo
mich der Feind mit Trauben und gehakten Eisen beschoss. 2.
Mann von der leichten Infant: wurden getodtet, und 1. Offr:
hart verwundet. Wir erhielten auch heute die Nachricht,
dass der ObristLt: Webster mit seinem Corps bey Coinghog
glüklich angekom̄en sey. Das 42^t Regt, die Queens Rangers und
die Volontairs von Irrland stiessen heute wieder zur Armée.

batteries fired a great deal, and our bombs were thrown so well that two of their small powder magazines in the first and second bastions blew up. A jäger was killed by a cannon ball. The troops recently arrived from New York were disembarked today on James Island at Hamilton's landing place.

We advanced our approaches last night and also raised a battery for three 6-pounders in the second parallel, right on the highway. The enemy fired briskly upon our working party with both cannon and musketry, to which we responded with many shells. Captain Hinrichs received orders to occupy the new work today. In the afternoon the rebels sent an officer out of the city to offer a capitulation, but since they wanted a free and honorable withdrawal of the garrison, negotiations were broken off. Toward evening a most severe gunfire ensued, lasting over two hours. *April 21*

Last night we built two demiparallels, about one hundred and fifty paces long, to the right and left of the approaches, while the enemy kept up a constant fire. Captain von Bodungen occupied the new work and was under fire from the enemy's musketry all day long, one of his jäger's being killed thereby. *22*

We advanced our approaches last night to within a stone's throw of the enemy's abatis. The batteries on both sides played throughout the night; we had one Englishman killed and five wounded. I occupied the new work today. The enemy fired upon me with grapeshot and scrap iron. Two light infantrymen were killed and an officer severely wounded. We received the news today that Lieutenant Colonel Webster has safely arrived with his corps at Cainhoy's. The 42nd Regiment, the Queen's Rangers, and the Volunteers of Ireland joined the army today. *23*

Aprl: Man hatte in der vergangenen Nacht die angefangene Arbeit
24. verbessert, wobey die Batterien von beyden Seiten die gantze
Nacht hindurch spielten. Capit: Hinrichs besezte heute die
Tranchées. Er war aber kaum auf seinem Posten, so thaten
die Rebellen, von ihrer linken, auf die frische Arbeit unserer
Rechten, wo der Lieut: v Winsingerode mit 30 Jägern, und
1. Offr: mit 50 Mann von der leichten Infant: stand, einen
Ausfall, dass der Lt: v: Winsingrode, da ihn die leichte Infant:
verliess, genöthiget war, bis in die 2te Paralelle sich zurük-
zuziehen. Es wurden hierbey 4. Jäger mit Bajonet-Stichen
hart verwundet, und 3 Jäger, nebst 1. Corp: und 8 Engländer
gefangen. Da aber die Feinde durch das Feuer der 2ten Paralelle
sehr gut empfangen wurden, so zogen sie sich so geschwind
wieder zurük, dass man 13 Gewehr und etliche Hüthe auf
ihrem Wege fand, welche vermuthlich von ihren getodteten
oder verwundeten müssen gewesen seyn. Der Feind konnte,
wenn er Hertz gehabt hätte, bis in die 2te Paralelle dringen,
und sich als denn wieder in Ordnung zurüke ziehen.—Der
Lord Cornwallis hatte in der vergangenen Nacht mit den
Volontairs von Jrrland, den Sud und Nord-Carolinern, bey
dem Gouverneurs-Hausse, durch Hülfe unser bewafneten und
aufgefangenen Boats den Cooper-Fluss passiret um zu dem
Webster: Corps zu stossen, und das Comando zu übernehmen,
wobey ein feindlicher Caper von 6. Canonen denen bewafneten Boats in die Hände fiel, welcher mit Rum und Reiss
beladen, in völliger Sicherheit an den linken Ufer des Cooper
Flusses sich fest gefahren, und die Fluth erwartete. Er wird
nunmehro zugerichtet, um sich seiner zu bedienen. Der General Pattersohn kam heute mit dem 63ten Regt: zur Armée,
und das Regt: v: Dietforth nebst dem Braunischen Corps
haben unter Comando des Obrist v: Westerhagen die Redouten
auf Fennings-Point und bey Lennings-Hauss besezt.

25ten Man hatte in der vergangenen Nacht bis an den Rand des
Grabens approchirt, und längst demselben die 3te Paralelle

PLATE II

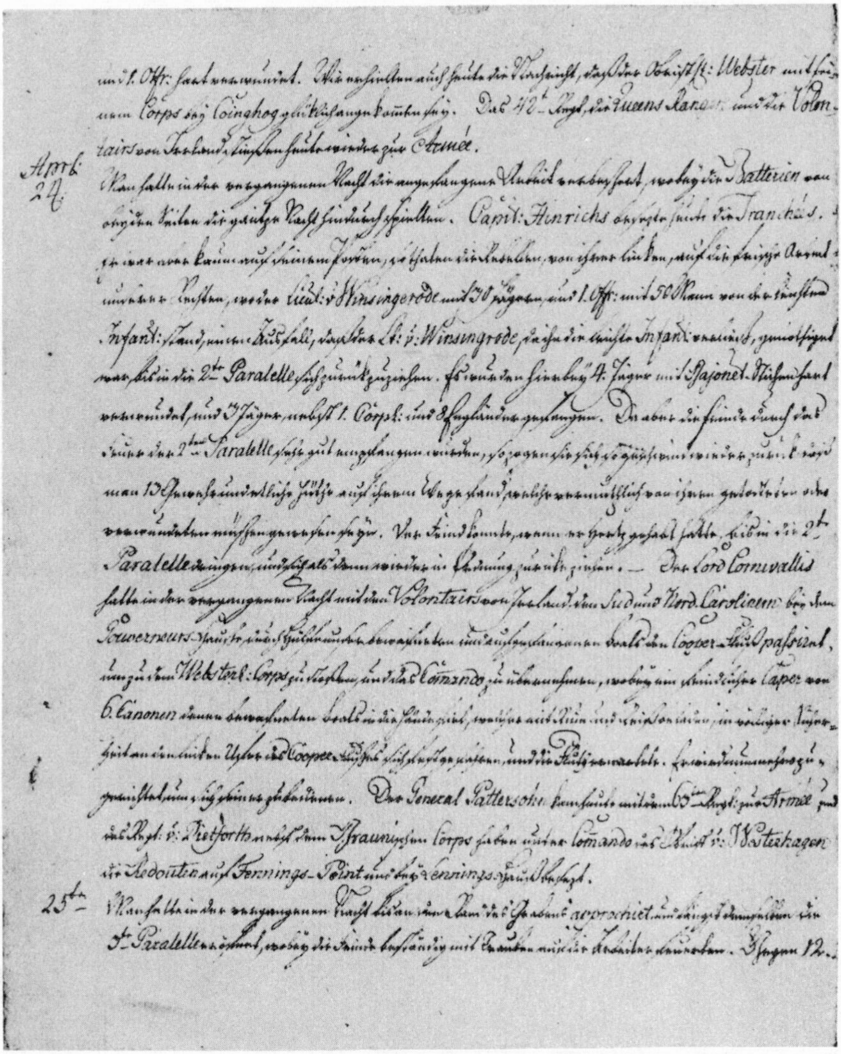

FACSIMILE PAGE OF EWALD'S DIARY
(Slightly reduced)

Last night the new works were improved. The batteries of both sides played all night. Captain Hinrichs occupied the trenches, but he was hardly at his post when the rebels made a sortie from the left upon the new work of our right, where Lieutenant von Winsingerode was posted with thirty jägers and another officer with fifty light infantry. Since the light infantry forsook him, Lieutenant von Winsingrode was obliged to withdraw into the second parallel. During this sortie four jägers were severely wounded with bayonets and three jägers, an English corporal, and eight rank and file were taken prisoners. However, since the enemy were very warmly received by the fire of the second parallel, they retired so fast that they left behind thirteen rifles and several hats, which, presumably, were those of their killed or wounded. Had they been courageous they could have advanced into the second parallel and then withdrawn in good order.—Last night Lord Cornwallis with the Volunteers of Ireland and the North and South Carolinians crossed the Cooper River at the Governor's house on our armed boats and some commandeered craft in order to join Webster's corps and take over the command. The armed boats captured a 6-gun privateer, which, loaded with rum and rice, had run aground on the left bank of the Cooper River and there, in complete safety, was waiting for the tide. She is now being conditioned for our service. General Paterson with the 63rd Regiment joined the army today. Von Dittfurth's Regiment and Brown's Corps, both under the command of Colonel von Westerhagen, occupied the redoubts on Fenwick's Point and at Linning's house.

Last night we advanced our approaches to the edge of the ditch and opened the third parallel alongside it. Our workmen were under a constant fire of grapeshot. Toward

eröfnet, wobey die Feinde beständig mit Trauben auf die Arbeiter feuerten. Gegen 12. Uhr fingen die Feinde ein heftiges klein Gewehr-Feuer längst ihrem Verhak zu machen an, wobey solche schrien: avance, tue, wodurch ein Schreken unter die Arbeiter und deren Bedekung kam, dass erstere davon liefen, und leztere sich nach der 2ten Paralelle theils ordentlich, theils unordentlich zurükezogen, welcher Schreken bis in die 2te Linie kam. Man sahe aller Orten Rebellen, man glaubte, es wäre ein Ausfall, man feuerte mit kleinen Gewehr über eine halbe Stunde lang, und kein Rebell hatte den Graben passirt, wodurch 1. Schottischer Officier nebst 4. Mann getödtet, 12. überhaupt von denen Engländern verwundet, 2 Hessische Grenad: getodtet, und 9. verwundet wurden. Der Lieut: Doepfer, welcher während diesem Zufall mit 20 Grenad: an dem Thor postirt war, mit dem Befehl, so bald der Feind das Thor eröfnen wollte, solchen anzuschiessen, hielt sich hier als ein braver Officier, und verliess zwischen diesen beyden Feuern seinen Posten nicht. Capit: Mallet welcher den nächsten Place d'armes besetzet hatte, verhielt sich ebenfalls bey dieser grossen Verwirrung sehr gut, und erwartete standhaft mit dem Bajonet in der Hand seinen Feind. Gegen 1. Uhr fand man sich wieder, allein das feindl: Feuer dauerte die gantze Nacht, und unsere Mörser Batterien beantworteten solches beständig. Capt: v: Bodungen besetze heute mit 60 Jägern die 3te Paralelle, und war dem gantzen Tag mit dem Feind engagirt. Die Rebellen hatten ihren 1ten Verhak, so bald es Tag war, verlassen. Wir hatten also ihr erstes Thor und abgebrochene Brüke über den Canal in unsern Händen.

April 26^t Man hatte in der vergangenen Nacht die neue Arbeit ver-

---

[1] These words ("Advance, kill") were retained in French, since they came most likely from the enemy's left wing front redoubt, which was occupied by Frenchmen (see pp. 235, 261).

[2] How unreliable a given diary may be in places is seen by comparing

twelve o'clock the enemy commenced a severe small-arms fire along their abatis, yelling at the same time *"Avance, tue,"* [1] which so filled our workmen and their guard with terror that the former ran away and the latter withdrew to the second parallel more or less in disorder. This terror also seized the second parallel. Everywhere they saw rebels. They believed the enemy had made a sortie and fired musketry for over half an hour, though not a single rebel had passed the ditch. [2] Our losses were one Scottish officer and four men killed, twelve Englishmen wounded, two Hessian grenadiers killed, and nine wounded. Lieutenant Doepfer, who during this engagement was posted at the gate with twenty grenadiers and was ordered to fire at the enemy as soon as they should attempt to open it, conducted himself like a good officer, not leaving his post between the two fires. Captain Mallet, who was occupying the nearest *place d'armes*, likewise conducted himself very well during this great confusion. Steadfastly, bayonet in hand, he awaited the enemy. Toward one o'clock our troops had collected themselves again. The enemy's fire, however, continued through the whole night, and our mortar batteries responded to it continuously. Captain von Bodungen with sixty jägers occupied the third parallel today and was engaged with the enemy all day long. By daybreak the enemy had left their first abatis. Thus we were masters of their first gate and the demolished bridge over the wet ditch.

During the past night the new work was improved and April 26

Ewald's entry for this day (April 25) with that of Hinrichs for April 24, and again both of these with the remarks of McIntosh, who, to be sure, reports from the other side. "Between 12 and 1 this morning," says McIntosh, "a heavy fire of cannon and musketry from our advanced redoubt, and the right of our lines, occasioned (it is said) by the enemy's advancing in column. It is certain they gave several huzzas, and abused us—calling us bloody dogs—being upon duty myself, and upon the lines all night; but whether they were out of their trenches is not so clear" (Simms, *op. cit.*, p. 134).

bessert, und 3 Batterien in der 3ten Paralelle angelegt, an welchem auch heute am Tage beständig gearbeitet wurde. Jch besezte heute die 3te Paralelle. Unsere Batterien spielten über 40 Bomben in die Stadt. Unser Verlust bestund in 1. Iäger, 2. leichte Infanteristen und 1. Canonier, dann 1. Offr: und 4. Grenad: verwundet.

April 27te Man arbeitete in der vergangenen Nacht an denen angefangenen Batterien, suchte solche durch Traversen gegen die feindl: Flanquen zu deken, und errichtete auch eine Batterie zur linken vor 2.6. ttor in der 2te Paralelle, wobey die feindl: Batterien beständig auf die Arbeiter spielten, welches wir mit Bomben beantworteten. Die Feinde unterhielten seit der vergangenen Nacht zu ihrer Sicherheit 3 Feuer zwischen ihren beyden Verhaken, welches sehr böss vor unsere Arbeiter war, und ich kann noch nicht begreiffen, warum nicht auf diejenigen, welche das Feuer anlegten und unterhielten, beständig mit kleinem Gewehr gefeuert wurde. Capit: Hinrichs muste heute die gewöhnlichen Oerter besetzen. Unsere sowohl als die feindl: Batterien spielten den gantzen Tag über. Unser Verlust bestand aus 1 Engl: Grenad todt, und 1. blessirt.

28. Man arbeitete in der vergangenen Nacht an den Batterien, wobey die Feinde beständig mit kleinem Gewehr auf die Arbeiter schossen, so wie beyderseitige Batterien die gantze Nacht feuerten. Capt: v: Bodungen besezte die 3te Paralelle und war wie gewöhnlich mit dem Feind in Feuer. Man brachte heute die Mörser in die 3te Paralelle, und einige in den demi place d'armes zwischen der 2ten und 3ten Paralelle, welche gute Dienste thaten, da der Feind fast den gantzen Tag seine Batterien spielen liess, und die unsrigen bis auf 2.24. ttor in No: 6. ohne unsern Werken Schaden zu thun, nicht mehr feuern durften. Ich weiss nicht, warum man nicht gleich die Batterien mit denen Paralellen mitgenoṁen, besonders da diese zu weit ablagen, und den Feind keinen grossen Schaden thun konnten. Ein Mann von der leichten Infanterie wurde heute getödtet.

three batteries were thrown up in the third parallel, on which work was continued during the day without interruption. I occupied the third parallel today. Our batteries threw more than forty shells into the city. Our losses consisted of one jäger, two light infantrymen, and one gunner [killed?] and one officer and four grenadiers wounded.

Last night we continued work on the new batteries, April 27 attempting to make them secure against the enemy's flanking fire by traverses. We also raised a battery for two 6-pounders in the left part of the second parallel. The enemy's batteries kept up a constant fire upon the workmen, to which we responded with shell. Since last night the enemy have kept three bonfires burning between their two abatis. This precautionary measure was very bad for our working parties. I do not understand why we did not keep up a constant fire of small arms upon those who started the fires and kept them burning. Captain Hinrichs was ordered to occupy the customary places today. Our batteries as well as the enemy's played the entire day. Our losses consisted of one English grenadier killed and one wounded.

Last night we continued work on the batteries, the enemy 28 incessantly firing small arms upon the workmen. The batteries on both sides also fired the entire night. Captain von Bodungen occupied the third parallel and was, as usual, engaged with the enemy. Some mortars were taken into the third parallel and several into the demiparallel between the second and the third parallels. They served us very well, for the enemy let their batteries play almost the entire day, and our pieces, except for two 24-pounders in No. 6, could not fire any more without damage to our works. I cannot understand why the batteries were not advanced with the parallels, especially since they were too far away to do great damage to the enemy. One man of the light infantry was killed today.

Aprl In der vergangenen Nacht wurde aus dem demi place
29ten d'armes, zwischen der 2ten und 3ten Paralelle gegen den Haupt-
Dam̃ approchiret, um die Schleusse zu ruiniren. Das feindl:
Canonen und Flinten Feuer war diese Nacht heftig, und
wurde von uns sehr schwach beantwortet. Ich besezte wie
gewöhnl: mit 60 Jägern die neu angefangene Approche, nach
welcher die Feinde stark bombardirte, weil sie merkten dass
man am Tage in selbiger arbeitete. Von den Arbeitern wurden
in voriger Nacht von den Engländern 2 Grenad: getödtet und
2 hart verwundet, dann 2 Hess: Grenad: leicht blessirt. Am
Tage wurden 2. Engländer todtgeschossen, und 2 nebst 1. Jäger verwundet. Es lief auch heute die angenehme Nachricht
ein, dass die Feinde die Verschanzung auf Lambergs-Point
verlassen, und sich nach der Stadt gezogen habe, worauf
der Lord Cornwallis solche besetzet, 4 Canons nebst vieler
Munition und eine Anzahl kleiner Schiffe erbeutet, wodurch
die Feinde nun gänzlich eingeschlossen seyn.

30^{t} Man arbeitete in der vergangenen Nacht an denen Batterien
in der 2ten und 3ten Paralelle und approchirte gegen den Dam̃,
so dass man schon den Rand des Grabens durchstochen hatte.
Das Feuer derer Batterien war bis nach Mitternacht heftig,
allein gegen Morgen wurde es still. Capt: Hinrichs muste
heute die neue Approche, und 3te Paralelle besetzen. Währender Nacht wurde 1 Hess: Grenad und Nachmittage 4.
Engländer bey der Arbeit verwundet. Man hat nun mehr,
seit der Zeit am Tage gearbeitet worden, die 400 Arbeiter in
2 Theile getheilt, wovon die eine Hälfte die Nacht, und die
andere am Tage arbeitet. Die Besetzung der Tranchée bestehet
aus 1,200. Mann.

Maij Man arbeitete vorige Nacht, die Batterien zu montiren, und
1te die Wasser Arbeit war so weit gekom̃en, dass solches am
Tage, schon einen merklichen Abzug hatte. Das Feuer war
währenden gantzen Nacht von beyden Seiten heftig, wodurch
2. Engl: und 1 Hess: Grenad: getodtet, und 2. Engl: nebst

Last night we advanced an approach toward the main dam from the demiparallel lying between the second and the third parallels so that we could demolish the lock. The enemy's cannon and musket fire was severe during the night and was answered only very weakly from our side. As usual, I and sixty jägers occupied the new approach, which was severely bombarded by the enemy, for they saw that we were working in it during the day. Of the working party two English grenadiers were killed last night, two severely wounded, and two Hessian grenadiers slightly. During the day two Englishmen were killed, while two others and one jäger were wounded. We received the pleasant news today that the enemy had deserted the fortifications on Lempriere's Point and withdrawn into the city, whereupon Lord Cornwallis occupied the abandoned works, capturing four guns together with much ammunition, as well as a number of small vessels. Now the enemy are completely surrounded.

Last night we continued work on the batteries in the second and the third parallels and advanced the approach toward the dam. The wall of the ditch has already been pierced. The batteries fired fiercely until midnight; but toward morning they were silent. Captain Hinrichs was ordered to occupy the new approach and the third parallel. During the night one Hessian grenadier was wounded and in the afternoon four Englishmen while at work. Now that we have been working also during the daytime, the four hundred workmen have been divided into two shifts, one of them working by night, the other by day. The force in the trenches consists of twelve hundred men.

Last night we were engaged in mounting guns in the batteries. The work at the ditch had progressed so far that today there was a noticeable drainage. The fire of both sides was severe through the entire night. We lost two English and one Hessian grenadier killed and two English and one

1. Hess: Grenad: verwundet wurden. Capit: v: Bodungen muste heute die 3te Paralelle besetzen. Es wurde 1. Jäger durch eine Canonen Kugel getödtet, und einem andern der Arm abgeschossen, auch 1. L. Infant: durch ein Stük Bombe getödtet. Heute Abend wurde der Befehl gegeben, dass 200. M. nur die erste Paralelle, und die übrigen alle die 2te und 3te Paralelle besetzen sollten. Gegen Abend spielten unsere Mörser Batterien über 1. Stunde lang, wodurch die feindlichen zum Stilleschweigen gebracht wurden.

Maij In der vergangenen Nacht arbeitete man, so wie in der Nacht
2te zuvor ohngeachtet der Feind ein starkes Geschütz und Mousqueten-Feuer machte, welches blos unsere Mörser beantworteten. Jch besezte heute die Tranchée. Die Feinde fingen eine Stunde vor Tage heftig zu feuern an, und da ihre Batterien die grosse Strasse kreuzten, so machte mir dieses das Einrüken in die Tranchée sehr sauer. Die Rebellen hatten von einem Deserteur, wie uns ein feindl: Uiberläufer versicherte, die Zeit erfahren, wenn die Jäger in und ausser die Tranchées marchirten, dahero sie ihnen zu Ehren einige Stüke auf die Strasse gerichtet hatten. Die feindl: Batterien schikten uns heute viel gehaktes Eisen und Glass in die Tranchées, und wir feuerten gar wenig. Unser Verlust war 1. Hess: Artill: Offr: hart verwundet, 1. Jäger und 1. L. Jnfant: leicht blessirt.

3te Man arbeitete Tag und Nacht an dem Ablassen des Wassers aus dem Canal, und an denen neuen Batterien. Die feindl: Batterien feuerten stark, und unsere spielten nur eine kleine Anzahl Bomben. Es wurden 3. Mann von der leichten Infanterie getödtet, und 1 Engl: Soldat hart verwundet. Am Tage war das beyderseitige Canonen Feuer nicht gar zu stark, doch wurde 1 Engl: Grenad: todtgeschossen, und 4 Mann von dem 63ten Regt: nebst 1. Pionier hart verwundet. Gegen Abend wurde das feindl: Canonen Feuer über 2. Stunden lang sehr heftig, welches auf die Ablössung gemüntzet war.

4ten In der vorigen Nacht hatte man sich mit der Arbeit wie zuvor

Hessian grenadier wounded. Captain von Bodungen occupied the third parallel today. One jäger was killed by a cannon ball and another had an arm shot off; also one light infantry-man was killed by a piece of shell. This evening orders were issued that only two hundred men should occupy the first parallel and that all the rest should go to the second and the third. Toward evening our mortar batteries played for over an hour, silencing those of the enemy.

We worked last night, just as the night before, in spite May 2 of the fact that the enemy fired briskly with guns and small arms, to which only our mortars responded. I occupied the [advance] trench today. The enemy opened a severe fire an hour before daybreak, and since their batteries raked the highway, I had a great deal of trouble getting into the trench. The rebels—so one of their deserters told us—had learned from one of our deserters the time when the jägers go into and leave the trenches; hence, to pay them their respects, they directed several of their pieces upon the highway. Today the enemy's batteries threw a great deal of scrap iron and glass into the trenches; but we fired very little. We had one Hessian artillery officer severely wounded and one jäger and one light infantryman slightly wounded.

Both day and night were spent bleeding the ditch and 3 working on the new batteries. The enemy's batteries fired briskly, ours playing only a few shells. Three men of the light infantry were killed and one English soldier was severely wounded. During the day the gunfire on both sides was not particularly severe. Nevertheless, one English grenadier was killed, and four men of the 63rd Regiment and one pioneer were severely wounded. Toward evening the enemy's cannon-ading was very violent for more than two hours. This was intended for our relief.

Last night our work was the same. From the demiparallel 4

beschäftiget, und aus demselben demi place d'armes rechts eine neue Approche angefangen, um sich dem Canal zu nähern, und das Wasser völlig aus dem selben zu leiten, weswegen die Feinde ein heftiges Geschütz und kleines Feuer die ganze Nacht hindurch machten, welches auch den ganzen Tag dauerte. Capit: v. Bodungen muste heute die 3 ^{te} Paralelle und die neue Approche besetzen. Bey dem Einmarch in die Tranchées wurde einem Jäger das rechte Bein abgeschossen, und 4. derselben verwundet. Gegen Mittag wurde 1 Jäger und ein UOffr: von den Hess: Grenad: todtgeschossen.—Gegen Abend schikte Lord Cornwallis 20 Gefangene ein, welche Tarlton bekom̃en hatte, unter diesen war Major Rutschelet ein Sohn des Gouverneurs von Charlestown und 2. Capitains. Unsere bewafneten Boats hatten auch in der vergangenen Nacht, ein 3 Mastiges Fahrzeug, welches mitten in dem Cooper-Flusse lag und kranke Negers am Bord hatte, ge- nom̃en. Das 64 ^{te} Regt stiess heute von dem Corps des Lord Cornwallis wieder zur Armée.

Maij
5 ^{te}

Gegen 10 Uhr gestern Abend fing das feindl: Geschütz und klein Gewehr-Feuer so heftig an, und dauerte die gantze Nacht bis am hellen Morgen, dass unsere Arbeiter wenig thun konnten. Ich besezte mit 50 Iägern die avancirten Werke, gegen welche der Feind von seiner Rechten aus eine Contre Approche in vergangener Nacht angefangen hatte, welche die unsrige Flanquirte, und an welcher der Feind den gantzen Tag über arbeitete. Ich suchte solches soviel möglich zu verhindern, allein er war schon tief in der Erde, und hatte 100 M. zu Bedekung der Arbeiter. Besonders aber muste ich mein Augenmerk auf die Embrassures richten, und konnte mithin nur 8. Jäger entgegen setzen. 1. M. von der L. In- fant: wurde todtgeschossen, und 1. Engl: Grenad: leicht ver- wundet.

6 ^{te}

Man arbeitete an den neuen Batterien, und führte Geschütz und Munition hienein. Die Arbeit nach dem Dam̃, war so

at the right a new approach was begun, so that we could get to the ditch and drain it completely. For this reason the enemy kept up a severe cannon and small-arms fire all night and all day. Captain von Bodungen was ordered to occupy the third parallel and the new approach. On his march into the trenches one of his jägers had his right leg shot off, while four others were wounded. About noon one jäger and a noncommissioned officer of the Hessian grenadiers were killed. Toward evening Lord Cornwallis sent in twenty prisoners captured by Tarleton, among them Major Rutledge, a son of the governor of Charleston,[1] and two captains. During the night our armed boats took a three-masted vessel which lay in the middle of the Cooper River and had sick Negroes aboard. The 64th Regiment left the corps of Lord Cornwallis today and joined the army again.

Toward ten o'clock last night the enemy's guns and mus- May 5 ketry opened a violent fire, lasting throughout the night and into the morning, with the result that our working party accomplished but little. I with fifty jägers occupied the advanced works, against which, last night, the enemy had begun a counterapproach on their right, flanking our new approach. They continued work on it the entire day, which I tried to prevent as much as possible. However, they were already deep in the ground and were, moreover, covered by a hundred men. Since it was especially important to watch the embrasures, I could oppose them with only eight jägers. One man of the light infantry was killed and an English grenadier slightly wounded.

We resumed work on the new batteries and took guns and 6 munitions into them. The sap leading to the dam had pro-

---

[1] The prisoner referred to is Captain Edward Rutledge, brother of the governor of South Carolina. Captain Hinrichs (p. 277) makes the same erroneous statement about his relation to the governor.

gut gelungen, dass der Canal an verschiedenen Orten kein Wasser mehr hatte. Die Feinde machten die gantze Nacht hindurch, ein anhaltendes klein Gewehr-Feuer, und endlich thaten wir ein gleiches auf diejenigen welche die Feuer anzünden wollten. Capit: Hinrichs besezte heute die 3te Paralelle und Approche. Das feindl: Canonen und Mousqut: Feuer war heute nicht stark. Wir verloren an Todten 1. Pionier-Offr: und 1. Mann von der leichten Infant: und 1. Engl: Grenad: wurde verwundet.

Maij 7ten In der vergangenen Nacht hatten wir unsere Batterien in der 2ten und 3ten Paralelle bis zum öfnen fertig gemacht, welche mit 23. Stüken, 2. Haubitzen und etl: und 20. Mörser, unter welchen ein 13. und 1.10 zölliger war, besezt waren. Die Feinde machten die gantze Nacht ein anhaltendes Geschütz und klein Gewehr-Feuer, wogegen unsere Batterien nur wenige Bomben spielten. Der Capit: v: Bodungen besezte heute die Tranchées, und wurde wie gewöhnlich warm gehalten. 1. Engl: wurde getödtet, Lt: Oehlhaus v. Graf: Gren: Batt: 1 Hess: Grenad: und 3 Englische Soldaten verwundet. Heute Morgen erhielten wir auch die freudige Nachricht dass der Admir: Arbuthnot, Sulivans Eiland nebst dem Fort Multric eingenoñen habe, und 150 Gefangne gemacht, benebst 20. Stüken erbeutet, wodurch wir nunmehro von dem gantzen Hafen Meister sind. Die Rebellen ergaben sich sobald sie sahen, dass eine Anzahl Mariniers und Matrosen auf dem Oestl: Theile gelandet und zum Sturm fertig waren. Zugleich erhielten wir die gute Nachricht, dass der Obriste Tarlton etl: 30 Dragoner an dem Santee Fluss gefangen, und viele niedergehauen habe, welches sich auf folgende Art zugetragen hat: Der Lord Cornwallis schikte den Lieut: Asch mit der berittenen L. Inf: gegen Lenons Ferry, welcher, da solcher der Nase nach patrouillirte, von denen Obristen Wassington und White gefangen wurde. So bald der General diese Nachricht erhielt, so schikte selbiger sogleich den Obristen Tarle-

gressed so far that the ditch was dry in several places. Through the entire night the enemy kept up a constant fire of musketry. At last we responded by firing at those sent out to start the bonfires. Today Captain Hinrichs occupied the third parallel and the [new?] approach. The enemy cannon and musket fire was not severe today. We had one officer of the Engineers and one man of the light infantry killed and an English grenadier wounded.

Last night we finished our batteries in the second and the third parallels, but did not open them. These mounted twenty-three pieces, two howitzers, and some twenty mortars, among them one of thirteen and one of ten inches. Throughout the night the enemy kept up a constant fire of cannon and small arms, while our batteries played only a few shells. Captain von Bodungen occupied the [front?] trenches today and was kept warm, as usual. One Englishman was killed; Lieutenant Oehlhaus of the Grenadier Battalion von Graff, another Hessian grenadier, and three English soldiers were wounded. This morning we received the good news that Admiral Arbuthnot had taken Sullivan Island and Fort Moultrie, with one hundred and fifty prisoners and twenty pieces, so that we are now masters of the entire harbor. The rebels surrendered as soon as they saw that a number of marines and sailors had landed on the eastern part and were ready to make an assault. At the same time we received the good news that on the Santee River Colonel Tarleton had taken some thirty dragoons prisoners, cutting down many others. All this happened as follows: Lord Cornwallis had sent out Lieutenant Ash with the mounted light infantry in the direction of Lenud's Ferry. He patrolled carelessly and so was made prisoner by Colonels Washington and White. As soon as the General received this information, he immediately

May 7

ton mit der Cavallerie der Legion dem Feind nach, welcher auch solchen zu Lenons Ferry einhohlte, sogleich auf selbigen fiel, zwischen 20 und 30 Drag: nieder hieb, etl: 30 zu gefangen machte, und 100 Pferde erbeutete. Die beyden feindl: Obristen, nahmen mit ihrer Partey die Flucht nach dem Santée-Fluss, und es wird vermuthet, dass der gröste Theil, in diesem Ufer ersoffen, oder in dem morastigen Ufer erstikt sind. Der Feind hatte schon den Lt: Asch und seine Leute in Boats gesezt, um sie über den Santée-Fluss in Sicherheit zu setzen. Da dieser aber seine Freunde an dem rechten Ufer des Flusses erblikte, schmiss solcher die Bedekung in Fluss, und kam glükl: zum Col. Tarleton.

Maij 8ten et 9ten   Das Feuer derer feindlichen Batterien und des kleinen Gewehrs, war die gantze Nacht hindurch anhaltend, welches man von unserer Seite mit einigen Schüssen von No: 6, und einiger Bomben beantwortete.—In allen Belagerungen in der gantzen Welt ist es gewöhnlich gewesen, dass das Feuer des Belagerer (um die feindl: Batterien zu demontiren) stärker als des Belagerten seyn muss. Nur hier ist has Gegentheil. Denn es sind 5. feindliche Stüke gegen eines von uns. Ich muste heute mit 50 Jägern, die 3te Paralelle besetzen. Sobald es helle war, so wurde die Stadt zum 2ten mahle aufgefodert wornach die Unterhaltung bis den 9ten Maij Abends 9. Uhr dauerten. Da aber die Rebellen, ohngeachtet ihre Provision zu Ende war, noch aus einem hohen Tone redeten, so wurde wieder abgebrochen, und die Feinde fingen um diese Zeit, nachdem sie uns 2. Tage am Seil herumgeführet, ihre Schuss-Scharten geändert, und Tag und Nacht gearbeitet hatten, unter Freuden Geschrey und Glocken-Spiel ihre Batterien aufs neue zu öfnen an, welches von unsern Batterien, so viel möglich beantwortet wurde. Diese beyderseitige heftige Canonate, welche mit einem anhaltenden Mousqueten Feuer begleitet war, dauerte die gantze Nacht hindurch.

10ten   Dieses ausserordentlich starken Feuers aber ohngeachtet,

sent Colonel Tarleton with the cavalry of the Legion in pursuit of the enemy. At Lenud's Ferry he caught up with them, attacked them, cut down between twenty and thirty dragoons, made some thirty prisoners, and captured a hundred horses. The two colonels fled with their party to the Santee River, and it is assumed that the greater part have either drowned in the river or sunk in the swamps along its banks. The enemy had already taken Lieutenant Ash and his men into boats in order to bring them to safety on the other side of the Santee. But when the latter saw their friends on the right bank of the river, they threw their guard overboard and safely reached Colonel Tarleton.

The fire of the enemy's batteries and small arms continued May 8 all night. It was answered from our side by some shots from and 9 No. 6 and by several shells. It is customary everywhere for the fire of the besieging army to be more severe than that of the besieged in order to dismount the latter's batteries. Only here the opposite is true, for there are five enemy pieces to every one of ours. I occupied the third parallel with fifty jägers. As soon as it was light the city was summoned a second time. The negotiations lasted until nine o'clock at night, May 9. But since the rebels, notwithstanding the fact that their provisions were spent, still spoke in a haughty tone, negotiations were broken off again. After leading us about by the nose for two days, after changing their embrasures and working day and night,[1] the enemy opened their batteries again with cries of joy and ringing of bells. Our batteries responded to their fire as well as possible. The heavy cannonading of both sides, which was accompanied by a constant fire of musketry, lasted through the entire night.

Yet in spite of this hot fire we dug a sap from our right 10

[1] Compare, however, De Brahm and Simms, who reproach the British for continuing their work during the truce. Simms (op. cit., p. 147) cites De Brahm as his only authority.

hatte man doch aus unserer rechten Paralelle bis an den Canal
Sappirt und an einer neuen Batterie angefangen. Capit: v:
Bodungen besezte heute die gewöhnl: Oerter, und das grosse
und kleine Feuer hielt von beyden Seiten den gantzen Tag
über an. Unser Verlust an Todten und Verwundeten bestehet
heute aus etlich und 20 Mann, mit welchen leztern 1 Engl:
Offr: und der Lieut: Fritsch von dem Graf: Battaill: und 1.
Iäger war.

Maij   Man hatte in der vergangenen Nacht an erwehnten Orte eine
11ten Gallerie über das Canal verfertiget, den 1te Verhak passirt,
und ein Logement nicht über 30. Schritte von den feindl:
Werken verfertiget, wobey das Feuer von beyden Seiten die
gantze Nacht hindurch anhielte. Ich besezte heute die 3te
Paralelle. Da· man sich aber in dem Logement noch nicht
halten konnte, so wurde dieses nicht besezt, doch troz dem
feindlichen Feuer am Tage daran gearbeitet.

Beyderseitiges Geschüz und Mousqueten Feuer continu-
irte beständig. Von 5. bis 7. Uhr Morgens wurde 1 L. Jnfant: 4. Hess: Grenad: und 2. Matrosen durch Stük-Kugeln
getödtet, und von leztern 3 hart verwundet. Gegen 9. Uhr
wurde den Batterien der Befehl ertheilet, die Stadt mit Feuer-
Kugeln zu beschiessen, wodurch 7. Häusser in der Vorstadt
in Brand geriethen, und das feindl: Feuer ein wenig stille
wurde. Wie die Häusser in Brand waren, so befahl der gross-
müthige General en Chef, denen Batterien so lange als es
brennte, zu schweigen, um diesem hartnäkigten Volk Zeit
zu geben, sich zu besinnen. Da es aber zu feuern fort fuhr, so
fingen unsere Batterien auch von neuen an, welches bis gegen
2. Uhr dauerte, wo der Feind chamade schlug, und ein Adjut:
des Rebellen Generals Lincoln mit einem Schreiben an unsern
Gen: en Chef aus der Stadt kam. Es wurde also Stillestand
auf beyden Seiten gemacht, und ich hatte das Glük gehabt,
die ersten und lezten Kugeln aus Charlestown gehört zu
haben.

parallel to the wet ditch and also began a new battery. Captain von Bodungen occupied the usual places today. The fire of the guns and the small arms continued the entire day on both sides. Our losses in killed and wounded amounted to some twenty today. Among the wounded were an English officer and Lieutenant Fritsch of Graff's Battalion as well as one jäger.

Last night we built a gallery over the ditch, passed the May 11 first abatis, and constructed a lodgment not more than thirty paces from the enemy's works, the fire of both sides continuing all night. I occupied the third parallel today. However, since the lodgment was not yet strong enough, we did not occupy it, but continued working on it during the daytime in spite of the enemy's fire.

The gun and musket fire continued on both sides. Between five and seven o'clock in the morning one light infantryman, four Hessian grenadiers, and two sailors were killed by cannon balls and three sailors severely wounded. Toward nine o'clock the batteries were ordered to fire hot shot into the city, which set fire to seven houses in the suburbs and lessened the enemy's fire somewhat. As soon as the houses had caught fire the generous Commander-in-Chief ordered the batteries to be silent while they burned in order to give this stubborn people time to think it over.[1] Since they continued to fire, our batteries, too, began anew and kept it up till almost two o'clock, when the enemy beat a parley and an adjutant to the rebel general Lincoln came out of the city with a letter to our Commanding General. A truce was observed on both sides, and I was fortunate enough to hear the first as well as the last shot out of Charleston.

[1] This statement is corroborated by Captain Hinrichs in his entry for April 13 (p. 249) and makes one skeptical of the following remarks of Edward McCrady: ". . . on all such occasions the British increased their fire, directing their shot and shells at the smoke" (*History of South Carolina in the Revolution, 1775–1780* [New York, 1901], p. 464).

Nachmittags 4. Uhr wurde die Stadt aufgegeben, und 1
Comp: Engl: und Hessischer Grenads, nebst 4 Canon: besezten
die feindlichen Werke, und das 7te 63te und 42te Regt: nahm
Besitz von der Stadt, und der Admiral von den Werken welche
den Hafen deken und von denen Schiffen.—Die Garnison,
welche aus 7. Gener: 16 Obrist: 42 ObristLts: 105 Capit: und
zwischen 4. bis 5,000 Mann bestand, strekte das Gewehr
zwischen den feindl: Verhaken, und wurde zu Kriegsgefan-
genen gemacht; 343. Canonen, worunter 21. Metallene waren,
3 Metallenen Mörser, einige Haubitzen und Cohorns, sehr
vieler Munition, nebst grossen Magazins von Rum, Reiss und
Indigo wurden erbeutet, welches ein unersezlicher Verlust
vor die Rebellen ist. Die Officiers behielten zwar ihre Equipage und Degens, da sie sich aber den 13ten gegen Abend übel
aufführten, und es schiene, als wenn solche einen Tu.nult
erregen wollten, wobey solche laut schrien: Es lebe der Congress, so wurden selbigen die Degens abgenoṁen. Ein feindlicher Officier versicherte mir, dass sie am meisten durch die
Iäger, Bomben, und kleines Gewehr-Feuer gelitten hätten,
und dass durch unsere Büchssen-Kugeln Leute in den hintersten Werken, ja sogar in der Stadt wären getödtet und
verwundet worden. Man siehet uns auch, da die gantzen
Einwohner der Stadt, Rebellen sind, und unter dem Gewehr
gestanden haben, so gerne als einen Preussischen Officier nach
dem vorlezten Kriege in Dresden.—Uiber dieses fielen nach-
stehende feindl: 27. Schiffe in unsere Hände: die Fregatte
Boston â 36. C. (nunmehro Charlestown) die Providence
â 32. C., der Ranger â 24. C. (nunmehro Halifax, der Avan-
turier â 24. C. ein Bulako â 18. C. und 5. 3 Mastige Fahrzeuge
nebst 17. kleineren. Dann waren 9. Schiffe versenkt, worunter
ein altes Ostindisch: Schif â 50 Can, die Fregatte Queen of
France â 32 C. nebst 2. 3 Mastern. In dem Wandaw Fluss sind
dem Corps des Lord Cornwallis in die Hände gefallen 13.
Fahrzeuge mit Gütern beladen, unter welchen ein 3 mastiges

At four o'clock in the afternoon the city was surrendered, and one company of English and Hessian grenadiers with four guns occupied the enemy's works, while the 7th, 63rd, and 42nd Regiments took possession of the city, and the Admiral of the ships and works covering the harbor. The garrison, which consisted of 7 generals, 16 colonels, 42 lieutenant colonels, 105 captains, and between 4,000 and 5,000 men, piled arms between their two abatis and were made prisoners of war. We took 343 guns (including 21 brass cannon, 3 brass mortars, and several howitzers and coehorns), a great deal of ammunition, and large stores of rum, rice, and indigo—all of which was an irreparable loss for the rebels. The officers, to be sure, kept their equipage and swords, but, since they misconducted themselves toward evening of the 13th and it looked as if they were going to stir up a tumult with their shouts "Long live Congress," their swords were taken away from them. An enemy officer assured me that they suffered most from the jägers and the shell and small-arms fire, and that our rifle balls killed and wounded people in the rear works and even in the city. Since all the inhabitants of the city are rebels and have been under arms, we are liked about as well as a Prussian officer in Dresden after the Seven Years' War. The following twenty-seven vessels came into our possession: the *Boston* frigate (now called *Charlestown*), 36 guns, the *Providence*, 32 guns, the *Ranger* (now called *Halifax*), 24 guns, *L'Aventure*, 24 guns, a polacre, 18 guns, and five three-masted ships as well as seventeen smaller ones. Then there were nine ships submerged, among them an old East Indiaman of 50 guns, the *Queen of France* frigate, 32 guns, as well as two three-masted ships. In the Wando River the corps of Lord Cornwallis came into possession of thirteen vessels and their cargoes, among them a three-masted ship. Thus we

ist. Auch hat man bey der Stadt 120 Boats von allerhand Sorten gefunden. Uiberhaupt also wurden 49 Schiffe erbeutet.

Maij D. 15ten Heute Nachmittage gegen 1. Uhr, da die Artillerie beschäftiget war, die Gewehre der Gefangenen in ein Gebäude zu legen, welches ein Pulver-Magazin des Feindes war, flog dasselbe in die Luft, wodurch 6. Gebäude, unter welchen ein Portel und ein Armen-Hauss war, durch die Flam̃en verzehret wurden. Es gingen hierdurch über 200. Menschen verlohren, unter welchen der Hauptmann Collin, und 1. Offr: von der Artillerie, der Lt: Macloi von dem 42ten Regt, 17 Engl: und 2. Hess: Artill: 1. Hess: Grenad: und verschiedene Engl: und Hessisch: Soldaten waren, ohne die Einwohner und Soldaten deren Rebellen, welche in dieser Gegend sich befunden hatten, mitgerechnet. Ich habe, so lange ich Soldate bin, manchen traurigen Auftritt im Kriege gesehen, allein noch keinen solchen schreklichen als diesen. Etlich und 20 verbrannte und verstüm̃elte, grub man aus den Trüm̃ern hervor. Etliche waren gegen die eine Kirche geschlagen, dass man keine menschliche Figur aus demselben machen konnte. Eine grosse Anzahl war halb todt, die sich vor Schmertzen des Brandes wie Würmer auf dem Erdboden krümten, und hier und da fand man Stüke von menschl: Körpern zerstreut liegen. Es wurde viele, welche den Brand stillen wollten, durch die losgegangenen Gewehr, verwundet. Ein Schlachtfeld konnte nicht trauriger aussehen. Und dieses Unglük ist blos durch die Unachtsamkeit der Engländer entstanden. Entweder ist ein Gewehr der Gefangenen welche geladen, und nicht abgeschossen waren, da man sie in der Eile in das Gewölbe hienein warf, loss gegangen, und hat das Pulver angezündet, oder es ist durch Bossheit der Rebellen, welches eher zu glauben ist, angezündet worden, welches beydes Nachlässigkeit der Engländer ist, wie ich denn am Cooper-Fluss ein starkes feindl: Pulver-Magazin offen, und nur mit 1. Schildwacht besetzet fand, welches mich bewog dem nächsten Regt: und dem Gen:

took forty-nine ships in all. Furthermore, we found near the
city one hundred and twenty boats of various kinds.

Toward one o'clock this afternoon when the artillery May 15
were engaged in putting the muskets of the prisoners away
in a building which had been used as a powder magazine by
the enemy, the building blew up, and the ensuing fire destroyed six houses, including a brothel and a poorhouse.
Over two hundred persons lost their lives, among them Captain Collins and one subaltern of the Artillery, Lieutenant
Maclow [?] of the 42nd Regiment, seventeen English and
two Hessian artillerymen, one Hessian grenadier, and several
other English and Hessian rank and file, not to mention the
inhabitants and rebel soldiers who happened to be near by.
During the years that I have been a soldier I have witnessed
many a sad spectacle of war, but never such a horrible one
as this. Some twenty charred and maimed persons were dug
out of the débris. Some had been blown against a neighboring
church, and were so mutilated that one could not make out
a human figure. A great many were half dead and, suffering
from burns, writhed like worms on the ground. Here and there
one found parts of human bodies scattered about. Many of
those who sought to put out the fire were wounded by muskets discharging. A battlefield could not look sadder. This
disaster was brought about by the carelessness of the English.
Either a prisoner's loaded musket was not shot off and, when
hurriedly thrown into the building, discharged and ignited
the powder, or the powder was ignited maliciously by the
rebels, which is more probable. In either case it must be
attributed to the carelessness of the English. I once found on
the Cooper River a large open powder magazine with only
one sentinel over it, which induced me to make a report to
the nearest regiment as well as to General Leslie. But I had a

Leslie solches zu melden, wobey ich viele Mühe hatte sie zu
bewegen darnach sehen zu lassen. 5,000. Gewehr nebst den
Degen der gefangenen Offrs schmelzten und flogen in die
Luft, deren Stüke noch viele in der Ferne tödteten, und ver-
wundeten. Und beynahe hätte dieses Unglük noch sehr ver-
grössert werden können, wenn das nur 200 Schritte davon
entfernte 2te Pulver-Magazin, worinnen 400 barils waren,
Feuer gefangen hätte.—Gegen Abend marchirten die beyden
Regimenter v: Dietforth und v: Hayne in die Stadt, um die
Garnison zu verstärken.

Anmerkung über die Stadt.

Die Stadt siehet einem schönen Dorfe ähnlich, und bestehet
etwa aus 800 Häussern, sie ist am Ende des Nuks zwischen
den Cooper und Ashley Fluss erbauet, ohngefehr über eine
gute Engl: Meile lang, und eine halbe Meile breit. Die Stras-
sen sind breit, und rechtwinkligt angelegt. Die meisten Gebäude sind von Holz und klein. Doch nach den Flüssen zu
siehet man schöne Gebäude von gebrannten Steinen, hinter
welchen gemeiniglich schöne Gärten angelegt sind. Man
findet hier viel Teutsche Franzossen und Spanier. Soviel man
von Ansehen schlüssen kann, so leben diese Leute mit vielen
Geschmak und in grösseren Luxum, als in den Nördlichen
Provintzen.—Was die Werke betrift so bestehen solche nach
der Land-Seite, aus einem Regulären Hornwerk mit 18 Can:
welches das alte Königswerk genennet wird, und dessen
Scarpe mit einer Mauer von Auster Schalen, und einem Kütte
davon 2. Fuss dik bekleidet ist. Es hat einen etwas morastigen
Graben, über welchen eine steinerne Brüke gehet. Das Thor
welches in der Mitte der Courtine ist, wird durch eine von
Erde aufgeführte lunette gedekt, welche einen doppelt verpallisadirten Graben hat. Nach der Stadt ist dieses Werk,
durch eine starke Brustwehr zugemacht, um welche man
ebenfalls einen doppelt verpallisadirten Graben angeleget

great deal of trouble to make them take the necessary precautions. Five thousand muskets and the swords of the captured officers melted and flew into the air, killing and wounding many at a considerable distance. This calamity might have been even greater had the fire spread to the second powder magazine, which was only two hundred paces away, and in which were four hundred barrels of powder.—Toward evening von Dittfurth's and von Huyn's Regiments marched into the city to strengthen the garrison.

REMARKS CONCERNING THE CITY

The city looks like a beautiful village and consists of about eight hundred houses. It is built at the end of the Neck between the Cooper and Ashley rivers and is approximately a good English mile long and half a mile wide. The streets are broad and intersect one another at right angles. Most of the buildings are of wood and are small; but near the rivers one sees beautiful buildings of brick, behind which there are usually very fine gardens. Many Germans, Frenchmen, and Spaniards live here. If one can judge from appearances, these people show better taste and live in greater luxury than those of the northern provinces.—Now a few words about the works. On the land side they consist of a regular hornwork with eighteen guns, called the old royal work, the escarp of which is faced with a wall of oyster shells and mortar[1] two feet thick. It has a rather muddy ditch, over which leads a stone bridge. The door, which is in the center of the curtain, is covered by a lunette of earth. This lunette is strengthened by a double-picketed ditch. On the city side the work has a

[1] This building material is commonly called "tapia" or "tappy" and consists of approximately equal parts of raw oyster shells, lime, sand, and water.

hat. Unter dem kleinen Gewehr-Schuss von diesem Werk ist
ein Retranchement en Redans in Form eines nach der Stadt
eingehenden halben Mondes angelegt, welches einen doppelten verpallisadirten Graben von 6 Fuss Breite, und eben so
viel Tiefe hat, der durch einen guten Verhak gekrönet ist. Der
Eingang in dieses Werk wird ebenfalls durch einen halben
Mond, der einen Graben hat, und durch bewegliche Spañische
Reuter gedekt. Zu beyden Flanquen dieses Werkes hat man
unter dem kleinen Gewehr-Schuss 2. detachirte Werke, von
welchen, das zur rechten an den Cooper-Fluss, und das zur
linken an dem Ashley Fluss gestützet ist, angelegt, welche
beyde, etwas rükwärts des Retranchements durch 2 andere
wieder gedeket werden. Die gantze Fronte dieser Werke, ist
durch einen Morast verwahrt, welcher durch die beyden
Flüsse Ebbe und Fluth hat, durch Hülfe dessen man einen 6
Fuss tiefen und 12 Fuss breiten Canal in der Entfernung von
100. Schritten von dem Retrenchement gezogen, und das
Wasser durch Däme über den Morast in den Canal gebracht,
welcher Graben ebenfalls an der Seite des Retranchements
einen guten Verhak hatte, hierüber war eine Brüke portatif,
und der Eingang durch den Verhak, mit einem wohlver-
wahrten Gatter Thor versehen. Diese detachirte Werke hingen
mit dem Retranchement durch Pallisaden und Graben anein-
ander, und man hatte das zur rechten, während der Belagerung durch eine Courtine zusañen gehenket, und das zur
linken ebenfalls durch dieses Mittel zusañen hängen wollen,
allein wir waren zu nahe, und eben dieses machte den feindl:
linken Flügel sehr schwach. Denn wenn man Meister von
diesen detachirten Werken war, so konnte man das übrige
im Rüken wegnehmen. Der Frantzössische Ingenieur du Por-
taille, welcher 14 Tage vor der Uibergabe von dem General
Wassington nach dieser Stadt geschiket wurde, fand es sehr
übel, dass diese detachirten Werke offen waren. Es war auch
die Ursache, dass das Hornwerk in der Kehle zugemacht

parapet and again a double-picketed ditch. Within musketry range of this work is a trench of redans in the shape of an inward crescent, with a double-picketed ditch six feet wide and equally deep, which is crowned by good abatis. The entrance to this fortification is given protection by a work constructed in the form of a half moon and having a ditch, and also by movable chevaux-de-frise. On both flanks of this work, within musketry range, there have been raised two detached works, that on the right resting upon the Cooper River and that on the left upon the Ashley. These detached works are [again] covered by two others situated a little behind the ditch. The entire front of these works is protected by a swamp which, because of the two rivers, has high and low tide. A hundred paces from the ditch they have dug a canal six feet deep and twelve wide, into which they have led water from the swamp by means of dams. This canal also has a good abatis on the side nearest the ditch. A portable bridge leads over the wet ditch, and the entrance through the abatis is provided with a well-covered gate-work. These detached works were connected with the lines by means of palisades and ditches. During the siege the one on the right was provided with a curtain, and they had intended to do this also on the left. However, we were too close upon them. The fact that the left work was still detached during the siege made it very weak, for, once one was master of these detached works, he could easily take those in the rear. The French engineer Duportail, whom General Washington had sent to this city two weeks before the capitulation, thought it very bad for these detached works to be open. He also saw to the hornwork's being closed in the rear. Had we come upon them less quickly, their works would certainly have been put in a respectable condition. The works which protect the

wurde, und wären wir diesem nicht mit unserer Arbeit so geschwind auf den Halss gekom̄en, so würden gewiss diese
Werke in einen ansehnlichen Stand gesetzet worden seyn. Was
die Werke betrift, welche die Stadt längst denen Warften und
den Hafen bedekte, so bestanden sie aus starken Batterien,
von welchen eine die andere dekte, und waren mit Courtinen
zusamen gehenkt. Besonders war der Theil, welchen man das
Königswerk nannte, mit gebrannten Steinen, oder mit einer
Mauer von Auster-Schalen bekleidet, und die Brustwehren,
welche 18 Fuss dike waren, mit Coffres von gantzen Cabbage
Bäumen, dessen Holz so zähe wie Kork ist, welche mit Sand,
der eingestampft war, gefüllet sind. Am Ende des Necks lag
ein Fort, welches ein langes Dreyek, so wie der Neck for-
mirete und den Haven dekte, und von eben diesen Materien
mit Terrassen erbauet, 3 Lagen Canons ausmachte, welche in
27. – 24 ttor und 18 ttor bestanden. Wollte man die Stadt von
der Wasser-Seite angreiffen, so war es nicht anders möglich
als solche durch schwim̄ende Mörser Batterien, oder Bombardier Gallioten bombardiren zu lassen, indem eine Stük-Kugel
gegen das Cabbage-Holz nicht den geringsten Effect thut.
Der Cooper Fluss war mit 14. gesenkten Schiffen versperret,
und der Canal, welchen man offen gelassen hatte, lag unter
dem kleinen Gewehr-Schuss dieser Werke. Nach der Seite des
Aschley-Flusses hatte man alle Werfte, von welchen man
vermuthete, dass solche nicht gut von den Batterien bestrichen werden konnten, durchstochen, und die Werke waren
mit Hundert und etlichen schweren Canonen besezt.—Der
commandirende General liess den 13 ten Maij nachfolgendes
Danksagungs-Schreiben, der Armee, über ihr gutes Verhalten,
während der Belagerung publiciren.

"Der com̄andirende General halten sich verbunden, der
"Armee das Lob zu ertheilen, welches dieselbe durch ihre

wharves and the harbor consist of strong batteries covering
one another and are connected by curtains. The part called
the royal work is faced with bricks or with a wall of oyster
shells, while the breastworks, which are eighteen feet thick,
are made of coffers of whole cabbage trees, the wood of which
is as tough as cork. These are filled with impounded sand.
At the point of the Neck there is a fort in the shape of a long
triangle, like the Neck itself, which protects the harbor and
which is built in terraces, also of palmetto logs and oyster
shells. It has three tiers of guns, consisting of twenty-seven
24- and 18-pounders. If one wanted to attack the city from
the water side, it could be done only by means of floating
mortar batteries or bombarding galiots, for cannon balls
have not the least effect upon palmetto wood.[1] The Cooper
River was barricaded with fourteen submerged ships, and
the channel which was kept open was within range of the
small-arms fire of the works. All the wharves on the Ashley
River which the enemy thought could not readily be raked
by their batteries have been provided with embrasures. Some
hundred heavy guns were mounted on the works.—The
Commanding General issued on the 13th of May the following
proclamation thanking the army for their good behavior during the siege:

"The commander in chief receives the highest pleasure in
giving the Army, by whose Courage and Toil he has reduced
this important place, the Tribute of Praise & of Gratitude
they so well deserve.—

[1] Both Captain Ewald and Captain Hinrichs make repeated reference to
the usefulness of the wood of the palmetto, commonly called "cabbage
tree." Hinrichs speaks at length of the protection it would afford seamen
during an engagement if the ships were lined, where the guns are mounted,
with this tough wood (see p. 349).

"Tapferkeit, und saure Arbeit, wodurch dieser wichtige
"Platz erobert worden, so wohl verdienet hat, und seine
"Excellenz finden ein unaussprechliches Vergnügen darinne,
"ihre Dankbarkeit im höchsten Grade abzustatten.—Sr:
"Excellenz sind dem Gen: Lieut: Lord Cornwallis, dem
"Gen: Leslie, v: Hyne, v: Cospoth, und dem Brigadier
"Batterson ohnentlich verbunden, vor die während der
"Belagerung geleisteten Dienste.—Denen sämtlichen Of-
"ficiers von der Artillerie, sowohl Engländer als Hessen,
"denen Officiers vom Iäger Detachement, dem Capitain
"Elphingston, denen See-Officiers und Matrosen, welche am
"Lande Dienste gethan, versichern Sr: Excellenz, dass Sie
"sich jederzeit ihnen höchst verbunden halten werden, vor
"den Eifer mit welchem dieselben alle ihre Operationes
"unterstützet haben.—Sr: Excellenz erstatten ferner ihren
"Dank dem Col: Webster und dem Corps mit welchem der-
"selbe, die völlige Communication den Feinden abgeschnit-
"ten, und besonders dem Obristen Tarlton, der Cavallerie
"und Infanterie von der Legion, vor das gute Betragen.
"—Der cõmandirende General sind dem Maj: Ferguson
"vielen Dank schuldig, vor die erwiesene Geschiklichkeit
"in der Feld-Fortification.—Dem Major Montcrief aber,
"welcher den Plan zur Belagerung gemacht, und ihn mit
"so vieler Beurtheilung, unermüdeten Fleisse, und Tapfer-
"keit ausgeführet, und die unter ihm dienende Ingenieurs,
"wünschen Sr: Excellenz Worte zu finden, um Ihre Dank-
"barkeit in einem höheren Grade ausdrüken zu können.

Maij Gestern und heute wurde der Militz erlaubet, auf ihr Ehren-
19 et 20 Wort nach ihren Wohnungen zu gehen, und der grösste Theil
der feindl: Officiers wurden nach Hatterals Point geschikt,

"His Excellency presents his warmest thanks to Lieu^t: Genl: Earl Cornwallis, Major Gen^{ls}. Leslie, Huyne, Kospoth, and Brigadier Genl. Paterson for their animated Services during the Seige:

"To the Officers and Soldiers of the Royal Artillery, of every Corps British and Hessian, of the Jägers, and to Captⁿ: Elphinston & the Officers and Seamen of the Royal Navy, who have acted with us on shore, His Excellency also addresses the assurance that he holds himself under the most permanent obligations to them, for having so well seconded in their spirited efforts all his operations.

"His Excellency further expresses his great obligations to Lieu^t. Col^l. Webster, and the Corps with which he broke in upon the most essential of the Rebel Communications; and particularly to Lieu^t: Col^l. Tarleton and the Corps of Cavalry & to the Infantry of the Legion, for the Soldierly conduct & Gallantry which gave them such Brilliant advantages over the Enemy.

"To Major Ferguson the General declares himself much indebted, for his great activity and good Services, & particularly for the useful application made of his Talents in field Fortification.

"But to Major Moncrieff who planned & Conducted this Seige, with such great Judgement, such unrelaxed assiduity, & so much intrepidity, & to the very Capable Officers under him, as well as to every other person in this department: His Excellency could wish to convey impressions of His Gratitude greater than he is able to express."[1]

Yesterday and today the militia were paroled to their May 19 homes, and the greater part of the enemy officers were sent and 20

---

[1] This proclamation is an exact transcript of von Huyn's copy in the von Jungkenn Papers. It is signed by John Despard, deputy adjutant general.

wo ihnen erlaubet ist, 6. Meilen weit in dem Land herum zu gehen.

Maij 21ᵗ Heute mit Anbruch des Tages marchirte die Engl: leichte Infant: das 42ᵗᵉ Regt, und die Queens-Rangers gegen Dorchester und Strawberg, um die in den Land von dem Feinde verstekte Effecten aufzusuchen. Sie haben auf 6. Tage Provision mitgenoñen. Die Armee ausser der Garnison von Charlestown erhielt auch heute den Befehl sich zum Embarquirung fertig zu halten. Wir erhielten auch die Nachricht, dass die Feinde, sobald Lord Cornwallis mit seinem Corps zu Mannigault angekoñen war, Georgetown verlassen, und sich gegen Campden gezogen hätten.

22ᵗ 23 24. Abends 8 Uhr marchirte das Detachement Jäger, die Engl: Grenad: und 3 Bataill: Hessischer Grenadiers unter dem Gen: Cospoth nach Ashley Ferry, um die leichte Infant: welche den Cyprus passiret, und ihre Partey weit in das Land, bis Oranienburg schikte, zu unterstützen. Unser Lager wiñelte hier von allerhand Arten von Schlangen, und man wurde an dem morastigen Ufer des Ashley-Flusses mehr dann 8. Crocodills gewahr. Wir erhielten auch Nachricht, dass Lord Cornwallis vor 3 Tagen den Santee-Fluss passiret und gegen Campden marchiret sey. Es kam heute eine gantze Comp: wohlgesinnter Einwohner aus den Gebürgen von Sud-Carolina hier an, welche Waffen und Munition verlangten, um sich an ihren Unterdrükern zu rächen. Es sollen sich schon 2000 M. Königs-Freunde zusañen geschlagen haben, welche sich theils hier, theils bey Lord Cornwallis befinden, und mit Gewehr versehen sind.

25ᵗ Heute brachte eine Engl: Fregatte die angenehme Nachricht, dass die Spanier nachdem solche erfahren hatten, dass der Adm: Ross ihre Provisions-Flotte genoñen, die Belagerung von Pensacola aufgehoben haben.

26ᵗ Des Morgens marchirten wir wieder in unser altes Lager zurük.

to Haddrell's Point, where they are permitted to go about the country within a radius of six miles.

At daybreak the English light infantry, the 42nd Regiment, and the Queen's Rangers started out toward Dorchester and Strawberry to search for the property which the enemy had hidden in the country. They took six days' provisions with them. The army, except the garrison of Charleston, was ordered today to keep itself in readiness to embark. We received the news that the enemy had left Georgetown and retired toward Camden just as Lord Cornwallis was arriving with his corps at Manigault. May 21

At eight o'clock in the evening the jäger detachment, the English grenadiers, and three battalions of Hessian grenadiers started off for Ashley Ferry under General Kospoth in order to support the light infantry which had crossed the Cypress and was sending advance parties as far into the country as Orangeburg. Our camp was alive with all kinds of snakes, and we saw at least eight crocodiles on the marshy bank of the Ashley River. Also, we received information that Lord Cornwallis had crossed the Santee River three days ago and was marching toward Camden. Today an entire company of loyal inhabitants arrived from the mountains of South Carolina, desiring arms and ammunition in order to avenge themselves on their oppressors. Two thousand loyalists, all armed, are said to have gathered already, some here, some with Lord Cornwallis. 22, 23,
and 24

Today an English frigate brought us the welcome information that the Spanish, after learning that Admiral Ross had captured their provision fleet, have raised the siege of Pensacola. 25

In the morning we marched back to our old encampment. 26

Maij
28^t

Kam das Corps des Obristen Abercramby wieder zurük, und bezog sein altes Lager.

29. 30 et 31
Iunij 1^t
und 2^t

D. 29ten blieb noch alles ruhig, den 30ten und 31ten wie auch den 1ten und 2ten, wurden das Iäger Detachement, die Engl: und Hess: Grenad: die leichte Infant: das 42te Regt: und die Queens Rangers, unter dem Gen en Chef: Sir Henry Clinton Gen: Leslie, und v Cospoth embarquirt.

3. 4. 5.
6. 7te

D. 3ten und 4ten passirten sämtl: Schiffe die Estacade, und den 6ten und 7ten die Bar.

8 bis 17te

Den 8ten ging die ganze Flotte in die See, und d. 17ten warf solche nach einer 10 Täg: glükl: Schiffart bey N. Yorck in der Narrows die Anker.

19te

Den 19ten Iunij, wurden sämtl: von Charlestown gekomene Truppen, unter dem General Leslie zu Staaten Eiland debarquiret.

ENDE.

ANHANG

Die unter Comando, des als Gouverneur und Comandant der Südlichen Provinzen zurükgebliebenen Earl Cornwallis, daselbst gebliebene Truppen, bestehen: als

Das 7te 63te und 64te dann Dittforth und Hynische Regt: zur Besatzung von Charlestown. Dann 2. leichte Infant: Comp: v. 71. Regt:, 1. v. 16ten Regt: 1. v. 60ten Regt: 2. Grenad: Comp: v. 71ten Regt: 1. von 16ten und 1. von 60ten Regt: Das 23te 33te und 71te Regt:, Brauns Corp: Yorck Volont., South und North Caroliner Volont:, South und North Carolin: Miliz, Fergusons und Rawdons-Corps, Ein Auszug von Yorck Provinzial:, die Legion zu Pferd und zu Fuss, 3. Trupp von 17ten Drag: Regt: Savannah Leicht Hors, Ein Corp: Artilleristen und Pioniers.

Colonel Abercrombie's corps returned, going into its May 28
former camp.

On the 29th everything remained quiet; on the 30th and 29, 30,
31st, as well as on the 1st and 2nd of June, the jäger detach- and 31,
ment, the English and Hessian grenadiers, the light infantry, June 1
the 42nd Regiment, and the Queen's Rangers embarked under and 2
the Commander-in-Chief, Sir Henry Clinton, and Generals
Leslie and von Kospoth.

On the 3rd and 4th all the ships passed the stockade and 3, 4, 5,
on the 6th and 7th the Bar. 6, and 7

On the 8th the entire fleet put to sea and on the 17th, 8 till 17
after a good journey of ten days, we cast anchor in the Narrows near New York.

On the 19th of June all the troops arriving from Charleston 19
disembarked on Staten Island under General Leslie.

END

APPENDIX

Lord Cornwallis, as governor and commandant of the
Southern provinces, had these troops under his command:

The 7th, 63rd, 64th, and Dittfurth's and Huyn's Regiments as garrison of Charleston. Then two light infantry
companies of the 71st, one of the 16th, and one of the 60th
Regiment; two grenadier companies of the 71st Regiment,
one of the 16th, and one of the 60th. In addition, the entire
23rd, 33rd, and 71st Regiments, and, lastly, the following
corps, troops, and detachments: Brown's Corps, the New
York Volunteers, the South and North Carolina volunteers,
the South and North Carolina militia, Ferguson's and Raw-
don's Corps, some New York provincials, the Legion (both
mounted and dismounted), three troops of the 17th Dragoon
Regiment, the Savannah Light Horse, and one corps of
artillery and pioneers.

DIARY
OF
CAPTAIN JOHANN HINRICHS

AUSZUG

aus dem Hand-Iournal des Staabs-Capit: Hinrichs vom Hochlöbl: Feld-Iäger-Corps, auf der See-Reise von New-York nach Georgien am Bord des Apollo, Transport-Schiffes, unter Coṁando des Hl: Major v: Wurmbs.

Decembr: Nachdem alles dasjenige, was zur vorhabenden Expedition
1779. erfoderlich war, seit Anfange dieses Monats war verordnet, und die respectiven Regimenter und Corps von dieser Embarkation waren avertiret worden, so wurde, nachdem die Schiffe mit 70 Täge Provision versehen waren, der Anfang mit dem embarkiren gemacht. Die Truppen waren folgende:

Brittische Grenadiers	1,008.	Mann.
" Light Infanterie	1,012.	"
" 23te Regiment	300.	"
" 33te do:	350.	"
" 42te do	750.	"
" 63te do	300.	"
" 64te do	350.	"
Hessische Grenadiers	1,200.	"
" Iäger	250.	"
" Chasseurs	120.	"
" Regiment Hayne	450.	"
Detachement vom 71ten Regt:	150.	"
Guides und Pion:	100.	"
Fergusons Corps	150.	"
Lord Cathcarts Legion	700.	"

[1] The 42nd Regiment was countermanded just before embarkation (see p. 367). It formed part of the reinforcements sent later (see p. 67).

EXTRACT

from the Private Journal of Staff Captain Hinrichs of the Jäger Corps, describing the Voyage from New York to Georgia, on Board the *Apollo* Transport, under the Command of the Honorable Major von Wurmb

Since everything necessary for the proposed expedition December, had been ordered since the beginning of the month, and the 1779 regiments and corps had been notified, the embarkation was started, the ships being provisioned for seventy days. The troops were the following:

British grenadiers...............................	1,008 men
" light infantry............................	1,012 "
" 23rd Regiment............................	300 "
" 33rd Regiment............................	350 "
" 42nd Regiment [1]	750 "
" 63rd Regiment............................	300 "
" 64th Regiment............................	350 "
Hessian grenadiers..............................	1,200 "
" jägers..................................	250 "
" chasseurs [2]	120 "
" Regiment Huyn.........................	450 "
Detachment of the 71st Regiment.................	150 "
Guides and pioneers.............................	100 "
Ferguson's Corps...............................	150 "
Lord Cathcart's Legion.........................	700 "

---

[2] This is the chasseur company of Captain George Hanger (see p. 13, note 1, and p. 24, note 1).

New-York Volunteers........................   400. Mann.
Althausens Riflemen.........................   35.   "

                                               6,625. M.
Dann das Brittische 7te Regiment...............   350.   "

                      Summa T: 6,975. Mann.

und diese Truppen wurden auf etlich und 80. Schiffe vertheilt.

Decemb: Nach der gestern empfangenen Ordre wurde das Detache-
d. 19ten ment des Hochlöbl: Feld-Iäger Corps, als Major von Wurmb,
Capit: Ewald, Hinrichs, v: Bodungen, Lieut. v: Winsinge-
rode, Schæfer, v. Bartholomæi und Kling, 24. Unter-Officiers,
3. Feldschers, 3 Waldhornisten, 3 Halbmondbläser und 250.
Jäger heute Morgen 10 Uhr unter Gewehr beordert, und
marchirten nach New-York zum embarquement.

Decbr: Capt: Ewald, Lieut: v. Winsingerode und 50 Jäger kamen be-
20.-22.   nebst der Bagage, Recruten u.s.w. der Hessischen Regter: v
Trumbach und v. Wissenbach auf das Schiff Fan; weil dieses
aber auf dem East-River auf einen Felsen fuhr, und sich be-
schädigte, so wurde das Detachement noch vor unserer Abfahrt, so gut nur thunlich in der Flotte eingetheilt.

Die übrigen Iäger embarkirten unter Comando des Hl. Major
v Wurmb auf dem Schiffe Apollo. Dieses Schiff führt 24.
Canonen, hatte aber die Hälfte davon in New York zurück
gelassen, um Raum für die Bettstellen zu verschaffen. Es war

[1] Correct total is 7,975.

[2] The total number of transports in the embarkation list (see the facsimile
facing p. 108) is eighty-eight. However, there is at least one ship missing
from this list, namely, the *Lady Crosby*, which, with two others, the *Swift*
and the *Henry* (manuscript letter of Major Baurmeister, March 26, 1780),
was taken by the rebels and brought into Charleston. It is interesting to
compare this list with Hinrichs' account as to the total force under Sir
Henry Clinton. That given in the facsimile is probably the more dependable,
since it was sent to Baron von Jungkenn by Major Carl Baurmeister, an
adjutant to Lieutenant General von Knyphausen. To this number must be
added some 4,000 reinforcements as well as 450 seamen and marines who
performed land duty. On the other hand, there must be subtracted 250 recruits

New York Volunteers.............................	400 men
Althausen's Riflemen	35 "
	6,625 men
Then the British 7th Regiment...................	350 "
Sum total	6,975 men [1]

These troops were distributed among some eighty ships.[2]

In compliance with orders received yesterday the detach- Dec. 19
ment of the Jäger Corps was under arms this morning at ten
o'clock, whereupon it marched to New York to embark.
This detachment was made up of the following officers and
men: Major von Wurmb, Captains Ewald, Hinrichs, and von
Bodungen, Lieutenants von Winsingerode, Schaefer, von Bartholomæi, and Kling, 24 noncommissioned officers, 3 regimental surgeons, 3 trumpeters, 3 buglers, and 250 jägers.

Captain Ewald, Lieutenant von Winsingerode, and fifty Dec. 20–22
jägers, as well as the baggage, the recruits, etc., of the
Hessian regiments von Trümbach and von Wissenbach[3] went
on board the *Fan;* but since she was damaged from running on
a rock in the East River, this detachment was distributed in
the most expedient manner over the fleet before our departure.

The rest of the jägers embarked on the *Apollo* under the
command of the Honorable Major von Wurmb. This ship
carries twenty-four guns; but she left half of them in New
York to make room for berths. She is a ship of four hundred
tons and commanded by a Scotsman named John Adimson [?].
Since the cavalry was still to be embarked, we lay at the wharf

---

for the Hessian regiments at Savannah and 150 Hessian and Anspach
chasseurs, as well as the 35 Riflemen who were on the *Anna*, which was
driven to England.

[3] The Regiment von Trümbach is the old Grenadier Regiment Rall,
which after the Trenton disaster was reorganized and successively commanded by von Woellwarth, von Trümbach, and d'Angelelli. This regiment
and von Wissenbach's were stationed at Savannah.

gross 400 Tonnen, und wurde geführt von einem Schottländer Nahmens Iohn Adimson. Weil noch die Cavallerie zu embarkiren war, blieben wir bis heute den 22ten an dem Wharft zu New-York liegen, und trafen, als wir gegen Mittag bey Sandyhook ankamen, noch die daselbst für England bestim̃te Flotte mit Invaliden etc etc an, welche aber den andern Morgen mit herrlichem Winde und unter Bedekung von 6. Kriegs-Schiffen in die See stach.

Decbr: 23.-25.   Der Wind war so vortheilhaft wie möglich für unsere Fahrt, weil aber den 25ten des Nachmittags erst die lezten zu unserer Flotte gehörigen Schiffe von New-York kamen, musten wir die Gelegenheit des günstigen Windes unbenutzt lassen, und wir blieben bis den andern Morgen innerhalb der Hook vor Anker liegen.

Decbr: 26.   Schon gestern Nachmittag war der Admiral mit seinem Geschwader aus dem Hook geseegelt, und über nachtete bey Never-Sink. Heute Morgen folgte die Flotte um 10 Uhr mit vortreflichen Winde nach. Der Tag war angenehm, und der Anblik der Flotte, wie jeder sich drängte, durch den Canal zu erst zu kom̃en, unterhaltend. Unsere Flotte war überhaupt 96. Seegel stark. Die Bedekung war folgende:

Europa.	64. Canonen.	V. Admir. Mar: Arbuthnot.
Ryssel.	74. "	Comodore
(Copper bottom)		
Robust.	74. "	Capt:
Raisonable.	64. "	"
Defiance.	64. "	"
Renown.	50. "	"
Roebuck.	44. "	" Sir And. Snape Hammond.
(Copper bottom)		
Romulus.	44. "	" Clinton
	32. "	"
Perseus.	20. "	"
(Copper bottom)		

[1] Names of ships' captains supplied from W. L. Clowes, *The Royal Navy* (London, 1897–1903), IV, 48.

at New York until today, the 22nd. Upon arriving at Sandy
Hook toward noon, we encountered a fleet destined for
England with invalids, etc., etc. This fleet put to sea the
following morning with a splendid wind and under cover of
six men-of-war.

The wind was as favorable as possible for our journey; Dec. 23–25
but, since the last ships belonging to our fleet did not arrive
from New York till the afternoon of the 25th, we could not
make use of this fair wind. We lay at anchor within the
Hook until the following morning.

The Admiral and his squadron sailed out of the Hook Dec. 26
yesterday afternoon and spent the night at Never Sink. At
ten o'clock this morning the fleet followed with an excellent
wind. It was a pleasant day, and we enjoyed the sight of the
fleet, every ship anxious to get through the channel first.
The entire fleet consisted of ninety-six sail. The convoy was
as follows:

Europe	64 guns	Vice-Admiral Marriot Arbuthnot [Captain Wm. Swiney] [1]
Russell (copper-bottomed)	74 "	Commodore [F. S. Drake]
Robust	74 "	Captain [Phillips Cosby]
Raisonnable	64 "	" [T. Fitzherbert]
Defiance	64 "	" [Max Jacobs]
Renown	50 "	" [Geo. Dawson, acting]
Roebuck (copper-bottomed)	44 "	" Sir Andrew Snape Hamond
Romulus	44 "	Clinton [Captain Geo. Gayton]
[ ]	32 "	[ ]
Perseus (copper-bottomed)	20 "	" [Honorable G. K. Elphinstone] [2]

[2] The 74's and the 64's did not remain at Charleston. However, several
vessels came as convoys with the Cork fleet. Major General von Huyn (p.
379) says five, though the editor can account for only the *Richmond* and the
Raleigh. (The other three may have been frigates and armed ships.) Several
other men-of-war arrived as convoys with the reinforcements sent from New
York. The list given by Clowes, *loc. cit.*, needs to be corrected.

Sr: Excellenz der commandirende General war am Bord des Romulus, und der Earl of Cornwallis am Bord des Roebuck.

Decbr: 27.
39.° 16.'
North.
66. Meilen.

Wir hatten heute einen guten Tag für unsere Farth. Der Wind
war mittelmässig, und die Kälte erträglich. Der Schifs-Capt:
schien ein stiller ordentlicher Mann zu seyn; unser Schiff war
eines der grösten, und erst 5 Iahr alt. Wir hatten 19. Matrosen
(die Anzahl sollte 25. seyn) worunter verschiedene handfeste
und erfahrne Mann.

Decbr: 28.
91. Meilen.

Eine hohe See, und allen Anschein zum Sturm. Gegen
Mittag wurde der obere Mast herunter gelassen, gegen Abend
war nur noch ein Seegel aufgespannt, und um 3 Uhr die Nacht
das Steuer fest gebunden. Unser Schiff ging 12½ Fuss im
Wasser, und wurde sehr geworfen; denn es hatte nicht seine
gehörige Ladung. Kein Stük blieb an seiner ihm angewiesenen Stelle, was nicht sehr fest gebunden war. Es war
keine Möglichkeit zu kochen, und die Leute musten mit
Zwiebak und Rum sich begnügen, Gegen 2. Uhr die Nacht
kam ein Anspach: Iäger in die Kajüte gestürzt, und wollte
melden: dass das Schif an einer Seite eingefallen wäre, und
einige Iägers schon todt. Es war stokfinster in dem Raum wo
sie lagen, die Bettgestellen waren 2 Reihen über einander, in
jeder lagen 6. Mann, und 4 von diesen Bettgestellen waren es,
die auf einmal durch das Geschaukel sich lossrissen und
einstürzten, und wo folglich die obenliegenden Iäger mit
samt dem Bette auf die darunter liegenden fielen; und als nun
durch dieses Gepolter die wenigen, welche noch schliefen,
auch aufwachten, alles munter war, iedes kreischte, und in
demselben Augenblik eine grosse unhöfliche Welle oben ins
Loch hieneinstürzte, da war ein panisches (aber sich leicht
zu entschuldigendes) Schreken über das ganze Schiff verbreitet.

Mit dem Lichte der Lampe klärte sich das Gesicht des
erschrokenen Jägers wieder auf.

His Excellency the Commanding General was on board the *Romulus*, and Earl Cornwallis on board the *Roebuck*.

It was a fair day for our voyage. The wind was moderate and the cold endurable. The master of our ship seemed to be a quiet, decent fellow. Our ship was one of the largest and only five years old. We had nineteen sailors (there should have been twenty-five), among them several sturdy and experienced men.

A heavy sea and every indication of a storm. Toward noon the main-topgallant was lowered; by evening only one sail was still set, and about three o'clock in the morning the helm was lashed. Our ship drew twelve and one-half feet of water. She pitched a good deal, for she had not sufficient cargo. Nothing remained in its proper place unless firmly secured. It was impossible to cook anything, and the men had to be satisfied with biscuit and rum. Toward two in the morning an Anspach jäger came rushing into the cabin with the report that one side of the ship was stove in and that some of the jägers had already been killed. It was pitch dark in the hold where they lay; the berths were arranged in two tiers and accommodated six men each.[2] The rolling of the ship had caused four of the berths to come loose and collapse, so that the jägers in the upper berths had fallen, berths and all, upon those lying beneath. This crash had awakened the few still asleep. At this moment, with all wide awake and shouting, a big rude wave had rushed in through the opening above and a panicky, but easily excusable fear had spread over the entire ship.

By the light of the lamp the face of the frightened jäger cheered up again.

[1] He probably means nautical miles.

[2] J. G. Seume, the German poet, who arrived in Halifax in 1782 with a contingent of Hessians, also speaks of six men being put away in each berth when four more than filled one (*Mein Leben*, in *Prosaische und poetische Werke* [Hempel ed., Berlin, 1875], I, 55).

Margin notes:

Dec. 27
39° 16′
north
66 miles[1]

Dec. 28
91 miles

Decbr: 29.
47. Meilen.

Der Sturm dauerte diesen Morgen noch alles fort; das Spritzen der Wellen zeigte aber an, dass er anfing schwächer zu werden. Gegen 10. Uhr seegelten wir wieder bey einer gewaltigen hohen See, und mit sehr veränderlichen Winde weiter. Die Luft war gemässigt, den Nachmittag sahen wir See-Enten und See-Hunde. Gegen Abend ging der Wind westlich und fing an etwas sicherer zu wehen. Die See legte sich nach und nach wieder und der Anschein zum Nordlichen Winde war da. Dieser Sturm war auf einer glüklichen, von Felssen und Sandbänken reinen Küste, indem wir zwischen Cap May und Cap Charles ohngefehr 70–80. Leag: Oestl: vom Lande waren, nemlich zwischen den 74 und 75°. West longitudo von London, und den 39 und 37° North latitudo vom Aequator. Wir hatten eine ziemlich ruhige Nacht.

Decbr: 30.
35.° 46.
67. Meilen

Noch etwas unruhige See am Morgen, die aber gegen Mittag ruhig ward; veränderlicher und schwacher Wind bis gegen Nachmittage, dann Nördlicher Wind, der gegen Abend ziemlich stark wurde: Jn der Nacht von 11. bis 3 Uhr gingen wir 7. Meilen in einer Stunde. Den Nachmittag wurde der Obere Mast wieder aufgesezt, und wir fuhren den Nachmittag mit 7 Seegeln. Es war ein Vergnügen zu sehen, mit welchem gesunden Magen Speiss und Trank von statten ging.—

Das unangenehmste beynahe von allem bey einer Winter-Farth zur See ist: das *Feuer*, welches man wegen der Kälte gezwungen ist, in der Cajute anzumachen, und wo dann der Stein Kohlen Dampf einen immerwährenden unangenehmen Geruch durch die ganze, auf die Luftröhre würkende Atmosphäre, und so Kopfschmerzen und Uiblichkeiten verursachet.

Gegen Abend war Wetterleuchten (der gewisse Vorbothe eines sich nahenden Sturmes in Winter-Zeiten) und um 2 Uhr ein heftiger Wirbelwind (Squal) mit Regenwetter. Wir waren in Gefahr. Unser Schif kam hinter den Wind, und der Admiral gerade auf uns ein, dem wir in den Weg getrieben waren. Ein Augenblik mehr so war unser Schiff in Grund

The storm continued through the whole forenoon, but the splashing of the waves showed that it was beginning to slacken. Toward ten o'clock we sailed on again with an extremely high sea and a variable wind. The air was moderate. In the afternoon we saw gulls and seals. Toward evening the wind shifted to the westward and began to be more steady. Gradually the sea grew calm again, and everything promised a north wind. Fortunately, the storm had struck us on a coast free of rocks and sandbanks, for we were between Cape May and Cape Charles, about seventy to eighty leagues[1] east of the coast, namely, between 74° and 75° longitude west of London and 39° and 37° latitude north of the equator. We had a rather quiet night.

The sea, though somewhat rough in the morning, became calm toward noon. Until well into the afternoon there was a variable breeze followed by a north wind, which became rather strong toward evening. Between eleven at night and three in the morning we made seven miles an hour. In the afternoon the main-topgallant was raised again, and we carried seven sails. It was a joy to see how everyone now relished food and drink.

The most unpleasant thing of all during a voyage in winter is, it seems, the necessity of having a *fire* in one's cabin, for the coal fumes impregnate the entire atmosphere with an everlasting disagreeable odor, affecting the windpipe and causing headaches and nausea.

Toward evening there was sheet lightning, in winter the certain forerunner of an approaching storm, and at two o'clock we had a violent squall with rain. We were in danger. Our ship was running before the wind, and the flagship, into whose course we were driven, was heading straight for us. Another moment and our ship would have been run down.

[1] He must mean nautical miles.

geseegelt, allein die Geschwindigkeit mit der der Man of War sich wendete, rettete uns. Der Wind blies stark, das Wetter klärte sich auf, der Wind ging nach Osten, und bey einer Sternhellen Nacht fuhren wir 5–6 Meilen in der Stunde;

Decbr: 31.
92 Meilen

Der Russel und Perseus machten diesen Morgen Jagd auf 4. Schiffe, die sich vor der Flotte sehen liessen. Gegen Mittag brachten sie sie ein. Es waren 4 im lezten Sturm aus der Flotte verschlagene Pferde Schiffe.—Herrliches Wetter und vortreflicher Wind. Wir würden, wenn wir nicht aus Besorgniss für Cap Feare Lookout und Hatteras, zu weit in die See gestochen, dass wir iezt in den Current kamen, ein ziemliches Stük Weges gemacht haben; allein dies schlug uns gewaltig zurük. Die Bewandniss hiemit ist folgende: Der Golf of Mexico ist ein grosser Ocean in West-Jndien, in welchen viele und reissende Flüsse von Carolina, Louisiana etc sich ergiessen. Alles dieses Wasser drängt sich durch eine schmale Enge, genannt die Strasse von Bahama. Welchen Druk dieses Wasser daselbst machen muss, ist leicht zu begreifen, und der Current ist so reissend, dass man, mit dem besten Winde kaum dagegen halten kann. Er läuft von Bahama längst der Küste von North-America, North by East, und ist bis Cap Hatteros am reissesten; verliert sich von da bis Cap Cod etwas, und bekom̄t durch diese hervorragende Land-Enge wieder einen neuen Druk, so dass er wieder mit vieler Geschwindigkeit läuft, und deswegen auch die Farth um Cap Cod südlich, hauptsächlich im Frühjahr sehr erschwert, und wegen der dasigen Felssen und Sandbänken gefährlich macht.— Iezt sehe man ein, von welchem Vortheil uns Rhode Island als See-Haven war; indem, so lange wir es im Besiz hatten, die New Englænder, welche die stärkste Marine haben, uns unsern Haven in New York nicht unsicher machen konnten.

Januar. 1.
1780.
34°. 08'.
25 Meil:

Wir hatten einen herrlichen Wind, der uns 6–7 Meilen in 1 Stunde führte. Wir fuhren S.W. hatten den Current gegen

However, the speed with which the man-of-war tacked saved us. The wind blew briskly, the weather cleared up, the breeze veered to the east, and under a starlit sky we made five to six miles an hour.

In the morning the *Russell* and the *Perseus* chased four ships that appeared before the fleet. Toward noon they brought them in. They were four horse transports separated from the fleet during the recent storm. Beautiful weather and an excellent breeze. We would now have made pretty good time had we not, in our attempt to clear safely Cape Fear, Cape Lookout, and Cape Hatteras, stood too far to sea and so got into the current, which held us back seriously. The nature of this current is as follows: The Gulf of Mexico is a large sea in the West Indies into which empty many swift rivers from Carolina, Louisiana, etc. All this water rushes through a narrow channel, called the Straits of Bahama. What pressure the water must exert there is easy to conceive. The current is so swift that even with the best wind it is hard to hold one's own. From Bahama it runs along the coast of North America, north by east. It is swiftest up to Cape Hatteras. From there to Cape Cod it loses some of its force; but this prominent neck of land gives it renewed force, so that it again flows with great velocity. This makes the sailing south around Cape Cod, especially in spring, very difficult and, because of the presence of rocks and sandbanks, very dangerous. One must realize now what an advantage Rhode Island was to us as a seaport, since, so long as we had it in our possession, the New Englanders, who have the strongest navy, could not make our harbor in New York unsafe.

We had a splendid breeze and could have made six to seven miles an hour; but since we were heading SW. we had

Dec. 31
92 miles

Jan. 1,
1780
34° 08′
25 miles

uns, und machten statt 146. Meilen nur 25. Den Nachmittag wurde das Wetter trübe und wolkicht, den Abend im̄er stürmischer, und die Nacht ein völliger Sturm. Alles ging im Schiffe wieder durcheinander, ein Seegel wurde nach dem andern eingebunden, und die Nacht war böse.

Jan: 2. Und so war der folgende Tag. Gegen Mittag wurde das Steuer fest gebunden, und wir trieben vor dem Haupt-Seegel. Der Wind war den Morgen N. und N.O. wir trieben W und S.W. Gegen Mittag als der Sturm in der völligsten Wuth war, spürte man an der Farbe der Wellen, dass der Grund nicht tief seyn müsse. Wir wurfen das Senkbley, und fanden nur 25 Faden Wasser. Dies war eine unangenehme Nachricht! Der Wind blies uns gerade aufs Land zu; wir waren nicht gewiss ob Cap Feare schon passirt war, und daselbst ist Untiefe von 25 zu 16. zu 3 Faden Wasser. Der Sturm schien jeden Augenblik heftiger zu werden, und nicht der geringste Anschein war da, dass das Wetter so bald sich ändern würde. —In der That, dies war keine Frühlings-Sonne die uns anlächelte! Gegen 4. Uhr den Nachmittag ging der Wind O.S.O. und um 6. Uhr war er S.O. und da der Sturm von 4½–5 Uhr minder wüthete wie vorher und nachher, so benuzte der Admiral die Gelegenheit sich mit der Flotte zu drehen, und eine andere Stellung anzunehmen, und diese war so vortheilhaft, wie möglich. Denn indem der Wind von S.O. kam, trieben wir S.W. und weil wir den Current gegen uns hatten, waren wir sicher, nicht weit verschlagen zu werden, und da der Wind vom Lande kam, waren wir sicher, nicht an die Küste gewehet zu werden. Aber des Geschaukels, Geknatters etc war kein Ende, und zu kochen war auch keine Möglichkeit.

Jan: 3. Dieser Tag war nicht besser, wie der vorige; ja viel mehr
33.° 02′. noch schlim̄er. Wir trieben, der Wuth der Wellen, und des Windes überlassen, mit festgebundenem Steuer vor einem Seegel südlich, indem der Wind Westlich war. Von der ganzen

the current against us, and so we made only 25 miles instead of the 146 that we might have made. In the course of the afternoon it became gloomy and cloudy. In the evening it grew stormier and stormier, and during the night we had a real storm. Everything on board the ship was topsy-turvy; one sail after another was furled. The night was bad.

And so was the following day. In the morning the wind Jan. 2 was N. and NE., driving us W. and SW. Toward noon the helm was lashed and we lay to before the mainsail. From the color of the waves we could tell that the sea was not deep. We cast the lead and found only twenty-five fathoms of water. This was unpleasant news! The wind was driving us straight toward land, and we were not sure whether we had passed Cape Fear, where the sea is only twenty-five to sixteen, and at some places but three fathoms deep. The storm seemed to be increasing every moment, and there was not the least prospect of the weather changing soon.—Indeed, it was no spring sun that smiled on us! Toward four o'clock in the afternoon the wind shifted to ESE., and by six o'clock it had veered to SE. Since the storm abated somewhat between half-past four and five, the Admiral made use of this opportunity to tack with the fleet, which proved to be most advantageous, for, while the wind came from SE., we drifted SW., and, the current being against us, we were safe against being carried too far, and when [later?] the wind came offshore, we were safe against being blown upon the coast. But there was no end of rolling, creaking, etc., and there was no opportunity to cook.

Today was no better than yesterday; in fact, it was worse. Jan. 3 Left to the fury of wave and wind, we drifted southward 33° 02′ with helm lashed and before one sail, the wind being westerly. Of the entire fleet we saw this morning only one man-of-war

Flotte sahen wir heute Morgen nur noch 1. Man of War und 17. Seegel.—Dass die stärkste Campagne nicht mehr angreiffen kann als eine solche Reisse, ist gewiss. Denn 1) Kein ordentliches Essen zu zurichten. 2) Mit der grösten Mühe und Unbequemlichkeit jeden Bissen zu sich zu nehmen. 3) Keinen Augenblick Schlaf, wegen des gewaltigen Schaukelns und Getöse, das an keiner Stelle des Schiffes ärger ist als in der Cajute. Dennoch waren wir alle bis jezt gesund und heiter, obgleich etwas entkräftet.

Jan: 4.
32.° 27'.
36. Meil:

Die vorige Nacht war nicht besser, wie die vorhergehende, und der heutige Tag auch nicht, wo nicht noch schliṁer, indem es so trübe, so dunkel war, dass wir auch in der Nacht die Flotte verlohren hatten. Wir sezten deswegen, ohngeachtet des bösen Wetters, heute Morgen um 8 Uhr 4. Seegel auf, kamen gegen Mittag wieder bey die Flotte, und legten dann wieder bey. Der Wind war N.W. und wir trieben S.W.—Von der ganzen Flotte waren nur 48 Schiffe da; es fehlte aber auch der Russel, Renown, und Robust, die vermuthlich den grösten Theil der übrigen Flotte bey sich haben werden. Und da der Renown fehlte, so hoften wir, dass die Anna, Transport, auf welchen die Chasseur-Compagnie des Capit: v: Hangers war, und welche im ersten Sturm den Haupt- und Hinter-Mast verlohren hatten, noch lebte, indem die Renown sie nach dem ersten Sturm gezogen hatte.

Jan: 5.
34.° 49'.
69. Meilen.

Heute Morgen fuhren wir einige Stunden, aber es wüthete wieder so heftig, dass gegen Mittag das Steuer wieder angebunden wurde, und alle Seegel bis auf einen eingezogen. Den ganzen Tag und die Nacht sahe und hörte man nichts als Noth-Flaggen und Noth-Schüssen von Schiffen, die Unglük erlitten hatten, allein niemand konnte ihnen helfen. Wir hatten heute Mittag auch einen Lek unter der Cajute beym Steuer, allein es war leicht zugemacht, indem man ohne Mühe dabey koṁen konnte. Der Wind war N.W. und wir fuhren S.W.

PLATE IV

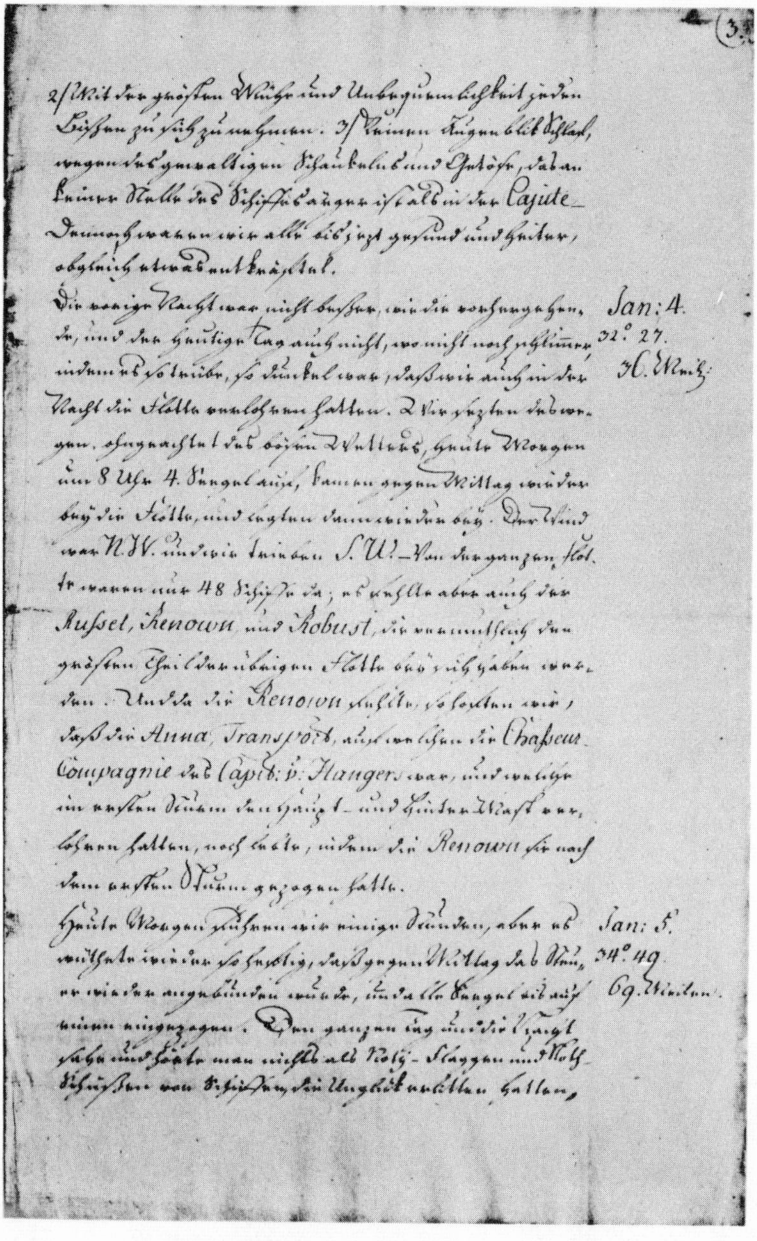

FACSIMILE PAGE OF HINRICHS' DIARY
(About one fourth of original size)

and seventeen sail.—It may be safely said that the most strenuous campaign cannot be as trying as such a voyage; for (1) one cannot prepare a decent meal; (2) one takes every morsel with the greatest difficulty and discomfort; (3) one enjoys not a moment of sleep because of the fearful rolling and noise, which is worse in the cabin than in any other place in the ship. Nevertheless, so far we have all been well and in good spirits, although somewhat weakened.

Last night was no better than the previous night, nor was the day any better—if anything, it was worse. It was so gloomy and dark that we lost sight of the fleet during the night. Hence, in spite of the abominable weather, we set four sails at eight o'clock in the morning. Toward noon we rejoined the fleet and then lay to again. The wind was NW. and we drifted SW. Of the entire fleet only forty-eight ships were together; but among the missing were the *Russell*, the *Renown*, and the *Robust*, which presumably were with the greater part of the missing ships. The absence of the *Renown* allowed us to hope that the *Anna* transport, which was carrying Captain von Hanger's company of chasseurs and had lost her mainmast and mizzenmast in the first storm, was still afloat and the chasseurs alive, for she had been taken in tow by the *Renown* after the first storm.

Jan. 4
32° 27′
36 miles

This morning we sailed for a few hours, but then the storm began to rage again so violently that toward noon it was necessary to lash the helm again and furl all sails except one. The entire day and night one could see and hear nothing but the flags and shots of ships in distress. However, no one could go to their assistance. At noon our ship, too, sprung a leak below the cabin, near the helm. But it was easily stopped since one could get to it without trouble. The wind was NW. and we stood SW.

Jan. 5
34° 49′
69 miles

Jan: 6. Sturm, Regen, Hagel, Schnee, und das Wasser der schäu-
menden Wellen bis oben über die Cajute, war unsere heutige
Observation. Wir zählen 52. Seegel. Der Wind war N.W. und
N.E. [*sic*] und wir trieben N.W. und N.N.O.

Jan: 7. Allezeit dasselbe Wetter! Wir waren die Nacht wieder etwas
10. Meilen von der Flotte gekoñen, und fuhren von 2–7. Uhr den Nachmittag mit 2. Seegeln, und dann wieder eingebunden, und
das Schif treiben lassen. Das Wetter wurde iñer diker, und
die See höher wie vorher. Der Wind war W.N.W. und das
Schif trieb W.S.W.

Jan: 8. Der Wind war so heftig wie vorher, und stand von gestern
30.° 16'. Nachmittag bis heute Mittag S.W. Das Schif trieb W.S.W.
Wir fingen diesen Nachmittag einen Shork. Er wog etwa
200 Pf. und war von Kopf bis Schwanz 9 Fuss 2½ Zoll. Ich
habe einen Theil seiner Haut aufbewahrt, sie ist so scharf,
dass sie zu einer feinen Säge in der mechanischen Werkstatt
kann benutzet werden. Es ist ein Raub-Fisch, und geht nie
ohne einen kleinen braunen, mit gelben Punkten bezeigneten
Fisch, der deswegen Pilot heisst. Dieser schwimet vor ihn
her, und zur Zeit einer herannahenden Gefahr klemmet er
sich unten an den Bauch des Fisches. Seine Iungen retten sich
dann in dem Leibe des Shorks (wie die Kröte) So fanden wir
auch über 40 junge lebendige Shorks in dem Eingeweide des
Alten. (Ich habe einige hievon in Spirit aufbewahrt) Der
Pilot hing an seinem Bauch, ging aber beym hienaufziehen
verlohren. Wenn er etwas erwischen will, so legt er sich auf
den Rüken, und sein Maul, wovon nur die untere Kinnlade
beweglich ist, und welches unter dem Kopfe sitzt, kann als
dann, wenn es geöfnet ist, eines erwachsenen Menschen Bein
auf einmal hienein spatzieren lassen. Sein Alter erkennet man
an der Reyhe Zähne, dieser hatte 3 Reyhen, und war 3 Jahr
alt. Man fängt ihm mit grossen Haaken am Strike mit einem
Stüke Fleisch, das hinten über die Cajute hienunter gelassen
wird. Denn da dieses der Ort ist, wo die Seeleute ihr Salz-

Storm, rain, hail, snow, and the waves breaking over the Jan. 6
cabin, such was today's observation. We were fifty-two sail.
The wind was NW. and NE. and we drifted NW. and NNE.

Always the same weather! In the night we were again Jan. 7
separated somewhat from the fleet and from two till seven 10 miles
o'clock in the afternoon we were going before two sails.
Then they were furled again, and the ship was allowed to
drift. The weather became thicker and thicker and the sea
higher than at any time before. The wind was WNW., and
the ship drifted WSW.

The wind was as violent as before, and from yesterday Jan. 8
noon until noon today it was SW. The ship drifted WSW. 30° 16'
In the afternoon we caught a shark. It weighed about two
hundred pounds and measured nine feet and two and one-half
inches from head to tail. I kept a piece of its skin, which is
so sharp that it can be used as a fine saw in a mechanic's
shop. The shark is a predatory fish and never moves about
except in the company of a brown, yellow-spotted fish,
which swims ahead of the shark (for this reason called
"pilot") and, when danger approaches, clings to his belly. The
shark's young then take refuge inside its body (as do toads).
So we found over forty young living sharks in the viscera
of the old fish. I preserved some of them in alcohol. The pilot
was clinging to his belly, but was lost in hauling up our
catch. When pursuing its prey the shark turns over on its
back, for its mouth, only the lower jaw of which moves, is
on the under side of its head. It is large enough to let a grown
person's leg pass in. One can tell its age by the number of
rows of teeth. This one had three rows and was therefore
three years old. It is caught with a large hook baited with
a piece of meat, which is let down on a rope abaft the cabin.
Since this is the place where seamen hang their salt meat in

Fleisch zum Einwässern, in ein Netz aushängen; so ziehet sich der Shork gewöhnlich dahin, und es ist schon manches Matrosen gehofte Mahlzeit von einem Shorke vorgegessen worden. Man isset von ihm nichts, als das Hintertheil desselben, soweit er nicht aufgeschnitten worden beym Ausnehmen. Dies ist ohngefehr von diesem 9 füssigen Fische, 2 Fuss. Dieses wird an der Luft getroknet, mit kalten Wasser aufgekocht, und dann mit einer Brühe gegessen. Besser aber soll es noch schmeken, wenn er erst gekocht, und hernach in Scheiben geschnitten, in der Pfanne wie beef stak zu bereitet wird.

Jan: 9.
29°. 53'.

Die ganze vorige Nacht S.W. Sturm; um 12 Uhr in der Nacht war der Wind W.S.W. und heute Morgen um 10 Uhr N. by W. das Steuer wurde lossgemacht, und wir fuhren bis 2. heute Mittag 9. Meilen W by N. Um 2 Uhr ging der Wind nach Norden, und der Sturm legte sich. In der Nacht war Windstille.

Jan: 10.
29°. 55'.
43 Meil:

Um 7 Uhr diesen Morgen sezten wir den Obern quer Mast wieder auf, und alle Haupt-Seegel wurden aufgespannt. Wir hatten 55 Schiffe. Um 10 Uhr kam ein Lüftchen aus S. by W. mit welchem wir W. bey N fuhren. Das Meer war in kurzer Zeit so ruhig, so unschuldig sahe es aus, dass man sich beynahe in dieses betrügliche Element verlieben sollte. Besonders glüklich waren wir, dass auch nicht ein einziger Jäger krank geworden war. Wir schmeichelten uns alle iezt in wenigen Tagen wieder ans Land zu kommen; allein schon um 2 Uhr den Nachmittag ging der Wind nach W. zu.

Jan: 11.
113. Meilen

Heute Morgen war der Wind S.W. völlig entgegen, und jeder Zoll den wir fuhren, entfernte uns mehr von dem Ort unserer Bestimung. Wir lavirten bald S. bald N. Den Nachmittag war ein kleiner Aufstand zwischen den Schifs-Capit: und seinen Leuten, welche sich über ihre Provision beschwerten, es war aber wieder beygelegt.

nets in order to soak it, sharks usually trail along here, and many a sailor's hoped-for meal has been devoured by a shark. None of the shark is eaten except the hind end, to which it is cut open when it is disemboweled, that is, about two feet of this nine-foot fish. It is dried in the air, put into cold water to cook, and is eaten with broth. It is said to taste even better if it is first boiled and then cut into slices and fried in a pan, like beefsteak.[1]

Up to midnight last night we had a SW. storm; about twelve o'clock in the night the wind was WSW., and around ten o'clock in the morning it was N. by W. The helm was unlashed, and we made nine miles W. by N. before two in the afternoon. At two o'clock the wind veered to the north and the storm abated. During the night there was a calm. Jan. 9
29° 53'

At seven o'clock in the morning we again raised the top-yard and set all mainsails. We were fifty-five ships. Around ten o'clock there came a gentle breeze from S. by W., before which we stood W. by N. In a short time the sea had become so calm and looked so innocent that one could almost come to love this treacherous element. We were especially happy because not a single jäger had become ill, and flattered our-selves that we would be able to land within a few days; however, at two o'clock in the afternoon the wind veered to W. Jan. 10
29° 55'
43 miles

This morning we had a head wind (SW.), and every inch we moved we went farther from our destination. We plied from S. to N. and from N. to S. In the afternoon there was a little mutiny among the crew, who complained to the ship's master about their rations. But everything was adjusted. Jan. 11
113 miles

[1] This account of the shark and pilot, though obviously based on ob-servations, is inaccurate in details: The pilot (remora) is striped rather than spotted; the young sharks had not taken refuge in the adult, but, rather, had not yet been born; and the number of tooth rows is not an index of the shark's age.—Carl L. Hubbs, Curator of Fishes, University of Michigan Museum.

Jan: 12.
31°. 41'.
64 Meil:

Der Wind blieb im̄er widrig, allezeit S.W. und wir fuhren N.W. Gegen Nachmittage war das Wetter ziemlich gut, aber bitter böse kalt. Starker Wind, hohe See, das Schif wurde sehr geworffen.

Jan: 13.
32°. 04'.
54. Meil:

Alles dasselbe! Im̄er Westl: Wind! Wir kreuzten auf und nieder. Ein böses Wetter! Schnee, Regen, Hagel, Sturm, schäumende Wellen, und eine bittere Kälte! Gegen Mittag stekte die Iudith Transport (auf welcher Faschinen und Ingeni: geladen sind) eine Noth-Flagge aus. Sie hatte einen Lek, und dazu alle Quer-Maste verlohren. Sie fuhr ans Admiral Schif, und bekam Hülfe. Gegen Abend wurde es heller, aber der blaue horizont zeigte scharfe Kälte an. Die Nacht ging der Wind etwas nach N. so mit als N.W. wir fuhren W.S.W., und hoften, er würde noch mehr nach Norden gehen. In dieser Hofnung schliefen wir ziemlich zumahl da das Schif nicht so sehr wie gewöhlich [sic] wankte, indem der Schnee und Hagel die Wellen etwas niedergeschlagen hatten.

Jan: 14.
31°. 28'.
59 Meil.

Allein unsere Hofnung war vergeblich, der Wind blieb wie er war, und wurde diesen Morgen noch mehr Westl: Wir kreuzten auf und nieder, das Wetter war ziemlich gut, allein, obgleich heute Nachmittag der Mond ins 1te Viertel trat, war dennoch kein Anschein zur Veränderung des Windes da.

Jan: 15.
31°. 14'.
55. Meil:

Einer unserer angenehmesten Täge, obgleich der Wind noch widrig war. Das Wetter war wie im Maij in Teutschland, und der Wind gelinde. Wir fuhren heute S.W. Heute Nacht kamen 3 Schiffe in die Flotte, und wir zählten 58. Seegel.

Jan: 16.
29°. 24'.
58. Meil:

Schönes herrliches Wetter, aber noch im̄er widrigen Wind! bis 9 Uhr heute Morgen fuhren wir S. und dann N. Wir sahen heute Morgen einen fliegenden Fisch, und hernach einen Soufleur von etwa 20 bis 30 Fuss gross. Er war ein Spermaceti, und er kam̄ dichte an unser Schif. Die Nasenlöcher, aus welchen er 3 Fuss hoch Wasser spritzte, waren etwa so gross als eine 48 pfündige Kugel.—Gegen Nachmittag wurde von dem Admirals-Adjut: Capt: Tomkins, das

The wind remained contrary, always SW., and we were
going NW. Toward afternoon the weather became fairly
good, though it was bitter cold. A strong gale and a heavy
sea, tossing the ship a good deal.

Everything the same! Still a westerly wind! We cruised
up and down. Terrible weather! Snow, rain, hail, storm,
foaming waves, and bitter cold! Toward noon the *Judith*
transport, carrying fascines and engineers, hoisted a flag of
distress. She had sprung a leak and, furthermore, had lost
all her yards. She approached the flagship and obtained assistance. Toward evening it cleared up, but the blue horizon was
a foreboding of severe cold. During the night the wind
veered somewhat to N., so that it was about NW. We stood
WSW. and were hoping for the wind to shift still more to
the north. With such hopes we slept fairly well, especially
since the ship did not roll as much as usual, for snow and
rain had beaten down the waves somewhat.

However, we had hoped in vain; the wind remained the
same, backing even more to the westward in the morning.
We cruised up and down. The weather was rather good, but
there was no indication of any change of wind in spite of the
fact that the moon entered the first quarter in the afternoon.

One of our most pleasant days, though the wind was still
contrary. The weather was like that of a May day in Germany, and the breeze was gentle. We sailed SW. During the
night three ships joined the fleet again, so that we now
numbered fifty-eight sail.

Beautiful, glorious weather, but still head wind! Until
nine o'clock in the morning we sailed S. and after that N.
In the forenoon we saw a flying fish and later a blower about
twenty to thirty feet long. It was a sperm whale and came
close to our ship. The nostrils, from which water spouted
three feet high, were approximately as large as a 48-pound
cannon ball. Toward afternoon the Admiral's adjutant,

Signal für die Schifs-Capitains ausgestekt, sogleich zu ihm
an Bord zu kom̃en. Sie erhielten daselbst die Ordre, sogleich
zur geschwinden Ausschiffung des Transport-Schiffes George,
welches, eine Noth-Flagge ausgesteket hatte, behülflich zu
seyn. So traurig dieser Anblik war, die Leute über Hals und
Kopf ihre Sachen und sich selbst in die Boote stürzen zu sehen,
so angenehm war der Anblik, so aufheiternd zu sehen: dass
die Vorsehung das Wetter ruhig genug liess, um mit Boote
an das Schif zu kommen. Eine Menge Transport-Schiffe und
2 Fregatten hatten sich in einer gewissen Entfernung um
dasselbe herumgelegt, und noch eine grössre Menge kleiner
Boote fuhren ab und zu. Es waren 4. Compag: light Infant:
am Bord. Weil es schon gegen Abend ging, und die See anfing
unruhig zu werden, und Anschein zum Sturm da, so musten
sich die Leute eilen, und es wurde von dem Cargo nichts
gerettet, sondern, nachdem die Leute, benebst ihrer Bagage
waren davon genom̃en worden, wurde das Schif sich selber
überlassen. Da die Flotte, wegen dieses Umstandes halte gemacht hatte, gab der Admiral um 7. Uhr den Abend ein Signal mit 8. Canonen mit mehreren Seegeln zu ihm zu stossen,
welches Signal der Perseus mit 3 Laternen beantwortete. Es
war viel Ansehn zum Sturm da, und es ging ziemlich rasch.
Das Schif muste die Nacht gewaltige Stösse aushalten.

Jan: 17.
30°. 15'.
58. Meil:

Wir hatten schon gestern Abend unsere Seegel halb wieder
eingezogen, und der Obere Mast wurde in der Nacht herunter
gelassen; Auch heute Morgen sahe es dem Sturme noch sehr
ähnlich, allein gegen Mittag klärte es sich auf, der Wind
aber war noch stark genug, um 3 Meilen in der Stunde zu
seegeln. Das Meer war sehr unruhig und der Wind noch widrig. Wir gingen den Tag Nordlich. Noch waren wir nicht
aus dem Current gekom̃en, und er trieb heute gewaltig N.
Oestlich. Das wenige Westl: welches wir also steuerten, wurde
durch diesen Current wieder aufgehoben, indem das Schif
$2\frac{1}{2}$° vom Cours wich. Wir zählten heute 57. Seegel.

Captain Tonken, hoisted the signal for the ships' masters to attend on board his ship at once. There they received orders to assist immediately in the quick debarkation of the *George* transport, which had hoisted a flag of distress. Sad as was the spectacle of the men throwing their belongings and themselves head over heels into the boats, it was a pleasant sight and a cheering thought that Providence permitted weather calm enough for us to reach the ship with boats. A number of transports and two frigates stood by, and a considerable number of small boats went back and forth. There were four companies of light infantry on board. The rescuers had to hurry, for evening was drawing near and the sea was becoming disturbed, having all appearances of a storm. Hence nothing was saved of the cargo, and, after the men and their baggage had been brought to safety, the ship was left to her fate. Since this incident had caused the fleet to lie to, the Admiral signaled at seven o'clock in the evening with eight guns for several sail to join him. This signal was answered by the *Perseus* with three lights. The weather was threatening, and the storm came quickly indeed. The ship had to withstand terrific pounding during the night.

Yesterday evening we reefed our sails and in the night Jan. 17 we lowered the main-topgallant. In the morning it was still 30° 15' quite stormy, but toward noon it cleared up. However, the 58 miles breeze continued to be fresh enough for us to make three miles an hour. The sea was very rough and the wind was contrary. We cruised north during the day. We had not yet got out of the current, which had a strong NE. drift today. The little steering west we did was thus counteracted by the current, the true course of the ship being two and one-half degrees off the course steered. We numbered fifty-seven sail today.

Jan: 18. Alles derselbe Wind, und ein heftiger Current. Wir steuer-
31°. 20'. ten N.W. Eine angenehme Luft! Das Schif Swan war sehr le-
71. Meil: kicht, und stekte eine Noth-Flagge aus. Es fuhr ans Admiral.
Die Schiffe machten den Nachmittag halt. Das Wetter war
gemässigt, mehr warm als kalt, und gegen Abend war beynahe Windstille. Dies liess uns hoffen, der Wind würde
sich gegen Morgen nordlich wenden, da auch nicht ein
Lüftchen, nicht die geringste Land-Wolke mehr am Horizont
war. Allein so herrlich auch der Abend und die Nacht war,
war dennoch unsere Hofnung vergeblich, indem der Wind eben
derselbe blieb. Den Abend waren wir nahe daran mit dem
Schif Bellona zusam̃en zu stossen.

Jan: 19. Ein ziemlich kalter Morgen für diese warme Gegend und eine
31°. 43'. wolkichte Luft, und im̃er, im̃erhin widriger Wind. Um 8.
53 Meil: Uhr heute Morgen mussten die Schiffe beylegen, und die
Truppen von Transport Schwan, wurden auf andere Schiffe
vertheilt bis auf ein Detachement, das denen Matrosen an
der Pumpe half. Der Current schien heute nicht so stark zu
seyn als gestern, ob wir gleich noch nicht so nahe am Lande
waren um Grund lootsen zu können. Besonders ist es, dass
der Current nach der Aussage eines unserer Matrosen 20
leaques vom Lande gerade entgegen gesezt läuft, nemlich
S.W. Er wusste mir die Ursache davon nicht anzugeben.
Sollte vieleicht das Cap Hatteros Schuld daran seyn? dass
nemlich der Current, der an dasselbe sich vorbey dränget,
und mehr Oestl: wegen dieses Drukes des Vorgebürges sich
wendet, das Wasser was aus den Flüssen südlich Cap Hatteras
fliesst, zurükstosset? Gegen Mittag wurde der Wind im̃er
heftiger, und unser Oberer Mast (main top galen) wurde
ganz herunter genom̃en. In der Nacht war der Sturm mit
seiner völligen Wuth da. Noch nie hatte der Wind und das
Wasser so getobet, noch nie war das Schif so geworfen worden,
musste es solche gewaltige Stösse abhalten, wie diese Nacht.
Allein weil der Sturm mit einmal so heftig anfing, war zu

The same wind exactly and a swift current. We steered Jan. 18
NW. Pleasant air! The *Swan* was very leaky and hoisted a 31° 20′
flag of distress. She came up close to the flagship. The ships 71 miles
lay to in the afternoon. The weather was moderate, warm
rather than cold, and in the evening there was almost a calm.
This gave us hope that the wind would change to the north
toward morning, especially since there was not the slightest
breeze and not even the smallest cloud on the horizon. However, beautiful as were evening and night, our hopes were in
vain, for the wind remained the same. In the evening we came
near colliding with the *Bellona*.

A rather cold morning for this warm region, a cloudy sky, Jan. 19
and always, always contrary wind. At eight o'clock this 31° 43′
morning the ships had to stand by, and the troops of the 53 miles
Swan transport, except for a detachment which assisted the
sailors at the pump, were distributed among other ships.
The current did not seem to be so strong as it was yesterday,
although we were not yet close enough to land to be able to
find bottom with the lead. It is strange that twenty leagues
from land the current should run in an exactly opposite direction, namely, SW., as I was informed by one of our sailors,
who was unable, however, to tell me the reason for this
phenomenon. Might this not be because of Cape Hatteras?
Owing to pressure from this promontory the current running
past it must flow more to the east, and the water from
the rivers south of Cape Hatteras will then cause the drift
to turn back. Toward noon the gale increased in violence,
and our main-topgallant was lowered completely. During
the night the storm broke in all its fury. Never before had
the wind and the water raged so; never before had the ship
been battered as it was last night. However, since the storm
had come up so suddenly, it was to be expected that it would
not last more than twenty-four hours. This afternoon I had

vermuthen, dass er nicht über 24. Stunden anhalten würde.
Die Geschiklichkeit der Englischen Marine hatte ich heute
Nachmittag noch Gelegenheit zu bewundern. Mitten im
heftigsten Sturm, da das Steuer schon angebunden war, sahe
der Schifs-Capt: ein kleines Boot (joli boat) von ferne treiben,
das vermuthlich von dem Verdeke eines andern Schiffes war
weggespielet worden. Der Capit: machte das Steuer loss,
stellte sich selber daran, und wusste bey dem gewaltigem
Gewerfe der Wellen, das Schif so zu lenken, dass das kleine
Boot ganz dichte an das Schif treiben muste. Einige Matrosen
hatten während dessen einen kleinen Anker des long boats
los gemacht, und wie das Boot jezt am Schif trieb, wussten
sie den Anker so geschikt hienunter zu werfen, dass der eine
Haaken desselben eines der Ruderbänke fasste, weil aber
unglüklicher Weisse diese Bank loss war, so gab der Anker
nach, und die Mühe war vergebens.

Jan: 20.   Diesen Morgen noch immerhin Sturm, gegen Mittag gab er
31°. 53′.   nach, und gegen Abend war beynahe Windstille. Allein Calm
18. Meil: und Sturm war gleich. Der Wind war und blieb Westl:. Wir
sahen heute wieder ein Schif in unserer Flotte, das den hintersten Mast verlohren hatte, und das Schif des Hl: Hauptm:
v. Eschwege schien sehr lekicht und beschädigt zu seyn. Wir
sprachen mit dem Schif Success Increase, das im 2ten Sturm
verschlagen gewesen war, gestern wieder in die Flotte gekommen war, und so viel Wasser geschöpfet hatte, dass es war
gezwungen gewesen, das Flattboat über Bord zu werfen, und
in verschiedenen andern Schiffen fehlte das Flattboat.

Jan: 21.   Heute Mittag war voller Mond, die Luft war trübe und
47 Meil: regnicht, und alle Anzeigen zur Veränderung des Windes. Der
Wind wurde immer schwächer, und um 12. Uhr die Nacht war
Calm, dann S.S.W. Wind. Wir steuerten W.N.W. Eine reine
angenehme Luft.

Jan: 22.   Bis 7 Uhr diesen Morgen hielt sich der Wind Westlich und wir
63. Meil: steuerten Nördlich, dann wurde es NW by N. und um 10

occasion to admire the skill of the English seamen. In the
midst of the most violent storm, when the helm was already
lashed, the captain saw at some distance a drifting jolly boat
that apparently had been washed from the deck of another
ship. He unlashed the helm, took it himself, and in spite of
the frightful tossing of the waves, he succeeded in steering
the ship into such a position that the little boat drifted right
against our ship. Some of the sailors had in the meantime
unfastened a small anchor of the longboat, and the moment
the boat drifted against the ship, they threw the anchor
down so skillfully that one of its flukes caught under one
of the thwarts. Unfortunately, this thwart was loose and
tore off. Thus all their labor was in vain.

This morning we still had the storm; by noon, however, Jan. 20
it had abated, and toward evening there was almost a calm. 31° 53'
But this was no better than the storm. The breeze was and 18 miles
remained westerly. Today we saw in our fleet another ship
which had lost her mizzenmast. The ship of Captain von
Eschwege appeared to be very leaky and damaged. We spoke
the *Success Increase*, which had been driven out of its course
during the second storm and rejoined the fleet yesterday.
She had shipped so much water that she was compelled to
throw her flatboat overboard. Several other ships were also
without flatboats.

It was full moon at noon today. The air was murky and Jan. 21
rainy, and everything pointed to a change of wind. The 47 miles
breeze became fainter and fainter. At midnight there was a
calm, and after that the breeze was SSW. We stood WNW.
Pure, pleasant air.

Until seven o'clock this morning the breeze remained Jan. 22
westerly, and we steered northward. Then it shifted NW. by 63 miles
N. and at ten o'clock NNE. We steered W. by S. although,

Uhr N.N.O. Wir steuerten W. by S. ob ich gleich wegen der Drift vermuthete, dass wir W. by N. gingen. Alle Seegel wurden so weit nur möglich aus gelassen, und die hintersten Schiffe hatten 15–20 Seegel auf. Iedes Gesicht war aufgeheitert.

Jan: 23.
32°. 08'.
125 Meil:

Wir sahen heute 3 fremde Schiffe rechts in der Ferne, wahrscheinlich von der Flotte im Sturm verschlagene. Mit dem herrlichsten Wind fuhren wir 5–7 Meilen in einer Stunde. Seit heute Mittag muste der Perseus vor dem Admiral 5–6 Meilen her sondiren, da der Sturm, wie ich vermuthe oder vielmehr die vielen Stürme, die Rechnung des geschiktesten Seemañes vereitelt haben.—Wir zählten heute 60. Seegel.

Jan: 24.
76 Meil:

Unser Schif war iezt eines der ersten in der Flotte, und fuhr mit guten Winde besser, als es mit widrigen Cours that. Bis 6 Uhr heute Morgen fuhren wir mit mittelmässigen Winde W. und dann W.S.W. Diesen Nachmittag war rechnicht Wetter, der Wind schwach und veränderlich, bald südlich, bald westlich bald nördlicht.

Jan: 25.
31°. 21'.
56 Meil:

Der Wind war die Nacht mittelmässig stark, aber heute Morgen ging es ziemlich rasch. Den Nachmittag hatten wir Regen, und eine ziemlich hohe See. Der Current war schwächer, und den Nachmittag sezte der Admiral ein Boot aus, um ihn zu messen. Die Nacht war ruhig indem das Schiff bey beständigen Winde feste an einer Seite lag. Der Wind war W. und N.W.

Jan: 26te
31°. 37'.
63 Meil:

Unsere Seegel mussten wir wieder kürzen. Wir waren iezt eines der vordersten Schiffe. Das Wetter war rechnicht, und Landschauer. Gegen Morgen ging der Wind nach Osten, nach Süden, und wurde dann wieder Nordlich. Den Nachmittag bliess er aus N.W. und zu befürchten war, dass er bald noch mehr Westl: blassen würde. Wie steuerten W.S.W. Schon gestern sahen wir einige Spitzen Grass in der See schwimmen, und seit einigen Tagen liessen sich See-Enten, u.s.w. sehen. Wir fuhren bey einer sehr kalten Luft 2–3. Meilen in der Stunde.

owing, I suppose, to the drift our true course was W. by N.
We let the reefs out of the sails, and the sternmost ships
carried fifteen to twenty sails. Every face was cheerful.

We saw today some distance to starboard three strange Jan. 23
ships which, apparently, had been separated from the fleet 32° 08′
in the storm. With a splendid breeze we made five to seven 125 miles
miles an hour. Since noon today the *Perseus* has been obliged
to take soundings five to six miles ahead of the flagship, for
the storm, I suppose, or rather the many storms, have made
futile the reckoning of even the best seamen. We numbered
sixty sail this day.

Our ship was now one of the first in the fleet, sailing Jan. 24
relatively better with a good wind than with an adverse one. 76 miles
Until six o'clock this morning we sailed with a moderate
breeze, first W. and then WSW. In the afternoon the weather
was rainy, the wind faint and changeable, now from the
south, now from the west, and again from the north.

During the night the breeze was moderate; but in the Jan. 25
morning we sailed fairly fast. In the afternoon we had rain 31° 21′
and a rather high sea. The current was less swift, and in the 56 miles
afternoon the flagship put out a boat in order to determine
its velocity. We had a quiet night since the ship, with a
steady breeze, listed continually to one side. The wind was
W. and NW.

We were compelled to shorten our sails again. Our ship Jan. 26
was now one of the first. The weather was rainy, and we had 31° 37′
some land showers. Toward morning the wind changed to the 63 miles
east, then veered to the south, and later shifted to the north.
In the afternoon it blew from the NW., and we feared that
it would soon blow even more westerly. We stood WSW.
Yesterday we saw some blades of grass floating on the water
and for several days we have been seeing gulls, etc. We made
two to three miles an hour. The air was very cold.

Jan: 27.
32°. 44′.
64 Meil:
Die Nacht war N.W. Wind, und Wellen und Wind dem Sturm gleich. Wir waren von gestern Abend nördlich gesteuert, und musten wegen des scharfen Windes den Obern-Mast herunter lassen.

Jan: 28.
32°. 50′.
53 Meil:
Bis die Nacht war der Wind Westlich geblieben, und wir fuhren von gestern Nachmittag 4. Uhr Südlich. Gegen Mitternacht ging der Wind nach Norden, und stand so bis heute Morgen 9. Uhr, wo Calm war. Um Mittag hatten wir schwachen N.W. Wind, womit wir, bis die Nacht S.W. steuerten. Wie wurfen diesen Morgen das Senkbley, und fanden bey 25 Faden Wasser, einen kiesartigen sandigen Boden.

Jan: 29.
32°. 35′.
112 Meil:
Mit missvergnügten Herzen legten wir uns gestern zur Ruhe, denn mit Einbruch der Nacht hatten wir wieder widrigen Wind. Allein gegen Mitternacht ging der Wind auf einmal nach Norden, und heute Mittag N.O. der herrlichste vortheilhafteste Wind der sich denken lässt, und dieser war so stark, und der Admiral liess so viel Seegel aufspannen, dass wir 7 bis 8 Meilen in der Stunde machten, Noch nie hatten wir so einen herrlichen Tag für unsere Farth gehabt. Um 10 Uhr den Morgen fanden wir 9 Faden Wasser und einen sandigen Boden, und gegen Mittag konnte man die Küste Georgien vom Obern-Mast mit blossen Augen sehen. Allein wir hatten ein gar zu grosses Stüke zu durchschneiden, um noch den Abend in Tybee einlaufen zu können. Deswegen legte der Admiral den Nachmittag bey, und als die hintersten Schiffe angekoñen waren, fuhren wir mit wenigen Seegeln die Nacht südlich, um nicht auf Bänke oder Felsen zu gerathen. Diesen Morgen war der Roebuck in unsere Flotte wieder gekommen, und den Nachmittag der Renown und Robust. Auch war seit einigen Tagen ein Englischer Privateer von 3 Masten nebst dessen tender zu der Flotte gekommen, und blieb seit der Zeit bey uns. Wir zählten heute 70 Schiffe.

Jan: 30.
31°. 45′.
46 Meil:
Weil wir die Nacht uns Südlich gehalten hatten, so waren wir heute Morgen mehr vom Lande entfernt, als gestern. Der

During the night the wind was NW. It blew hard and the sea ran high. Since last night we have been steering northward, and because of the stiff gale we had to lower our main-topgallant.

Until night the wind remained westerly, and since four o'clock yesterday afternoon we have been sailing southward. Toward midnight the wind changed to the north and remained there until nine o'clock this morning, when it became calm. About noon we had a gentle NW. breeze, before which we stood SW. until night. We cast the lead this morning and found at twenty-five fathoms a gravel-like, sandy bottom.

With cheerless hearts we lay down to rest last night, for since nightfall we had been having head wind. However, toward midnight the wind suddenly shifted to N. and at noon today to NE., the best, the most favorable wind imaginable. It was so strong that, when the flagship had us carry a press of sail, we made seven to eight miles an hour. Never before had we had such a splendid day for our voyage. At ten o'clock in the morning we found nine fathoms of water and a sandy bottom, and toward noon we could see with the naked eye the coast of Georgia from the main-topgallant. We were too far out, however, to be able to enter Tybee in the evening. Therefore the flagship lay to in the afternoon. After the last ships had arrived we stood southward during the night, with but few sails, so as not to run onto banks or rocks. This morning the *Roebuck* joined the fleet again, and in the afternoon the *Renown* and the *Robust*. Several days ago a three-masted English privateer and her tender had also joined the fleet and have been with us since then. We numbered seventy ships today.

Since we had stood to the southward during the night, we were farther from land this morning than we were yesterday.

Jan. 27
32° 44'
64 miles

Jan. 28
32° 50'
53 miles

Jan. 29
32° 35'
112 miles

Jan. 30
31° 45'
46 miles

Wind war stille. Gegen Mittag mussten die Schifs-Capitains am Bord des Adjut: Capit: Tomkins, woselbst sie die Ordre bekamen das Transport Schiff [   ] ieder mit 1. Tonne Wasser zu versehen, (indem dieses Schif fast kein Wasser mehr hatte, und die Leute am Bord desselben schon seit langer Zeit von 1. Nössel Wasser des Tages hatten leben müssen) hievon waren aber die Schiffe ausgenoⁱ̃men, welche ein Flattboat am Bord hatten, indem dieses sie hinderte das Fass aus dem Verdek zu langen,—und so war auch unseres davon befreyet. Wir zählten heute 50 Seegel; Wahrscheinlich hat der Rest näher an die Küste gehalten, und ist uns auf die Art aus dem Gesicht gekoⁱ̃men, und diese Schiffe koⁱ̃men sicher eher in Haven als wir. Capit: Saunders von dem Transport Schif: Success Increase kam heute zu unsern Schifs-Capit: und wir erfuhren von ihm, dass er im 2ten Sturme von der Flotte verschlagen gewesen sey, und 18 Tage die Flotte verlohren hätte. Sein Schiff war durch Unachtsamkeit in Brand gerathen, einen neuen Haupt-Seegel hatte er verlohren, und so viel Wasser geschöpft, dass er war gezwungen gewesen das Flattboat über Bord zu werfen. Während dass er verschlagen gewesen war, sprach er mit einem 2 mastigen Schiffe von Iamaica, das alle Mäste verlohren hatte, und einen Noth-Mast (Jury Mast) aufgesetzet hatte. 3 Tage tobte der Wind zu stark, ehe er diesem verunglükten Schiffe, das nur noch 50 Pf. Zwiebak an Provision hatte, konnte zu Hülfe koⁱ̃men. Dem half er aus, mit Brod, Fleisch, Mehl, u.s.m. und es blieb bey ihm, bis gestern Mittag, wo die Flotte zu geschwinde seegelte, es wird aber, wenn kein Unglük dazwischen koⁱ̃mt, nachkommen. Von diesem Schiffe erfuhr der Capit: Saunders: dass d'Estaing an seinen Wunden sollte gestorben seyn, und dass die Französ: Flotte zu Martinique, und Guadaloupe läge.—Weil der Capit: Saunders von der Flotte verschlagen war, erbrach er seine zu Sandy-hook erhaltene Ordre, worinne er fand: dass der Sammelplatz der Flotte zu Tybée-Island sey.

It was calm. Toward noon the ships' masters were ordered to attend on board the ship of the adjutant, Captain Tonken, where they received orders to supply the transport [   ] with one tun of water apiece, since this ship had hardly any water left and for a long time the men on board had been obliged to get along on one pint of water a day. However, the ships having flatboats on board were excepted, because these made it difficult to unload the casks. For this reason our ship was exempted. We numbered fifty sail today. The rest had probably kept closer to the coast and thus got out of our range of vision. These ships will certainly enter the harbor before us. Captain Saunders of the *Success Increase* came to our ship's master, and from him we learned that he had lost the fleet in the second storm and had not seen it for eighteen days. Through carelessness his ship had caught fire; she had lost a new mainsail and had shipped so much water that he was compelled to throw the flatboat overboard. While he was lost he spoke a two-masted vessel from Jamaica that had lost all her masts and raised a jury mast. For three days the wind raged so furiously that he could not come to the assistance of this damaged ship, which had no provisions left, except fifty pounds of biscuit. He supplied her with bread, meat, flour, etc., and she remained with him until yesterday afternoon, when the fleet began to outsail her; but she will follow if she does not meet with misfortune. From this ship Captain Saunders had learned that d'Estaing is said to have died of his wounds,[1] and that the French fleet was lying at Martinique and Guadeloupe. While Captain Saunders was separated from the fleet he broke open the orders he had received at Sandy Hook, in which he found that the fleet was to rendezvous at Tybee Island. The ship had on board part of the 33rd Regi-

[1] This rumor was untrue. D'Estaing was wounded, but not seriously, at Savannah, October 9, 1779.

Das Schif hatte einen Theil des 33ten Regiments, unter Commando des Major Densys am Bord. Um 1 Uhr den Mittag fanden wir nur noch 13 Faden Wasser. Den Nachmittag kam der Commodore von Savannah Capt: Henry auf der Fowey Fregatte, benebst einer Sloop of war in die Flotte, und begab sich zum Admiral. Wir fuhren W. by N. Der Wind war S.W. und mit diesem Winde konnten wir nicht einlaufen, indem die Flotte mehr nördlich war als der Canal. Wir legten deswegen gegen Abend bey, und fuhren die Nacht Südlich mit wenigen Seegeln und mittelmässigen Winde. Um 3 Uhr den Nachmittag gab der Admiral das Signal zum Ankern bereit zu seyn, um 4 Uhr sahen wir das Land N.N.W. ohngefehr 8–9 Meilen von uns, und fanden 9. Faden Wasser. Die Nacht fuhren wir unter Anführung des Adjut: Capit: Tomkins auf dem Transport-Schiffe Iohn, indem die man of wars bey anbrechender Nacht alle in die See stachen, um an der Küste zu kreutzen.

Jan: 31.
64. Meil:

Gegen Morgen konnten wir wieder das Land erkennen, es war aber so neblichtes Wetter, dass die Flotte nicht wagen durfte einzulaufen. Gegen Mittag hatten wir bald 10. bald nur 4 Faden Wasser. Die Mann of war waren diesen Morgen wieder zu der Flotte gekommen. Weil nun der Nebel sich nicht legen wollte, und dazu der Wind beständig S.W. blieb, so gab der Romulus den Nachmittag 3 Uhr das Signal zum ankern, und um 4½ Uhr wurfen wir Anker, bey 7½ Faden Wasser auf der Rheede von Georgien, zwischen Tybée und Port-Royal. Wir waren aber nur 37 Seegel die hier unter Anführung des Romulus und der Sloop of war, welche gestern von Savahnah gekoṁen ist vor Anker lagen. Der Rest der Flotte war mehr Südlich, die Luft war angenehm, so gemässigt wie der May in kältern Gegenden, aber von dem Lande konnte man nichts, wegen des diken Nebels erkennen. Die

---

[1] Captain Henry (according to Hinrichs, commodore at Savannah) probably was naval agent at Savannah. He was John Henry, captain of the *Renown*, which on the Charleston expedition was commanded by George

ment under the command of Major Dansey. At one o'clock
in the afternoon we found only thirteen fathoms of water.
In the afternoon the Commodore from Savannah, Captain
Henry,[1] accompanied by a sloop of war, met the fleet in the
Fowey frigate, and repaired on board the flagship. We were
sailing W. by N., the wind being SW. With this wind we
could not put into port, since the fleet was north of the channel. Therefore we lay to in the evening and during the night
we stood southward with but few sails and a moderate
wind. At three o'clock in the afternoon the Admiral gave the
signal to be ready to cast anchor. At four o'clock we sighted
land NNW., about eight to nine miles distant. We found nine
fathoms of water. During the night we sailed under the
command of the adjutant, Captain Tonken, on board the
John transport, for the men-of-war had put to sea at nightfall
to cruise along the coast.

Toward morning we could again descry land, but it was so Jan. 31
foggy that the fleet did not dare run in. Toward noon the 64 miles
depth of the water varied from ten to four fathoms. The men-
of-war had joined the fleet again in the morning. Since the
fog did not disperse and, moreover, the wind was continually
SW., the *Romulus*, at three o'clock in the afternoon, gave the
signal to cast anchor. So we came to anchor at half-past four
in seven and one-half fathoms of water in the roadstead of
Georgia,[2] between Tybee and Port Royal. But we were only
thirty-seven sail riding at anchor here under the command of
the *Romulus* and the sloop of war that had come from Savannah yesterday. The rest of the fleet was farther south. The air
was pleasant, as moderate as in May in colder regions; but
because of the thick fog we could not make out land. Through

Dawson, master of the frigate *Iris* (Gt. Brit. Hist. MSS. Comm., *Report on
American Manuscripts*, II, 107, 135, 136; Clowes, *op. cit.*, III, 406, 509).

[2] The roadstead of Georgia is Tybee Roads.

ganze Nacht hindurch feuerte der Admiral alle halbe Stunde 1
Canone, um die noch nicht vor Anker liegenden Schiffe an
sich zu ziehen, welches Signal der Romulus jederzeit beantwortete. Dies war der 43te Tag, seit wir auf dem Schiffe
waren, und der 36te unserer Farth. In diesen 36 Tagen hatten
wir 15 Täge Sturm gehabt, 25. Tage widrigen Wind, und
waren 1851. Meilen gefahren.

Febr: 1. Der Nebel dauerte heute Morgen noch immer fort. Gegen
Mittag schien der Wind sich etwas zu bessern, und der
Romulus gab ein Zeichen zum Anker lichten. Um 12. Uhr
fuhren wir S.O. bis 3 Uhr den Nachmittag, und dann wendeten
wir uns, und fuhren W. by S. Gegen 4. Uhr bekamen wir
einige vor Anker liegende Schiffe im Gesichte, es waren die
Europe, Robust, Raisonable und Rüssel; Allein der admiral
war nicht mehr auf seinem Schiffe, und der Comodore hatte
die Comodors-Flagge ausgesezt. Wir fuhren hinter dem Romulus weg, wo wir die Ordre bekamen N.W. dem Romulus zu
folgen. Um 5. Uhr sahen wir Tybée Island S.W. by W. und
den Leucht-Thurm bey 3½ Faden Wasser. Wir passirten den
Romulus und den Roebuck, auf welchen der Admiral sich
befand, und fuhren W. by N. bis zum light-house, allein wer
kann vor Unglük? Auf einmal sassen wir auf einer Sandbank,
auf welcher wir bey der Flut nur 11. Fuss Wasser fanden.

Febr: 2.   Das Schif legte sich diese Nacht ziemlich auf eine Seite.
Um 1 Uhr die Nacht kamen mehrere Flatboats auf Befehl
des Adjut: Tomkins, um uns bey einer etwanigen Gefahr aus
zu schiffen. Weil diese Debarkirung aber in der Nacht mit
vieler Unordnung und Verderbung an Ammunition u.s.w.
verknüpft war, und wir bey den Sondiren fanden, dass die
Bank aus reinem Sande bestund, der Wind dazu vom Lande
kam, auch nicht der geringste Anschein zur hohen See war,
so blieben wir auf dem Schiffe, behielten aber zu mehrerer
Sicherheit die Flatboats so lange bey uns, bis gegen Morgen
die Flut uns befreyete, seegelten dann gegen Mittag so weit,

the entire night the Admiral fired a gun every half hour to attract the ships not yet anchored, which signal was answered by the *Romulus* every time. This was the forty-third day we have spent on board the ship, and the thirty-sixth day of our voyage. During these thirty-six days we had fifteen days of storm and twenty-five days of contrary wind. We have sailed 1,851 miles.

The fog lasted all morning. Toward noon the wind Feb. 1 seemed to improve somewhat, and the *Romulus* gave the signal to weigh anchor. At twelve o'clock we stood SE., and at three o'clock we tacked and sailed W. by S. Toward four o'clock we descried some ships riding at anchor. They were the *Europe*, the *Robust*, the *Raisonnable*, and the *Russell*. However, the Admiral was no longer aboard his ship and the Commodore had hoisted the Commodore's flag. When we were astern of the *Romulus* we received orders to follow her NW. At five o'clock, in three and one-half fathoms of water, we sighted Tybee Island SW. by W. and also the lighthouse. We passed the *Romulus* and the *Roebuck*, the Admiral being aboard the latter, and stood W. by N. as far as the lighthouse; but who can foresee misfortune! Before we realized it we were aground on a sandbank, on which we found only eleven feet of water at high tide.

The ship heeled a good deal during the night. At one Feb. 2 o'clock several flatboats arrived under the command of Adjutant Tonken to take us off in case of danger. But such a debarkation in the night involves much disorder and destruction of ammunition, etc. Furthermore, by taking soundings we found that the bank consisted of pure sand. In view of these considerations we decided to remain on board the ship, especially since the wind was blowing from the land and there was not the least indication of the sea running high. For safety's sake, however, we kept the flatboats until the tide set us free early in the morning. We sailed far enough before

dass wir das light-hous ohngefehr $\frac{1}{2}$ Meile hinter uns liessen, und wurffen den Nachmittag bey $3\frac{1}{4}$ Faden Wasser, den Anker in Savannah Sound hart an Great Tybée Island.

Febr: 3.   Der Perseus war das einzigste Kriegs Schiff, das so weit mit uns herauf kom̄en konnte, ausser dem war noch die Vi-gilant hier, und 4 Ruder Galeeren lagen zwischen hier und Savannah town auf Station. Von unserer Flotte fehlen uns 10 Schiffe, benebst der Defiance man of war, weil aber ein anderes Transport-Schif, das im Sturm verschlagen gewesen, und in der See wieder zu uns gekommen war, einmal unter dem 30.°, 11 Seegel gesehen hatte, so war Hofnung da, dass sie noch kom̄en würden. Die fehlenden Schiffe waren folgende:

DeFiance, Man of war.

Smirna-Galley	Brittisch: Grenad: 4. Comp:
Lord Mulgrave	63te Regt: 4. do:
King George	64. '' ''
Eleonora	Legion Cavallerie.
Fidelity	Legion Infant:
Anna	Hangers Chasseurs, Althausen Riflemen und 30 Jäger von Capt. Ewalds Detachement.
Little Daly	Quarter Master Gen: Departement.
Remembrance	Ingenieurs.
Russian Merchand	Artillerie.
Greyhound	1 Comp: vom 63ten Regimt:

Der com̄andirende General ging heute mit dem Admiral und Earl Cornwallis nach Savannah. Die Schifs-Capit: bekamen Ordre so viel möglich, und so geschwind Wasser schöpfen zu lassen. Die Boate musten deswegen 12. Meilen den Fluss hinauf nach 5 Fathom hole Nacht und Tag fahren. Weil der Capit: Ewald, und der Lieut: v. Winzingrode ohne Iäger auf dem Schiff Spring bey einem Detachement des Regt: Hayne sich befanden, auch dieses Schif war beordret worden, nach Savannah zu fahren, so kamen sie heute zu uns auf unser Schif.

noon to have the lighthouse approximately half a mile astern, and in the afternoon, in three and one-fourth fathoms of water, we cast anchor in Savannah Sound, hard by Great Tybee Island.

The *Perseus* was the only warship that could come up with Feb. 3 us as far as this. Besides the *Perseus*, the *Vigilant* was also here, and four row-galleys were stationed between here and Savannah. Ten transports as well as the *Defiance* man-of-war were missing from the fleet. But since another transport which had been lost in the storm and then joined us again on the high sea had seen eleven sail under the thirtieth degree, we had hopes they would still arrive. The missing ships were:

Defiance man-of-war	
Smyrna galley	British grenadiers, four companies
Lord Mulgrave..............	63rd Regiment, four companies
King George................	64th Regiment, four companies
Elenora....................	Legion cavalry
Fidelity...................	Legion infantry
Anna......................	Hanger's chasseurs, Althausen's Riflemen and thirty jägers of Captain Ewald's detachment.
Littledale.................	Quartermaster General's Department
Remembrance...............	Engineers
Russia Merchant............	Artillery
Greyhound.................	One company of the 63rd Regiment

Today the Commanding General, the Admiral, and Earl Cornwallis went to Savannah. The masters of the ships received orders to provide themselves as quickly as possible with all the water they could get. Therefore the whole day and night the boats plied twelve miles up the river to Five-Fathom Hole. As Captain Ewald and Lieutenant von Winzingrode (but no jägers) had been on the *Spring* transport with a detachment of the Regiment Huyn, they joined us on board our ship today, for the *Spring*, too, had been ordered to go to Savannah.

Febr: 4.   Heute Morgen um 3 Uhr fuhr ich mit unsern Wasser
Boate, hinauf bis 5 Fathom hole, lies mich daselbst ans Land
setzen, und ging von da mit Hülffe des Compasses und der
Charte bis Savannah zu Fusse.

Georgien war vormals mit unter dem allgemeinen Nahmen
von Carolina begriffen. Wahrscheinlich wurde dieses Land zu
erst von Cabat im Jahr 1497 entdeket, allein es wurde kein
Besitz davon genoīen. Die Spannier landeten im I. 1512. auf
der Küste von Florida, und machten daselbst manche Versuche Colonien anzulegen. 1562 schikte der berühmte Französ:
Admiral Coligni 2. Schiffe, unter Ribauts Commando nach
der Küste von Florida. Dieser landete nördlich des Flusses
Alatamaha an mehreren Plätzen, und nahm von diesen Besitz
in Nahmen des Königes von Frankreich Charl IX., dem zu
Ehren er das Land Carolina nannte, und legte an der Mündung
des Albermarle Sound, Charles Fort an. Allein innerliche
Unruhen in Frankreich waren die Ursachen, dass er ohne
Unterstützung von Hause blieb, und sich gezwungen sahe mit
seinen Leuten wieder nach Europa zurük zu kehren. Dennoch
liess er sein Vorhaben nicht fahren, und schikte 1564 und 65.
6 Schiffe unter Ribaut und Landoner wieder nach Carolina.
Die Spannier waren davon benachrichtiget worden, kamen
mit einer grossen Macht dazu, nahmen Charles Fort weg,
Ribaut und eine Menge Leute wurden getödtet, und Landoner
muste mit dem Uiberrest wieder nach Frankreich zurük
kehren. Iezt machten die Spannier Miene ihre Besitzungen
zu behaupten, allein 1567. überfiel sie der Französ: Capit: de
Gorgues, tödtete den grösten Theil von ihnen, und demolirte
die Werke, musste aber wegen der innerlichen Unruhen die in
Frankreich herrschten wieder zurük gehen. So blieb Carolina
unbesezt, bis den 24ten Mart: 1663. König Carl der 2te in
England ein Patent an verschiedene angesehene Engländer
ausfertigen liess: Kraft desselben ihnen das Eigenthum, und

At three o'clock this morning I went with our water Feb. 4
boat up to Five-Fathom Hole. I went ashore and walked to
Savannah with the help of a compass and a map.

Georgia formerly was part of what went under the more
general name of Carolina. It seems that this land was first
discovered by Cabot in the year 1497; but it was not taken
possession of then. The Spaniards landed on the coast of
Florida in the year 1512 and made several attempts to estab-
lish colonies there. In 1562 the famous French admiral
Coligni sent two ships to the coast of Florida under Ribaut's
command. The latter landed at several places north of the
River Altamaha and took possession of them in the name of
the King of France, Charles IX, in whose honor he called the
land Carolina. At the mouth of Albermarle Sound Ribaut
established Charles Fort. However, because of political dis-
turbances in France he received no support from home, and
therefore found himself compelled to return to Europe with
his men. But Coligni did not give up his plans and in 1564
and '65 he again sent six ships to Carolina under Ribaut and
Laudonnière. The Spaniards, having been advised of this,
came with a large force and took Charles Fort. Ribaut and a
great number of men were killed and Laudonnière had to
return to France with the rest. Now the Spaniards seemed
intent upon maintaining their possessions. However, in 1567
the French captain de Gourgues surprised them, killed the
greater part of them, and demolished their works. But
because of the internal unrest prevailing in France he was
compelled to return. So Carolina remained unoccupied until
March 24, 1663, when King Charles II of England granted
letters patent to several eminent Englishmen, conveying to
them property and jurisdiction over it. These colonists took
as their lawgiver the great Locke, whose basic principle was

die Gerichtsbarkeit (Property and jurisdictien) übertragen wurde. Diese Eigenthümer nahmen den grossen Locke zu ihren Gesetzgeber an, dessen erster Grundsatz: eine gänzliche unumschränkte Religions-Freyheit für jede Religion und Sekte war. Dieses sowohl, als die freye Austheilung des Landes, gegen die geringe Abgabe, von jährl: 2 Coppers per Acre, und ein Zuschuss von 12,000. Pf. Sterl:, die die Eigenthümer unter sich zusamen legten, brachten eine Menge Pflanzers in dieses Land und machten ihnen ihren Auffenthalt erträglich. 1665 bekamen die Eigenthümer ein neues Patent, welches die alten Gerechtsamen bekräftigte, und die Gränzen des Landes bestimte. Nemlich vom Atlantic, bis zum Missisippi Westlich, und von 30°. 37'.–36°. 31'. Nord. d.i. alles Land zwischen Virginien und Florida, und dieses ist 700 Meilen lang und 380 breit.

Anfänglich war dieses Land ziemlich ruhig, allein ihre eigene Schuld brachte ihnen einen Indianischen Krieg auf den Halss, und als durch die geschikte Bemittelung ihres Gouverneurs Joseph West, dieses beygelegt war, wurden sie unter sich selbst uneinig. Die bösesten Streitigkeiten für einen Staat, sind Religions Streitigkeiten. Diese herschten daselbst. Ihr Gesetz gab jedem Religions-Verwandten die Freyheit daselbst sich niederzulassen. Dies brachte eine grosse Anzahl Sekten zusamen; Ieder hatte seine eigenen Begriffe, Interesse, u.s.w., und jeder neidete, hasste, bekriegte, bevortheilte den andern. Dies machte dass 1705. die Königin Anna sich schon ins Mittel schlug, und die Eigenthümer waren nahe daran ihre Freyheiten und Gerechtsame zu verlieren.—Auch dieses wurde wieder beygelegt.—Als aber kurz darauf ein neuer Indianischer Krieg ausbrach, und innerliche Unruhen, Partheyen u.s.w. im Lande selbst noch herrschten, wurden die Colonien so herunter gebracht, dass 7. Eigenthümer ihr Eigenthum und Gerichtsbarkeit (property and jurisdiction) der Krone für 24,000. Pf. St. verkauften. Der Earl Granwille

complete, unlimited freedom of conscience for every religion and creed. This fact, as well as the free distribution of land in return for the small annual quitrent of two coppers per acre and a subsidy from a fund of £12,000 sterling which the proprietors had made up among themselves, attracted many planters to this land and made their life tolerable. In 1665 the proprietors received new letters patent, which reaffirmed their jurisdiction and determined the boundaries of the province, namely, from the Atlantic west to the Mississippi, and from 30° 37′ north to 36° 31′, i.e. all the land between Virginia and Florida, which is an expanse 700 miles long and 380 broad.[1]

At first the province was fairly quiet, but through their own fault the settlers brought on an Indian war, and when by the skillful mediation of their governor, Joseph West, this was terminated, they began to quarrel among themselves. The worst disputes for a state are religious disputes. These prevailed in Carolina. Their laws gave the right of settlement to adherents of all religions. This brought together a great number of sects. Everyone had his own ideas, interests, etc., and everyone envied, hated, fought, and took advantage of the others. This caused Queen Anne to intervene in 1705, and the proprietors came very near losing their privileges and jurisdiction. Fortunately this, too, was adjusted; but when shortly afterward a new Indian war broke out and internal unrest, party strife, etc., still prevailed in the province, the colonies declined to such an extent that seven proprietors sold their property and jurisdiction to the Crown for £24,000 sterling. Earl Granville kept his seventh [sic], approximately

[1] By the first charter the boundaries were 31° in the south and 36° in the north, but in 1665 they were enlarged to 29° south and 36° 30′ north, from the Atlantic to the Pacific.

behielt seinen 7^{tel} Antheil von etwa 60 Meilen, zwischen dem Atlantic und der South-See. Dieser Tractat der Krone mit den Eigenthümern wurde 1728. vom Parliament confirmiret. Die Provinz wurde hierauf in North und Sud-Carolina getheilt, die Constitutiones, welche mit den Engländischen nicht übereinstimten, abgeschaft, und Friede und Ruhe kam wieder ins Land.

Allein obgleich Georgien mit unter diesem Lande begriffen war, war doch bis iezt noch keine Colonie daselbst etabliret worden. Im Iahre 1732. wurde erst der erste Versuch gemacht. Das Land wurde nun in 3 Provinzen getheilt: North, South-Carolina und Georgien. Dies lezte begriff alles Land, was südlich des Savannah-Rivers bis Florida lag. In der Charter von 1732. wurde dieses an 23 privat Persohnen übergeben. Das erste Project zur Pflanzung dieser Colonie war von einigen patriotisch gesinnten Männern, blos aus Mitleiden für arme und hülfebedürftige Famielien in Grossbrittanien und Jrrland, unternomen worden. Sobald wie die Charter war gegeben worden, wurde eine Subscription angestellt, und diese war ansehnlich genug, so dass noch vor Ausgang Octobr: 100 der ärmsten, und hülfebedürftigsten Leuten, mit allen Nothwendigkeiten versehen von England abseegelten. Sie landeten d. 20ten Febr: 1733. in Port Royal, und Mr. Oglethorpe, ihr Oberaufseher, legte kurz darauf den Plan aus, zur ietzigen Stadt Savannah.—Die Subscription hatte während dessen noch mehres in England eingebracht, und das Parliament schenkte 10,000 Pf. St: hierzu, die es aus der Verkauffung des Landes in St: Christopher gehoben hatte. Mehrere Famielien wurden jezt hienüber geschikt, und jedes Iahr sahe man augenscheinlich diese Colonie aus ihrem Chaos sich heraus-winden, wachsen und blühen.—Allein dieses währte nur so lange, als Mr: Oglethorpe die Direction hatte. Kurze Zeit hernach kam Streit, Uneinigkeit unter den Colonisten, und alles kam in solche Verwirrung, dass die Bevollmächtigten

sixty miles, extending from the Atlantic to the South Sea. This transaction between the Crown and the proprietors was confirmed by Parliament in 1728. The province was then divided into North and South Carolina. Those articles of the constitution which did not conform with the English constitution were abolished, and peace and quiet prevailed once more in the province.

Though Georgia was part of this province, no colony had by this time been established there. Not until 1732 was the first attempt made. The land was now divided into three provinces: North and South Carolina and Georgia. The latter included all the land south of the Savannah River as far as Florida. In the charter of 1732 this was granted to twenty-three private persons. The first project for the establishment of this colony was undertaken by some patriotically minded men solely out of compassion for poor and indigent families in Great Britain and Ireland. As soon as the charter had been granted subscriptions were solicited. These were large enough to enable one hundred of the poorest and most indigent people, provided with all necessities, to depart from England before the end of October. They landed in Port Royal on the 20th of February, 1733, and Mr. Oglethorpe, their governor, soon afterward laid out the present city of Savannah. The subscription in England had in the meantime brought in additional sums. Furthermore, Parliament granted £10,000 sterling, which had been raised by the sale of land in St. Christopher. Several families were now sent over, and every year one could plainly see this colony extricating itself from its chaos and growing and flourishing. But this lasted only while Mr. Oglethorpe was in charge. A short time afterward quarrels and discord set in among the colonists, and everything was in such confusion that the authorites and pro-

und Eigenthümer ihre Charter im Iahr 1752 dem Könige wieder zurück gaben. Von dieser Zeit war diese Provinz unter der unmittelbaren Iurisdiction der Engländischen Gerichtsbarkeit. Diese untersuchte die Zwistigkeiten, änderte vieles in der Handhabung der Iurisdiction ab, und sezte sie auf den Fuss auf welchem die Caroliner stunden.—Sie war die lezte Provinz die zu der ietzigen Vereinigung der Rebellischen Staaten beytrat, und ist die erste, welche ganz wieder dem Könige gehöret. Denn am Ende des Iahres 1778. ging ein Theil der Königl: Armee unter Comando des Obrist-Lieut: Campbell's von Neu-York, und bemächtigte sich der Stadt Savannah nach geringer Gegenwehr, während dass der General Major Prevost von St. Augustin aus zu Lande bis Turisburg [sic] vorrükte, dieses weg nahm, sich mit dem Obrist Lieut: Campbell conjungirte, in kurzen das Land von Feinden reinigte, bis Charlestown vorrükte, und im Anfang des Iahres 1779. mit Beyhülfe des vormaligen und iezt wieder eingesezten Königl: Gouverneurs Wright das alte Civil Gouvernement in seiner völligen Stärke einführte. Im Monat Septembr: suchte die vereinigte Macht des Galliers und Americaners unter Anführung des Comte d'Estaing und Gen: Maj: Lincolns, die sich in Savannah verschanzte Armee gefangen zu nehmen, allein dieses Vorhaben schlug ihnen zu ihrem grossen Nachtheile fehl, und die Provinz ist iezt mehr als jemals von Feinden gesäubert, so, dass ohne die geringste Gefahr der gröste Theil der Truppen in einzeln Plantationen im Lande vertheilet liegen.

Die Lage Georgiens ist dem Aequator schon nahe genug, um das Clima im Somer wegen seiner Hitze beynahe unerträglich zu machen. Schon im Ianuar ist sie so gross, dass der zu mehrerer Kälte gewöhnte Teutsche sie bey nahe unerträglich findet. Der ganze Boden ist da, wo nicht Morast oder Holz ist, tiefer Sand, der im Somer so brennend ist, dass ein Ey in wenig Minuten darinne siedet (dieser Winter ist nach

prietors surrendered their charters to the King in the year 1752. From this time on the colony was under the immediate jurisdiction of the English government. It investigated the disputes, made many changes in the administration of the laws, and put the colonists on the same footing as the Carolinians. Georgia was the last province to join the federation of the rebellious states and is the first to belong entirely to the King again, for at the end of the year 1778 part of the Royal Army under the command of Lieutenant Colonel Campbell left New York and took possession of the city of Savannah, meeting with but little opposition, while Major General Prevost advanced by land from St. Augustine to Purysburg. Having seized the latter, he joined Lieutenant Colonel Campbell, and before long the country was cleared of the enemy. They advanced as far as Charleston, and early in 1779, with the aid of the former and now reinstated Royal Governor Wright, the old civil government was introduced again in all its strength. In the month of September the united forces of France and America, under the command of Count d'Estaing and Major General Lincoln, tried to capture the army entrenched in Savannah. But, to their sorrow, this attempt was unsuccessful. The province is now more than ever cleared of the enemy, so that the greater part of the troops can lie dispersed in isolated-plantations in the country without the least danger.

Georgia is situated close enough to the equator to make the climate in summer almost unbearable because of the heat. Even in January it is so hot that a German, accustomed to a colder climate, finds the heat nearly intolerable. The soil where there is no marsh or woodland is deep sand, which is so hot in summer that an egg will cook in it in a few minutes. (According to the account of a thirty-year-old inhabitant of

der Aussage eines 30 jährigen Einwohners von Savannah der
kälteste den er erlebet hat: Eis hat es die Nacht in der Stube
gefrohren, und einmal sogar am Tage ein wenig geschneyet;—
unerhörte Dinge in diesem Lande!)

Die ganzen Südlichen Provinzen von Cap Hatteras an, haben
ein flaches Ufer (die Ursache warum so wenige Häven in
diesem Theile Amerikens sind, und warum diese mit so vielen
Bänken und Untiefen angefüllet sind. Dies lässt uns einsehen,
von welchem Vortheile der Besitz von Charlestown dem
Feind oder uns ist) Diese Fläche des Landes erhöhet sich
allmählich, so dass je weiter man im Lande zurükgehet, je
höher das Land, je gesünder die Luft, je besser der Boden
wird. Und dieses geht bis an die berühmten Apalachisch:
Gebürge.—Dass solch eine Küste, in einem seit wenigen
Iahren erst angebautem Lande mit unreinen Dünsten muss
angefüllet seyn, ist begreiflich. Die Holzer sind undurch-
dringlich, und die Moräste und Gebüsche, welche den grösten Theil des Landes jezt noch ausmachen, machen dieses
Land auf alle Fälle zu einen ungesunden. Das Wasser der
Flüsse, welches sich durch diese Moräste durcharbeiten muss,
die ein imerwährender Wald der Reinigung und Läuterung
der Sonne beraubt, ist aus diesen natürlichen Ursachen mit
unreinen mit unedlen Theilen angefüllt, und dem Cörper
schädlich. Die Hitze des Somers, welche bey der geringsten
Bewegung den Cörper abmattet, alle pores eröfnet, und durch
die Transpiration schwachet, verlangt, dass man viele Ge-
tränke zu sich nehmen muss, und die Folge ist—das Fevrée
and aguee, welches Jahr aus, Iahr ein hier wüthet, und
manchen dahin reisst, und jedem den es befällt, seiner edelsten
Säfte beraubt, und ihm vor der Zeit altern lässt.

Die ganzen Plantationen der Europeer in Georgien liegen
längst dem Savannah und der See-Küste: natürlich die fläch-
sten Theile des Landes, und so die ungesundesten. Die Absicht
Englands bey der Pflanzung dieser Colonien war, um Wein,

Savannah, this winter has been the coldest he has experienced. There has been ice in the rooms at night and once it even snowed a little during the day—unheard-of things in this part of the country.)

All the provinces south of Cape Hatteras have a flat coast. (That is the reason why there are so few harbors in this part of America and why they are filled with so many banks and shoals. It makes one realize what an advantage the possession of Charleston is to the enemy as well as to us.) This lowland gradually rises, so that the farther inland one goes the higher the land, the healthier the air, and the better the soil. And this continues to be true as far as the famous Appalachian Mountains. It is only natural that such a coast in a country cultivated for only a few years should be filled with effluvia. The woods are impenetrable, and the marshland and brushwood, which still constitute the greater part of the country, certainly make this land unhealthy. The water of the rivers must find its way through these swamps, which by endless woods are deprived of the purification and clarification of the sun, and for such obvious reasons is full of impure and base particles and harmful to the body. The heat of the summer, which fatigues the body upon the slightest movement, opens all pores, and through perspiration weakens the constitution, demands that one partake of much liquid. The result is fever and ague, which rages here year in and year out and snatches away many a one, and robs him whom it seizes of his most noble humors, causing him to grow old before his time.

All the plantations of Europeans in Georgia are situated along the Savannah and the seacoast, the flattest parts of the country and, consequently, the most unhealthy. England's intention in establishing this colony was to cultivate grapes,

Oel und Seide selbst zu bauen, und auch schon im Iahr 1739
wurde eine Probe Seide nach England geschikt, und von
denen dasigen Manufacturisten für so gut befunden, als die
beste italienische rohe Seide. Allein, eine schwache Colonie
in einem gänzlich wilden Lande, kann ohnmöglich Manu-
factur bearbeiten, da sie alle Hände voll hat, um den blossen
Lebens-Unterhalt sich zu verschaffen. Sie muss erst mit
überflüssigen Händen angefüllet seyn, ehe es möglich ist
Manufactur-Waaren von ihr wohlfeiler als von einer Nation
zu erhalten, welche seit langer Zeit schon diese Waare unter
ihre Landes-Producte gerechnet hat.

Die Haupt-Beschäftigung dieser Colonie ist: der Reiss, Türki-
scher Waizen (indian Corn) und der Indigo, benebst dem
Handel mit Holz. Es wird aber auch Waitzen, Haver, Car-
toffeln, daselbst gezogen. Erbsen und Bohnen und andere
Garten-Kräuter wachssen hier mit dreymaliger Ernde in
einem Iahre, doch gerathen sie besser, je weiter im Lande man
kom̄t. Der Weinstok wächsst wild, und ist im Iunij reif.
Aepfel und Apricosen, schwarze und weisse Maulbeeren,
Orangen, und Oliven, alles dasjenige, was die warme Zone
hervorbringt, wird hier unter die Landes-Producten gerechnet.
—Geflügel giebt es hier genug, und bey nahe alle wild.—
Tyger und Wölfe, und Bären kom̄en bis zu denen Plantationen; Schlangen unzähliger Arten, giftige und unschädliche,
sind so wie das Crocodill und Opossum dem Einwohner ganz
bekannte Thiere.—Wann der Herr einer Plantage seinen
Negro zu seinen Nachbarn schikt, oder auf die Iagd geht, so
umwikelt derselbe sich die Beine mit diken Tüchern, um den
Biss der Schlangen minder gefährlich zu machen.

Savannah und Augusta sind die beyden berühmtesten Oerter
in dieser Provinz. Erster bestehet aus etwa 150 hölzernen
Häussern, die in recht winklichten Gassen, auf einem sandigten, und von der daran liegenden Gegend erhabenen Boden,
am Savannah River, erbauet worden ist. Sie liegt 15 Meilen

olives, and silk, and as early as 1739 a sample of silk was sent to England and was found by the manufacturers as good as the best Italian raw silk. However, a weak colony in an entirely wild country cannot possibly engage in manufacturing, since the settlers have their hands full procuring a mere subsistence. A colony must first be full of superfluous hands before it can produce manufactured wares more cheaply than a nation which for a long time has counted these wares among her staple products.

The main occupation in this colony is the cultivation of rice, Indian corn, and indigo, as well as the sale of timber. Wheat, oats, and potatoes are, however, raised too. Peas, beans, and other garden produce yield three crops a year; but they grow better the farther inland one goes. Grapes grow wild and ripen in June. Apples and apricots, black and white mulberries, oranges and olives, in fact, all the products of the warmer regions are grown in this province. Fowl are plentiful, mostly wild. Tigers, wolves, and bears prowl around the plantations. Countless varieties of snakes, venomous and harmless, as well as crocodiles and opossums, are animals very familiar to the settlers. When a Negro is sent to a neighbor, or when the master goes hunting, he wraps his legs with thick rags to make the snake bites less dangerous.

Savannah and Augusta are the two best-known towns in this province. The former lies on the sandy bank of the Savannah River, higher than the surrounding region, and consists of about one hundred and fifty wooden houses[1] built along streets intersecting one another at right angles. It is situated fifteen miles from the sea and can be reached by ships of four hundred to five hundred tons, since the river as far up as

[1] Perhaps a mistake of the copyist; should read "four hundred and fifty." There were then in Savannah about four hundred and thirty houses, most of which were wooden structures (C. C. Jones, *History of Georgia* [Boston 1883], II, 378).

von der See, und der Haven bis zur Stadt hällt 3–3½ Faden
Wasser, so dass Schiffe von 400–500 Tonnen bis vor die Stadt
koñen köñen. Oberhalb derselben kann aber nur mit 1 mastigen Schiffen und grossen Kähnen der Fluss bis an Augusta
(welcher Ort der Stapel des Indianischen Tausch-Handels ist)
befahren werden. Der ganze Fluss ist mit Krümmungen und
Jnsuln und Bänken angefüllt, der Strom in demselben reissend, und eine Ebbe und Fluth bis Savannah von 9½ Fuss.

In der Stadt sind 2. Kirchen, Stadthaus und Markt, und
vor der Stadt waren Baraquen für 600 Mann, die bey der Ankunft der Franzossen und Rebellen am Ende des vorigen
Iahres niedergerissen wurden, weil sie der Fortification im
Wege standen.

Westlich stösst diese Provinz an die Upper und Lower Creeks,
Chikesaues und Cherokees Indians (von lezten sind iezt 300 in
Savannah zu unserer Armée gestossen und noch 1000 werden
stündlich erwartet) Diese Indianer sind nicht so roh wie man
glaubt; sie haben ihre Grund-Sätze von Ehre, Diebe, Religion,
Freundschaft und Rache, etc. Ich sahe einen dieser in Savan-
nah. Sein ganzer Kopf ist geschoren, bis auf eine runde
Platte oben am Hintertheil des Kopfes. Diese Haare werden
zusamen gebunden, und sie schmüken sie mit Corallen,
Bändern, Federn und Muscheln. Der ganze übrige Theil des
Kopfes und Gesichtes ist mit bunten Farben bemahlet, Ohren,
Nasse, und alles. Die rothe Farbe ist hier die Haupt-Farbe.
Iezt tragen sie wollene Deken, und lange blaue tüchene
Strümpfe bis über das Dikbein. Keiner geht ohne sein Pulver
und Bley und Tomahawkée. Dieses ist eine von denen Euro-
peern ihnen verhandelte Pfeiffe, an welcher ein Beil an einer
Seite ist und ein Hañer an der andern. Der Hañer ist inwendig
hohl, und hienein stopfen sie den Tobak, und der Stiel
welcher inwendig hohl ist, dienet ihnen zum Rohre. Sobald
man mit ihnen sich einlässt, ist das erste, dass sie einem die
Hand reichen, dann setzen sie sich gleich ohne Umstände

the city has a depth of three to three and one-half fathoms. Above the city the river can be navigated only by single-masted ships and large boats as far as Augusta, which is the staple of the Indian trade. The entire river is full of turns and islands and banks. The current is swift, and at Savannah the difference between high and low tide is nine and one-half feet.

The city has two churches, a city hall, and a market. Outside the city there were barracks for six hundred men, which were torn down late last year on the approach of the French and the rebels, since they hindered the fortification of the city.

To the west of this province live the Upper and Lower Creek, the Chickasaw, and the Cherokee Indians (three hundred of the Cherokee have just joined our forces at Savannah and one thousand more are hourly expected). These Indians are not so savage as one imagines them to be. They have definite principles concerning honor, stealing, religion, friendship, revenge, etc. I saw one of them in Savannah. The Indian has his whole head shorn except for a round spot on the crown. The hair is tied together and is adorned with corals, ribbons, feathers, and shells. All the remaining parts of his head and face are painted in gay colors—ears, nose, and everything. Red is the predominant color. At present they are wearing woolen blankets and long blue cloth stockings reaching above the thigh. No Indian ever goes about without his powder, lead, and tomahawk. This is a pipe given them by Europeans in trade, which has a hatchet on one side and a hammer on the other. The hammer is hollow, and in it they put tobacco, the hollow handle serving as a pipestem. When one has any dealings with them they first extend their hands in greeting; then they sit down without more ado, whereupon the host lights a pipe of tobacco. After taking a few puffs he gives it to his neighbor, and so the pipe makes the rounds until

nieder, sobald muss eine Pfeiffe Tobak von dem Wirth angezündet werden; Dieser thut dann einige Züge, gibt sie seinem Nachbar, und so gehet die Pfeiffe herum, bis sie alle ist.
Hernach raucht ieder wann er will. Diesen Gebrauch habe
ich auf die Art zu erklären gesucht. Ihre Pfeiffen sind ihr
Hand-Gewehr, und die Mittheilung desselben von einem zum
andern, ist ein Zeichen der Freundschaft, als wollte der
Indianer sagen: Hiermit gebe ich mein Gewehr in deine Hand,
damit du siehest, dass ich keine böse Absicht auf dich habe,
und von dir vermuthet bin.—Im Streit aber ist ihr erstes, dass
sie nach ihrem Gegner mit dieser Pfeiffe werfen, und die
Geschiklichkeit, mit welcher sie dieses Instruments sich
bedienen, ist fast unbegreiflich, indem sie das kleineste Mahl-
zeichen in einer Entfernung von 20 und mehreren Schritten,
mit der Spitze des sehr geschärften Beiles berühren. Als Soldaten sind sie für einen, an Kugel und Bley und Handgemenge
Gewöhnten, nichts weniger als gefährlich. Sie setzen keine
Posten und Piquetter aus, sondern ganz verzettelt legen sie
sich im Holze bey kleinen Parteyen, aber nur einzeln hin,
und bey dem geringsten Alarm ziehen sie sich zusam̃en, und
verlieren sich nie. Sie haben ein erstaunliches Gehör und
scharfes Gesicht.—Allein sie halten keinen echeç ab. Sich in
Laub und Busch zu verbergen, und einzelnen Leuten auf den
Schuss zu passen, und wann sie die geringste Gegenwehr
sehen, mit erstaunenswürdiger Leichtigkeit dann zu fliehen,
eben so geschwind wieder an einer andern Stelle hervor zu
kom̃en, darinne bestehet ihr Haupt-Militair. Nur um die
ganzen Indianer zu unsern Freunde zu behalten, ist es, warum
der König sucht einige davon in seinem Sold zu nehmen.
Denn im Grunde kosten sie unzählig mahl mehr als ordentliche Soldaten, und ruiniren mehr als sie Vortheil schaffen.——

[1] Cf. letter of Governor Sir James Wright to Sir Henry Clinton, March
18, 1780: ". . . however these people may be thought useless in the field—

it is empty. After this everyone smokes when he pleases. This custom I have attempted to explain in the following manner. Their pipes are their weapons, and passing them from one to another is a sign of friendship, as if the Indian were to say: "Herewith I put my weapon into your hand so that you may see that I have no evil intentions toward you and need not be suspected by you." But the first thing they do in a fight is to throw this pipe at their opponent. The skill which they exhibit when making use of this instrument is almost inconceivable, for they hit the smallest mark with the point of the keen-edged hatchet at a distance of twenty and more paces. As soldiers, they are anything but dangerous to one accustomed to balls, lead, and hand-to-hand combat. They do not station outposts and pickets, but scatter about in the woods and lie down in small bands, but each man by himself, and at the slightest alarm they assemble, never losing touch with each other. They have a marvelous sense of hearing and sharp eyesight. But they cannot stand a repulse. Hiding in bushes and behind trees, waiting to take a shot at someone, and upon meeting with the slightest resistance taking flight with amazing agility, but showing up at another place just as quickly—these are their principal military virtues. The only reason why the King attempts to have some of them in his pay is to have all Indians as his friends, for in reality they cost many times more than real soldiers and do more harm than good.[1]

---

your Excellency will be pleased to recollect that I had the honor to mention to you here my opinion of the consequences of Indians, and that if they were against us they would harrass the King's Troops in any march & receive the Rebels amongst them, and I feared we could never subdue the rebellion" (Gt. Brit. Hist. MSS. Comm., *op. cit.*, II, 104).

Ich besahe sogleich die Festungs-Werke und die Attaque des Comte d'Estaing; Aber ich fand keine in vorigem Kriege von Gallien so sehr berühmte Ingenieurerie und Disposition! Da die ganze Relation, von dieser wirklich berühmten Belagerung sowohl, als die Plane davon iezt schon sicher bis nach Europa gekomen sind, so will ich mich mit der Zergliederung desselben nicht aufhalten, sondern blos einige allgemeine Bemerkungen über das Betragen des Feindes und unsere Truppen hier beyfügen.

Dass dem Engländer Unachtsamkeit im Dienst beygemessen wird, ist bekannt. Ob dieses Nachlässigkeit, Uibermuth und Eigendünkel, oder Bewustseyn eigner Grösse, edler Stolz, Zutrauen auf persöhnl: Stärke, und Uiberzeugung von der Uiberlegenheit über den Feind ist, will ich unentschieden lassen.—Genug es ist.—Nur von dieser Seite betrachtet, lässt sich die Frage beantworten: warum die Engländer nicht eher und nicht sicherer einen Ort verschanzten, der den Besitzer zum Herrn der Provinz Georgien machte, bis dass der Feind vor derselben war? Und wo konnten sie, seit der Krieg mit dem Bourbonischen Hause declarirt ist, wo, in welcher Nord Americanischen Provinz konnten sie sich einen feindlichen Besuch eher vermuthen, als in den Südlichen, an welchen Spanien und Frankreich, vor dem Pariser Frieden, einen grössern Anspruch nach unserm Europæischen, uns selbst gebildeten Natürlichen Rechte, hatten, dann England oder irgend eine andere Europäische Nation? Und wäre auch dieses Recht nicht, liess es sich schon aus dem Grunde vermuthen, um 1) Charlestown desto sicherer und fester zu machen, und 2) hauptsächlich um dem West-Indischen Handel der Engländer zu schaden, und ihren eigenen zu sichern. Denn: *da der Current aus dem Golfo von Florida alle Flotten aus der Havanna sowohl, wie die von den Windwards Islanden zwingen, bey der Heimfart bis zum Cap Hatteras allezeit längst der Americanischen Küste heraufzufahren,* so lässt sich blos durch die

I immediately inspected the fortifications and studied the attack made by Count d'Estaing. But I did not find any of the engineering feats or dispositions for which the French were so much lauded in the last war. Since a detailed account of this really famous siege as well as the plans thereof have by this time surely arrived in Europe, I shall spend no time discussing it in detail, but shall make only a few general remarks concerning the conduct of the enemy and of our troops.

It is well known that the English are charged with heedlessness in military service. Whether this be carelessness, haughtiness, and conceit, or consciousness of their own greatness, inborn pride, confidence in personal strength, and the conviction of their superiority over the enemy, I do not care to decide. The fact remains that it is there. Only when looked at from this angle can we answer the questions: Why did the English not fortify the city strongly before the enemy was upon it, since whoever is in possession of it is master of Georgia? Where, since war with the House of Bourbon had been declared, where, in what North American province could they more reasonably expect the enemy than in the southern provinces, to which Spain and France, according to European and common law, had a greater claim prior to the treaty of Paris than England or any other European nation! Even if they had no such right to these provinces, they could have been expected there for the following reasons: (1) to make Charleston all the safer and stronger; (2) to hurt the West India trade of the English and to strengthen their own. This alone would have been sufficient cause, for *the current from the Gulf of Florida compels all fleets on the return voyage from Havana and the Windward Islands to sail along the American coast as far as Cape Hatteras*. The mere men-

Anführung dieses Facti, ohne den geringsten Commentar die Wichtigkeit des Havens Savannah und Charlestown schon erklären.

Unbekannt konnten sie hiemit nicht seyn, eben so wenig als mit der Stärke d'Estaings in den West-Jndien sowohl zur See als zu Lande, und dennoch, ja nicht einmal nach der verlohrnen See-Schlacht des Admiral Byrons fingen sie an sich in Bereitschaft zu setzen; sondern als Lincoln schon bey Ebenetzer stand, und d'Estaing schon in Georgien gelandet war, war Savannah noch halb offen, und die durch Krankheiten u.s.w. schon so sehr verringerte Besatzung, noch in der Provinz bis in South-Carolina, bis in Beaufort verzettelt! —Dieses wäre nicht zu vergeben gewesen, wenn nicht der Ausgang ihnen günstig gewesen wäre. Allein so unvortheilhaft sie sich vorher zeigten; so gross, so vortheilhaft zeigten sie sich bey der Belagerung selber, und kein reitzender Anblik kann sicherer für einen Sodaten seyn, als durch die demolirten, ganz unordentlich von blossem Sande und wenigen Brettern aufgeworfene Werke des wahrhaftig grossen Moncrieffs zu gehen, und jede demolirte Batterie, jede halb dahinter aufgeworfene neue, jeder Fuss durchwühltes Land zeigt mit Uiberzeugung, dass ein Gran Gegenwart des Geistes, eine wieder alle Regeln, aber zu rechter Zeit und am rechten Fleken hier aufgeworfene Wehre, viel tausendmahl mehr werth ist, als die köstlichste theoretische Probleme. die mit übertriebener Genauigkeit auf dem Papiere entworfen wurden, und unter Tausend Fällen, nie anders als im Buche anzuwenden sind.—Aber wie es mit Savannah, mit der Besatzung ausgesehen, wäre Capit: Moncrieff erschossen worden, ehe der Feind sich zurükzog?—Gewiss nicht zum besten! Die ganze Besatzung bestand, ehe Obrist-Lieut: Maitland zu ihnen stiess aus keine 1000 Mann Engländer, Hessen, und Provinzialisten, unter welchen etwa 60 Pferde waren, und diese musten ein Terrain besetzen von mehr denn 12,500 Fuss; denn so viel ist die

tion of this fact without the least comment will show how important are the harbors of Savannah and Charleston.

They must have been aware of this, just as they must have known d'Estaing's strength in the West Indies, on water as well as on land. Nevertheless, they made no preparations, not even after Admiral Byron's fleet had been defeated. As a matter of fact, when Lincoln had advanced as far as Ebenezer and d'Estaing had already landed in Georgia, Savannah was still half open, and the garrison, considerably weakened by disease, etc., scattered in the province, even as far as Beaufort, South Carolina. All this would have been considered unforgivable negligence had not the whole affair turned out favorably. Though they had shown themselves in a bad light hitherto, during the siege itself they displayed valor and good judgment. There is no more fascinating sight for a soldier than that of the demolished works of the truly great Moncrieff, thrown up, as they were, in a disorderly fashion only out of sand and a few boards. Every demolished battery, every new half-completed work in the rear of it, every foot of torn-up ground shows convincingly that a grain of presence of mind, that a barrier hastily thrown up, but in the nick of time and at the right spot, is worth many thousand times more than the most splendid theoretical problems, which, though they be drawn on paper with exaggerated exactness, cannot one in a thousand cases be carried out in practice. But how would Savannah, how would the garrison have fared had Captain Moncrieff been killed before the enemy withdrew? Certainly none too well! The entire garrison before Lieutenant Colonel Maitland joined it consisted of fewer than a thousand men, made up of English, Hessians, and provincials, amongst whom were approximately sixty horse. These had to occupy a territory of over 12,500 feet, i.e. the line from the river on one side of the city to the river

Lienie von einer Seite des Flusses bis zur andern. Der Boden ist tiefer Sand, und nur ein von der Land Seite offenes Werk (double tenaille) eine 4 ekigte redoute an der Ebenezer road, und 2 andere, zwischen dieser und der double tenaille, welche diesseits der Stadt am Savannah river liegt, war die ganze Verschanzung, ausser einem Verhau um die ganze Lienie. Die rechte Flanke, nemlich von der Ebenezer road, bis an Savannah, oberhalb der Stadt, umgab ein Morast und kleiner Bach. Die Werke waren halb verfallen, von blossem Sande und wenigen Faschienen aufgeworfen, und keine 12 Fuss stark. Kein Sandsak, kein Schanzkorb, nichts war im Vorrath, um die, in solchen schwachen Brustwehren mit Geschütz leicht zu machende Oeffnungen wieder auszu bessern.—Dies war die wahre Lage der Truppen Septembr 3. als Comte d'Estaing mit 51 Seegeln sich vor Tybée zeigte, und aus der Provinz Nachricht einlief: dass General Lincoln mit einem starken Detachement Rebellen über den Savannah, ohnfern Ebenezer ging, und sich der Stadt näherte. Allein zum grösten Vortheil der Belagerten, verzoge sich die Landung der Franzosen bis den 12ten (bey Bewlie etwa 14 Meilen von der Stadt) und ihre Annäherung bis 3 Meilen vor der Stadt, und Vereinigung mit denen Rebellen bis den 16ten. Dieses und die geschikte scheinbare Unterhandlung des General Prevost, womit er den Feind, unter Hofnung der Uibergabe bis zum 18ten von Feindseeligkeiten abzuhalten wuste, gab dem unermüdeten Ingenieur Capt: Moncrieff Zeit, aus diesem Undinge von Verschanzung, eine nach Ort und Zeit gute Verchanzung der Lienien zurechte zu bringen; dem Maitland Zeit von Beaufort aus, mit 800 streitbaren Männern zu dem Gener: Prevost zu stossen, und der Garnison Zeit sich einzugraben. Diese Verstärkung sowohl, als die Demontirung verschiedener

---

[1] The correct form of this name is Beaulieu, though Captain Hinrichs' spelling is frequently found.

on the other. The ground is deep sand, and the entire fortification consisted of a double tenaille open on the land side
and situated this [the east] side of the city on the Savannah
River, a rectangular redoubt on the Ebenezer road, two
others between the latter and the double tenaille, and abatis
around the entire line. The right flank, i.e. from the Ebenezer
road to the Savannah River above the city, was surrounded
by a swamp and a narrow creek. The works were less than
twelve feet thick and half-crumbled, having been thrown up
of mere sand and a few fascines. No sandbags, no gabions,
nothing was in readiness that could be used to repair the
breaches easily made by guns in such weak breastworks.
This was the true situation of the troops on September 3,
when Count d'Estaing appeared before Tybee with fifty-one
sail and when from the province came the news that General
Lincoln with a strong detachment of rebels was crossing the
Savannah in the neighborhood of Ebenezer and approaching
the city. However, to the greatest good fortune of the besieged the landing of the French at Bewlie,[1] about fourteen
miles from the city, was delayed till the 12th[2] and their
approach to within three miles of the city and junction with
the rebels till the 16th. This delay, as well as General Prevost's clever pretense of negotiations, which made the enemy
hope for a surrender and kept them from opening hostilities
till the 18th,[3] gave the indefatigable engineer, Captain
Moncrieff, time to make out of this weak fortification of the
lines a strong one, considering, of course, place and time.
Furthermore, it permitted Maitland, who was approaching
from Beaufort, to join General Prevost with eight hundred
effective men, and also gave the garrison time to entrench
itself. This reinforcement, as well as the increase of men and

---

[2] On this day only about twelve hundred men could be landed, stormy
weather making further debarkation impossible.

[3] Hostilities commenced an hour before sundown on the 17th.

Schiffe, und der Zuwachss, welcher dadurch an Artillerie und
Menschen den Belagerten anwuchss, gab der Sache eine vor-
theilhafte Wendung. Denn von 300 Negroes wurden iezt 15
Batterien aufgeworfen, diese mit 76. Canonen besetzet, und
mit Mariniers und Matrosen bemannet, zwischen denen alten
Redouten mehrere, nemlich 13 aufgeworfen, und aus 1000
Mann, waren iezt, die Matrosen und Einwohner Savannahs
(welche auch in den Werken zu fechten gezwungen wurden)
mitgerechnet, 2350 Mann erwachssen.—Unbegreiflich ist es
mir, dass d'Estaing (welcher in meinen Augen vormals Mons:
la Resourçe war) sich entschlüssen konnte, die geringste
Verzögerung gleich nach den 12ten statt finden zu lassen, und
nicht viel mehr, ehe die Canonen aus den Schiffen von denen
Belagerten konnten benutzet werden, ehe Maitland konnte zu
der Besatzung stossen, und ehe die redouten, batterien, linien
und Traversen konnten gemacht werden, sogleich den 13ten
oder doch den 16ten des Morgens, mit dem Bajonet au bout
du fusil diesen elenden Sand Haufen stürmte, und wegnahm?
Dieses, dieses kann ich nicht begreiffen, ist mir unerklär-
bar! Seine Force bestand aus 1700. Europaischen regularen,
1000 Mariniers, und 3100 Westindischen Truppen, der Rebellen nicht zu gedenken. Noch weniger möchte ich seine
Arbeit billigen. Seine Haupt Batterie liegt etwa 400 Schritt
vom feindlichen Werke. Zur Bresch-Batterie zu weit entfernt, und zur demontir und ricochet Batterie zu nahe. Hätte
er ricochet geschossen, (und das Terrain zwischen beyden
Werken erlaubet es,) gewiss hätte er grossen Schaden angerichtet, wollte er aber iezt Kern schiessen, so gingen die
Kugeln über die Lienien weg in die ledigen Häuser, oder
richtete er niedriger, so schlugen sie im Sande vor die Lienie

---

[1] The various accounts differ slightly. This, however, is the number
given in Rivington's *Royal Gazette*, which Hinrichs may well have seen.

[2] This passage, a bit of sarcasm, may be rendered freely: "It is incon-

artillery resulting from the dismantling of several ships, gave an advantageous turn to the affair. Three hundred Negroes were put to work raising fifteen batteries. These were mounted with seventy-six cannon and manned by sailors and marines. Between the old redoubts thirteen more batteries were thrown up, and the thousand men had by then increased to 2,350,[1] counting sailors and the inhabitants of Savannah, who were also compelled to fight in the works. It is inconceivable to me how d'Estaing (who formerly, I believe, was a M. La Resource)[2] could permit the slightest delay after the 12th. Why did he not on the 13th, or at least on the morning of the 16th, storm and take this miserable sand pile with fixed bayonets before the besieged could use the cannon from the ships, before Maitland could join the garrison, and before the redoubts, batteries, lines, and traverses could be raised? It is this, this that I cannot understand, that is puzzling to me! D'Estaing's force consisted of 1,700 European regulars, 1,000 marines, and 3,100 men from the West Indies,[3] not to mention the rebels. Even less can I approve of his works. His main battery lies about four hundred paces from the enemy's works. For a breach battery it is too far away, and for a demounting and ricochet battery, too close. If he had used ricochet fire (and the ground between the two works permits of it), he would certainly have done great damage. But at this distance a point-blank shot would go over the lines into the empty houses,[4] or, if aimed lower, would strike into the sand and die. And with this *feux*

---

ceivable to me how d'Estaing, who formerly, I believe, was always resourceful . . . ."

[3] According to the most accurate calculations, d'Estaing's force, given by Hinrichs as 5,800, consisted of no more than about 4,500, while the Americans numbered some 2,000 (C. C. Jones, ed., *Siege of Savannah* [Albany, 1874], p. 39).

[4] Many houses were struck and set on fire, but comparatively little damage was done to the fortifications.

und erstikten. Und mit diesem Feux d'artifice amusirte sich der d'Estaing bis den 9ten Octobr: des Morgens, als am welchen Tage er mit 6000 Franzosen und Rebellen, mit Hülfe eines diken Nebels, an der Ebenezer road, bis in den Verhau vorrükte, und in einem kleinen defilée, das der Bach zwischen der Ebenezer road und dem Savannah river overhalb der Stadt machte, sich Formirte (also hatten die Engländer daselbst, an diesem schwächesten Theil der Verschanzung weder Piquet noch Posten?) mit der grösten Hitze adtaquirte, und die Caroliner Redoute berennete. Sicher hätte er den Sieg zweifelhaft gemacht, wo nicht davongetragen, wann nicht zum Glüke der Belagerten der Comte d'Estaing sowohl, wie Pulavsky, zwey von Grund aus brave Männer, am Verhake, hart bey einander niedergeschossen worden. Dies aber brachtĕ den ersten Halte zu wege, (eine gefährliche Sache beym Sturm) und da der Feind, die Französ: lieblings Methode: en Colonne zu adtaquiren, auch hier beybehalten hatte, und rechts und links, bis 20. Schritt vor dem Verhau, an der Ebenezer road, Morast ist, und so diese Colonne in Division zum deployiren aufgeschlossen, auf die Strasse vorrükten, und vor dem Verhau nicht deployirten, sondern en Colonne auftrang, und vom Avant-Corps nichts separirt commandirt war, um die an der rechten Flanque der Caroliner Redoute liegende Batterie von 5. Canonen weg zu nehmen, so richtete diese mit Carteschen ein so mördendes Feuer unter die Colonne an, dass statt 250–300, die der Feind nur bey der Attaque verlohren hatte, die Retraite ihm zwischen 12–1300 todte und blessirte kostete. D'Estaing und Pulavsky war iezt so gut als todt, die Rebellen abgeschrekt, und der Feind zog sich wieder zurük, ohne das geringste der Schande mit sich davon zu führen! Hätte d'Estaing die Colonne gleich links und rechts

---

[1] The greater part of the attacking force did not advance along this road; most of those who did were slaughtered, as were those that collected here from the swamps.

d'artifice d'Estaing amused himself till the morning of the 9th of October, when with six thousand French and rebels under cover of a thick fog, he advanced on the Ebenezer road[1] as far as the abatis and formed ranks in a narrow defile made by the creek between the Ebenezer road and the Savannah River above the city. (It seems that the English had neither pickets nor posts at this, the weakest part of their fortification.) In the heat of the first onrush he attacked and stormed the Carolina redoubt. Count d'Estaing might have been victorious; certainly the outcome would have been doubtful had not he and Pulaski been shot down close together at the abatis. The loss of these two excellent men changed the luck of the besieged, for it caused the first halt, a dangerous thing in an assault. The enemy attacked in column formation, a favorite method with the French. However, to the right and left of the Ebenezer road to within twenty paces of the abatis there are morasses, and so the closed column which was to have deployed advanced as one division on the road without deploying before the abatis. They rushed on in column formation, not even detailing a separate detachment of the vanguard to take the five-gun battery situated to the right of the Carolina redoubt. This battery sent such a murderous fire of grapeshot into the column that, instead of the mere 250 to 300 which the enemy had lost in the attack, their retreat made their losses mount to between 1,200 and 1,300 killed and wounded. D'Estaing and Pulaski were now as good as dead; the rebels were disheartened; and the enemy withdrew without taking with them the least of their disgrace.[2] If d'Estaing had made the column deploy right and left just as

---

[2] The German passage is not clear and was, therefore, translated literally. It seems to imply that they withdrew without taking with them any of their dead or wounded, the victims of a disgracefully directed assault. Upon withdrawal of the allied forces from the field a truce of four hours was granted for burying the dead and collecting the wounded.

deployiren lassen, so bald er den Morast passiret war, oder wollte er diéses nicht, hätte er die Attaque in 3 Reserven eingetheilt, z.B. die erste attaquirt, die 2te Formirt unterdessen im Defilée, und die 3te rükt langsam die Ebenezer road herunter, und fällt da auf wo der Feind just anfängt zu wanken, und hätte dann die Avant in 2 Theile getheilt, eine Division dann auf die Caroliner Redoute rüken lassen, während die andere die 5 Canonen Batterie bestürmet hätte, auch eine Batterie an der Sandsbergs Strasse, da wo das Rebellen Piquet stand, und eine andere an der Ebenezer road, am Ausgange des Waldes, jede von etwa 4 bis 6. 18 und 24 Pfünder aufwerfen lassen, und damit während der Attaque den bestürmenten Fleken per ricochet (distance 750. Schritt) Flanquirt—und wäre dann nicht selber gefährlich blessiret worden, so möchte es wohl schlim mit dieser Garnison ausgesehen haben! Denn an bravour fehlte es dem Feinde nicht; sie waren schon auf der Brustwehr, schon in dem Eingang der Caroliner redoute. (Ich habe selbst einen Englischen Officier gesehen, dem bey Vertheitigung des Eingangs in dieser Redoute, von einem Franzosen die Nase vom Kopfe herunter gehauen ist, der es aber mit dem Leben bezahlen muste, und in dem Eingang der Redoute liegen blieb.)

Ohne hier der vielen Nachtheile zu erwähnen, die uns der Verlust dieser Garnison und Stadt gezogen hätte, den Muth den die Rebellen dadurch wiederbekoṁen hätten, das Mistrauen welches die Königl: Gesinnten Americaner auf unsere Stärke gesetzet hätten, wann sie sahen, welchem traurigen Schiksaal iezt Georgien ausgesezt sey, und blos weil es sich für uns erkläret hatte (denn die Rebellen wären gewiss barbarisch mit ihnen umgegangen) alles dieses vorausgesezt, so

¹ Much of this criticism is just and shows that Captain Hinrichs was a good tactician. Not all his censure, however, is quite fair, for some of the movements he claims d'Estaing should have made had actually been planned, but for various reasons were not carried out. The most decisive

soon as they had passed the swamp, or, in case he did not want to do this, had he divided the attacking column into three parts, then the first could have attacked while the second might have formed in the defile, and the third, in the meantime, could have slowly advanced down the Ebenezer road and stormed the line wherever the enemy began to falter. Furthermore, he might have divided the van into two parts, one of which could have attacked the Carolina redoubt while the other stormed the five-gun battery. He should, moreover, have thrown up a battery on the Sunbury road, where the rebel picket was posted, and another on the Ebenezer road at the edge of the forest, each battery consisting of about four to six 18- and 24-pounders. During the attack these should have been fired by ricochet, range 750 paces, at the flanks of the work being stormed[1]—and then, if d'Estaing himself had not been dangerously wounded, the garrison probably would have fared very badly, for the enemy were not lacking in valor. They had already ascended the breastworks and had gained the entrance to the Carolina redoubt. (I myself saw an English officer who, in the defense of the entrance to this redoubt, had his nose struck off by a Frenchman, who, however, had to pay for this with his life, falling in the entrance.)

It is not necessary to mention the many disadvantages which the loss of this garrison and the city would have entailed; for example, the courage which it would have given to the rebels and the distrust which the American loyalists would have had in our strength had they seen to what a deplorable fate Georgia was exposed merely because this province had declared its loyalty to us (for the rebels would certainly have treated the inhabitants barbarously). All this

factor, of which Hinrichs seems to have been ignorant and which contributed most toward the allied disaster, was the intelligence of their plans, which was supplied by a deserter.

hätte auch im Gegentheil die Wegnahm Savannahs vieleicht den ersten Zank-Apfel zwischen Frankreich und den Rebellen gegeben; indem d'Estaing im Anfange der Belagerung durch Aufforderung der Garnison: *Im Namen des Königes von Frankreich*, schon genug zu verstehen gab, dass er nicht im Willens habe, so geschwind wieder die Provinz zu verlassen, als die Rebellen etwa vermuthen mochten.

Febr: 5. Nachdem ich mich heute Morgen noch etwas in Savannah umgesehen hatte, mich so viel die Kürze der Zeit und Gelegenheit erlaubte nach der politisch und oeconomischen Lage der Provinz erkundiget hatte, fuhr ich mit contrairen Winde in 4½ Stunden wieder zurük nach Tybée auf unser Schif. Die 4 auf Station gelegenen Ruder-Galeeren waren schon gestern Nachmittag nach Tybée gegangen, und zu gleicher Zeit die Vigilant mit 2 Provision Schiffen nach Dawfoskée Sound gefahren. Die Schifs-Capitains musten heute alle auf 10 Täge Provision für die am Bord habende Truppen, vorräthig haben, oder sich von den Proviant-Schiffen liefern lassen.

Febr: 6. Heute Nachmittage kam der Lord Mulgrave ein, seit den 4ten Tag unserer Fart war er von der Flotte gewesen, und hatte seit der Zeit mit keinem Schiffe gesprochen, aber einige von ferne gesehen, zu den er nicht komen konnte. Auch kam heute ein Agent des Admirals an unser Schif, und lass denen

---

[1] William Gordon also had his suspicions concerning d'Estaing's summons. "Lincoln," he says, "remonstrated to d'Estaing on his summoning Prevost to surrender to the arms of France *only*, while the Americans were acting in conjunction with him; the matter was soon settled, and the mode of all future negotiations amicably adjusted" (*History of the Rise, Progress, and Establishment of the Independence of the United States* [London, 1788], III, 327). Charles Stedman, referring to "this hasty proceeding" of Count d'Estaing, remarks: "by some it was thought to be a plain indication that the French meant to conquer for themselves" (*History . . . of the American War* [London, 1794], II, 125). The editor found the following remarks in a manuscript letter of Major Carl Baurmeister to Baron von Jungkenn, Dec.

may be taken for granted. On the other hand, the reduction of Savannah might have been the first apple of discord between France and the rebels, for when at the beginning of the siege d'Estaing summoned the garrison to surrender *in the name of the King of France*, he made it plain enough that he would not be willing to leave the province so quickly as the rebels might have expected.[1]

In the morning I looked around in Savannah and inquired into the political and economic conditions of the province as much as time and opportunity permitted. Then, with contrary wind, I returned to our ship at Tybee, the trip taking four and one-half hours. The four row-galleys that had been stationed offshore had come in to Tybee yesterday afternoon. At the same time the *Vigilant* and two provision ships had gone to Daufuskie Sound. The ships' masters were ordered to have ten days' supply of provisions for the troops on board and to have the provision ships make up any shortage. Feb. 5

This afternoon the *Lord Mulgrave* arrived. She had been separated from the fleet since the fourth day of our voyage and during that time had not spoken a single ship, although she had sighted several at a distance without being able to reach them. An agent of the Admiral came to our ship and Feb. 6

13, 1779: "General Lincoln had a heated argument with Count d'Estaing for summoning General Prevost to clear Georgia in the name of his sovereign, which Lincoln had meant to do in the name of Congress. Count d'Estaing, however, believing that all of Georgia was in British possession, thought to have good reasons to conquer it for France." Again, there is the postscript of d'Estaing's second communication to General Prevost, dated Sept. 16, to wit: "I apprise your Excellency that I have not been able to refuse the army of the United States uniting itself with that of the King." This, W. B. Stevens remarks, "is a strange piece of diplomacy, for it implies that he had endeavored to prevent it, when his very purpose in coming to Georgia was to effect it" (*History of Georgia* [Philadelphia, 1859], II, 207, 224).

Matrosen eine Ordre des Admirals vor, in welcher ihnen bey schwerer Strafe das Plündern der Häuser, bey Landung der Truppen verboten wurde.

Febr: 7. Der General und Admiral kamen heute von Savannah zu der Flotte, und erster ging am Bord des Agenten Schifs lezter am Bord des Perseus. Die Transport Schiffe bekamen Ordre Morgen bis auf 30. Täge Provision für die Truppen zu empfangen,—so werden wir wahrscheinlich nicht durch die Jnnland route, sondern an der Küste weg nach Port-Royal fahren. Ein gewaltiges Wetter war heute. Horicane, Regen Hagel, Gewitter von S.W. Es kamen heute wieder 2 Schiffe an.

Febr: 8. Sehr kalt, und scharfer Wind, hohle See. Die Truppen am Bord der Peggy Transport, wurde heute auf die Empress of Russia gebracht, und die Peggy Transport ging nach Savannah, weil sie zu lekigt war. Gegen Abend bekamen die Transport Schiffe Ordre sich sogleich seegelfertig zu machen, um den andern Morgen nach North-Edisto River zu fahren, woselbst die respv: Truppen sollten debarquiret werden. Auch wurde zu gleicher Zeit durch ein Signal vom Admiral-Schif der Flotte bekannt gemacht, dass jeder von der Flotte sich sogleich an Bord seines angewiesenen Schiffes begeben sollte, auch keinem Boode mehr sollte erlaubet seyn, ans Land zu fahren.

Febr: 9ten Gegen Mittag wurde nach gegebenen Signal der Anker gelichtet, wir fuhren mit W.N.W. und angenehmer Luft N.O. und machten bey Trensch Eiland einer 10 Meilen grossen, mit Fichten bewachssenen grossen Insul halte. Weil der Wind

---

[1] Cf. Arbuthnot to Elphinstone: "Memo. Roebuck off Tybee Island. 5 February, 1780. It is the Admiral's direction that the respective Agents for Transports announce to their different divisions previous to the sailing of the Armament that if any of the crews are detected in, and proved to be guilty of, plundering the Country people, they will be delivered up to the Provost Marshall of the Army, to be punished in so exemplary manner as will sufficiently deter them from a repetition of the like atrocious practice" (*Keith Papers*, I, 145–146). That Elphinstone, to whom the agents were

read to the sailors an order from the Admiral forbidding them, under pain of severe punishment, to plunder the houses on the landing of the troops.[1]

The General and the Admiral came from Savannah today Feb. 7 to join the fleet again. The former went on board the agent's ship, the latter on board the *Perseus*. The transport ships received orders to procure tomorrow thirty days' provisions for the troops. So, presumably, we shall not take the inland route, but sail along the coast to Port Royal. Had a terrible storm today from SW.—hurricane, rain, hail, thunderstorm. Two more ships joined the fleet today.

Very cold, sharp wind, and a high sea. The troops on Feb. 8 board the *Peggy* transport were embarked on the *Empress of Russia* today; the *Peggy* went to Savannah, because she was too leaky. Toward evening the transport ships received orders to prepare immediately to sail and proceed to the North Edisto River the next day, where the troops are to be disembarked. At the same time the fleet was notified by a signal from the Admiral that everyone should at once betake himself on board the ship to which he was assigned; nor should any more boats be permitted to go ashore.

Toward noon, at a given signal, we weighed anchor. The Feb. 9 air was pleasant and before a WNW. wind we stood NE. We stopped at Trench Island,[2] an island ten miles long and covered with pines. Since the breeze was too faint and the last

---

directly responsible during the land operations, took these orders seriously, but that, nevertheless, some plundering on the part of the seamen did occur, may be seen from a letter by Captain Chads, agent for transports, to Captain Elphinstone: "I am sorry you should have complaints . . . , but I am afraid the Men of War's boats from Five Fathom Hole have made some visits that way and suppose they did not go off empty handed" (*ibid.*, p. 171).

[2] Trench Island, now Hilton Head Island. Its present name was in use before the end of the seventeenth century, as Professor Verner W. Crane has kindly informed me.

zu schwach war, und die lezten Schiffe aus dem Haven nicht
zu uns koм̃en konnten, wurde Nachmittag der Anker geworfen, wir funden 3 Meilen von Trensch Eiland einen sandigen Boden, bey 7 Faden Wasser.—Der Robust und Renow
kamen diesen Morgen in die Flotte.

Febr: 10ᵗʳ Den Morgen 10 Uhr lichteten wir den Anker, und fuhren mit
gelinden Winde und angenehmer Luft längst der Südwestl:
Küste herunter. Die Nacht war der King Georg wieder in die
Flotte gekoм̃en. Um 2 Uhr des Nachmittags war es, dass wir
den Anker in Nord-Edisto River wurfen, wir hatten 5½ Faden
Wasser. Das Signal für die Zurechtmachung der Flattboats
zur schleunigen Debarquirung, wurde sogleich ausgesezt, und
die Schifs-Capitains bekamen Ordre denen an Bord habenden
respve: Truppen auf 2 Tage Provision mit auf das Land zu
geben.

JOHANN HINRICHS
Staabs Capit: im Jäger Corps.

ships could not get out of the harbor to join us, we cast anchor in the afternoon. Three miles from Trench Island we found a sandy bottom at seven fathoms of water. The *Robust* and the *Renown* joined the fleet again in the morning.

At ten o'clock in the morning we weighed anchor and Feb. 10 sailed with a gentle wind down the southwest coast [of Trench Island]. The air was pleasant. During the night the *King George* had joined the fleet again. It was two o'clock in the afternoon when we cast anchor in the North Edisto River, where we had five and one-half fathoms of water. Immediately the signal was hoisted to prepare the flatboats for quick debarkation, and the ships' masters received orders to supply their respective troops with two days' provisions for land.

JOHANN HINRICHS
Staff Captain in the Jäger Corps

AUSZUG.

Aus dem Hand Journal des Staabs Capitaine Johannes Hinrichs vom Hochlöblichen Feld-Jaeger Corps, in der Expedition nach South Carolina

2ter Theil. Von der Landung zu North Edisto bis zur Eröffnung derer Tranchéen, Feb. 11, Marz 31. 1780.

Der Feind welcher durch unssere zu lange Fahrt, durch den Sturm und das Verschlagen, kaum den Gedancken mehr hegte, dass wir noch in Carolina landen würden, war noch mehr durch unssern Auffenthalt in Tybee, durch die dasselbst vom Hauptquartier mit Fleiss manchmal laut ausgegebene Ordres, durch die unterm General Patterson unter March-Ordre stehende Regimenter (und welche auch würcklich schon nach Piurisburg zu, vorgerückt waren,) irre gemacht worden. Er hatte seine Augen auf Beauforth gerichtet, seine Trouppen bis Pompan vorrücken lassen, und lies uns ruhig, ihm im Rücken auf John's Jsland landen.

Febr. 11– Den Anfang machte heüte Nachmittag die Light Jnfanterie, Brittische Grenadiers und 2 Compagnien Hessische. Regenwetter und Nacht verhinderten uns zu folgen; die Armée war in folgende Brigaden eingetheilet—

[1] Cf. Clinton to Prevost, February 18, 1780: "The Rebels seem to have collected their whole force for the defence of Charlestown which renders it expedient that I shou'd be prepared for every opposition they will be able to make. I find it therefore necessary to reverse my plan of operations in the back country for the present and request that the 71st Regiment, the light Companies, the Legion Infantry, Ferguson's Corps, N. & S. Carolinians

EXTRACT

From the Private Journal of Staff Captain Johann Hinrichs of the Jäger Corps on the Expedition to South Carolina

Part Two. From the Landing in the North Edisto to the Opening of the Trenches, February 11—March 31, 1780

Because of our extremely long voyage and because of severe storms and the scattering of many of our ships, the enemy no longer seriously thought that we would still land in South Carolina. They were, furthermore, confused by our stay at Tybee, by certain orders given publicly at headquarters for the purpose of deceiving them,[1] and by the movements of the regiments under the command of General Paterson, who had already actually advanced toward Purysburg. The enemy were looking for developments near Beaufort, their troops having advanced as far as Ponpon. Thus we were able to land unmolested on Johns Island in the enemy's rear.

This afternoon the light infantry, the British grenadiers, Feb. 11 and two companies of Hessian grenadiers began the disembarkation. Rain and darkness prevented us from following. The army was divided into the following brigades:

& York Volunteers may be in readiness to join us under B. Gen[1] Paterson. But as I wou'd not abandon the advantage we may derive here from an invasion being supposed to impend the back settle[ts] I request you will let the publick and the troops remain in that opinion, and let every arrangement seem to tend to the movement first intended" (Gt. Brit. Hist. MSS. Comm., *op. cit.*, II, 91–92).

Light Jnfantery
Brittish Grenadiers } Gen: Maj: Leslie
Hessische Grenadiers—Gen. Maj. v. Kosboth } Mylord Cornwallis.

7.
23. } Oberst Lieut: Clarcke

Jäger
33. } Oberst Lieut: Webster.
71.

N^{ta} Von dem 71^t R^{gmt} war das 1te Bat: mit General Patterson, und das 2te wurde mit General Leslie noch erwartet, indem es bey unsser Abfahrt von Tybee den Savannah River noch nicht heruntergekommen war.

63
64 } General Major Huyne.
Huyne

Der Landungsplatz war Simmon's Point, auf Simmon's Jsland, Einer auf jeder Charte dem Namen nach unbekanten Jnsul,—Sie ist ein Stück von John's Jsland, öde und salzicht, voller Cabbage Trees—. Die Landung geschahe unter Anführung des Capitaine Elphingstone von dem Perseus, der 2 Jahre vorher, hier eine Batterie demoliret, und die ganze John's Jsland durchstreift hatte. Der commandirende General und Lord Cornwallis waren an der Spizze der leichten Jnfanterie, rückten bis Simmon's House und Bridge vor, und die Generals blieben im Regen und Morast im Holze.

Febr. 12. Während dass wir heüte und der Rest der Trouppen landeten, rückten die light Jnfantery bis Wilson's House vor, die Brittish Grenad: 3 Meilen von Simmon's House, Hauptquartier war diesses, und die beyden Hessischen Grenadier Compagnien blieben bey demsselben; Unssere Landung ging geschwinde genug von statten, obgleich wir 2 Meilen zur

[1] The name "Simmons Island" appears, however, on Henry Mouzon's map of 1775. On the Clinton maps (William L. Clements Library) the name appears as "Simond's Island." Its present name is "Seabrook Island."

[2] Perhaps Captain Elphinstone was here on the 24th of June, 1779, when one column of Prevost's force touched this point on their march to Purys-

Light infantry ⎫
British grenadiers ⎬ Major General Leslie   ⎫
Hessian grenadiers—Major General von Kospoth   ⎬ Lord Cornwallis
                                                  ⎭

7th   ⎫
23rd ⎬ Lieutenant Colonel Clarke

Jägers ⎫
33rd   ⎬ Lieutenant Colonel Webster
71st   ⎭

Note: The 1st Battalion of the 71st Regiment was with General Paterson, and the 2nd with General Leslie, who had not yet come down the Savannah River when we departed from Tybee.

63rd ⎫
64th ⎬ Major General Huyn
Huyn's ⎭

The landing place was Simmons Point on Simmons Island, unmarked by name on any map.[1] It is a part of Johns Island, desolate and salty, and full of cabbage trees. The landing was effected under the direction of Captain Elphinstone of the *Perseus*, who had demolished a battery here two years ago[2] and had roamed all over Johns Island. The Commanding General and Lord Cornwallis were at the head of the light infantry. They advanced as far as Simmons' house and bridge, the generals remaining with the men as they marched through the woods in swamp and rain.

While we and the rest of the troops were landing, the Feb. 12 light infantry advanced as far as Wilson's house and the British grenadiers to within three miles of Simmons' house. The latter was used as headquarters, and the two Hessian grenadier companies remained there. Our landing was effected in good enough time, although we had to go two miles in

burg. The editor has been unable to ascertain whether there was a battery here that Elphinstone might have demolished. Clinton marched his troops along practically the same route that this column had taken the year before (Clinton map, 307).

See fahren musten, aber der March bis zum Hauptquartier war desto beschwerlicher; durch eine Wildniss von unge-heüren Sande, Moräste, undurchdringliche Gehölze, wo nie Menschen Händen hingekoṁen sind, mit einer Colonne durch zu arbeiten, Selbst Elphingstone, der unsser Guide war, führte uns auf 2 meilen um. Wir musten manchmal auf $\frac{1}{2}$ Meile durch einen Morast und Gehölze, 1 bey 2 uns drängen und stehlen.—Welches Land zum Krieg führen—! Wir kamen gegen Nachmittag beym Hauptquartier an, gingen noch $1\frac{1}{2}$ Meile weiter vor, und rückten lincks am Weege, hart am Bohiskit River ins Lager, rechts an uns, stiess das 33 ^{te} R^{gmt} und an diesse die Hessische Grenadiers.

Wir waren hier von James Chapel 22 Meilen, von Simmons bridge $1\frac{1}{2}$. von Charlestown 25 Meilen entfernet.

Febr. 13 Heüte Morgen rückten wir vor bis Wilson's House, und 1 Bat: Light Jnfantery marschirten nach Fennings Ferry, und das 2te Bat: light Jnfantery nach Chesum Ferry, das 33te R^{gmt} hatte seinen lincken Flügel am Bohiskit River gestüzt, und unsser rechter standt mit zurück weichender Front an einem starcken Nadeln Holze, bis auf dem Weege nach Che-sum Ferry. Der Weg von unsserm vorigen Lager bis hier, war eine 8 Meilen lange, schnur gerade gehauene Allée N.E vom starcken Nadeln Holze.—Von hier war 8 Meilen Haupt-Quartier, 8 Meilen Stono Ferry, $5\frac{1}{2}$ Meilen Fenning's Ferry, 5 Meilen Chesum Ferry, 7 Meilen New cut Creek.—Während diessem waren unssere Ruder Galeeren den North Edisto und Wadmelow River herauf gegangen, im lezten so weit als New cut.—Und weil die Provision bey denen Trouppen diessen Abend fällig war, so sondirte der Capt Elphingstone den Bohiskit River, wie weit dersselbe Flach Boots herauf lassen wolte, indem wir den Stono und Wadmelow uns nicht bedienen durften, bis wir den Posten von jensseitigen Ufer zu Stono Ferry hatten, wosselbst jezt Pulawsky's Legion

boats; but the march to headquarters was the more arduous.
A column making its way through a wilderness of deep sand,
marshland, and impenetrable woods where human feet had
never trod! Even Elphinstone, our guide, led us two miles
out of our way. Sometimes we had to struggle, singly or two
abreast, through marsh and woodland for half a mile.—What
a land to wage war in!—Toward afternoon we arrived at
headquarters, advanced another one and one-half miles and
made camp on the left of the road, close to the Bohicket
River. At our right was the 33rd Regiment, and next to it
were the Hessian grenadiers.

We were encamped twenty-two miles from James Chapel,
one and one-half miles from Simmons' bridge and twenty-five
miles from Charleston.

In the morning we advanced as far as Wilson's house; the Feb. 13
1st battalion of light infantry marched to Fenwick's Ferry
and the 2nd battalion to Chisholm's Ferry. The left wing of
the 33rd Regiment rested upon the Bohicket River, and our
right wing, with its front turned back and extending as far
as the road to Chisholm's Ferry, stood before a dense pine
woods. The road from our previous encampment to this one
was an avenue hewn straight as a string eight miles long and
to the NE. of the dense pine woods. From here it was eight
miles to headquarters, eight miles to Stono Ferry, five and
one-half miles to Fenwick's Ferry, five miles to Chisholm's
Ferry, and seven miles to New Cut Creek. In the meantime
our row-galleys had come up the North Edisto and Wadmalaw rivers, in the latter as far as the New Cut. Since the
provisions for the troops were expected this evening, Captain
Elphinstone sounded the Bohicket to ascertain how far flatboats could come up, for we could not make use of the Stono
and the Wadmalaw until we should have possession of the
post on the other bank at Stono Ferry, where now stood

(die nach Pulawsky's Todt der franz: Major Vernier commandiret) standt.

Febr. 14. Diessen Morgen rückten wir und 33 bis Stono Ferry, die Grenadiers bey Dr Well's House, die Fusileers bey Jsaac Watts, und ein Theil der Huyneischen Brigade bey Wilson's House vor; Vom 1^t Bat: leichte Jnfantery waren 3 Compagnien unter Major Camphell bey Gibbon's House detachirt worden; Wir marchirten unter Comando des Oberst Lieut: Webster, und unsser Guide, war ein aufgefangener Negroe Junge: Wir fragten ihn, ob er den Weg nach Stono Ferry wüste, er sagte ja.—und er brachte uns bis—ans Wasser. Jch muss gestehen, noch überfällt mir ein Schauder, wenn ich mir diesse Lage vorstelle, 600 Mann auf einem 1000 Schritt langen Kiessel Damme, der an beyden Seiten mit unergründlichen Morästen umgeben ist, am jenseitigen Ufer Feind, Anhöhen und Wercke, und der Fluss zwischen uns 100 Schritte breit—dies war unssre Lage—. Der Feind hatte keine Canonen, ward selber durch unsser Aufdringen bestürzt und liess uns Zeit, ohne Verlust uns wieder bis hinter den Morast, und dann zurück zu ziehen. Wir rückten Stono Ferry in der Front rechts, und 33 lincks ins Lager, und hatten unser Haupt-Augenmerck auf unssern Rücken, dann zwischen unsserm rechten Flügell und Gibsons House wo Major Camphel standt, waren noch 4 Hauser am Stono, die alle eine Anfurth hatten und unbessezt waren (der übrige Theil des Flusses, war mit einem breiten Moraste für jeder Landung gesichert.) Und 3 Meilen vor unsserm lincken Flügel war New cut Creek, *hier stand nichts, und bey der Ebbe war das Wasser keine 2 Fus tief, und auf dem jenseitigen Ufer waren Anhöhen:* 2 Ruder Galeeren gingen bey Chesum Ferry den Stono River diesse Nacht herauf, und legten sich zwischen Fenning's und Chesum Ferry vor Ancker, wenn wir jezt den Plan zur Hand nehmen, werden wir die Position vortheilhaft finden, indem der Feind den Orth unssers Ubergangs nicht errathen konte—

Pulaski's Legion (since Pulaski's death commanded by the French major Vernier).

This morning we and the 33rd Regiment advanced to Feb. 14 Stono Ferry, the grenadiers to Dr. Wells' house, the fusiliers to Isaac Watts', and part of Huyn's brigade to Wilson's house. Three companies of the 1st battalion of light infantry were detached to Gibbes' house[1] under Major Campbell. Our commander was Lieutenant Colonel Webster, and a captured Negro boy our guide. We asked him if he knew the way to Stono Ferry; he said he did, and he took us to the river. I must admit that I still feel a shudder when I think of our situation: six hundred men on a pebble bar a thousand paces long, bordered on both sides by bottomless swamps; on the opposite bank the enemy, on higher ground and in possession of works, and the river between us a hundred paces wide. Such was our situation! The enemy had no guns. They were dumfounded by our approach, and gave us enough time to withdraw behind the swamps without loss. With Stono Ferry in front of us to the right we pitched camp with the 33rd Regiment at our left, always carefully watching our rear, for between our right wing and Gibbes' house, where Major Campbell was posted, there were four houses on the Stono, all with boat landings and unoccupied. A wide morass prevented landing at any other place. Three miles in front of our left wing was New Cut Creek, *unoccupied, and at low tide with water less than two feet deep, and higher ground on the other bank*. This night two row-galleys went up the Stono River past Chisholm's Ferry and came to anchor between Fenwick's and Chisholm's ferries. If we now look at the map we shall find our position advantageous, for the enemy could not surmise the place of our crossing. They would only know

[1] There were three Gibbes' houses, one on Simmons Island, this one on Johns Island, near the Stono River, and a third on the Neck of Charleston.

nur so viel: dass wir gesonnen waren, uns Meister von Stono zu machen. Gegen Abend sezte der Feind einen Shooner, der am jenseitigen Ufer lag, in Brand, aber welchen Fehler, dass er ihn nicht in den Canal trieb und da versenckte? Die Provision Boote kamen den Nachmittag den Bohiskit River bis Johns Jsland Church bey Dr Well's House, herauf

Febr. 15. Heüte Morgen recognoscirte die Generalitaet die jensseitigen Wercker und den Fluss, wir meldeten ihnen von dem verbrennten Shooner, und der vom Feind bey der Prescotschen Expedition hier an diessem Ufer verbranten Ruder Galeere the Rattelsnake (bey welchen Capt Wolf und 60 Grenadiers damals waren erschossen worden) Der General und Moncrieft gingen mit Jägern hinnunter, konten aber für klein Gewehr nicht nahe genug ankommen, und musten sich mit unsserm Rapport begnügen lassen: dass keines von beyden Schiffen im Canal lägen: Den Nachmittag erfuhre ich, dass bey Sucky Staniards Hauss ein kleines gesundes Boot läge, und bey Abraham Wats ein grosses, Jch recognosscirte es, fand das grosse für 50 Mann gut, nahm beyde unter eine Wache und meldete es schrifftlich durch Capt. St George ins Hauptquartier.

Febr. 16– Gegen Morgen ging ein Bat. light Jnfantry bey Sucky Staniards über, mit Hülfe einiger zusammen geraften Boote, und landeten auf Jnglis Plantation, eine hübsche Anhöhe: Kaum war der Feind von der Landung der ersten Boots benachrichtiget worden, verliess er seinen Posten bey Stono Ferry, und zog sich um 9 Uhr des Morgens über Wallis und Randoff's Bridge und brach die Brücke hinter sich ab, 1 light Jnfantery

---

[1] Cf. David Ramsay, *History of the Revolution of South Carolina* (Trenton, 1785), II, 71–72: "About the same time sixty grenadiers of the British army, with two fieldpieces and musketry, attacked the American schooner Rattlesnake, from the banks of the river Stono. Her gallant commander, Captain Frisby, defended himself with the greatest bravery, repulsed the assailants with the loss of their captain, and the greatest part of his men; but finding

that we were planning to make ourselves masters of Stono [Ferry?]. Toward evening the enemy set fire to a schooner that lay against the opposite bank. But what a mistake not to drive it into the channel and sink it there! In the afternoon the provision boats came up the Bohicket River as far as Johns Island Church, near Dr. Wells' house.

This morning the staff of generals reconnoitred the works Feb. 15 on the other side of the river as well as the river itself. We made a report to them concerning the burnt schooner and a burnt row-galley, the *Rattlesnake*, which had been set on fire by the enemy at this bank during Prevost's expedition, when Captain Wolf and sixty grenadiers were killed.[1] The General and Moncrieff went down with some jägers, but they could not get close enough because of musketry. Hence they had to be satisfied with our report, which vouched that neither of the vessels was lying in the channel. In the afternoon I heard that at Sucky Staniard's house there was a little sea-worthy boat and at Abraham Watts' a large one. I reconnoitred and found that the large one would carry fifty men; so I placed a guard over both boats and made a written report to headquarters through Captain St. George.

Toward morning a battalion of light infantry crossed the Feb. 16 river at Sucky Staniard's in several boats which had been secured, and landed at Ingles' plantation on pleasant, rising ground. As soon as the enemy was informed of the landing of the first boats, they left their post at Stono Ferry and retired at nine o'clock in the morning over Wallace's and Rantowle's bridges, destroying them behind them. At daybreak the 1st

---

it impossible to retreat with his vessel, set her on fire, and conducted his wounded men with the rest of his crew, safe through the country." The sixty grenadiers referred to were from the Regiment von Trümbach, Rall's old regiment. In other words, they were Hessian and not British grenadiers (Edward J. Lowell, *The Hessians and the Other German Auxiliaries of Great Britain in the Revolutionary War* [New York, 1884], p. 241).

Bat. rückte mit anbrechendem Morgen nach Stono Ferry in die vom Prevost voriges Jahr aufgeworfene, jezt vom Feind *verlassene* und nicht *demolirte* Wercke. Mehrere Boote kamen jezt unter Bedeckung eines Canonen Boots, durch New cut creek mit der Fluth herauf und Jäger und 33 gingen über. So bald wir am jensseitigen Ufer posto gefast hatten, recognoscirte der General unter Bedeckung des 1 B. light Jnf. bis Wallisbridge, 3½ M. von Stono Ferry. Den Nachmittag kamen die beyden Fusilier Rgmtr. 7. 23. herüber und bessezten die Wercke. Unssere Brigade rückte links in Front, und 1 Light Jnf. Bat. rechts in Fronte im Lager, in der Form eines halben Mondes, vom Ufer des Stono rivers lincks, bis rechts an densselben. Das ganze commandirt General Major Leslie, der mit dem Snow Paquet von Savannah gekom̃en war, und den Nachmittag zu uns. Oberhalb der Wallisbridge war eine Furth, neben diesse kamen die feindliche Cavalleristen mit Patrouillen von 10 zu 30 M. und recognoscirten diessen Abend unssere Vorposten.

Febr. 17– Mit Anbruch des Tags ging eine patrouille von denen hier stehenden R^{gmtrn} 7 M. auf der Strasse nach Cocky Swamps und Pompan vor, und brachten gegen Mittag, ohne etwas vom Feind angetroff[en]* zu haben, Pferdte, Vieh und Negroes ein. Gegen Nachmittag kamen 18 Cavalleristen bis vor unssere Posten. Sie konten diesses ziemlich sicher thun, da wir keine Cavallerie hatten, und unssere Commandeurs keine Embuscaden und streifende Partheyen ausschickten.

Febr. 18. Während dass wir auf diessem Posten stunden, war Capt Elphingstone mit unermüdetem Eifer bemühet durch Wadmelow river, New cut creek und Stonoriver bis an Wappoe creek, Canonen, Amunition und Provision herauf zu schaff[en]. Unssere Men of War creüzten vor der Bar von Charlestown, und unssere Transportschiffe machten sich p.

---

* Here and elsewhere a bracketed ending indicates that the original has only a wavy line.

battalion of light infantry advanced to Stono Ferry and went into the works which had been raised by Prevost the year before and which the enemy had just *abandoned* without, however, *demolishing* them. Now several boats under cover of a gunboat came up New Cut Creek with the tide, and the jägers and the 33rd crossed over. As soon as we had taken post, the General, with a guard consisting of the 1st battalion of light infantry, reconnoitred as far as Wallace's bridge, three and one-half miles from Stono Ferry. In the afternoon the 7th and the 23rd Fusilier Regiments came and occupied the works. Our brigade encamped on the left front and the 1st battalion of light infantry on the right front, thus forming a crescent with the points resting upon the river. The entire contingent was commanded by Major General Leslie, who had come from Savannah on the *Snow* packet and had joined us in the afternoon. Above Wallace's bridge was a ford, to which enemy cavalry advanced in patrols of from ten to thirty men and reconnoitred our outposts this evening.

At daybreak a patrol of the regiments stationed here advanced seven miles on the road to Cocky Swamp and Ponpon, returning toward noon without having met any of the enemy, but bringing with them horses, cattle, and Negroes. Toward afternoon eighteen enemy cavalrymen came close to our posts. They could do this without great risk, since we had no cavalry[1] and our commanders had sent out neither ambuscades nor scouting parties.

While we were at this post Captain Elphinstone made great efforts to get cannon, ammunition, and provisions up through Wadmalaw River, New Cut Creek, and Stono River as far as Wappoo Creek. Our men-of-war cruised before the

Feb. 17

Feb. 18

[1] Most of the horses of the cavalry and artillery had been thrown overboard, because the transports carrying them had become very leaky (see pp. 23, 373). Furthermore, one cavalry transport, the *Swift*, with twenty-eight horses, was captured by the rebels (see p. 371 and embarkation list).

Brigade 1, worauf die Bagage gepackt wurde, fertig, um Johns Jsland herum, zwischen diessem und James Jsland mit Bagage us.m. herauf zu fahren. 2 Bat. light Jnf. marchirten heüte nach Mathews, rechts an Fennings, und Hess. Gren: nach Fennings Ferry. Capt Ewald machte heüte eine Patrouille, ohne Feind und Vieh an zu treffen, Er war bey Smiths Hauss gewessen.

Febr. 19 Was wir von Uberlaufern erfahren konten, war, dass der Feind jetzt Nacht und Tag an den Verschanzungen der Stadt arbeitete, und sichere Miene machte, seinen Posten zu behaupten, und dass die bey Dorchester und Pompan stehende Detachements sich eins nach dem andern der Stadt näherte, mit Zurücklassung kleiner Partheyen und Avertissemens Posten. Eine kleine Ruder Galeere von uns gerieth diessen Nachmittag bey New cut creek durch Unvorsichtigkeit in Brand, und flog in die Luft, und die Crane Galley ging heüte nach Wappoe cut.

Febr. 20. Gegen Abend ging 1^t Bat. light Jnf. wieder zurück über die Ferry um bey dem baldigen Ubergang nach James Jsland nahe zu seyn und 2 starcke Fusileer Piquets besezten das von der Light Jnfant: verlassene Lager. Die Britañia Transport war heüte zu Edisto angekoṁen, und der Major Robertson kam zu uns, Sie hatten seyd 8 Tagen die Defiance Men of War in sehr schlechten Umständen verlassen.

Febr. 21 Die etwas verfallene Schanzen wurden heüte wieder ausgebessert, und 2 Offrs und 20 Pioniers kamen heüte zu uns, um die Batterie en Barbette die auf der Strasse zwischen denen Redoutten lag, und den Verhack aus zu bessern.

Mit Anbruch des Tags gingen Light Jnf. und Grenadiers, mit Major Moncrief an der Spizze, bey Hamiltons House über nach James Jsland und rückten so weit vor als Newtown new cut, und Forth Johnston

[1] The Major Robertson mentioned here is Lieutenant Colonel Archibald Robertson, who arrived on the *Briton*, Feb. 20, 1780 (see his *Diaries and*

Bar of Charleston, and the transports (one per brigade) with the baggage, etc., made ready to sail around Johns Island and come up between it and James Island. The 2nd battalion of light infantry marched to Mathews' today to the right of Fenwick's, while the Hessian grenadiers went to Fenwick's Ferry. Captain Ewald went on patrol today without encountering either enemy or livestock. He was at Smith's house.

We found out from deserters that the enemy were working   Feb. 19 day and night on the fortifications of the city, that they were firmly determined to maintain their post, and that the detachments posted at Dorchester and Ponpon were one by one approaching the city, leaving behind small parties and observation posts. Through carelessness one of our small rowgalleys caught fire and blew up this afternoon near New Cut Creek. The *Crane* galley went to Wappoo Cut today.

Toward evening the 1st battalion of light infantry went   Feb. 20 back over the ferry in order to be near for the anticipated crossing to James Island. Two strong fusilier pickets occupied the camp vacated by the light infantry. Today the *Briton* transport arrived in the Edisto, and Major Robertson[1] joined us. A week ago the *Briton* had left the *Defiance* man-of-war in very bad shape.

Today the somewhat crumbled entrenchments were re-   Feb. 21 paired, and two officers and twenty pioneers joined us in order to repair the abatis and the battery in barbette situated in the road between the redoubts.

At dawn the light infantry and the grenadiers, Major Moncrieff in command, crossed near Hamilton's house to James Island and advanced as far as Newtown New Cut and Fort Johnson.

Sketches in America, pp. 213–214). The *Briton* is most likely the *Royal Briton*, since the *Briton* was used as a horse transport (see embarkation list).

Febr. 22. 1 Offr. und 8 M. Pioniers wurden heüte Nachmittag ½ Meile vor die Posten derer Fusileer Piquets geschickt, um aus William Ashly's House ein Schleifstein zu holen, Sie hatten Ober und Unter Gewehr mit: Eine feindl: Patrouille von 20 Pferdten, nahm sie bey dem Hausse, ohne einen Schuss zu thun, in Empfang, ein Negroo brachte die Nachricht. ½ Stunde nachher rückte das Fusileer Piquet und ich mit 20 Jägern mit Gr. Leslie, OberstL^t Webster und Clarke so weit vor, um zu sehen, welchen Weeg sie genommen.

Febr. 23. Jch muste heüte mit 20 Jäger und 30 Engländer bey dem Hausse wosselbst Gestern die Pioniers waren gefangen worden, in Embuscade liegen; Allein es kame niemand.

Febr. 24. Light Jnf: rückte so weit vor als Wappoo cut, Brittish Grenadiers standten jensseits Newtown new cut und Hessische Grenadiers bey Forth Johnston: Gen. Maj. Leslie ging heüte von uns, um das Commando über die Light Jnfanterie und Brittish Grenadiers zu übernehmen, und OberstL^t Webster war der nächste zum Com̃ando Diessen Morgen gingen von jeder Brigade 100 Mann aus, von uns nach Pompan Road, und die Fusileers nach Walis Bridge, um Vieh ein zu treiben. Das Detachement von uns kam gegen Mittag wieder mit einer Menge Vieh us.m. Das von denen Fusileer blieb bis gegen Nachmittag aus; Vernier hatte sich mit seiner Cavallerie auf Walis Road embusquiret, da wo 2 Wege zusammen laufen und dann lincks und rechts ein dicker Morast und Gebüsche ist, folglich ein starck Defilée war, in der Mitte desselben war eine Brücke: Er hatte die Helfte der Cavallerie abssizzen lassen. Die Engländer, wie gewöhnlich ohne Arrier garde, ohne zu laden, Menschen und Vieh durch ein ander, die Strasse herunter, die Cavallerie sezte ein, und die Fusileer hatten 3 blessirte mit Lanzen, ehe noch einer geladen hatte, Jch war gerade vor unssern Posten spazieren, rafte 8 Jäger zusammen, und eilte nach diessem Hauffen Engländer, Rebellen und Vieh, welche alle durch einander waren. Capt.

This afternoon an officer and eight pioneers were sent half
a mile beyond the posts occupied by the fusilier pickets to
fetch a grindstone from William Ashley's house. They had
their muskets and their side arms along; but an enemy patrol
of twenty horse captured them at the house without firing a
shot, according to the report given us by a Negro. Half an
hour later the fusilier picket and I with twenty jägers, as
well as General Leslie and Lieutenant Colonels Webster and
Clarke, pushed forward far enough to see which way they
had gone.

With twenty jägers and thirty English I had to lie in
ambush today near the house where yesterday the pioneers
were taken prisoners, but no one came.

The light infantry advanced as far as Wappoo Cut; the
British grenadiers were posted on the other side of Newtown
New Cut and the Hessian grenadiers at Fort Johnson. Major
General Leslie left us today to take over the command of the
light infantry and the British grenadiers; Lieutenant Colonel
Webster is to command in his absence. In the morning each
brigade sent out a hundred men (ourselves to the Ponpon road
and the fusiliers to Wallace's bridge) in order to drive in
livestock. Our detachment returned toward noon with a
number of cattle, etc.; that of the fusiliers stayed away till
early afternoon. Vernier and his cavalry had lain in ambush
at Wallace's road, at a place where two roads meet and where
on both sides there are marshes and dense brushwood forming
a very narrow defile, with a bridge about half way. He had
ordered half of his cavalry to dismount. The English were
coming down the road, as usual without rear guard and without having loaded their muskets, men and livestock in confusion. The cavalry charged and wounded three fusiliers with
their lances before our men had loaded a single musket. I
happened to be strolling in front of our post. Quickly I
gathered eight jägers and hurried toward this motley crowd

Ewald kam mit einem Peloton aus einer andern Ecke, und obgleich OberstLieut: Webster uns zu rief, wir solten halten bleiben, liefen wir doch vor bis an die Brücke, da wir die Gegend kannten. Es war gerade Zeit, dann die abgesezte Cavallerie kam schon lincks und rechts die Strasse herunter, und feüerten die Strasse herunter. Einige Büchssenchüsse brachten sie zum halten und retiriren. Die Engländer hatten 6 blessirte, und OberstLᵗ Webster bedanckte sich bey uns.

Febr. 27. Weil jezt die erforderliche Artillerie und Provision grösten-theils herauf war, auch wir Herr von James Jsland waren, und so unssere Schiffe gerade den Stono River herauf fahren kon-ten, gingen wir heüte zurück über Stono Ferry und zogen unssere Brigade bey Sucky Staniards Hauss, und die Fusiliers lincks am Wege, Front New cut Creek im Lager, und liessen zur Bessezung der Redoutt[en] ein Detachement von beyden Brigaden von 1 Capt. und 100 Mann zurück. Die Nacht lag Vernier bey William Ashlew's House in Embuscade und kam den Morgen so weit, als wo unssere Posten vorher gestanden hatten.

Febr. 28. Die feindliche Fregatte Providence, die mit noch 3 andern in dem Canal bey Sullivans Jsland lag, kam heüte Nachmittag herunter und legte sich hart unter Forth Johnston lincks am Ufer, und cannonirte unssere Grenadiers, die 2 Mann dadurch verlohren und ihr Lager bessen [= besser] zurück schlagen mussten. Es wurden dieser Tagen einige Batterien eine im demolirten Forth Johnstone und 2 lincks an demsselben auf-geworfen, doch wurden sie nur ganz leicht gemacht, auch ka-men keine Canonen hinnein, vermuthlich nur dem Feind eine Blendung zu machen. Die Piquets der Hessischen Gre-nadiers gingen von der Mündung des Newtown new cut bis Lighthouse Jsland. Den Mittag ging noch ein Transport von 4 Shooner mit schwerem Geschüze den Fluss hinnunter bis Wappoo Auf James Jsland wurde ein Hospital aufgerichtet, es waren viele Krancke in der Armee.

of English, rebels, and livestock. Captain Ewald came with a platoon from another direction, and although Lieutenant Colonel Webster called to us to halt, we nevertheless rushed to the bridge, for we knew the lay of the land. We arrived in the nick of time, for the dismounted cavalry coming down the road right and left had begun to fire. A few rifle shots made them halt and retire. The British had six wounded. Lieutenant Colonel Webster gave us his thanks.

Since by now the greater part of the necessary artillery Feb. 27 and stores had come up and, moreover, since we were masters of James Island, and our ships could therefore come right up Stono River, we retired today across Stono Ferry, our brigade going into camp near Sucky Staniard's house and the fusiliers to the left along the roadside, facing New Cut Creek. We left in the redoubts a captain and one hundred men taken from the two brigades. During the night Vernier lay in ambush near William Ashley's house, and in the morning he advanced to the place where our pickets had been posted.

The enemy frigate *Providence*, which with three others had Feb. 28 been stationed in the channel at Sullivan Island, came down [up] the river this afternoon, anchored right below Fort Johnson on the left bank and cannonaded our grenadiers, who lost two men and were compelled to encamp farther back. During these days several batteries were erected, one in the demolished Fort Johnson and two to the left of it. But they were built only very lightly, nor were any guns mounted in them. They were intended, apparently, only as blinds. The pickets of the Hessian grenadiers extended from the mouth of Newtown New Cut to Lighthouse Island. In the afternoon four more schooners with large pieces went down [up] the river to the Wappoo. On James Island a hospital was erected, for there were many sick in the army.

Febr.29. Gegen Abend kame die Cavallerie bis nahe vor unssere Posten auf Stono Ferry, unssere Jäger schossen sich mit ihnen herum. Auf James Jsland war alles ruhig.

März 3– Das 2te Bat: 71 war heüte zu uns gestossen, und rückten in das Lager der Fusileer R^{gmtr}, welche den Nachmittag nach Mathewsins marchirten, und den andern Morgen nach James Jsland übergingen, und zu denen Brittischen Grenadiers stiessen.

März 6   Ging das 2 Bat. 71 auch zurück, und bey Mathewsen über den Fluss, und zog bey Hamilton, wo Huyne und 64 standt ins Lager, 63 lag in Gibson's Hauss, weil $\frac{2}{3}$ des R^{gmts} kranck war, Es hatte die Fahrt von York aus, auf einem ehemaligen Hospital Schiff gethan. Während dass wir diessen Posten hatten wurden täglich Partheyen auf marode in Johns Jsland von unsser Brigade ausgeschickt, und eine starcke Anzahl Vieh zusammen getrieben.

März 7.   Um 3 Uhr diessen Morgen marchirte unssere Brigade nach Mathewsen wosselbst sie um 9 Uhr ins Lager rückte, das Detachement auf Stono main und denen Redouten von 1 Capt 100 M. blieb stehen: es hatte keine Canonen, und wäre ein bösser Posten gewessen seyn, wenn unssere Nachrichten nicht zu sicher waren, dass blos Cavallerie gegen ihnen stundt. Die Strasse nach Mathew'sen läuft fast alle gerade, und ist ein pine Wood, und blos da wo plantationen liegen, ausgehauen Die Light Jnf: hatte eine Brücke über Wappoo cut, und eine andere über Wappoo creek gemacht und warteten auf unsere Ankunft, um auf Stono main ab zu gehen.

März 8–   Vorige Nacht solte die Light Jnf. über Wappoo bridge auf Stono main die feindl: Cavallerie unter Oberst Blandt, der bey Gouverneur Bull's Plantation stand, überfallen und marchirten desswegen mit einbrechender Nacht über die Brücke lincks durch Moräste und über schmale Dämme hinter Sa-

Toward evening the enemy cavalry came close to our Feb. 29
pickets at Stono Ferry. Our jägers exchanged some shots with
them. On James Island all was quiet.

Today the 2nd Battalion of the 71st Regiment joined us. March 3
They went into the camp of the fusilier regiments, which in
the afternoon marched to Mathews' and the following morning crossed over to James Island to join the British grenadiers.

The 2nd Battalion of the 71st left us again. They crossed March 6
the river at Mathews' and went into camp at Hamilton's,
where Huyn's and the 64th were encamped. The 63rd was
quartered in Gibbes' house, since two thirds of the regiment
were sick. It had made the voyage from New York in a former
hospital ship. Ever since we have been at this post our brigade
has sent out daily foraging parties into Johns Island; thus a
great quantity of livestock has been driven in.

At three o'clock in the morning our brigade marched to March 7
Mathews', where it went into camp at nine o'clock. The
detachment in the redoubts on Stono mainland, a captain
and a hundred men, was maintained. They had no guns and
their situation would have been deplorable indeed if our
intelligence, namely, that only cavalry opposed it, had not
been so reliable. The road to Mathews' is straight almost all
the way. It is hewn through a pine woods which is cleared
only where plantations are situated. The light infantry had
built a bridge over Wappoo Cut and another over Wappoo
Creek and were waiting for our arrival before departing for
Stono mainland.

Last night the light infantry was ordered to cross the March 8
Wappoo bridge to Stono mainland in order to surprise the
enemy cavalry under Colonel Bland,[1] who was posted at
Governor Bull's plantation. They marched at nightfall to

[1] Hinrichs is mistaken. It was Colonel William A. Washington who was
harassing the British with his cavalry. Among them were the remains of
Bland's Light Horse.

vage und Loan's Plantation weg. Capt Nash von der Cavallerie light Jnf: hatte seinen Bedienten mit, diesser ritte die
gerade Strasse, vermuthlich um zu plündern; Ein feindlicher
Posten nahm ihn gefangen, der Anschlag wurde verrathen,
um 2½ Uhr zog sich die Cavallerie zurück, und um 3 Uhr
kam die light Jnfanterie bey der Plantation im Rücken an,
und fand das leere Nest.—13 Mohren von Joungs Plantation
auf Wadmelow Jsland kamen heüte geflüchtet. Vernier war
durch New cut creek gesezt und hatte diesse Plantation ge-
plündert, er war aber nicht so hoch als Widow Carses Hauss
gekommen, und noch weniger über den Bohiskit River, 3
Comp: von 71, gingen heüte nach Lighthouse Jsland, um bey
dem Ubergang der Schiffen und Ausladung der Canonen zu
helfen und zu decken.

März 9. Weil die Schiffe jezt beordert waren von North Edisto herum
nach Stono zu kommen, so musten die Matrossen aus den
Flachboots genommen werden, und auf die Schiffe zurück,
dies war die Ursache, warum wir hier so lange liegen musten.
Gegen Mittag fuhren wir über nach Hamiltons Hauss, statt
Matrossen waren es Soldaten von 64 und statt flachboots eine
Art schmale pettioquer. Es war eine ziemlich gefährliche
Fahrt, 33 kam die Nacht um 12 Uhr erst, Bagage und Pferdte
ging bey Johns Ferry über. Wir rückten diesseits Newton
new cut ins Lager. Unsser Commando auf Stono Ferry ging
heüte auch ab, und kam mit 63 herüber.

Forth Johnstone welches vom Feinde selbsten war demo-
lirt worden war ein von Backsteinen und Cabbage Tree auf-
gebauetes 4 Eck. Es lag zu hoch um Schiffen viel Schaden
thun zu können, so bald sie den Canal bey Forth Sullivan
passirt waren: indem sich der Canal alsdann hart unter James
Jsland weg ziehet. Von der Spizze des Forths ging eine Sandbanck in den Canal hinnein, bis Lighthouse Jsland, folglich

the left over the bridge, through marshes and over narrow bars, passing Savage's and Loan's plantations. Captain Nash of the cavalry of the light infantry had his servant along, who was captured by an enemy outpost while riding by the straight highway (presumably in order to plunder). Our plot was betrayed. At half-past two the cavalry retired, and at three o'clock the light infantry arrived in the rear of the plantation only to find that the birds had flown. Today came thirteen Negroes fleeing from Young's plantation on Wadmalaw Island. Vernier had crossed New Cut Creek and plundered this plantation. However, he had not proceeded as far as Widow Carr's house and certainly not across the Bohicket River. Three companies of the 71st went to Light-house Island to aid and cover the crossing of the ships and the unloading of the guns.

Since the ships had been ordered to come around from the March 9 North Edisto to the Stono, the sailors had to leave the flat-boats and return to the ships. It was because of this that we were stationed here so long. Toward noon we crossed over to Hamilton's house. In place of sailors we had soldiers from the 64th and instead of flatboats, craft somewhat like narrow pettiauguers.[1] It was a rather dangerous crossing; the 33rd did not arrive till twelve o'clock at night. Baggage and horses crossed at Johns Ferry. We went into camp on this side of Newtown New Cut. Our command also left Stono Ferry today and came over with the 63rd.

Fort Johnson, which was demolished by the enemy them-selves, was quadrilateral, built of bricks and palmetto logs. It was situated too high to do much damage to ships after they had once got through the channel at Fort Sullivan, for the channel beyond that passes close below James Island. From the point of the fort a sand bar extends into the channel

[1] A pettiauguer, also called perriaguer, or pirogue, is a dugout, i.e. a canoe hollowed out with tools rather than burned out in Indian fashion.

müssen unssere Schiffe, wenn sie herauf wollen, hart am Forth Sullivan, jezt *Forth Moultrie* genannt, im Kernschuss der Batterien vorbey—. Die Distance von hier aus, war zu weit, um die Stadt beschiessen zu können.

Forth Moultrie liegt am östlichen Spizze der Jnssul, und ist, wie gewöhnlich die Bevestigung des Haven en amphitrate construirt, die Materie ist Backstein und Cabbage Tree, diesses ist ein biegsames, sehr starckes, zähes Holz, welches der Gewalt nachgiebt, aber nicht dadurch zerstöret wird: 150 Mann war die Besazzung unter Oberst Scott und 20–30 Canonen, wovon 24 lb: die schweresten waren. Durch eine Brücke nach Mount pleasant auf welcher eine Tete de pond genannt die Bridge Battery liegt, mit dem vesten Lande zusammen gehängt ist. 4 feindl. Fregatten und 4 Ruder Galeeren lagen im Canal bey Sullivans Jsland, 1 Fregatte lag unter der Stadt, 2 Fregatten, 2 Ruder Galeeren und 2 Scooner in der Mündung des Ashly Rivers, in der Linie mit dem Ausfluss des Wappoe Creek. Das Fort in der Spizze der Stadt und die Verschanzung der Stadt längst dem Ashly River war beynahe geendiget, und nach der Landseite zu war an den angefangenen königl: Fortificationen eine Linie an beyden Seiten nach den Flüssen zu, angehängt worden, die eine Art von redans mit untermischten semi-Bastionen in meinen Augen zu seyn schienen. Die Artillerie in Charlestown bestand aus mehr denn 200 Stücken von 2 pfündig[en] Französischen bis 32 Pfünder; die Bessazzung war 6000 Mann mit Miliz, Bürger, Matrossen und Artillerie. Unssere Position war: Hauptquartier und light Jnfantery bey Wappoo bridge, Brittish Grenadiers und Fusiliers bey Mr Scots Hauss, Jäger, 33, bey Newtown New cut. Hess: Grenadiers 1½ Meile diesseits Forth Johnstone, Huyne, 63, 64, 2 Comp: von 71 bey Hamilton's Hauss, 3 Comp: 71 auf Lighthouse Jsland,

as far as Lighthouse Island. Consequently, our ships in coming up will have to pass close to Fort Sullivan, now called *Fort Moultrie*, within point-blank range of the batteries.—The distance from here is too great to fire upon the city.

Fort Moultrie is situated on the eastern point of the island and is constructed like the usual fortifications of a harbor *en amphitheatre*. The material is brick and palmetto, a pliable, very strong, and tough wood, which yields to an impact without breaking. The fort has a garrison of one hundred and fifty men commanded by Colonel Scott, and twenty to thirty guns, 24-pounders being the heaviest. A bridge with a *tête de pont*, called "bridge battery," leads to Mount Pleasant, thus connecting the island with the mainland. Four enemy frigates and four row-galleys are riding at anchor in the channel at Sullivan Island and one frigate below the city, while two frigates, two row-galleys, and two schooners are stationed in the mouth of the Ashley River in a line with the outflow of Wappoo Creek. The works on the point of the town and the fortifications along the town side of the Ashley River are almost finished. On the land side, lines have been joined to both ends of the unfinished royal fortifications, extending them toward the rivers. The entire line, it seems to me, is a series of works resembling redans and interspersed with demi-bastions. The artillery in Charleston consists of more than two hundred pieces, ranging from French 2-pounders to 32-pounders. The city is garrisoned with six thousand men,[1] including militia, inhabitants, seamen, and artillery. Our position is as follows: Headquarters and light infantry at Wappoo bridge, British grenadiers and fusiliers at Mr. Scott's house, jägers and the 33rd at Newtown New Cut, Hessian grenadiers one and one-half miles this side of Fort Johnson, Huyn's, the 63rd, the 64th, and two companies of the 71st

[1] Six thousand is much too large a number, especially since Woodford's reinforcements had not yet arrived (see p. 211, note 2).

die Bagage Schiffe mit 1 Ruder Galeere und 2 armirten Booten lagen beym Hptquartier.

Marz 10. Heüte Morgen rückte Light Jnf:, brittish Grenadiers und Fusileers mit 4 leichten 6 l^br über Wappoo, nach Stono main und marchirten nach Fenning's point ins Lager, Jäger und 33 über Wappoo bridge zwischen Fenningspoint und Hauptqrtr bey Tomrosen's Plantation, hess: Grenad: Linsing, Lengercke beym Hauptquartier, wo light Jnf. gestandten hatte, 64 und 71 2 Comp: bey Scot's wo brittish Grenadiers und Fusiliers gestandten hatten; Vacant und Graff blieben bey Forth Johnston stehen. Die vom General Prevost voriges Jahr zur Deckung der Wappoe Brücke aufgeworfene 2 Redoutten bessezten 2 Comp: von 33 und 1 Capt u 60 Jäger hatten das avancirte Piquet, $\frac{1}{2}$ Meile rechts an unsserm Lager auf der Kreüz Strasse nach Ashly Ferry und Fennings point, dies war 4 Meilen von Church Creek, $4\frac{1}{2}$ Meilen von Ashly Ferry und $2\frac{1}{2}$ M. von Fennings Point, rechts an diesses piquet sties $\frac{1}{2}$ Meile Distance 2^t Bat: light Jnf: und lincks waren kleine Jaeger und 33 piquets mit einem Morast in Front, welche mit denen Redouten piquetten an Wappoe bridge zu sammen hängen.

Jch hatte diesses piquet und detachirte 1 Soffr und 12 M. in Fronte, 1 – und 6 lincks und rechts, Vernier war schon wieder da mit seinen Cavalleristen, zog sich aber den Abend über Church Creek zurück. Weil wir jezt unsser Separirtes Piquet hatten, und freye Hand auf demsselben, so legte ich den Abend gleich eine Embuscade. Es kam die Nacht nichts. Die Parthey brachte mir einen Mohren mit, von dem ich erfuhr, dass die feindliche Cavallerie einem Deserteur war nach geritten gewessen, sich über Church Creek durch eine

1 A German regiment or battalion was called "vacant" when no regular colonel, or lieutenant colonel, was in command. The battalion referred to

at Hamilton's house, three companies of the 71st on Light-house Island, while the baggage ships, a row-galley, and two armed vessels are stationed at headquarters.

This morning the light infantry, the British grenadiers March 10 and fusiliers, and four light 6-pounders crossed the Wappoo to Stono mainland and encamped on Fenwick's Point; the jägers and the 33rd crossed over Wappoo bridge and went into camp at Tom Rose's plantation between Fenwick's Point and headquarters; Linsing's and Lengerke's Hessian Grena-diers moved near headquarters, where the light infantry had been stationed; while the 64th and two companies of the 71st went into camp at Scott's, where the British grenadiers and fusiliers had been. The Vacant[1] and Graff Battalions remained at Fort Johnson. The two redoubts that General Prevost had thrown up last year to cover the Wappoo bridge were occu-pied by two companies of the 33rd, while a captain and sixty jägers formed the advanced picket, half a mile to the right of our camp on the crossroad to Ashley Ferry and Fenwick's Point. This was four miles from Church Creek, four and one-half from Ashley Ferry, and two and one-half from Fenwick's Point. Half a mile to the right of this picket was the 2nd bat-talion of light infantry, and to the left behind a swamp were posted several small pickets of jägers and the 33rd, which were in touch with the redoubt pickets at the Wappoo bridge.

Since I was in command of the advanced picket, I detached a noncommissioned officer with twelve men to the front and two with six men each to the right and the left. Vernier was about again with his cavalry, but withdrew in the evening over Church Creek. Since we now had a separate picket and I had a free hand to do as I saw fit, I laid an ambuscade the first evening. No one came during the night. However, the return-ing party brought along a Negro, from whom I learned that

here is the old Grenadier Battalion von Minnigerode, which was later commanded by von Loewenstein.

Furth zurück gezogen hätte, und dass die Brücke über densselben abgebrandt seye; ½ Meile lincks lag Savitsh Plantation, 1¼ M. rechts an der Strasse vorwärts Gouverneur Bull's
und 1¾ Meile Thom Fuller's

März 11. Gegen 3 Uhr Nachmittag liessen sich die feindliche Cavalleristen wieder in der Front sehen, aber sie kamen nicht so nahe
als Savitsh Plantat: um in eine an 2 Stellen gelegte Embuscade
zu fallen. 64 war heüte auch nach dem Hauptqrtr gekoṁen.
Huyne und 63 standten bey Mr Scots Hauss

März 12– Heüte Morgen fouragirte unssere Brigade und 1 Bat. light
Jnfant: Governeur Bull's Plantation. Light Jnfanterie mar-
chirte um 6 Uhr nach Bull's, Church Creek in Front, und wir
um 7 Uhr lincks von Savitsh durch das Holz nach Ashly
Road zu. Jch muste mit meiner Division die lincke Flanque
decken, und hatte Communication mit der Light Jnf. bey
Hammon's Plantat. 33 blieb bey Savitsh, Ewald auf Ashly
Road in Front der light Jnf: und der Rest der Jaeger zwischen
Ashly Road und Savitsh: Wie wir aus dem Holze kamen,
(1000 Schritt Distance) sprengten 7 Cavalleristen aus Savitsh
Plant: nach Ashly Road zu, wie aber da die light Jnf. standt,
machten sie hier zurück und auf einen Fuspfadt zwischen
Savitsh und Hammons durch, und nach Ashly Road oberhalb
Bull's zu, hier hielten sie die ganze Zeit, während wir foura-
girten, und hielten mehrere Canonen Schüsse ab, *die der Oberst-*
Lt Abercrombie auf 7 Lighthorse thun liess, statt einige Jäger hinten
herum ihnen in Rücken zu schicken, ehe sie sich zu rück zogen.

März 13. So bald wie die Grenadiers und Fusiliers waren auf Fennings-
point ins Lager gerückt, wurde der Anfang zu einer Batterie
an dem Ausfluss des Wappoo Creek gemacht, um theils die
Stadt von dersselben aus zu beschiessen—es war 1900 Yard
Distance, theils aber und hauptsächlich um die feindlichen
Schiffe aus Ashly River ab zu halten, und diessen Fluss in
unssere Gewalt zu bringen. Die Batterie wurde heüte ge-

the enemy cavalry had pursued a deserter and had withdrawn over Church Creek through a ford, since the bridge over it had been burned. Half a mile to the left lay Savage's plantation, one and one-quarter miles in front of us, on the right of the road, Governor Bull's, and one and three-quarter miles, Tom Fuller's.

Toward three o'clock in the afternoon the enemy cavalry March 11 appeared again in front of us; but they did not proceed as far as Savage's plantation, where we had ambuscades at two places. The 64th came to headquarters today; Huyn's and the 63rd were stationed at Mr. Scott's house.

This morning our brigade and the 1st battalion of light March 12 infantry foraged on Governor Bull's plantation. The light infantry marched to Bull's about six o'clock, Church Creek in front of them, and we at seven o'clock from Savage's through the wood in the direction of the Ashley road. I covered the left flank with my detachment and was in touch with the light infantry at Hammond's plantation. The 33rd stayed at Savage's, Ewald on the Ashley road in front of the light infantry, and the rest of the jägers between the Ashley road and Savage's. As we came out of the woods we saw a thousand paces away seven cavalrymen rushing out of Savage's plantation and heading for the Ashley road; but when they saw the light infantry there, they withdrew and followed a footpath between Savage's and Hammond's, which took them to the Ashley road above Bull's. Here they stayed while we foraged in spite of several cannon shot, *which Lieutenant Colonel Abercrombie had ordered to be fired at seven light horse, instead of sending a few jägers around to their rear* before they left.

As soon as the grenadiers and fusiliers had gone into camp March 13 on Fenwick's Point, preparations were made for a battery near the mouth of Wappoo Creek, partly in order to fire upon the city, the distance being 1,900 yards, and partly—this was the principal object—in order to keep the enemy's shipping out of the Ashley and thus get control of the river. This

schlossen und hatte Bettungen und Schiessscharten für 6,
32 ^{1br} wovon 2 rechts den Fluss enfilirten, und 4 quer auf die
Stadt geöffnet waren, die Canonen zu diesser und denen
übrigen noch zu errichtenden Batterien, waren, 2 metallene
24. l ^{br} und die leichteren Calivers ausgenoͤmen, aus der Europe
und Raisonable, welche nach Port Royal geschickt wurden
war. Der Admiral befandt sich auf dem Roebuck.

März 14. Die ganze Nacht und heütige Tag ruhig, Embuscaden lagen
die ganze Zeit aus, aber es kam niemand. Die Nacht wurde
ein light Jnf. Piquet noch ausgessezt, zwischen unsser Piquet
und dem 2 ^{t} Bat. light Jnfant: um Communication auf der
Strasse zu erhalten. Jch hatte es den Morgen an Mylord Cornwallis vorgestelt, dass sehr leichte und gewiss Negroes
zwischen unsserm Piquet und dem 2 ^{t} Bat. leichte Jnf: durch-
gehen könten, indem die freye Passage jedem erlaubt wäre.
Allein jezt war eine vollkommene Chaine vom Haupt-Qrtier
bis an Ashly.

März 15– Diessen Morgen fouragirten unssere Brigade und 2 B. Light
Jnf: Tom Fuller's Plantat: 2 ^{t} Light Jnf: pousirte bis church
creek, die Brücke war ab, und jensseits ein feindl: Lighthorse
Piquet. Unssere Brigade passirte lincks auf Randots Road
bis Loans Plantat: Durch Detachements von Jäger und 33
war Communicat: bis Savitsh erhalten.

März 16– Ausser der für 6 32 ^{1b} verfertigten und jezt bessezten Batterien, wurde 500 Yard besser lincks von Ashly gerade in der
Flanque der feindl: Wercke nach dem Lande zu, eine andere
Batterie für 2 32 ^{1br} und 1 – 7 Zoll Haubize verfertiget—die
Haubize blos um der Schiffe willen—die Distance von feindlichen Wercken war 2350 Jard. Grenadiers, Fusiliers und light
Jnfanterie waren Tag und Nacht mit flechtung von Horden
beschäfftiget, die bey Gen. Maj. Leslie Quartier aufgestüzelt
wurden; So bald die 6 Gun Batterie konte eröffnet werden,
musten die feindl: Fregatte Queen of France und übrige an

battery was finished today. It had platforms and embrasures for six 32-pounders, two of which enfiladed the river to the right, while four opened straight across upon the city. With the exception of two brass 24-pounders and some of smaller caliber the guns for this battery as well as for those that were still to be erected were taken from the *Europe* and the *Raisonnable*, which had been sent to Port Royal. The Admiral was on the *Roebuck*.

The entire night and day everything quiet. Ambuscades March 14 were posted all the time, but no one came. Also, during the night a picket of light infantry was sent out to take post between our picket and the 2nd battalion of light infantry in order to maintain communication on the road. In the morning I had pointed out to Lord Cornwallis that it was very easy, especially for Negroes, to pass between our picket and the 2nd battalion of light infantry, since everyone was granted free passage. Now, however, there was a complete chain extending from headquarters to the Ashley.

This morning our brigade and the 2nd battalion of light March 15 infantry foraged on Tom Fuller's plantation, the latter advancing as far as Church Creek. They found the bridge demolished and on the other side an enemy picket of light horse. Our brigade proceeded to the left on Rantowle's road as far as Loan's plantation. By detachments of jägers and the 33rd we maintained communication to Savage's.

Besides the battery of six 32-pounders, which was now March 16 manned, another battery for two 32-pounders and a 7-inch howitzer was raised on the Ashley, five hundred yards farther to the left, in the flank of the enemy's works to landward. The howitzer was to be used only against the ships, the distance from the enemy's works being 2,350 yards. The grenadiers, fusiliers, and light infantry were busy day and night making hurdles, which were piled up at Major General Leslie's quarters. As soon as the 6-gun battery was ready to

der Mündung des Ashly liegende Schiffe die Ancker lichten, und sich um die Stadt herum in Coopers River legen. Auf James Jsland wurden beym Hauptquartier, wosselbst die Schiffe lagen und die Magazienen solten angelegt werden, 3 Redouten mit einem Verhack am Wappoe Creek bis zum Stono River auf geworfen, und längst dem Stono nach der See zu, waren alle nur mögliche Fahrzeüge zusammen gerafft worden, und in Sicherheit gebracht, um dem Feind alle Möglichkeit einer Landung von Johns Jsland aus, welches wir abandonirt hatten zu benehmen. Die beyden hess: Grenadier Bat. Vacant und Graff, waren jezt benebst Huyne, welches hinter denen Grenadiers campirte, auch nach dem Hauptquartier gekommen, und 63 nach Newtown new Cut, diesses und Huyne gab ein Commando von 2 Capt. unter Major M'Keen von 23 nach Forth Johnson, der nach Ankunft des Oberst Lieut: Balfourt beym R^{gmt} sich diesses Commando ausgebethen hatte.

März 17 Heüte wurde ein Rondeaus für klein Gewehr zur Deckung der beyden auf Fennings point liegenden Batterien verfertiget. Sie lag auf dem Damm, der zwischen dem Morast lincks und rechts nach diessen Batterien führte.

März 18. Vorige Nacht desertirten 2 Light Jnfanteristen von 63, und diesse Nacht wurde ein Posten von 33 von denen detachirten Piquetter in Front unsser Brigade, von einem feindlichen Jnfanteristen blessirt

März 19. Heüte kamen 2 feindl^e Officiers zu uns ein.

Die Marine hatte während der Zeit mit Hülfe der 3 Comp: von 71 auf Lighthouse Jsland, die untere Lage Canonen und Provision ausgeladen, und unter Bedeckung 2 Ruder Galeeren, welche über das B$\bar{a}$r gegangen waren, in 2 Transportschiffen nach Lighthouse Jsland geschickt, und laureten auf günstigen

---

[1] No doubt Thomas Mecan, who was then ranking captain.

[2] Since none of the French dictionaries give a meaning that fits here, this word is left untranslated. Captain Hinrichs, it seems to me, is referring to

be opened, the enemy's frigate *Queen of France* and the other ships stationed at the mouth of the Ashley were compelled to weigh anchor, pass around the city, and lie in the Cooper River. On James Island, near headquarters, where our ships lay and where the magazines were to be built, three redoubts were constructed and abatis thrown up along the Wappoo as far as the Stono River. Along the Stono toward the sea all kinds of craft had been gathered and brought to a safe place in order to deprive the enemy of every means of landing by way of Johns Island, which we had abandoned. The two Hessian Grenadier Battalions Vacant and Graff, together with Huyn's Regiment, which had been encamped behind the grenadiers, had by now also come to headquarters, while the 63rd had gone to Newtown New Cut. The latter and Huyn's supplied a command to Fort Johnson, consisting of two captains under Major M'Keen[1] of the 23rd, who had asked for this command after the arrival of Lieutenant Colonel Balfour in the Regiment.

To cover the two batteries on Fenwick's Point we built March 17 today a *rondeaus*[2] for small arms on a bar which extends through a swamp up to the batteries.

Last night two light infantrymen of the 63rd Regiment March 18 deserted, and this night a picket detachment of the 33rd posted in front of our brigade had a man wounded by an enemy infantryman.

Today two enemy officers came in. March 19

Aided by the three companies of the 71st which were stationed on Lighthouse Island the sailors unloaded the lower tiers of guns and stores, and brought them to Lighthouse Island in two transports under escort of two row-galleys that had crossed the Bar. They are now waiting for favorable

---

some sort of breastwork, probably a rideau. Colonel Oliver L. Spaulding, Jr., however, suggests that, perhaps, it is meant for roundhouse (blockhouse).

Wind, um selber über die Bar zu gehen. Mit unermüdetem Eifer war Capt Elphingstone von der Perseus beschäfftiget, den kleinen Dienst der Marine zu besorgen Mehr wie eine Nacht, brachte er mit dem Senckbley in der Handt, in Ashly River, unter Forth Moultrie und zwischen den feindlichen Kriegs-Schiffen zu, und kam allemal mit nüzlichen Nachrichten und vortheilhafften Berichten wieder zurück. Er sprach mit mehreren Commandeurs von feindl: Fregatten, und einmal mit dem Commandanten von Forth Moultrie (in der Nacht vom 18. auf 19) von dem er erfuhr, dass es ihm an Wasser fehlete. Die Flachboots wurden unter Aufsicht des Capt Tomkins beym Hauptquartier ausgebessert, und die stärksten davon bekamen eine neü erfundene 3- und 6 pfündige Canone in ihren Schnabel, welche Canonen nach der Stadt, in welcher sie sind erfunden worden, Caronaden genant werden.

Der Feind arbeitete mit unermüdetem Eiffer an Verschanzung der Stadt Eine Schanze, eine Batterie wurde an der andern aufgeworfen, wie Schwämme wuchssen sie aus der Erde. Von der Spizze der Stadt längst dem Ashly zählte ich blos 22 Schiesscharten. Die Einwohner verliessen ihre Hausser an diesser Seite der Stadt, und zogen sich nach der östlichen, indem sie bey Beschiessung der feindl: Schiffe in der Mundung des Ashly Rivers aus unsser 6 Canonen Batterie von Fennings point vor wenigen Tagen erfahren hatten, dass es uns ein leichtes wäre, Feuer Kugeln in die Stadt zu schicken. Jhre Besazzung hatte sich, wahrend dass wir gelandet waren mit 600 von North Carolina verstärkt, und ihre regulirten R^{gmtr} machen 3000 M. aus, das üþrige waren Miliz, Negroes und Bürger der Stadt, ausser etlichen 100 Franzossen. Oberst Blandt war mit die Virginische Lighthorse 180 Pferdten,

---

[1] Though in the original *bloss* ("alone," "only") modifies the direct object, it is here translated as modifying the prepositional phrase. This is by no means the only case in which such liberties had to be taken.

wind to cross the Bar themselves. With untiring effort Captain Elphinstone of the *Perseus* performed a menial task for the advantage of the navy. He spent more than one night sounding the Ashley River below Fort Moultrie among enemy warships, returning every time with useful information and advantageous reports. He spoke with several commanders of enemy frigates and once with the commandant of Fort Moultrie (on the night of the 18–19th), from whom he learned that they were short of water. The flatboats were repaired near headquarters under the supervision of Captain Tonken, and the strongest of them had 3- and 6-pounders mounted in their bows. These pieces have been invented only recently and are called "carronades" after the city in which they were invented.

The enemy worked with untiring effort on the fortification of the city. One trench, one battery after another, was thrown up; like mushrooms they sprang from the soil. From the point of the city along the Ashley alone I counted twenty-two embrasures.[1] The inhabitants were moving from their houses on this side of the city to the eastern side, because several days ago when our 6-gun battery on Fenwick's Point opened fire on the enemy's ships in the mouth of the Ashley, they learned that it would be easy for us to throw hot shot into the city. Since our landing, their garrison has been reinforced by six hundred men from North Carolina. Their regular regiments amount to three thousand men;[2] the rest are militia, Negroes, and inhabitants of the city, as well as some hundred French. Several days ago Colonel Bland[3] came down with one hundred and eighty Virginia light horse. He and Major

[2] For a detailed estimate see Edward McCrady, *History of South Carolina in the Revolution, 1775–1780* (New York, 1901), pp. 507–508.

[3] See p. 197, note 1.

seyd einigen Tagen herunter gekommen, und er und Major Vernier observirten uns zwischen Ashly River und Randots. Jhre Jnfanterie war alle in der Stadt und d. 20^t standte nur noch 1 Offr. 25 M. mit 12 Pferdt[en] advertissements Posten bey Ashly Ferry jensseits dem Flusse, in dem vom General Prevost voriges Jahr zur Deckung seines Übergangs dasselbst auf geworfenen Teté de pond.

März 20. So standten die Sachen, als wir heüte Morgen 2 gute Nachrichten erfuhren, die 1): dass alle unssere destinirten Men of wars, vorige Nacht glücklich die Bar passirt wären, dies war eine sehr gute Nachricht, indem nach Ausladung der untersten Reihe Canonen und provision, die gröste Gefahr bey einem etwaigen Sturm unssere Esquadre bevor gestanden hätte. Sie fingen sogleich heüte Morgen an, Canonen etc. wieder ein zu nehmen. Die 2te Nachricht war,: dass streichende Partheyen von General Pattersons Corps sich schon um Stono Ferry hätten sehen lassen, Major Vernier war desswegen auch vor unssern Vorposten weg, und ging diessen entgegen, indem er diesses Land am besten kante, und die Virginier stunden gegen uns. Jch hatte heüte das Piquet, und Lieut: Kling und 9 Mann lagen seyd 3 Uhr in Embuscade. Um 5 Uhr den Nachmittag wurde ich abgelöst, ein Jäger von dem neüen Piquet hatte seinen Hund bey sich, diesser lief vor die Vorposten. Er pfiffe ihn mit dem gewöhnlichen Jäger Ton des Appels: Lt Kling mit dem ich Abrede genoṁen hatte, bis in die sinckende Nacht liegen zu bleib[en], glaubte ich hatte meinen Vorssaz geändert, und kam ein, kaum war er halb weges nach dem Lager, so kamen 20 feindliche Pferdte gerade an den Flecken, wo er gelegen hatte, dis war unglücklich! Jm Kriege, Glück ist die Hauptsache.—

März 21- So bald der Feind unssere Schiffe vor sich sahe, zog er alle seine Fregatten und armirte Schiffe in den Coopers River, versenckte zwischen Coopers Jsland und der Stadt 7 Scooner,

Vernier reconnoitred between the Ashley River and Rantowle's. All their infantry were in the city, and on the 20th
only an observation post of one officer and twenty-five men
with twelve horses was stationed at Ashley Ferry on the
other side of the river in the *tête de pont* which General Prevost
had thrown up last year to cover his crossing.

Such was the state of affairs when this morning we re- March 20
ceived the following news: (1) All the men-of-war assigned
to us have safely crossed the Bar during the night. This was
good news indeed, for, after the unloading of the lowest
tiers of cannon and stores, our squadron would have been in
greatest danger in case of a storm. They immediately began
to take on their guns, etc., again. (2) Scouting parties of
General Paterson's corps have been seen around Stono Ferry.
For this reason Major Vernier was no longer in front of our
advanced posts. He had gone in the direction of the approaching corps, for he was the one most familiar with that part
of the country. Now the Virginians are opposing us. I was
in command of the picket today, and Lieutenant Kling and
nine men had been lying in ambush since three o'clock. At
five in the afternoon I was relieved. A jäger of the new picket
had his dog along. Because this dog had run ahead of the
advanced post, his master called for him, whistling the recall
of the jägers. Hence Lieutenant Kling, though I had told him
to remain at his post until nightfall, withdrew, believing
that I had changed my mind. He was barely halfway to the
encampment when twenty enemy horse arrived at the very
spot where he had lain in ambush. This was unfortunate indeed! Luck is the main thing in war.

As soon as the enemy saw themselves confronted by our March 21
ships they withdrew all their frigates and armed ships into
the Cooper River and sank seven schooners, the frigate *Queen
of France*, and an old two-decker between Cooper Island[1] and

[1] Should read "Shutes Folly."

die Queen of France Frigate und einen alten 2 Decker, so dass unssere Schife, wenn sie auch Forth Moultrie passirt waren, ihnen die Retraite über den Coopers River nicht abschneiden konten. Zwischen der Sand-Bank an Forth Johnson und Sullivans Jsland, konte keine Versenckung angebracht werden, indem der Strom in dem Canal bey jeder Ebbe und Fluth dasselbst so reissend ist, dass nichts seiner Gewalt wiederstehen kann.

März 22– Da unssere Schife jezt über der Bar waren, unssere Batterien auf Fennings Point fertig, unssere Bagageschife und Magazine und Artillery beym verschanzten Hauptqrtr fertig waren, So bekamen wir den Morgen Ordre, gegen Mittag March fertig zu seyn, um mit unsser Brigade und der Light Jnf: den Ashly River herauf zu rücken, um über densselben zu gehen, wir waren vor jedem möglichen feindl: Fahrzeuge sicher, indem der Feind sie alle in Cooper River aufgeschlossen hatte, über das waren unssere Batterien auf Fenningspoint starck genug, jedes Unternehmen der Art zu hintertreiben.

Wir rückten vor bis Church Creek, ohne etwas vom Feind an zu treffen. Jensseits bey St Andrews Church, war ein feindliches Detachement Cavallerie, 3 Comp: Light Jnf: musten so gleich durch baden, der Feind liesse sie ans Land kommen, schoss seine Carbiener ab und retirirte. Die Light Jnfantery postirte sich in die Kirche und Capt Ewald muste mit seiner Division ihnen zum soutein gehen, und die Nacht dasselbst bleiben; Sogleich musten die Pioniers den Anfang zur Wieder Aufbauung, der vom Feind verbrandten Brücke machen; Während diessem rückte der Rest der light Jnf: diesseits der Church Creek ins Lager, und ich wurde vom Brigad: Webster beordert, nördlich am Church Creek hinnunter das Terrain zu recognosciren, und das Lager und Position diesser Brigade auszu sehen, Die Jäger deckten die Flanque und hatten ihren rechten Flügel am Church Creek und lincken am Dickigt und Morast gestüzt. 33 hatte diessen Creek in Front und commu-

the city, so that our ships, even though they should pass
Fort Moultrie, would not be able to cut off their retreat by
way of the Cooper River. Between the sand bar at Fort
Johnson and Sullivan Island they could not sink anything,
for the current in the channel, ebb or tide, is so rapid that
nothing can withstand its force.

Since our ships had crossed the Bar and inasmuch as the March 22
batteries on Fenwick's Point were finished and our baggage
ships, magazines, and the artillery at the entrenched headquarters were ready, we received orders in the morning to
be prepared to march by noon. Our brigade and the light
infantry were to advance up the Ashley River to effect a
crossing. We were safe from any hostile vessel whatever, since
the enemy had them all bottled up in the Cooper River. Moreover, our batteries on Fenwick's Point were strong enough
to frustrate every attempt at interference.

We advanced as far as Church Creek without meeting any
of the enemy. On the other side at St. Andrew's Church was
a detachment of enemy cavalry. Three companies of light
infantry were at once ordered to wade the creek. The enemy
allowed them to reach the bank, fired their carbines, and
retired. The light infantry took post in the church. Captain
Ewald went to their support with his detachment and remained there overnight. The pioneers began immediately with
the rebuilding of the bridge that had been destroyed by the
enemy. In the meantime the rest of the light infantry encamped this side of Church Creek. I was ordered by Brigadier
Webster to reconnoitre the territory to the north along
Church Creek and to look over the encampment and the
position of our brigade. The jägers were covering the flank,
their right wing resting upon Church Creek and their left
upon a thicket and a bog. The 33rd had the creek in front
and had communication with the 2nd battalion of light in-

nicat: mit dem 2ᵗ Bat: light Jnf: Ohnweit vor uns lag Moils Plantation. Hiesselbst kam ich in einem Vortheilhaften Posten ins Piquet. Um 9 Uhr des Abends erfuhr ich, dass ½ Meile besser nördlich noch eine Brücke über den Creek ginge, dass diesselbe noch Gestern Abend gestandten, und diesses der Ort sey, wo die feindl:e Cavallerie nach Verbrennung der Church bridge die patrouillen herüber gemacht hatte. So bald wie der Mond helle schien, ging ich mit 8 Mann—und mit 4 bis an die Brücke, und liess bey der Zuruckkunft sogleich an den Major v. Wurmb und Brigadier Webster schriftlich Rapport thun, die Brücke war noch in gutem Standte von vesten Balcken und starcken loossen Bohlen, 14 Fus lang und 9 breit, der Weg bis dahin sumpfigt und ausgefahren, aber leicht zu repariren.

März 23 Kaum war der Tag am Himmel, so wurde ich nach dem Brigadier gerufen er danckte mir vor die angezeigte Nachricht, sagte: dass die Brücke an der Kirche heüte nicht könte fertig werden, und bat mich sogleich zum commandirenden General zu reiten, und demsselben es zu melden, Jch traff densselben unterwegs bey Bull's Plantation an, und that ihm Rapport, er war so gütig sich zu bedancken, und befahl sogleich den Weeg durch Pioniers machen zu lassen, und die Brücke zu bessezen. Jch eilte zuruck, nahm 40 Jäger, zeigte den Pioniers ihre Arbeit und bessezte die Brücke mit 1 Peleton, rückte mit dem andern vor bis Lloyds und ging mit 4 Jägern bis Far's und recognoscirte das Terrain und den Weg nach Ashly Ferry. Die ganze Gegend jenseits der Brücke, war eine plaine mit Morästen durchschnitten, und Gestern Nachmittag waren noch 80 Pferde bis Lloyds gewessen, und 100 bis Far's, wie ich zurück kam, traf ich die Generalitaet bey Lloyds an, und als die Colonne (Jäger, 33, Light Jnf.) angerückt war, machte ich die Avantgarde bis in die Creüz strasse die nach Ashly Ferry, Andrews Church und Beecken's bridge führet. Hier muste ich halten, postirte meinen Troup en échelon auf die

fantry. A little in front of us was Moil's [?] plantation.
There I posted my picket at an advantageous spot. At nine
o'clock in the evening I learned that half a mile farther north
there was another bridge across the creek, which was still
standing last night, and that it was there that the patrols of
the enemy's cavalry had crossed after burning the Church
bridge. As soon as the moon shone brightly I set out with
eight men and went as far as the bridge with four. Upon
returning I made a written report to Major von Wurmb and
Brigadier Webster. The bridge was still in good condition.
It was fourteen feet long and nine wide, built of heavy beams
and strong, loose planks. The road leading to it was swampy
and full of deep ruts, but could be easily repaired.

Scarcely had the sky become light when I was called to
the Brigadier, who thanked me for the information I had
sent him. He said that the bridge at the church could not
be finished today and asked me to ride at once to the Commanding General to report the same to him. I met him on the
way, at Bull's plantation, and made my report. He was kind
enough to thank me and immediately gave orders for the
road to be repaired by the pioneers and for the bridge to be
occupied. I hastened back, took forty jägers, showed the
pioneers what to do, and posted a platoon at the bridge.
With the other platoon I advanced to Lloyd's, and with four
jägers I went to Farr's and reconnoitred the territory and the
road to Ashley Ferry. All the country on the other side of
the bridge was one large plain intersected by swamps. As
late as yesterday afternoon eighty horse had been as far as
Lloyd's and a hundred to Farr's. When I returned I found the
General's staff at Lloyd's, and after the column (the jägers,
the 33rd, and the light infantry) had arrived, I formed the
vanguard as far as the intersection of the Ashley Ferry-
Bacon's bridge road with the St. Andrew's Church road.
Here I had to make a halt. I drew up my detachment in

March 23

Strasse nach Ashly Ferry und Beckers bridge. Während dass die Coloñe anrückte recognoscirte der commandirende General Ashly Ferry, und ich muste ihn mit 12 Mann decken; Der General wünschte, wenn etwa einer diesseits ware, mit einem Boote um Nachricht von uns einzuziehn ihn zu überschnellen. Jch machte mich durch Graben und Gebüsche bis am Bauche im Wasser und Morast hinnunter, bis dichte ans Ufer, allein es war niemand diesseits; Jensseits hatten sie hart am Wasser, hinter einem Stein Aufwurf einen Posten von 4 M. stehen, der Dam einigemal durch stochen, am Ende desselben eine flesche mit einer Schiesscharte für 1 Canone (die Canone war nach der Stadt zurück gebracht worden, und oben war das von Prevost voriges Jahr aufgeworfene Werck mit einem Detachement bessezt. Die 4 Mann hielten wir leicht im Zaum, dass sie sich nicht blicken lassen durften, noch weniger einen Schuss thun, der General blieb eine Stundte da, ging dann zurück, und befahl mich, stehen zu bleiben, und recognoscirte die Strasse nach Beckers bridge vorwärts bis Midletown's Plantation, unter Bedeckung Jäger, 33, und Light Jnf: Ging hierauf zurück, und die Colone rückte unter Gen. M. Leslie bey Draytons ins Lager. Gen. Leslie schickte mir Ordre auf meinem Posten zu bleiben, und glaubte ich hätte meine ganze Division, Jch hatte aber nur 12 Mann. Jn Andrew's Church war 1 Comp: Light Jnf: detachirt worden

März 24. Die Nacht um 2½ Uhr zog der Feind den Posten von 4 Mann bis hinter den Damm zuruck. Um 7 Uhr Morgens wurde das Detachement in der Redoute von Charlestown aus, mit 25 M: abgelösset, um 12 Uhr recognoscirte der feindl:e General, kam aber nicht auf den Damm. Gegen Mittag kam das Grenad. Bat: von Linsing nach Church Creek, lössete die Comp: Light Jnf. in Andrews Church ab, und ein anderes Detachement kam den Nachmittag um 4 Uhr, um mich abzu lössen. Wie ich eben abgehen wolte, schickte der Feind wieder 4 Mann den Dam̃ herunter, um Posten am Wasser zu fassen. Jch fand

echelon formation on the road to Ashley Ferry and Bacon's
bridge. While the column was approaching, the Commanding
General reconnoitred Ashley Ferry, and I guarded him with
twelve men. The General wished us to surprise anyone who
might be on this side with a boat attempting to obtain information about us. I made my way down through ditches and
brushwood, up to my belly in water and morass, until I got
close to the bank; but there was no one on this side. On the
other side, close to the water, behind a stone barricade, they
had a post of four men. The bank was pierced at several
places, and at one end of it was a flèche with an embrasure
for a gun, which, however, had been taken back to the city.
Above that were the works thrown up by Prevost last year;
they were now occupied by a detachment. We easily kept the
four men in check, so that they dared not show themselves,
much less fire. The General remained there for an hour.
When he started back he ordered me to stay. He reconnoitred
the road to Bacon's bridge as far as Middleton's plantation
with a guard of jägers, the 33rd, and the light infantry. Upon
his return the column went into camp at Drayton's under
Major General Leslie. Believing I had my entire force with
me, General Leslie sent orders for me to stay at my post, but
I had only twelve men. A company of light infantry was
detached into St. Andrew's Church.

At half-past two in the morning the enemy withdrew the March 24
post of four behind the bank, and at seven o'clock the detachment in the redoubt was relieved by twenty-five men from
Charleston. At twelve o'clock the enemy general reconnoitred, but did not come up on the dam. Toward noon the
Grenadier Battalion von Linsing came to Church Creek and
relieved the light infantry company in St. Andrew's Church,
while another detachment relieved me at four in the afternoon. Just as I was about to leave, the enemy again sent four
men down the dam to take post by the water; this I thought

diesses vor unrecht, weil er bey Nacht ihn verlassen hatte,
postirte 4 Jäger in das Ferry Hauss, und ging am Wasser
spazieren. Wie sie bald herunter waren, gab ich das Signal
und 1 wurde todtgeschossen, 2 blessirt, und 1 lief zurück, ich
marchirte hierauf ab zum Corps, und die Grenadiers hatten
hierauf Ruhe.

März 25 Heüte kam Gen. Maj. Patterson mit 1500 Mann über Ebe-
nezer, Pompan, nach Wallisbridge. Die Jndianer hatte er zu
Savannah zurück gelassen, Er hatte bey sich 3 Troops von
17 Dragoner und Legion, 1ᵗ Bat: 71, South, North Carolina
Miliz, Fergusons Corps und 3 Bat: Light Jnf: neml: 2 Comp:
von 60 und die 16 unter Major Graham. Seine Erwartung
Einwohner mit zu bringen, war vereitelt; indem 4000 Stück
Gewehr, die in Newyork dazu bestimmt waren auf the russian
Merchand Transport, bey unsserer Fahrt hierher, verunglückt
waren.

März 26- Passirte Patterson die Wallis und Randolphs Creek, erstere
auf einer Nothbrücke, und leztere auf einer grossen Fähre,
die der Feind vernachlässiget hatte, bey Ruinirung der Brücke,
mit zu verbrennen. Der General Clinton ging mit 3 Comp:
light Jnfantery bis Rantolf's ihm entgegen. Jch hatte das
piquet vor unsserm Lager, das in der Front des 1 Bat. Light
Jnf:, auf der Strasse nach Beckers bridge standt, und den
Nachmittag wurde ein feindlicher Cavallerist, der zwischen
3 von mir gelegte Embuscaden, gefallen war, herunter geschossen, das Pferdt war so flüchtig, dass es nicht zu erha-

¹ Cf. letter of Sir James Wright to Sir Henry Clinton, March 18, 1780,
in which he laments the fact that the Creek Indians are to be stopped on
their way to join the British troops (Gt. Brit. Hist. MSS. Comm., *op. cit.*,
II, 103–104).

² For a more detailed account of the troops composing this reinforcement see McCrady, *op. cit.*, p. 446. McCrady, however, is mistaken when he
says that the entire 71st Regiment was with General Paterson. The 2nd
battalion of this famous regiment had joined Sir Henry Clinton's army on
March 3.

to be unfair, since they had deserted that post during the night. So I posted four jägers in the ferry house and strolled along the river. When they were almost down the dam, I gave the signal, and my men killed one and wounded two; the fourth man ran back. Thereupon I marched off to the corps, and the grenadiers were no more molested.

Today Major General Paterson arrived at Wallace's bridge **March 25** with fifteen hundred men, coming by way of Ebenezer and Ponpon. He had left the Indians at Savannah.[1] His command consisted of three troops from the 17th Regiment of Dragoons and the Legion, the 1st Battalion of the 71st, South and North Carolina militia, Ferguson's Corps, and three battalions of light infantry, namely, two companies of the 60th and the sixteen companies under Major Graham.[2] His hopes of bringing Georgians along were frustrated by the loss of four thousand muskets shipped for their use from New York on the *Russia Merchant*, which had foundered during our passage.[3]

Paterson crossed Wallace's and Rantowle's creeks, the **March 26** former on an emergency bridge, and the latter on a large ferry which the enemy had neglected to burn when they destroyed the bridge. General Clinton met him at Rantowle's with three companies of light infantry. I commanded the picket in front of our encampment and was posted ahead of the 1st battalion of light infantry on the road to Bacon's bridge. In the afternoon an enemy cavalryman who was caught between the three ambuscades I had laid was shot down from his horse. The horse ran away so fast that we could not catch it. The wounded man was Sergeant von Waik [?], a native of Boston, serving in the 1st battalion of Virginians. He died

---

[3] The *Russia Merchant*, a transport of 243 tons, foundered some time before the 19th of January. Her crew and "eighty persons, men, women, and children belonging to the artillery," were taken on board the *Lady Dunmore*, a privateer sloop, which joined part of the fleet on the 19th of January (Robertson, *op. cit.*, p. 208).

schen war, Es war der Sergeant von Waik, gebürtig aus Boston, im 1ᵗ Bat. Virginien Er starb die Nacht; Jch erfuhr von ihm, dass Oberst Blandt, seyd kurzem resignirt hätte.

März 27. Diessen Mittag um 1 Uhr, musten auf beym Hauptqrtr gegebenen Signal die Matrosen von den Transportschifen die 14 Flachboots und einige longboats an der Zahl 20 bemannen, und gingen mit anbrechender Nacht unter Bedeckung einer Ruder Galeere und 2 armirten Booten, durch Wappoo cut, nach Wappoo creek, wosselbst sie in einer Bucht, diessèits Fennings Point anhielten—. Die light Jnf. fouragirte heüte.

März 28. Diessen Morgen fouragirten und trieben Vieh und Pferdte ein, Jäger und 33, auf der Strasse nach Randoltens ohnweit Lloyds und Far's. Es war wenig da; den Mittag kam die Cavallerie vom Gr: Patterson, 300 Pferdte starck, unter Commando des Oberst Lᵗ Tarleton zu unsser Colonne, 1 Bat. 71 folgte nach. Der Rest ging unter General Patterson nach Tomrosens und Fennings point, und die Brittish und Hessische Grenadiers, Fusiliers und Leg: Jnfanterie, stiessen benebst 71 – 1 Bat. und die Cavallerie zu uns, und campirten hinter uns, und light Jnf. längst dem Ashly river in mehreren Colonnen.

März 29. Diesse Nacht kamen die Boote unter Commando des Capt: Tomkins und unter Bedeckung 2 armirter Boote, bis bey Gr. Maj. Leslie Quartier und mit Anbruch des Tages embarkirten 1) Jäger, light Jnf. und 1 Bat. Brittish Grenad: und landeten bey Tom Fuller's. Ein feindl: Cavallerie Piquet, das zwischen Tom Fuller's und Wahnests Hauss hielt, wurde durch einige Schüsse von armirten Booten, so gleich zurück gewiessen; die 2ᵗᵉ Division, als 2 Bat. brittish Grenad, und 4 Bat. Hess: Grenadiers, 2 engl: 6ˡᵇʳ und die Hessische Feld-Stücke gin-

¹ In November, 1779, Colonel Theoderick Bland received permission to retire from his post at Charlottesville, Virginia, where he was in charge of the convention troops. Some time in 1780 the General Assembly of Virginia elected him a delegate to Congress. Von Hinrichs obviously refers to

during the night. I learned from him that Colonel Bland had resigned some time ago.[1]

March 27At one in the afternoon, upon a signal given at headquarters, the sailors of the transports manned the fourteen flatboats and some longboats, twenty in all. At nightfall they proceeded under cover of a row-galley and two armed boats through Wappoo Cut into Wappoo Creek, where they stopped in a cove this side of Fenwick's Point.—The light infantry foraged today.

March 28This morning the jägers and the 33rd foraged on the road to Rantowle's not far from Lloyd's and Farr's, bringing in some cattle and horses. There was little to be had. At noon General Paterson's cavalry, a force of three hundred horse, arrived under the command of Lieutenant Colonel Tarleton. They were followed by the 1st Battalion of the 71st. This battalion, Tarleton's cavalry, the British and Hessian grenadiers, the fusiliers, and the Legion infantry joined our forces, going into camp behind us, while the light infantry encamped along the Ashley River in several columns. The rest of Paterson's command went to Tom Rose's and Fenwick's Point.

March 29The boats under the command of Captain Tonken, with an escort of two armed boats, came tonight as far as Major General Leslie's quarters, and at break of day the jägers, the light infantry, and the 1st Battalion of British Grenadiers embarked and landed at Tom Fuller's. An enemy cavalry picket stopping between Tom Fuller's and Wahnest's[2] house was immediately driven back by several shots from the armed ships. The second contingent, namely, the 2nd Battalion of British Grenadiers and the four battalions of Hessian grena-

---

his resignation from the Charlottesville post (*Bland Papers* [Petersburg, 1840], I, xxix–xxx).

[2] The former is called Benjamin Fuller's house by Captain Ewald; the latter the editor has been unable to identify.

gen hierauf bey Tom Draytons Hauss über, während dessen,
dass die 1te Division überging, deckte ich die Flanque von
Dorchester und Beckers bridge aus, mit meinem Piquet, und
bey Ubergang der 2^t Division bey welcher ich war, rückte
Legion und 23 vor. Hierauf folgte 7. 33. und 71 in der 3.
Division—Sobald alles herüber war, ging die Bagage unter
Bedeckung 23 u Legion und Cavallerie bis Ashly Ferry zuruck,
und wir sezten uns in March nach Ashly Ferry zu. Jch hatte
die Avantgarde und einige feindl: Cavalleristen schwebten
vor mir herum; machten es aber so gescheüt, dass ich nicht
an sie kommen konte. Wir marchirten in folgender Ordnung;
Jäger, Light Jnfant. Brittish Grenad:, Hess: Grenadiers 7.
33. 71.—2 Meilen jensseits Ashly Ferry rückten wir ins Lager, Hauptqrtr Quarterhouse, Jäger in Front, auf der Strasse
nach Charlestown, Light Jnf. hinter diesse im halben Mond.
Hinter diesse Brittish Grenad: und Hess: Bat. v. Linsing,
Front Charlestown 3 Bat. Hess: Grenadiers, Front Coopers
River, 7 mit zurück weichendem lincken Flügel lincks an die
Hessen, 33. und 71 in Rücken, Front Dorchester, Pioniers bey
der Ferry. Vom Feind liess sich nichts sehen,—Wir wurden
heüte von der Brigade des Oberst Webster genom̃en, und
standen unmittelbar unterm commandirenden General. Jn
der Fronte der light Jnf. waren beyde Bat. von 71. zum 33 R^{gt}
gestossen. So bald wir hier angekom̃en waren, wurde Bagage,
etwas Provision, und einige Französ: 4^{lbr} übergeschift und
23 und Legion gingen sodann nach Fenning's point

März 30. Gegen 9 Uhr heüte Morgen, brachen wir auf, und marchirten
in der gestrig[en] Ordnung bis Governor's Hauss, ehe wir
vom Feind etwas, einige Lighthorse ausgenom̃en, antrafen.
Wir machten hier halt, weil der General von diessem Hausse
aus, den Cooper River und die Wercke der Stadt an ihrem
rechten Flügel recognosciren wolte. Kleine Partheyen vom

diers, two English 6-pounders, and the Hessian fieldpieces, later crossed at Tom Drayton's house. While the first contingent was crossing, I with my picket covered the flank from the Dorchester and Bacon's bridge side. The crossing of the second contingent, to which I belonged, was covered by the Legion and the 23rd Regiment. Then followed the 7th, the 33rd, and the 71st—the third contingent. As soon as all had crossed, the baggage, covered by the 23rd, the Legion, and the cavalry, returned to Ashley Ferry, and we also set out on our march to Ashley Ferry. I had the vanguard. Some enemy cavalrymen hovered around in front of us, but they were wise enough not to let us fall in with them. We marched in the following order: jägers, light infantry, British grenadiers, Hessian grenadiers, 7th, 33rd, and 71st. Two miles on the other side of Ashley Ferry we went into camp, the Quarter-House being used as headquarters. The jägers were in front on the road to Charleston and the light infantry behind them in the form of a crescent. Behind the latter were the British grenadiers and the Hessian Battalion von Linsing facing Charleston, three battalions of Hessian grenadiers facing the Cooper River, the 7th with its left wing turned back at the left of the Hessians, the 33rd and the 71st in their rear facing Dorchester, and the pioneers at the ferry. Nothing could be seen of the enemy. Today we were detached from the brigade of Colonel Webster and were now immediately under the Commanding General. Both battalions of the 71st joined the 33rd Regiment and took post in front of the light infantry. As soon as we arrived here, the baggage, some provisions, and several French 4-pounders were ferried across, whereupon the 23rd and the Legion went to Fenwick's Point.

Toward nine o'clock in the morning we broke camp and March 30 marched in yesterday's order as far as the Governor's house before we met any of the enemy except a few light horse. Here we halted, for the General, using this house as a base,

Feind liessen sich jezt blicken, und einer unsserer Flanqueurs
schosse einen Offr vom Pferdte. Um 12 Uhr rückten wir
weiter vor; kaum aber waren wir etliche 100 Schritt gegangen fielen etliche Musketen Schüsse lincks am Weege, durch
welche der Lord Carney der in der Suite des Generals zwischen
unsser Avantgarde und dem Corps ritte, schwer in Leib
blessirt wurde: Wir deployirten sogleich lincks und rechts
vom Weege, attaquirten sie in geschwinden Jäger-Schritten,
und schlugen sie über 1½ Meile zurück bis in ihr Aussenwerck
(the Gate Work) eine Flesche in der Strasse, die rechts und
lincks durch einen Morast gedeckt wird; die Dämme und
Fuspfädte zwischen der Strasse und Ashly hatte der Feind
durchstochen und verhauen, und zwischen Coopers River und
der Strasse war kein Weeg. Wir waren schon im Morast der
ihre Flanque rechts und die Fronte bis an Weg umgab, und
wären auch einige stecken geblieben, wären wir doch gewiss
durch gedrungen, und hätten sie aus diessem offenen Wercke,
von welchem wir keine 40 Schritt mehr entfernt waren, her-
ausgeworfen; Allein der commandirende General kam selbst
und befahl uns, bis hinter dem Morast zu bleiben. Wir machten halt. Die light Jnf. marchirte hinter uns auf. 2 Comp:
light Jnf: mit 1, 6^{1br} rückten in der Strasse bis bey uns vor,
und 1 Comp: lincks an uns. Der Feind war etwa 300 M.
starck, worunter sehr gute Schüzzen waren, mit welchen wir
uns herum schossen. Es währete keine ½ Stundte, so kame
ein Bat: von der Stadt, diessen zum Soutien, und sie pflanzten ihre Fahne auf die Schanze. Wir schossen uns ziemlich
mit Jhnen an 2 Stunden herum; mit einmal deployirten sie,
und zogen sich hinter einen andern Morast, ohngefehr 1000
Schritt zu rück. Unsser Piquet nahm sogleich Besiz von dem
Wercke, und der General recognoscirte die Stadt. Es war von
hier etwa eine engl: Meile und alles eine einzige Plaine kein

wanted to reconnoitre the Cooper River and the right wing of the fortifications of the city. Soon small parties of the enemy appeared, and one of our flankers shot an officer from his horse. At twelve o'clock we advanced farther, but we had barely gone some hundred paces when several musket shots were fired from the left of the road, one of them inflicting a severe abdominal wound upon Lord Caithness, who was riding in the party of the General between our vanguard and the corps. We immediately deployed to the right and left of the road, attacked them at a quick jäger pace and threw them back more than one and one-half miles to their outer work (the gate-work), a flèche in the road protected on both sides by a morass. The enemy had cut up and barricaded all the dams and footpaths between the road and the Ashley. Between the Cooper River and the highway there was no road. We were already in the bog that surrounded their right flank and front as far as the road, and even though some of us had sunk into the morass we would certainly have pushed on and thrown them out of this open work, which was less than forty paces in front of us. But the Commanding General came in person and ordered us to remain behind the bog; so we stopped. The light infantry marched up behind us. Two companies of light infantry with one 6-pounder advanced on the road to where we were, and one company came up at our left. The enemy's force consisted of about three hundred men. Among them were very good marksmen, with whom we exchanged some shots. Before half an hour was up a battalion from the city came to their support and raised a standard on the earthwork. For about two hours there was a good deal of firing on both sides. Then they deployed and withdrew behind another bog about a thousand paces farther back. Our picket immediately took possession of the work, and the General reconnoitred the city, the distance being about an English mile. Before us was a large plain without a single

Hügel auf dersselben und jedes Hauss rasirt und jeder Baum und Busch um gehauen. Gegen Abend recognoscirte die feindl: Generalitaet unter Bedeckung 24^{1br} und 2 geschlossenen Bat: light Jnfant: und rückten bis ans Gate Work vor, Unsser Piquet zog sich auf 100 Schritt zurück, wie sie mit dem Bajonet und Cartetschen aufpreschten. Allein unssere Büchsen schwiegen nicht, in Zeit von $\frac{1}{2}$ Stundte, war kein Feind mehr zu sehen, Sie verlohren hierbey 2 Offr. 7 M. todt, und 3 Offr. 30 M. blessirt. Unter den ersten war ein Adjutant, und unter lezten der General Adjutant, welcher durch beyde Backen geschossen war. Wir hatten 1 Todten und 2 blessirte. Den Abend rückten wir am rechten Flügel der light-Jnfant. bey Gib's Plantation ins Lager. Hinter uns stunden brittish und hess: Grenadiers, von Williams Hauss am Ashly River (Hptqrtr) bis am [   ] House am Coopers. Den Rücken deckte ObL^t Webster, mit 33. 71. bey Governor's House, 23. marchirte nach Fennings Point. Legion und Cav: kam, nach einigen Tagen, herüber und lagerte sich in Front der Websterisch[en] Brigade. Newyork Volontairs stundten bey Gen. Leslie vormaligen Quartier auf Fenningspoint, in Linie mit Gibs Plant:, Huyne, 63. 64. im verschanzten Lager auf James Jsland bey denen Schiffen und Magazienen. South und North Carolina Militia hinter Tomrosens an Wappoe Creek.

März 31 - Die Ruder Galeeren, welche bey Ashly Ferry gelegen hatten, legten sich heüte herunter an Wappoe Creek, und die 2 Canonen Boote legten sich hinter Gibs plant: zur Deckung unsserer Communication über den Ashly. Unssere Communication mit den Schiffen war: Ein Landungsplaz hinter Gibs, in Linie mit unsserm Lager, nach die NYork Volontairs jensseits des Flusses, von da über Fenningspoint nach Wappoe Creek, wosselbst dies- und jensseits North u South Carolina Militia, und jensseits längst dem Wappoe durch den cut nach Huyne's

hill, every house razed and every tree and shrub chopped down. Toward evening the enemy general's staff reconnoitred under cover of two 4-pounders and two battalions of light infantry marching in close order. They advanced as far as the gate-work. Our picket withdrew a hundred paces when they attacked us with bayonets and grapeshot. Yet our muskets were not silent, and in half an hour's time there was not an enemy in sight. They had two officers and seven men killed, and three officers and thirty men wounded. Among the former was an adjutant and among the latter an adjutant general, who was shot through both cheeks.[1] We had one killed and two wounded. In the evening we went into camp at Gibbes' plantation, joining the right wing of the light infantry. The British and Hessian grenadiers were behind us between Williams' house on the Ashley River (headquarters) and [   ] house on the Cooper. The rear was guarded by Lieutenant Colonel Webster, with the 33rd and the 71st at the Governor's house. The 23rd marched to Fenwick's Point. The Legion and the cavalry came over several days later and encamped in front of Webster's brigade. The New York Volunteers were stationed at General Leslie's former quarters on Fenwick's Point in a line with Gibbes' plantation; Huyn's, the 63rd, and the 64th in the entrenched camp on James Island near the boats and magazines, and the South and North Carolina militia behind Tom Rose's on Wappoo Creek.

The row-galleys, which had lain at Ashley Ferry, came *March 31* down today into Wappoo Creek, and the two gunboats anchored behind Gibbes' plantation, so as to cover our communication across the Ashley. Our line of communication with the boats was as follows: from a landing place behind Gibbes' house, situated in line with our camp, to the New York Volunteers on the other side of the river and from there by way of Fenwick's Point to Wappoo Creek, on both

[1] See p. 50, note 1.

Brigade am Stono bey denen Magazienen. Eine herliche Disposition! Von heüte an kamen Horden, Schanz zeüg und Provision herüber, benebst in Stücken gelegte Mantelletten 14 Fus lang, und 10 Fus hoch, die zu Newyork waren verfertiget worden, und bey Gibs wosselbst die Jngenieurs und Artillerie hinrückten, zusammen gessezt wurden. Dies ist die schönste, leichste, sicherste Art, Batterien, Redoutten etc. in einem sandigten Bod[en] zu verfertigen. Der General und Jngenieur recognoscirten Tag und Nacht. Die Nachlässigkeit des Feindes, natürliche Graben nicht zu geworfen zu haben, deckten sie sehr, und ihre Furcht Deserteurs zu haben, die ihnen abhielt, streichende Partheyen aus zu schicken, machte die Recognoscirung ziemlich sicher.

Die Nacht wurde ein Weg durch den Verhau, der vom Feind rasirten Baume, 3000 Fus in Front unsseres Lagers, als wo der Major Moncrief seine Tranchéen eröffnen wolte, gehauen; Jch war mit einem Piquet und 20 Light Jnf: vom andern piquet aussen, Major Moncrief ging bis an feindlichen Verhack. Die Mantelleten (Plannels) wurden zusammen gessezt, und heüte kamen 2 Brass 24 ^{lbr}, 4 eisserne d°, 32, 2 – 18 lb. Brass, 1 – 7 Zoll 1 – 9 Zoll Haubize und 12 Kazzen Kopfe (royals) 2- bis 4½ Zöllige Kessell herüber, und die Nacht wurde unssere erste paralelle mit Verfertigung 3 Redoutten eröffnet.

[1] Cf. Robertson, *op. cit.*, p. 219. Henceforth it will be understood that "the Engineer" is Major Moncrieff.

[2] Either the scribe could not decipher the manuscript, which most likely had many corrections and additions, or he blundered in copying, for we are

sides of which were stationed North and South Carolina militia, and then along the far side of the Wappoo, through the cut, to Huyn's brigade on the Stono near the magazines. A wonderful disposition! From this day on hurdles, entrenching tools, and provisions were brought over, as well as disjointed mantelets fourteen feet long and ten feet high that had been built in New York and were being put together at Gibbes', where the engineers and artillery were taking post. This is the finest, easiest, and safest way to build batteries, redoubts, etc., in a sandy soil. The General and the Engineer [Moncrieff][1] reconnoitred last night as well as today. The negligence of the enemy in not having filled up the natural ditches afforded our officers good cover, and the enemy's fear of desertions, which kept them from sending out scouting parties, made the reconnoissance rather safe.

During the night a passageway was cut through the enemy's abatis, which was built of felled trees three thousand feet in front of our camp. Here Major Moncrieff intended to open his trenches. I was out there with my picket and twenty light infantry from the other picket. Major Moncrieff went as far as the enemy's abatis. The mantelets were put together, and during the day two brass 24-pounders, four iron do., 32,[2] two brass 18-pounders, one 7-inch and one 9-inch howitzer, 12 mortars (royals), and two bell-muzzles with bores from two to four and one-half inches were brought over. During the night our first parallel was opened, three redoubts having been finished.

---

not told how many 32's were brought over. Perhaps it should read: "four iron ditto, ditto 32[-pounders]," i.e. four iron 32's.

3ter Theil.
oder
Belagerung und Einnahme
von
Charlestown
April 1—Mai 12—1780.

Apr. 1. Da das gehörige Werckzeüg, Horden und etliche schwere
Stücke mit Amunition herüber war, auch die vors erste erforderliche Mantelletten zu sammen gessezet, so wurde die erste
parallele in der Nacht vom 1ten auf den 2ten eröffnet, und
zwar mit Verfertigung 3 Redouten die 1 auf dem Weege und
die andern beyden lincks an demsselb[en]. Jede Redoute
erforderte 16 Mantelletten, die von 400 Arbeiter getragen
worden, denen 100 mit Werckzeüg folgten. Diesses machte
125 Arbeiter auf jede Face, bey welchen 1 StaabsOffr, u 5
Cap^{ts} waren, folglich 500 M. p Redoute = 1500 Arbeiter für
die Nacht.—Mit einbrechender Nacht rückte Light Jnfanterie unter Comando des OberstL^t Abercrombie und Oberst
Lt Dandas, 100 Schritte vor die Arbeiter in einen natürlichen
Graben vor, Um 6 Uhr rückten die Arbeiter aus, und 500
Mann Reserve unter OberstL^t Webster, die in das vom 2^t
Bat. light Jnf. verlassene Lager rückten. Die Jngenieur Cap^{ts}
waren bey jede Brigade eingetheilt, und hatten ihre Assi-
stenten bey sich, die Arbeiter marchirten die Strasse, die nach
Gibs führet, und legten ihre Gewehre und Taschen in Front
des vom 1 Bat. light Jnf: verlassenen Lagers ab, und wurden
bey denen Manteleten eingetheilet. Um 7½ Uhr marchirte

Part Three
or
Siege and Reduction
of
Charleston
April 1—May 12, 1780

Since the necessary tools and hurdles, as well as several April 1
heavy pieces and ammunition, had been brought over, and a
sufficient number of mantelets had been put together, we
opened the first parallel with three redoubts the night of the
1st–2nd. One redoubt was on the road and the other two to
the left of it. Every redoubt required sixteen mantelets, which
were carried by 400 workmen who were accompanied by
another 100 with tools. Thus each face required 125 workmen (with whom were one staff officer [field officer?] and five
captains), which made a total of 500 men per redoubt and a
grand total of 1,500 workmen for the night. At nightfall the
light infantry under the command of Lieutenant Colonels
Abercrombie and Dundas advanced into a natural ditch a
hundred paces in front of the working party. At six o'clock
the workmen and 500 reserves set out under Lieutenant
Colonel Webster and went into the camp evacuated by the
2nd battalion of light infantry. Several captains of the Engineers and their assistants were detailed to each brigade. The
workmen marched out on the road leading to Gibbes' and,
when in front of the camp evacuated by the 1st battalion of
light infantry, they laid down their muskets and cartridge

Capt Sutherland von die Jngenieurs Mit der 1^t Brigade hinnaus, kurz darauf folgten die beyden andern in der grösten
Stille. der Weg war mit Stangen an welchen Pappier beve-
stiget war, gezeichnet, die Manteleten wurden angelegt,—
die Erde 12 Fus dicke angeschüttet. Die Arbeiter kamen
zuruck, die light Jnf. bessezte sie den Tag über,—der Tag
brach an, ehe der Feind das geringste gewahr wurde, noch
weniger Hinderniss im Wege legte. Gegen Abend eröffnete
der Feind 1—181^{br} aus dem Centro seiner Wercke.

Apr. 2. Die Ablössung ging allemal mit einbrechender Nacht, und so
bald sie hinnein war, gingen die Arbeiter heraus. G. Maj.
Leslie comandirte heüte (die 3, vorige Nacht verfertigte
Redouten, wurden hernach No 3, 4, 5, genant) Es wurden
die Redouten durch Laufgraben diesse Nacht zusammen
gehängt, und der Anfang einer 4 Redoute rechts am Weege
(No 2) gemacht, es wurde vom Feind haufig geschossen.
Lincks am Wege in Linie mit N°. 5 wurde ein Weg ruck wärts
über 2 Moräste mit Horden verfertiget, *N° 3 lag 3000 Fus in
Front des Lagers, 1800 Fus vom feindl: Verhacke und 2180 Fus
von der feindl: Linie im Centro*

Apr. 3. Gegen Mittag eröffnete der Feind eine maskirte Batterie von
2 metallen[en] 18 l^{br} in der semi Bastion rechts des Thors der
Stadt, amusirte sich hiermit den Tag über, ohne Schaden zu
thun. Gegen Abend eröffnete er 2—12 lbr in dem Front
Wercke des feindl: lincken Flügels (Franzossen hatten diesse
bessezt) welche die Strasse und N° 3 bestrichen. Diesse Nacht
wurde der Laufgraben von N° 5 lincks verlängert mit vor-
gehender Linie, und am lincken Flügel der Anfang einer Batterie (N° 6) für 9 Canonen mit geblendeten Schiessscharten
gemacht. N° 2, wurde geendigt, und besser rechts nach dem
Ashly zu, wurde der Anfang einer neüen Redoute (No 1) gemacht, diesse lag näher am Feind, denn die übrigen, und war
von der ersten paralele (No 3. u s.w.) durch einen Morast getrennet, und hatte einen starcken Morast, der bis in Ashly ging,
in Fronte.

boxes and were distributed over the mantelets. At half-past seven Captain Sutherland of the Engineers marched out with the 1st brigade. Shortly afterward the two other brigades followed very quietly. The way was marked with poles to which paper had been fastened. The mantelets were set up, and earth was piled against them twelve feet thick. The working party returned, and the light infantry occupied the redoubts in the course of the day. It was morning before the enemy had become aware of our activities; so they had not interfered in any way. Toward evening the enemy opened one 18-pounder in the center of their works.

The troops and the working parties were always relieved at nightfall. Major General Leslie had the command today. The three redoubts thrown up last night were later called Nos. 3, 4, and 5. This night the redoubts were connected by trenches, and a fourth redoubt was begun at the right of the causeway (No. 2). The enemy fired frequently. At the left of the road in line with No. 5 a road to the rear was built over two bogs by means of hurdles. *No. 3 lay 3,000 feet in front of the camp, 1,800 feet from the enemy's abatis, and 2,180 feet from the center of the enemy's line.* April 2

Toward noon the enemy opened a masked battery of two brass 18-pounders in the demibastion to the right of the city gate and had a good time with them without doing any damage. Toward evening they opened two 12-pounders in the advanced work of their left wing, which was occupied by Frenchmen; these raked the road and No. 3. This night the trench was continued to the left of No. 5 in an oblique line, where a battery (No. 6) was begun for nine cannon with masked embrasures. No. 2 was finished, and farther to the right, toward the Ashley, a new redoubt (No. 1) was begun. The latter lay nearer to the enemy than the others and was separated from the first parallel (No. 3, etc.) by a bog, while in front of it was a swamp extending to the Ashley. April 3

Apr. 4. Mit Anbruch des Tags muste das Jäger Detachement mit Jnf: Commando hinnaus, um N° 1- und N° 6 zu bessezen. Capt. Ewald und 50 Jäger kamen unter Cõmando des OberstL^t Webster in N° 6, Major v. Wurmb und der Rest der Jäger in N° 1 (Jch standt mit 50 M. im Piquet,) der Feind canonirte den Tag unbändig aus 12. 18. 24^{lbr} 5- und 6 Zoll Haubiz[en] und that, (die Fregatten mit gerechnet) über 600 Schüsse. Denn 2 feindl: Fregatten, lichteten gegen Mittag die Ankker, die eine kam diesseits N° 6 in welche sie einige broad Sides schickte. allein Sie konte kein Schaden thun, denn das Schiff lag zu tief, musten die Canonen einfallen lassen, und in der Batterie war inwendig ein Graben. Sobald wie die Schiffe unter Seegel gingen, brachte Major Moncrief 1 metallen[en] 24 l^{br} durch 80 Matrossen an lincken Flügel der 2^t light Jnf ans Wasser, und L^t M'clow von der light Jnf. Artill: brachte so gleich 2 Kugel ins Schiff, dass es um wenden muste. Canonen, Amunition u s w. wurde heüte herüber gebracht. Major Tralles commandirte die Artillerie Capt. Ewans von Raisonable 64. men of war mit 4 Offrs, und 100 Matross[en] zur Besazzung einer Batterie kam heüte auch an, und zog in Gibson's Garten ins Lager,—Die Jäger verlohren nichts.— Weil unssere erste paralele bey nahe geendiget ware, so gaben wir von heüte an, nur kleine Utroffrs piquetter in Fronte des Lagers. Den Nachmittag ging ich nach N° 3 um zu zeichnen, der Feind brachte einen 18 lb. Kugel bis Gen. Leslie Quartier, ich fand, dass sie aus einem metallenen Stück geschossen war, Diesse Nacht wurde N° 6 hinten geschlossen, um das Flanquiren der Schiffe zu hindern und Platforms gelegt. Am rechten Flügel wurde N° 1 geendigt. Gegen Morgen recognoscirte der Jngenieur, um in Front N° 5 eine avancirte Batterie an zu legen.

[1] Plunging fire.   [2] See, however, p. 45.

At break of day the jäger detachment went out with an April 4 infantry command to occupy Nos. 1 and 6. Captain Ewald and fifty jägers under the command of Lieutenant Colonel Webster went into No. 6; Major von Wurmb and the rest of the jägers into No. 1. I had a picket of fifty men. The enemy fired excessively with 12-, 18-, and 24-pounders and 5- and 6-inch howitzers, firing over six hundred shots, including those from the two frigates which weighed anchor toward noon. One of the frigates came this side of No. 6 and fired several broadsides into it. However, she could do no damage, for she lay too low—they had to let their balls drop[1]—and our men were further protected by a trench inside the battery.[2] As soon as the ships set their sails Major Moncrieff had eighty sailors take a brass 24-pounder to the river, close to the left wing of the 2nd battalion of light infantry, and Lieutenant M'Clow [?] of the artillery of the light infantry fired two shots into the ship, forcing her to withdraw. Today guns, ammunition, etc., were brought over. Major Traile[3] commanded the artillery. And Captain Evans of the *Raisonnable* man-of-war, 64 guns, arrived today with four [junior] officers and a hundred sailors to man a battery. He encamped in Gibbes' garden. The jägers had no losses. Since our first parallel was almost finished, we sent henceforth only small pickets in charge of noncommissioned officers in front of our camp. In the afternoon I went to No. 3 in order to make sketches. The enemy fired an 18-pound ball as far as General Leslie's quarters. I ascertained that it was shot from a brass piece. During the night No. 6 was provided with platforms and closed in the rear to make it secure against the flanking fire of ships. On the right wing No. 1 was completed. Toward morning the Engineer reconnoitred the ground in front of No. 5, where he intended to construct an advanced battery.

---

[3] In the Army List of 1781 Peter Trail[e] appears as a captain.

Apr. 5. Der Feind schoss heüte ohne Aufhören, über 700 Schüsse, der General schickte durch den Adjutant St Georg an die Batterien auf Fennings Point, denen Ruder Galeeren und Canonen-Boots Ordre, ihre Stücke spielen zu lassen, doch die Stadt nicht in Brand zu schiessen. Diesse machten ein gewaltiges Feüer, und die 32^{lbr} erschreckliche Verwirrung in der Stadt. man hörte nichts als o morder! o lord! Eine feindl: 12 lb. Kugel schlug bis in unsser piquet. Den Nachmittag musten wir besser vorrücken, indem das 3te Bat. light Jnfanterie zu uns gestossen war, und unsser Lager bezog. Diesse Nacht wurde N° 1 stärcker gemacht, 2, 24 lb. nach N° 6 gebracht, und die platforms in diesser Batterie geendiget. Eine Canone blieb im Morast stecken, sie musten über die Plaine gezogen werden, und die Wege über den Morast waren sehr leichtsinning gemacht.

Apr. 6. Von heüte Morgen bis retraite schoss der feind nur 40 Kugel und 6 Bomben meistens 9 u 12^{lbr} und einige 18^{lbr}. bey G^r Maj: v. Kosboths Quartier (da wo Apr. 4 der eine metallene 24^{lbr} war hingebracht worden) wurde eine Batterie für 1 metallenen, 1 eissern[en] 24^{lbr} gegen die Schiffe aufgeworfen, und die Stücke auf gefahren, 2 feindl: Fregatten Providence u Ranger gingen heüte am jensseitigen Ufer des Cooper Rivers hinauf, und legten sich an der Mündung des Wando vor Ancker. Verschiedene Boote ging[en] mit Weiber und Bagage heüte aus der Stadt nach Habcaw Ferry 7 eisserne 1 met. 24^{lbr} wurden heüte bis ans Gate way gebracht, um die Nacht desto näher zum transportiren zu seyn; Auf einer vom Pionier Major erfundenen Schleife mit 2 Räder vorne, wurde heüte durch 100 Matrossen ein Canonen Boot aus dem Ashly River, nach dem Coopers River zugebracht, um dasselbst zu Sondirung der versenckten Schiffe, Auffangung einzelner Scooner etc. gebraucht zu werden, den Mittag kam Capt. Collins von der royal Artillery mit 80 Artilleristen an, er war auf der russian Merchant Transport verschlagen gewessen, und kam

The enemy cannonaded incessantly today, firing over seven hundred shots. The General sent his adjutant, St. George, to carry orders to the batteries on Fenwick's Point and also to the row-galleys and gunboats to let their pieces play without, however, firing the city. It was a furious cannonade, the 32-pounders causing a fearful confusion in the city. One heard nothing but "Oh, murder! Oh, Lord!" An enemy 12-pound ball fell in the midst of our picket. In the afternoon we had to advance farther, for the 3rd battalion of light infantry had come up and taken possession of our encampment. During the night No. 1 was reinforced, two 24-pounders were taken to No. 6, and the platforms in this battery were finished. Since one cannon had been mired in the bog, the pieces had to be conveyed over the plain. The roads over the swamp had been built very carelessly.

Between morning and retreat the enemy fired only forty shots and six shells, mostly 9- and 12-pounders and a few 18-pounders. Near Major General von Kospoth's quarters (whither on April 4 one brass 24-pounder was taken), a battery was thrown up and provided with one brass and one iron 24-pounder, which were to be used against the ships. The two enemy frigates *Providence* and *Ranger* went up the opposite bank of the Cooper River and dropped anchor at the mouth of the Wando. Some boats with women and baggage left the city today and went to Hobcaw Ferry. Seven iron and one brass 24-pounder were taken as far as the gateway to be that much closer for transportation tonight. On a dray with two wheels in front, which had been invented by the Major of the Engineers, a hundred sailors today hauled a gunboat from the Ashley to the Cooper River. It was to be used in taking soundings over the submerged vessels and in capturing some schooners, etc. At noon Captain Collins of the Royal Artillery arrived from the Bermudas with eighty artillerymen. He had been lost on the *Russia Merchant*

jezt von die Bermudas, das Schiff war verlohren gegangen, so wie der Defiance Men of War. Die Nacht wolte der Feind wieder mit starck[em] Feüer unssere Arbeiter hindern, allein die Ruder Galeren und Batt: auf Fenningspoint zwangen sie nach zu lassen. Eine feindl: Kugel demontirte eine Canone auf Fenningspoint. Diesse Nacht wurde mit Transportirung Canonen in N° 6 zu gebracht, und mit Verfertigung eines Pulver Magaziens bey dersselben. Zu gleicher Zeit wurden die Schiessscharten ausgeflochten, 2 geöffnet, und die übrigen wieder maskirt.

Apr. 7. Nur etlich und 50 Schüsse that der Feind bis gegen Mittag. Den Nachmittag kam Succurs von 700 Mann unter General Woodford mit Provision etc etc in der Stadt von Habcaw Ferry über den Cooper River an; bey Retraite schoss der Feind ein Freüden Feüer aus allen Batterien und die Garnison gab ein 3 maliges Hurray von denen Werckern. und von 8–10 Uhr Abends spielten alle Glocken in der Stadt. Jch war gerade bey Major Tralles und niemand von uns zweifelte daran, dass der Feind nicht einen Ausfall gethan hätte und jedermann lief zum Gewehr, bis Rapport kam, von dem feindlichen Freüden Feüer. Diesse Nacht wurde ein anderer Weg nach N° 2. über die Moräste von gehauenen Stämen Nadeln Holz gemacht, und rechts an N° 2 der Anfang einer für 12 Stück grossen Batterie (sie wurde auch genant N° 2, oder the Sailors Battery) indem die Matrosen sie bessezzten) gemacht.

Apr. 8– Diessen Nachmittag war es, dass unssere Men of Wars Forth Moultrie passirten. Um 4 Uhr den Nachmittag kamen sie mit dem herrlichst[en] Winde, stärcksten Fluth und bedeckten Luft aus 5 Fathom Hole. Der Admiral fuhr in einem Joly Boat vorauf, und lootzte jedes Schiff durch. Die Avant hatte Sir Andrew Snape Hammond auf der Roebuck. Um 4½ Uhr war

---

[1] Captain Hinrichs has apparently been misinformed on this point. Other accounts, including the Admiral's report and the diaries of Captain Ewald and Major General von Huyn, agree that the Admiral was on the

transport, which later sank, as did also the *Defiance* man-of-war. During the night the enemy again attempted to hinder our working party by fiercely cannonading it, but the row-galleys and the batteries on Fenwick's Point compelled them to let up. An enemy ball dismounted a gun on Fenwick's Point. The night was spent in transporting guns into No. 6 and constructing a powder magazine near by; the embrasures were lined with wickerwork and two of them were opened up and the rest masked again.

By noon the enemy had fired only some fifty shots. In the April 7 afternoon General Woodford brought succor to the city, seven hundred men as well as provisions, etc., etc. He arrived by way of Hobcaw Ferry and Cooper River. The enemy expressed their joy by firing all their batteries at retreat, while the garrison gave three huzzas from the works. From eight to ten in the evening all the bells in the city rang out. I happened to be at Major Traile's. None of us doubted but that the enemy had made a sortie. Hence we ran for our arms. Soon, however, came information as to the cause of the enemy's rejoicing. During the night another road was built, to No. 2, by means of trimmed pine trunks laid across the bogs, and on the right of No. 2 a battery was begun for twelve pieces. It was also called No. 2 or "the sailors' battery," for it was manned by sailors.

This afternoon our men-of-war passed Fort Moultrie. At April 8 four o'clock they came out of Five-Fathom Hole with a splendid wind and a strong tide, and aided by fog. The Admiral went ahead in a jolly boat and piloted each ship.[1] Sir Andrew Snape Hamond led the vanguard with the *Roebuck*. At half-

---

Roebuck, thus leading the way, to be sure, but not in a jolly boat. Since the 74's and the 64's did not stay at Charleston, the Admiral had shifted his flag from the *Europe* to the *Roebuck*, which was commanded by Sir Andrew Snape Hamond. Hinrichs makes the same erroneous statement in the manuscript journal of the Jäger Corps (cf. Lowell, *op. cit.*, p. 247).

diesser am Forth, und Forth Moultrie fing an aus 40 Stücken,
gröstentheils 24^{lbr} zu speyen. So wie das Schiff in vollem
Stolze, ohne sich an alle Kugel zu kehren unter das Forth
kam, gab es seine Broad Side, und segelte ohne Verlust, ohne
Aufenthalt, vorbey, vor der Stadt weg und wurf die Ancker
bey Forth Johnston. Hierauf folgte der Richmond (er war von
Cork gekoñen) Diesser verlohr den vorderen Ober Mast.—
Der Renown machte die Arriére, und als er unter das Forth
kam, hielte er an, legte die Seegel zurück, und machte so ein
unbändiges, immerwährendes Feüer, dass das ganze Schiff ein
Bliz zu seyn, schiene, und deckte auf die Art den Rücken der
Esquadre. Ein Transport schiff fuhr veste, blieb sizzen und
wurde so sehr zusañen geschossen, dass das Volck es in Brand
sezzen muste und verlassen. Verschiedene Kugeln flogen durch
die Schiffe und ohne Schaden zu thun. Um 6½ Uhr lagen
unssere Schiffe diesseits vor Ancker mit Verlust von 7 Todten,
und 1 midshipmann und 13 Mann blessirten, wovon Renown
die meisten hatte. Welch eine Kleinigkeit bey einem so gewaltigen Feüer!—Der Feind hörte auf einmal auf zu schiessen, und staunend sahe er den stolzen Britten, den Herrn
des Meeres, jeder Gefahr, jeder Hinderniss, mit Verach-
tung und Hohn entgeg[en] gehen und bessiegen. Schrecken
und Staunen, Furcht, niedergeschlagener Muth und vereitelte
Hoffnung, schienen ihre Augen, Ohren und Herz so sehr zu
benebeln, dass sie auch nicht einen einzigen Schuss aus ihren
Wercken, auf unssere, auf die Brustwehre der Wercke ge-
sprungene Besazzung der Tranchéen thaten!—Diesse Nacht
wurde die Sailor's Batterie N° 2 fertig gemacht.—Heüte
wurde das Detachement Jäger in Front der Armé vertheilt.
Capt Ewald blieb in unsserm alten Lager, Capt. v. Bodungen
kam in Fronte des 1^t Bat. light Jnf: und ich kam zwischen der
Strasse und den Coopers River, in Front des 2^t Bat: light Jnf:
zu stehen.

Apr. 9. Der Feind feüerte heüte wenig. Ein Detachement von der

past four he passed the fort, which belched fire out of forty pieces, most of them 24-pounders. As soon as this ship in all her glory came under the fort she defiantly replied with a broadside and then sailed by without loss and without delay. After crossing below the city she cast anchor at Fort Johnson. Then followed the *Richmond*, which had come from Cork. She lost her fore-topmast. The *Renown* formed the rear guard, and when she arrived at the fort she lay to, took in her sails, and gave such an unrelenting, murderous fire that the whole ship seemed to flare up. Thus she covered the rear of the squadron. One transport ran aground and was so shot to pieces that the sailors had to set her afire and abandon her. Several cannon balls went through the ships without doing any damage. By half-past six our ships lay at anchor on this side, having seven killed and one midshipman and thirteen men wounded,[1] most of whom were on the *Renown*. What a trifling loss under so enormous a fire! The enemy suddenly stopped firing and, filled with amazement, saw the proud Briton, the master of the sea, meet and overcome every danger, every obstacle, with scorn and disdain. Horror, astonishment, fear, despondency, and shattered hopes seemed to befog their eyes, ears, and hearts to such an extent that they did not fire a single shot at our men, who had jumped upon the parapets of the works!—During the night the sailors' battery (No. 2) was finished.—Today the jäger detachment was scattered in front of the army. Captain Ewald remained in our old encampment, Captain von Bodungen went in front of the 1st battalion of light infantry, and I was stationed between the road and the Cooper River in front of the 2nd battalion of light infantry.

The enemy fired but little. A detachment from the city April 9

[1] Most accounts, including that of the Admiral, say that the ships had twenty-seven killed and wounded. Ewald states that their losses were seven killed and twenty wounded.

Stadt wurde heüte über nach Habcaw gessezt. Es schiene als hätte es 2 leichte Stücke bey sich. Eine feindliche Ruder Galere versuchte es, unssere zwischen der Stadt und Forth Moultrie vor Ancker liegende Schiffe zu beunruhigen Der Feind beschäfftigte sich den ganzen Tag mit Wegnehmung verschiedener schweren Stücke aus denen Wercken gegen uns, um sie gegen die Schiffe an der Mündung des Cooper Rivers auf zu führen. Unsser Canonen Boot, welches in den Cooper River übers Land war gebracht worden, fuhr heüte Nacht den Fluss herunter, und sundirte bis in South bay, gegen Morgen kam es wieder zurück, den Nachmittag musten die Commandeurs derer 3 Jäger Divisionen hinnaus in die Wercke gehen, um jeder für sich in den vor seiner Front liegenden Wercken, Posten für kleine Partheyen Jäger auszu suchen, welche alle Tage hinnaus solten und den Feind beunruhigen. Allein die Distance von feindlichen Wercken war zu gros, um den Feind, ausser bey einem Ausfalle, Schaden thun zu können. Und da diesse Nacht eine neüe Batterie (N° 7) 150 Schritt in Front von N° 5 angelegt wurde, so war diesses ein besserer Post[en]

Apr. 10. für die Jäger. Mit Anbruch des Tags muste 1 Capt. Ewald und 50 Jäger hinnaus, um diesse angefangene Batterie N° 7. zu bessezzen, sie war noch nicht halb fertig und der Feind schoss rasch, doch ohne Schaden zu thun. Faschienen zu Ausflickung der Batterien wurden heüte gebunden, mehrere Manteleten verfertiget, Mörsser und Canonen bis an den Gate way gebracht und von da in der Nacht nach N° 6. Der Feind machte in seinen an den Cooper angelegten Wercken und den noch [= nach] dem centro zu nächst gelegenen redans 13 neüe Schiesscharten gegen N° 6, ohne aber mehr denn 6 Stücke hinnein zu bringen. Diesse Nacht wurde N° 7 fertig, N° 6– und N° 2 bessezt, und in N° 7. kamen 3 – 24^{lbr} und 1, 12^{lbr}

Apr. 11– Wenig oder gar kein Feüer, und an beyden Seiten Tag und Nacht gearbeitet. N° 7 gab dem Feind neüe Arbeit; er öffnete den Nachmittag 5 neüe Schiesscharten aus seinem Centro

was ferried over to Hobcaw today. It seemed to be taking two light pieces along. An enemy row-galley tried to annoy our ships lying at anchor between the city and Fort Moultrie. The enemy was engaged all day in removing several heavy pieces from the works facing us in order to mount them against the ships at the mouth of the Cooper River. Our gunboat which had been taken overland into the Cooper went down the river tonight taking soundings as far as South Bay. Toward morning it returned. In the afternoon the commanders of the three jäger detachments went out into the works situated before their respective fronts to select posts for small parties of jägers, which were to go out every day to molest the enemy. However, the distance from these works was too great for rifle fire to be effective unless the enemy should make a sortie. During the night a new battery (No. 7) was erected one hundred and fifty paces in front of No. 5, affording the jägers a better post. At break of day Captain Ewald and April 10 fifty jägers went out to man the unfinished battery No. 7. It was not half completed, and the enemy fired rapidly, but without effect. Today we made fascines to repair our batteries, constructed several mantelets, and took some mortars and cannon as far as the gateway, and from there during the night to No. 6. In their works on the Cooper and in the redans closest to the center the enemy made thirteen new embrasures to be used against No. 6; but they got only six pieces into them. During the night No. 7 was finished, No. 6 and No. 2 were manned, and three 24-pounders and one 12-pounder were taken into No. 7.

Little if any cannonading, and both sides working day April 11 and night. No. 7 caused the enemy new work. In the course of the afternoon they opened in the center of their works five more embrasures against it. In No. 7 a powder magazine was

Wercke gegen sie. Diesse Nacht wurde in N° 7. das Pulver
Magazien angelegt, und es kamen noch 3 – 24 lb. hinnein. An
N° 7. lincks wurde eine blinde Batterie angelegt, und an diesse
lincks ein Laufgraben, der mit einspringendem Winckel auf
den ausspringenden Winckel der Front Redoute des Feindes
am Cooper mit obliquer Linie zu lief. Da unssere erste Paralele
auf die Art geendigt war, und die demontir-Batterien zum
Spielen fertig, so wurde der Major Crosby mit einer Aufforderung an die Stadt geschickt (vide Beylage), die auf eine
sehr höfliche Art abgeschlagen wurde

Apr. 12– Um 4 Uhr Morgens schickte Gr. Leslie zu mir, ihm sogleich 1
Offr und 20 Mann hinnaus zu schicken; Weil der Tag anbrach
und kein Saumen war, nahm ich selber 20 Mann und eilte
hinnaus. Jch bessezte den halb geendigten Laufgraben. Allein
es war noch zu weit Distance um mit Büchssen auf dem feindlichen Parapet Schaden thun zu können Unssere Batterien
waren alle beordert worden, auf den ersten Winck fertig zu
seyn. N° 2. als den rechten Flügel hatte Capt. Ewans von der
royal Navy 1 – 12 lb, 11 – 24 lb, 1 – 9 Zoll Haubize. N° 6 als
den lincken Flügel hatte Capt Lossum royal Artillery und
N° 7, ein Subaltern Mr Abbot—N° 6 hatte glühende Kugel—.
Um 11 Uhr kam Ordre, dass die Batterien den Tag nicht solten
geöffnet werden, Jch kam den Tag mit etlichen Bomben,
20–30 Cartetschen und Canon Schüssen ab—und verlohr keinen Mann. Den Nachmittag marchirte 23, 33, Legion rückwärts, um über den Coopers River zu gehen, und zu Cain
Hoy Posto zu fassen. Unssere Flotte von Newyork war ange-
kom̃en, und der General wolte keinen Augenblick verliehren,
jede Communication der Stadt ab zu schneiden. Wir gaben
desswegen statt der beyden Rgtr 1 Capt. 60 M. in N° 3. 4. 5.
Die Nacht wurde mit Amunition Tragung zugebracht.

Apr. 13. Etwas nach Anbruch des Tages, wurden unssere 3 Baterien

---

[1] General Clinton summoned the city to surrender on the 10th of April,
not on the 11th. Apparently Captain Hinrichs was too much occupied with
his military duties to make daily entries. The enclosure referred to here has

built, and three 24-pounders were taken into it. On the left of No. 7 a blind battery was thrown up and at the left of it a trench, which with a reëntering angle ran obliquely toward the salient angle of the enemy's front redoubt on the Cooper. Since our first parallel was now finished and the dismounting batteries were ready to play, Major Crosbie was sent into the city with a summons (*vide* enclosure),[1] which was refused in a very polite manner.

At four o'clock in the morning I received orders from General Leslie to send an officer and twenty men out to him. Since day was breaking and no time could be lost, I myself took twenty men and hastened out. I occupied the half-finished trench. However, the range was still too great to use our rifles effectively against the enemy's parapet. All our batteries had been ordered to be ready at a moment's notice. No. 2, with one 12-pounder, eleven 24-pounders, and one 9-inch howitzer, constituting the right wing, was commanded by Captain Evans of the Royal Navy; No. 6, the left wing, by Captain Lawson, Royal Artillery; and No. 7 by a subaltern, Mr. Abbot.—No. 6 had hot shot. At eleven o'clock orders came to the effect that the batteries should not be opened during the day. I got off with a few shells and twenty to thirty grapeshot and cannon balls, without losing a man. In the afternoon the 23rd, the 33rd, and the Legion marched to the rear in order to cross the Cooper River and take post at Cainhoy. Our fleet had arrived from New York, and the General did not want to lose a moment in cutting the city off from all communications. We therefore posted one captain and sixty men, in place of the two regiments, in Nos. 3, 4, and 5. The night was spent carrying ammunition.

A little after daybreak we opened our three batteries,

April 12

April 13

---

not been preserved with the diary, nor do the von Jungkenn Papers contain any of the other enclosures noted in these journals. However, the correspondence between the commanding generals has often been printed.

geöffnet, und spielten mit ziemlichem Effect. Die auf Fennings-
point secundirten mit immer anhaltendem Feüer. N° 2 brachte
zu erst eine mit 3 Ambrassen und 2, 18 lb bessezte Front
Redoute am Ashly zum Schweig[en] N° 6 schoss glühende
Kugeln, und die Stadt brandte an 3 verschiedenen Stellen, der
General lies das Feüer der Batterien immer schwächer und
schwächer werden, und gab dem Feind Zeit zu löschen. N° 7.
Litte am meisten, die Nacht wurde wenig geschossen, an
beyden Seiten war beschädigt und aus zu bessern, frische
Amunition an zu schaffen. Wir hatten 2 Todte 5 Blessirte
überhaupt vom Feind bekommen. Diesse Nacht wurde die
2te paralele eröffnet, die Sappe ging in Front N° 7 200 Schritt
über einen Morast, und die Paralele wurde rechts und lincks
etwa 100. Schritt lang eröffnet, und hatte einen andern
Morast lincks in Front—. Die 2te paralele lag im Centro 1300
Fus vor der ersten 500 Fus Distance vom feindlichen Verhacke
und Canale, und 880 Fus vom Centro Wercke.

Apr. 14. 1 Capt (Ewald) und 50 Jäger (mit Jnfanteristen melirt) musten
diesses Werck bessezzen und schossen sich mit dem Feind
herum. Der Feind zog seine Canonen aus der Front Redoute
zurück, und maskirte die Schiesscharten, und spielte den Tag
mit 12 lbr aus dem Hornwerck im Centro und enfilirten aus
die 18 lbr. seine Front Redoute des lincken Flügels N° 2
konte diesse Redoute nicht zum Stillschweigen bringen, sie
lag in obliquer Linie, und ricochet verstandten sie nicht,
welches das einzige Mittel war, eine Kugel hinnein zu
bringen, aber sehr delicat zu schiessen, indem ein breiter
Morast zwischen N° 2 und diessem feindlichen Wercke war—.
Diesse Nacht wurde die 2te Paralele lincks über 200 Schritt
verlängert, und der Weg über den Morast in der Sappe mit
Horden 20 Schritt breit gemacht; dies gab ziemlich klein
Gewehr Feüer. Um 11 Uhr des Abends war es so arg, dass ich

¹ See p. 85, note 1.

which played with rather good results. Those on Fenwick's Point seconded ours with a continuous cannonade. No. 2 began by silencing a front redoubt on the Ashley which had three embrasures and two 18-pounders. No. 6 fired hot shot and set fire to the city in three different places. The General let the fire of the batteries get weaker and weaker, giving the enemy time to extinguish the fires.[1] No. 7 suffered most. During the night there was but little cannonading, for both sides had to make repairs and procure fresh ammunition. We had a total of two killed and five wounded. During the night the second parallel was opened. The sap intersected a swamp two hundred paces in front of No. 7. The parallel was opened about one hundred paces on both sides. In front of it to the left lay another swamp. The center of the second parallel was 1,300 feet in front of the first, 500 feet from the enemy's abatis and wet ditch, and 880 feet from their central fortification.

Captain Ewald with fifty jägers and a sprinkling of in- April 14 fantry occupied the new work and exchanged many shots with the enemy, who withdrew their guns from the front redoubt and masked its embrasures. They let their 12-pounders in the hornwork in the center play upon us, while we enfiladed the front redoubt of their left wing with 18-pounders. No. 2 was unable to silence this redoubt, for it lay in an oblique line, and the men did not know how to fire ricochet, which was the only way of getting a shot into it.[2] This, to be sure, would have required very delicate firing, since a broad swamp lies between the two redoubts. During the night the second parallel was continued more than two hundred paces to the left, and the road in the sap through the swamp was made twenty paces wide by means of hurdles. This brought upon us a good deal of musketry. At eleven o'clock at night it was so

[2] Redoubt No. 2 was manned by the navy (p. 247), which accounts for the gunners' lack of familiarity with ricochet fire.

mit OberstL^t Abercrombie nach N° 7 hinnaus lief, um zu sehen, ob der Ausfall richtig sey. Jm Hingehen nach N° 7 begegneten uns die englische Arbeiter. Sie sagten: sie wären beordert worden ihre Gewehre zu holen (die hätten sie mit nehmen müssen) Die Arbeit wurde fertig, ohne grossen Verlust.

Apr. 15– 1 Capt (Hinrichs) 50 Jäger, 50 Gren. 50 Light Jnf: bessezten diessen Morg[en] die 2te Paralele, ich gab denen brittisch[en] Grenadiers den rechten Flügel weil diesser zu weit vom Schiessen war, (Um 11 Uhr, lössete Lt Burke mit 50 Hess: Gren: aus N° 7 die 50 brittish Gren. ab) Die LightJnf: und Jäger melirte ich. Der Feind hatte zwischen der Front Redoute und dem Verhack contre Approchen gemacht, und mit rifle men bessezt, mit denen wir uns den Tag herum schossen, 17 Cartetsch[en] Schüsse, 19 – 18 lb-Kugeln von der lincken Front Redoute des Feindes und 13 Bomben, 6–10 zöllige aus der rechten Front Redoute kam[en] in die Paralele. 2 Bomben sprangen mitten unter uns im Laufgraben; 5 auf der Banck, die übrigen crepirten, und nichts, nichts, denn 1 Gewehr zerschlagen, und wir alle mit Erde beschüttet. Jch liess einige Traversen machen. Unssere Batterien secundirten nicht gut, von klein Gewehr hatte ich 2 light Jnfanteristen blessirt. Die Bumben wurfe der Feind meisterhaft, hatte er so gut ricochet zu schiessen verstanden, aus denen 2 18 lbr seiner enfilirenden Front Redoute am lincken Flügel, so hätten wir viele Leüthe verlohren—. Diesse Nacht wurde diesser fertige Theil der 2^t paralele stärcker gemacht, und auftritte an dem parapet, rechts wurde der Laufgraben bis beynahe an der Strasse (Centrum) fort geführet, und im Laufgraben bey N° 7. eine Bomben Batterie für 12 royals und 1 – 7 Zoll Haubize ausgestochen, und bessezt, Magazine und amunit: dasselbst angelegt.

severe that Lieutenant Colonel Abercrombie and I ran out to No. 7 to see whether the enemy had really made a sally. On our way we met the English workmen. They told us they had been ordered to fetch their muskets. (They should never have been without them.) The work was completed without great loss.

I occupied the second parallel this morning with fifty April 15 jägers, fifty grenadiers, and fifty light infantry. I assigned the British grenadiers to the right wing because the distance was too great for musketry. (At eleven o'clock Lieutenant Burke with fifty Hessian grenadiers came from No. 7 to relieve the fifty British grenadiers.) I distributed the light infantry among the jägers. The enemy had built counterapproaches between their front redoubt and their abatis and manned them with riflemen, with whom we exchanged many shots in the course of the day. Into our parallel fell seventeen grape-shot, nineteen 18-pound balls from their left front redoubt, and thirteen shells, 6 to 10 inches, from the right front re-doubt. Two shells burst among us in the trench and five others on the parapet. The rest failed to explode. We had no loss, none whatever, except one broken rifle, and all of us covered with earth. I caused several traverses to be made. Our batteries did not support us well. Two of my light infan-trymen were wounded by the enemy's small-arms fire. They threw their shells in a masterly manner. Had they known as well how to fire ricochet from the two 18-pounders of their enfilading front redoubt on the left wing, we would have lost many men. During the night the completed part of the second parallel was reinforced, and banquettes were built on the parapet. On the right the trench was continued almost to the road (center). In the trench, at No. 7, a battery was thrown up for twelve royals and one 7-inch howitzer. A magazine was built, ammunition carried into it, and the battery manned.

Apr. 16   1 Capt. (v. Bodungen) bessezte heüte die 2te paralele am link-
ken Flügel, wurde gleichfals cannonirt und hatte 1 Light Jnf.
todt. Diesse Nacht wurde die Sappe am rechten Flügel
zwischen N° 2– u 3 geöffnet, zur 2^t Paralele. Ein natürlicher
Graben beschleünigete die Arbeit sehr, die 2^t Paralele wurde
450 Schritt in Front N° 2– u 3, auf 100 Schritt lang fertig.
Jch ging hinnaus des Nachts, um die Arbeit zu sehen, der
Feind schoss rasch, und unssere Bomben Batterien schossen
unaufhörlich 12 lb Kugel vom Feind schlugen ricochet in
der Nacht aus dem Hornwerck bis auf die Strasse diesseits
N° 3.

Apr. 17.   1 Capt. (Ewald) und 30 Jäger, bessezten die 2te Paralele
rechts, welche vorige Nacht war geöffnet worden. 1 Lieut.
(Kling) 30 Jäger die 2^t paralele lincks. Der Feind brachte
in seiner rechten Front Redoute 1 12^{lbr}, womit er diesses
Werck, doch ohne Schaden zu thun, enfilirte. Unssere Bomben
spielten gut. Diesse Nacht wurde der Laufgraben vom rechten
zum lincken Flügel geschlossen, und so die 2te paralele geendigt, auch über das die Sappe zur Eröffnung der 3^t paralele am lincken Flügel (in Linie mit N° 7) angefangen.

April 18.   Der lincke Flügel war der nächste am Feind, der angefangenen
Sappe zur 3^t paralele nicht zu gedenken; 1 Capt. (Hinrichs)
und 30 Jäger besezten sie, 1 Lieut. (v. Winzingeroda) und 30
kamen am rechten Flügel. Der Feind schickte mir aus seiner
Front Redoute rechts, 6 Bomben in Graben, noch ehe es
völlig Tag war, öffnete den Tag über aber keine andere Batterie als in der lincke Front Redoute. 2 – 18 lb., womit er
uns zu enfiliren suchte. 2 light Jnf: wurden getroffen, Gegen
Abend brachte er 3, 12 lbr. in der rechten Front Redoute,
womit er über die Banck einen Schuss auf N° 6 that; und
sogleich die Affette [= Lafette] von einer unsserer Canonen
zerschlug, unssere Bomben spielten herlich, besser als jemals.
Den Abend kam ein Überlaufer und sagte: dass die feindle:
Piquets und light Jnf: unssere Wercke am rechten Flügel

Captain von Bodungen occupied the left wing of the second parallel. He was likewise cannonaded and had one light infantryman killed. During the night the sap at the right wing between Nos. 2 and 3 was opened to connect with the second parallel. A natural ditch expedited the work considerably. The second parallel, four hundred and fifty paces in front of Nos. 2 and 3, was completed for a distance of one hundred paces. I went out at night to see what had been done. The enemy fired briskly, and our batteries bombarded them incessantly. Twelve-pound balls fired ricochet from the hornwork struck as far as the road this side of No. 3.

Captain Ewald and thirty jägers occupied the right of the second parallel, which was opened last night, while Lieutenant Kling and thirty jägers occupied the left. The enemy brought into their right front redoubt one 12-pounder, with which they enfiladed this work, doing no damage however. Our shells played well. During the night the trench from the right wing was connected with that from the left, and thus the second parallel was finished. Furthermore, a sap was begun at the left wing in line with No. 7 for the opening of the third parallel.

Of the second parallel the left wing was closest to the enemy. I occupied it with thirty jägers, while Lieutenant von Winzingeroda and thirty men went into the right wing. Even before it was completely light the enemy sent six shells from their right front redoubt into my trench; but through the whole day they opened no other battery except two 18-pounders in their left front redoubt, with which they attempted to enfilade us. Two light infantrymen were struck. Toward evening they conveyed three 12-pounders into their right front redoubt, one of which sent a shot over the barbette into No. 6, smashing the carriage of one of our guns. Our shells played splendidly, better than ever. In the evening there came a deserter who told us that the enemy's pickets

attaquiren wolte. Allein es kam nicht dazu, vieleicht weil der Deserteur vermist war, und sie es verrathen sahen. Diesse Nacht wurde das in voriger Nacht verfertigte Stück der 2^t paralele verstärkt, und die Schanzen ausgebessert, indem das Mondlicht zu helle war in Fronte zu Sappiren, und in der 2^t paralele am rechten und lincken Flügel eine Bomben Batterie angelegt, von beyden Seiten wurden die Nacht mehrere Bomben geworfen.

Apprl 19. 1 Capt. (v. Bodungen) mit 30 Jäger rechts, 1 Lieut. (Schaefer) lincks, besezten die 2te paralele (ausser die Jnf. Detachements) Den Abend um 9 Uhr gingen unssere Ruder Galeeren von Wappoe, nach Forth Johnston, indem der Admiral sie zu einer andern Bestimmung brauchte. Die feindl: Batterien am Ashly feüerten rasch, ich ging mit OL^t Abercrombie bis am Gate work, um das Feüer an zu sehen, und 2 feindl: 12 lbr. von der Half moon Battery, die zwischen dem Hornwerck im Centro und der rechten Flügel Front Redoute lag, ricochirten den Weg herunter, bis diesseits dem Gate Work, wie viel solte uns wohl jede Ablössung kosten, zwischen dem Lager und N° 3, da keine einzige Traverse, viel weniger Sappe, 1500 Schritt lang gemacht ist, wenn der Feind zur Zeit der Dämerung einige Stücke herunter die Strasse ricochetteren liess. und wäre diesses nicht unssere eigene Schuld? Diesse Nacht wurden die Sappen lincks zur Eröffnung der 3^t paralele 136 Schritt in Fronte avancirt, und zugleich eine 2te Sappe am rechten Flügel, zu einer 3^t paralele geöffnet.

Apr. 20. Ein Capt. (Ewald) und 30 Jäger lincks, und 1 Lieut. (Kling) und 30 rechts, besezten die Sappen zur 3^t paralele. Unssere Büchssen lincks hatt[en] Kern Schuss in denen Schiesscharten der feindl: Front Redoute am Coopers so dass diesse Canonen unsserm rechten Flügel nicht haufig enfiliren konten, Ein Jäger wurde getroffen, diesse Nacht wurde am lincken und rechten Flügel die 3te paralele geöffnet, lincks wurde nach dem coopers river zu, der Laufgraben aufgeworfen, und rechts

and light infantry intended to attack the right wing of our works. Nothing happened, however. Perhaps the deserter was missed, and they saw themselves betrayed. During the night that part of the second parallel which was finished the night before was reinforced and the earthworks repaired, for the moonlight was too bright to sap in front. On the right as well as on the left wing of the second parallel bomb batteries were built. Both sides threw some shells during the night.

Captain von Bodungen with thirty jägers occupied the April 19 right wing of the second parallel, Lieutenant Schaefer the left. There were some infantry detachments besides. At nine o'clock in the morning our row-galleys left the Wappoo and went to Fort Johnson, the Admiral needing them for some other purpose. The enemy's batteries on the Ashley fired briskly. I went with Lieutenant Colonel Abercrombie as far as the gate-work to observe the firing. Two enemy 12-pounders of the half-moon battery, which was situated between the hornwork in the center and the right front redoubt, ricocheted down the road beyond the gate-work. How much was every relief between camp and No. 3 likely to cost us? For there was not a single traverse, much less a sap, for a distance of fifteen hundred paces, and at dusk the enemy could ricochet down the road with several pieces. Would it not be our own fault? During the night the saps at the left for the opening of the third parallel were advanced one hundred and thirty-six paces and another sap for the third parallel was dug at the right wing.

Captain Ewald and thirty jägers occupied the left saps for April 20 the third parallel, and Lieutenant Kling and thirty men the right one. Our rifles at the left shot point-blank into the embrasures of the enemy's front redoubt on the Cooper, so that these guns could only infrequently enfilade our right wing. One jäger was struck. During the night the left and right wings of the third parallel were opened. On the left a trench

nach der Strasse zu, die Bomben Batterien in der 2^t paralele bessezt, und hinter der am lincken Flügel der 2^t paralele, Bettung und Pulver Magazien für 1 – 10 Zoll Haubize verfertiget, auch die 2te paralele mit mehreren Traversen und Auftritten versehen; Und da durch einen Uberlaufer die Nachricht gekomen war, dass der Feind einen Ausfall unternehmen wolte, so wurde in der Eile auf der Hauptstrasse in Linie mit dem feindlichen Thore, 160 Schritte hinter der 2ten Paralele, eine Batterie en barbette für 2 engl: 6^{lbr} und 2 hessische Feldstücke aufgeworfen, und die Stücke aufgefahren, Von dem Ausfall wurde nichts—. Der Feind warf die Nacht 41 Bomben auf die Arbeiter, ohne grossen Schaden anzurichten.

Apr. 21– Ein Capt. (Hinrichs) und 30 Mann, besezten die vorige Nacht geöffnete paralele und 80 engl: Grenadiers waren unter die Jäger melirt, 1 Lieut. (v. Winzingerode) und 30 M. an rechten Flügel, der Feind suchte uns en flanc zu enfiliren, nemlich von der Front Redoute seines rechten Flügels, nach unsserm rechten Flügel, und von seiner lincken Front Redoute nach unsserm lincken. 3 flanckirende Stücke seines rechten Flügels, brachten die Jäger zum Schweigen, so dass der Feind ohne Verlust sich nicht bey der Schiesscharte sehen lassen durfte. 2 andere Schiesscharten, die in obliquer Linie mit unsser paralele lief, brachte ich mit 7 Bomben zum Schweigen, indem ich aus der 2^t[en] paralele mir vom Capt: Lossum zwey Royals holen liess. Eine Bombe brachte ich gerade auf das Platform, sie sprang wie sie fiel, schleüderte 2 Artilleristen aus der Schiessscharte in Graben, und das feindliche Platform in die Luft. Gegen Mittag kam eine Flagg in truce heraus, die 6 Stunden Waffenstillstandt verlangte, um eine gute Capitulation zu machen, der Waffenstillstand wurde ihnen zugestand[en] und nach dem Admiral von unsserer Seite geschickt, weil ihre Forderung[en] aber übertrieben waren, so wurde aus der Capitulation nichts, (vide Beylage) und

was thrown up in the direction of the Cooper River and on the right a trench leading toward the road. The bomb batteries in the second parallel were manned. Behind the battery on the left wing of the second parallel a platform and a powder magazine were built for one 10-inch howitzer. Furthermore, the second parallel was provided with several traverses and banquettes. Since a deserter informed us that the enemy intended to make a sally, we built in great haste a battery in barbette for two English 6-pounders and two Hessian fieldpieces on the main road in line with the enemy's gate, one hundred and sixty paces behind the second parallel; the pieces were mounted, but nothing came of the sortie. In the course of the night the enemy threw forty-one shells at the working party without doing much damage.

With thirty jägers I occupied the left wing of the parallel *April 21* opened last night (there were eighty English grenadiers interspersed with the jägers), Lieutenant von Winzingerode and thirty men the right one. The enemy tried to enfilade us with flanking fire, i.e. our right wing from the front redoubt of their right wing, and our left from their left front redoubt. Three flanking pieces of their right wing were silenced by the jägers, and the enemy could not let themselves be seen at the embrasures without loss. Two other embrasures, which ran in an oblique line with our parallel, I silenced with seven shells from two royals which I had obtained from Captain Lawson and mounted in the second parallel. One shell I succeeded in getting right onto their platform. It burst as it fell, throwing two artillerymen from the embrasure into the trench and blowing up the enemy's platform. Toward noon a flag of truce came out, requesting cessation of hostilities for six hours in order to make a good capitulation. The truce was granted, and we sent for the Admiral; but because their demands were unwarranted nothing came of the capitulation (*vide* enclosure). At ten o'clock in the night our guns and

um 10 Uhr des Abends, spielten unssere Canonen und Bomben Batterien so starck, wie sie noch nie gethan hatten. Diesse Nacht wurde die 3te Paralele erweitert, sie lief nach dem Centro zu, vorwärts, so dass der rechte Flügel der paralele lincks und der lincke Flügel der paralele rechts, die nächste am feindl: Verhacke war, und ganz am lincken Flügel, der 3^{t} paralele lincks, da, wo ich gestern die 2 Royals hatte gebettet, wurde eine Bomb[en] Batterie von 12 royals und 1 – 7 Zoll Haubize ausgestochen und bessezt, am rechten Flügel der 3^{t} paralele rechter Hand, wurde eine andere Bomben Batterie ausgestochen.

Apr. 22. 1 Capt. (v. Bodungen) lincks, 1 Lieut. (Schaefer) rechts, bessezten die 3^{t} paralele. Unssere Jäger hatten schon allenthalben Kernschüsse, so dass der Feind nicht ohne Schaden zur lincken, seine Ambrasen öffnen durffte. Diesse Nacht wurde am rechten Flügel besser vorwarts Sappirt, und am lincken Flügel, das vorige Nacht aufgeworfene Stück der 3^{t} paralele verstärkt, und mit mehreren Traversen versehen, und Pulver Magaziens für die 2 avancirte Bomben Batterien angelegt.

Apr. 23. 1 Capt (Ewald) lincks, 1 Lieut. Kling rechts, besezten das avancirte Werck, und schossen sich mit denen feindlichen Büchssenschüzen herum, die an ihrem rechten Flügel contre approchen gemacht hatten, und an ihren lincken von der Brustwehr der Front Redoute feüerten. Diesse Nacht wurde die 3te paralele unssers lincken Flügels, rechts bis 10 Schritt vom feindl: Gatter Thor und Graben fort geführet, und am rechten Flügel wurde sie lincks bis aufs feindl:e Glacis erweitert, doch war der lincke Flügel der nächste, am lincken Flügel wurde eine neüe Bomben Batterie angelegt und bessezt.

Apr. 24. 1 Capt. (Hinrichs und 30 M. lincks, 1 Lieut. (v. Winzingeroda) und 30 Jäger rechts, wurden heüte Morgen um 3 Uhr vom General Major Leslie beordert, die Avancirten Wercke zu bessezzen. Wie ich an den vorige Nacht aufgeworfenen Theil kam, so liess ich meine Jäger halten, und recognoscirte mit

batteries played more violently than ever before. During the
night the third parallel was extended. It was intended to
come to a point in the center, so that the right wing of the
left parallel and the left wing of the right parallel were closest
to the enemy's abatis. At the extreme left of the left section
of the third parallel, at the same spot where I had mounted
the two royals yesterday, a battery for twelve royals and one
7-inch howitzer was thrown up and manned. Also, on the
right wing of the right section of the third parallel a bomb
battery was thrown up.

Captain von Bodungen occupied the left, Lieutenant April 22
Schaefer the right part of the third parallel. The enemy were
now everywhere within point-blank shot of our jägers, so
that they could not open their embrasures at the left without
loss. During the night new saps were advanced on the right
section, while on the left the new part of the third parallel
was reinforced and provided with several traverses. Also,
powder magazines were built for the two advanced bomb
batteries.

Captain Ewald occupied the advanced work on the left, April 23
Lieutenant Kling on the right. Both parties exchanged many
shots with the enemy's riflemen, who had built counterapproaches on their right wing and were also firing from the
breastwork of their left front redoubt. During the night the
left section of the third parallel was continued to the right
to within ten paces of the enemy's gate-work and ditch,
while the right section was continued to the left as far as
the enemy's glacis. The left section, however, was closest.
Here a new bomb battery was built and manned.

I was ordered by Major General Leslie at three o'clock April 24
this morning to take thirty men and occupy the left of the
advanced work, while Lieutenant von Winzingeroda with
thirty jägers was to proceed to the right. When I arrived at
the part thrown up last night, I had my jägers halt, while I

2 M. das Werck, indem ich unssere leichte Arbeit kannte, und wusste dass wir mitten unter den feindlichen Aussenwercken stachen, und keine einzige Traverse in einem 400 Schritt langen Graben sahe. Jch ging bis am feindl: Gatterwerck. Der Tag wolte aber anbrechen, und in demsselben Augenblick schickte der Feind 2 enfilirende Kugeln, uns aus seiner lincken Front Redoute in Graben, die eine enfilirte en flanc den ganzen Graben hinnunter bis wo die Sappe war: die andere en revers schlug 100 Schritt diesseits dem Gatterwerck in Rücken des parapetts. Jch liess meine 2 Jäger am Ende des Grabens halten, und ihr Augenmerck auf das Gatterwerck richten, lief zurück nach denen brittish: Gren: in d. 2^t parallele holte 1 Soffr. 12 M. (von der 42. Gren. Comp:) und liess ohngefehr im Centro des Laufgrabens eine Traverse machen, der General Leslie kam zu mir, und wunderte sich dass noch keine Jnfanterie da war, und danckte mir vor meine Mühe. Meine Jäger lies ich während dessen Sandsäcke holen, und auf das parapet legen, Kaum war ich 6 Schue in der Erde, so gab es eine Gekreisch im Centro (nemlich in dem Raum der zwisch[en] der 3. Paralele rechts—und lincks noch war) Jn demsselben Augenblick feüerte mein doppelter Posten, den ich oben hatte stehen lassen, und die Arbeiter die jensseits der Traverse stundten, kamen herüber gesprungen und riefen d...me the rebels are there. Jch sprang aufs Parapet, und als ich den Feind sahe, welcher aus einer an seiner lincken Flügel Front Redoute liegend[en] Bariere auf unssern rechten Flügel schon aufgeprescht war, und jezt aus dem Gatterwerck heraus drang, so liess ich meine Arbeiter zum Gewehr greifen, zog die 2 Jäger diesseits der Traverse, und liess ein immerwährendes Feüer längst dem unbessezten Theil der paralele bis zum Gatterwerck machen, der Feind war schon über 50 Schritt hinten uns,* indem er an unsserm rechten Flügel durch gedrungen war, und zwischen der 3^t und 2^t paralele zum Theil

* A partial correction from *hinten raus*.

myself and two men inspected the work, for I was aware of
our light way of building and knew that we were right
under the enemy's outer works. There was not a single traverse in a trench four hundred paces long. I went as far as
the enemy's gate-work. But as day was breaking, the enemy
sent two enfilading shots from their left front redoubt into our
trench, one of them enfilading *en flanc* down the entire trench
as far as the sap, while the other, *en revers*, struck the back
of the parapet a hundred paces this side of the gate-work.
I had my two jägers halt at the end of the trench to watch
the gate-work while I ran back to the British grenadiers in
the second parallel. I brought one noncommissioned officer
and twelve men (of the grenadier company of the 42nd Regiment) and had a traverse made approximately in the center of
the trench. General Leslie came and was surprised that no infantry was here yet. He thanked me for my labors. In the
meantime I had my jägers fetch sandbags and lay them on the
parapet. While in the trench, which was barely six feet deep
where I stood, I heard a loud yelling in the center, i.e. in
the space that was still between the right and the left section
of the third parallel. At the same moment the double post
I had left standing above fired, and the workmen on the other
side of the traverse came running over crying "D . . . me the
rebels are there." I jumped on the parapet and when I saw
the enemy, who were already pressing upon our right wing
from a barrier situated at their left wing front redoubt and
were also rushing out of the gate-work, I had my workmen
seize their muskets, withdrew the two jägers this side of the
traverse, and opened a continuous fire along the unoccupied
part of the parallel as far as the gate-work. The enemy, having penetrated our right wing, were already more than fifty
paces behind us, partly between the third and second parallels.
I ordered some jägers and Corporal Rubenkoenig behind the
traverse and had them fire behind the trench across the plain.

sich befandt. Jch wurf einige Jager mit dem Corporal Rubenkoenig hinter die Traverse, und liess sie hinter dem Graben,
längst der plaine feüern. Unssere 2te paralele fing an zu feüern,
dies brachte uns viele Kugeln im Rücken und als an unsserm
rechten Flügel die 2^t Paralele hervor preschte, so zog sich der
Feind, mit Zurucklassung 20 Gewehre zurück, deckte aber
seine Retraite mit so einem überschwenglichen Schauer von
Cartetsch[en], in welche alte zersprungene Bomben, zerbrochene Schippen, Hacken, Beilen, BügelEissen, Pistolen Laufe,
zerbrochene Schlösser etc etc geladen waren, (welche Stücke
wir im Graben fandten) enfilirte uns mit seiner am lincken
Flügel liegenden Front Redoute (15 Kugel stacken in der von
mir aufgeworfenen Traverse) dass kaum einer den andern, der
dichte bey ihm standt, hören konte. Es war noch dämericht,
der Dampf des Pulvers so dicke, dass man Freünd und Feind
nicht erkennen konte, und da ich nicht wissen konte, ob der
Feind schon retirirte, sprang ich aufs parapet und liess meine
Jäger und Grenadier längst dem Laufgraben und auf die
Schiesscharten, ein so immerwährendes Feüer machen, dass
nach ½ Stundte Canonade die feindlichen Batterien schwiegen.—Oberst Parcker wurde in der Schiesscharte mit mehreren Artilleristen erschossen, wie wir den Abend von einem
Uberlaufer erfuhren. Jch kam mit einem leicht, mit dem
Bajonet blessirten Engländer davon, das ganze Parapet wo
ich mit meinen Leüthen standt, war über 1 Fus vom feindl:
Batterie Feüer rasirt worden; Welches Glück! unsser rechter
Flügel wosselbst Lt Winzingeroda mit 30 Jägern und 25 light
Jnf: standt, kam nicht so gut weg, 1 light Jnfanterist wurde
erschossen, 5 blessirt, 2 Jäger mit dem Bajonet blessirt und
3 Gefangen, wovon einer einen Schuss in Leib hatte. Sie
musten auf die 2te paralele repliciren, da ihnen durch die
Nachlässigkeit der Engländ[e]r, der Feind zu geschwinde auf
den Halss kam, und sie ohne Unterstuzzung mit abgeschos-
senen Büchssen gegen Bajonetter ohnmöglich stehen konten.

Now our second parallel began to fire. This made many bullets fall in our rear. But when the second parallel pressed forward on our right wing, the enemy withdrew, leaving twenty muskets behind. But they covered their retreat with so excessive a shower of canisters which were loaded with old burst shells, broken shovels, pickaxes, hatchets, flat-irons,[1] pistol barrels, broken locks, etc., etc. (these pieces we found in our trench) and so enfiladed us at the same time from the front redoubt of their left wing (fifteen balls were embedded in the traverse I had thrown up) that one could hardly hear another close beside him. It was still dark, and the smoke of the powder was so thick that one could not tell friend from enemy. Since I could not know that the enemy had withdrawn, I jumped on the parapet and had my jägers and grenadiers keep up such a hot fire along the trench and upon their embrasures that after half an hour's cannonade the enemy's batteries were silent. A deserter told us in the evening that Colonel Parker and several artillerymen were killed in an embrasure. I suffered no loss except one Englishman slightly wounded with a bayonet. The entire parapet where I stood with my men was razed more than one foot by the enemy's battery. What luck! Our right wing, where Lieutenant von Winzingeroda was stationed with thirty jägers and twenty-five light infantry, did not get off so well. One light infantryman was killed, five wounded; two jägers had bayonet wounds and three, one of whom had a bullet wound in the abdomen, were taken prisoners.[2] They were compelled to repair to the second parallel because through the

[1] Colonel Oliver L. Spaulding, Jr., suggests "stirrup irons," translating *Bügeleisen* as though it stood for *Steigbügeleisen*.

[2] De Brahm and McIntosh agree that twelve prisoners were taken. Furthermore, Thomas Moultrie, brother of General Moultrie, was killed. The entire party consisted of two hundred Virginians and South Carolinians under the command of Lieutenant Colonel Henderson (W. G. Simms, *South Carolina in the Revolutionary War* . . . . [Charleston, 1853], p. 132).

Von Capt. Lossum von der Artillerie hatte ich 2 Stücke, welches eine Art Cohorns war, und die er wie Swivels hatte zurechte machen lassen, geliehen bekoen, Sie waren metallen und hatten eine Kammer, und waren auf der Delaware Fregatte erbeütet worden, diesse thaten mir heüte herrliche Dienste, indem meine Jäger keine patronen mehr hatten, (ich bekam um 10 Uhr 15 frische Leüthe) und 2 Comp: light Jnf. vom Lager aus zum Soutein). Diesse Lossums, (wie ich sie nennen will) trieben eine Hand Granade 1800 Fus, Jch schoss ausserdem 100 Mussketen Kugeln, 3 lb Case Shots und $\frac{1}{2}$ lb bogy Shots, und that den Tag über 130 Schuss damit. Der Feind suchte mit Canonen mich zum Schweigen zu bringen, ein Zeichen, dass Sie Dienste thaten, ich rückte aber von einer Stelle zur andern damit, und jagde manchmal 3–4 Schüsse, jeden mit 100 Musketen Kugeln in die feindliche Schiesscharten. Diesse Nacht ward diesser Theil der Paralele welcher ziemlich war ausgeschossen worden, wieder ausgebessert, und mit mehreren Traversen versehen, auch der Anfang einer neüen Sappe gemacht, am lincken Flügel der 3^t paralele lincks. Das Signal bey einem Ausfalle für die ganze Linie, war ein 3 maliges Hurray an unsserer Seite. Ein bösses Signal. Etwa 20–30 vom Feind liessen sich beym Gatterwerck sehen, unssere nächste Jnfanterie Posten der Bedeckung gaben das Signal und feüerten, Jeder rief das Signal die Arbeiter liefen zurück, die 2te paralele sahe diesse koen, hörte das Hurray, glaubte es wäre Feind und gab Feüer, und in kurzem war ein so überschwenckliches klein Gewehr, Canonen und Bomben Feüer von beyden Seiten, das bis um 2 Uhr in die Nacht währete, ehe der Jrthum allenthalben aufgekläret werden konte, als nur zu dencken möglich ist. Wir verlohren dabey 1 Offr todt (71) und mehr denn 50 todt und blessirt, und unssere Arbeiter konten wenig oder gar nichts die Nacht machen.

Apr. 25.   1 Capt. (v. Bodungen) etc. bessezte heüte die Fronte. Es war

negligence of the English the enemy was upon them too quickly, and without support they could not make a stand with discharged rifles against bayonets. From Captain Lawson of the Artillery I had borrowed two pieces resembling coehorns, taken on the *Delaware* frigate, which he had changed into swivels. They were made of brass and had a chamber. They served me splendidly today, for my jägers had no more cartridges. (At ten o'clock fifteen fresh men and two companies of light infantry came to support me.) These Lawsons, as I shall call them, threw a hand grenade 1,800 feet. I also fired 100-bullet canisters, 3-pound case shot, and ½-pound bogy shot, firing in the course of the day 130 shots. The enemy tried to silence me with cannon, a sign that our fire was effective. However, I moved from one place to another with my pieces and sometimes fired three to four 100-bullet canisters into the enemy's embrasures. During the night this part of the parallel, which was pretty well shot to pieces, was repaired again and provided with several traverses. Likewise, a new sap was begun on the left wing of the left section of the third parallel. The signal that the enemy was making a sortie along the whole line was a threefold "Hurray!" on our side—a fatal signal, indeed! About twenty to thirty of the enemy were seen at the gate-work. Our nearest infantry post on guard gave the signal and fired. Everyone repeated the signal; the workmen ran back; the second parallel saw them coming, heard the "Hurray!" believed they were enemies, and fired. Within a short time there was a tremendous fire of musketry, cannon, and shell on both sides. It was two o'clock in the morning before everyone realized that it was a mistake. We had an officer killed (71st) and more than fifty [men] killed and wounded. Besides, our working parties could accomplish little or nothing during the night.

Captain von Bodungen, etc., occupied the front today. April 25

ziemlich ruhig. Einige Tage nach dem Ubergang des OberstL^t
Webster, mit 23. 33. Legion, war 64. und die Cav: der light
Jnf: auch übergegangen, und 63 war ins verlassene Lager von
33 bey dem 71 R^{gt} von James island herüber gekommen; das
Commando von 63 und Huyne auf Forth Johnstone war von
2 Comp: des R^{gt} v. Ditfourths unter Commando des Major v.
Borks abgelösset worden, Heuyne stand bey denen Schiffen,
und 3 Comp: von v. Ditfourth standten bey der Ferry, wo die
Newyork Volontairs gestanden, die zu uns herüber kamen,
und grösten theils bey denen Canonen eingetheilet wurden.
42. war bey Gibsons ins Lager gerückt, und gab Commandos
mit in die Tranchéen. Queens Rangers stunden im Rücken der
Armée, bey Quarter House, wo die Legion gestandten hatten,
und Jrish Volontairs South- und North Caroliner, welche mit
dem General Patterson heüte herüber gekoṁen gingen diesse
Nacht mit Lord Cornwallis über den Cooper River, um zu
dem Detachement des OberstL^t Webster zu stossen; Es war
noch 1 Canonen Boot, und 2 Flachboots mit Caronaden über
Land nach dem Cooper River gebracht worden, und diesse
hatten einen feindlichen Scooner aufgefangen. Die 2 feindliche
Fregatten Providence und Ranger hatten sich unter den Canonen der Stadt hinter die Versenckung gelegt, und waren die
einzigen die noch Canonen inne hatten, die übrigen waren in
die Wercker gebracht worden; Brig: Gen: Patterson kam an
der Stelle des Lord Cornwallis von James Jsland herüber, um
den Dienst in der Linie zu thun. Der Lord Cornwallis sties
mit seinem armirten Flachboot auf einen feindl: Scooner, er
rief ihm zu, gleich die Seegel zu streichen. Diesser that es,
und das armirte Boot nahm—einen Scooner mit 4. 6 lb,
gefangen. Die vorige Nacht angefangene Arbeit, wurde diesse
Nacht fort gessezt, mehrere Traversen in der 3^t Paralele
gemacht, und am lincken Flügel der 3^t paralele lincks in

---

[1] The original does not make it clear whether two schooners were captured this day or whether this is the boat referred to just above. The latter

It was rather quiet. Several days after Lieutenant Colonel Webster had withdrawn and crossed over with the 23rd, the 33rd, and the Legion, the 64th and the cavalry of the light infantry crossed the river, while the 63rd arrived from James Island and went into the vacated camp of the 33rd, close to the 71st. The detachment of the 63rd and Huyn's at Fort Johnson has recently been relieved by two companies of the Regiment von Dittfurth under Major von Borck. Huyn's was stationed near the ships, and three companies of von Dittfurth's were posted at the ferry where the New York Volunteers had been. The latter came over to us and were for the greater part distributed among the guns. The 42nd had encamped at Gibbes' and furnished detachments for the trenches. The Queen's Rangers were stationed in the rear of the army at the Quarter-House, where the Legion had been. The Irish Volunteers and the South and North Carolinians, who came over today with General Paterson, went this night with Lord Cornwallis across the Cooper River to join the detachment of Lieutenant Colonel Webster. Another gunboat and two flatboats with carronades have been taken overland to the Cooper River and have captured an enemy schooner. The two enemy frigates *Providence* and *Ranger* have withdrawn behind the boom below the guns of the city. They were the only ones still in possession of cannon, the rest of them having been taken into the works. Brigadier General Paterson came over from James Island to do service in the line in place of Lord Cornwallis. The latter encountered with his armed flatboat an enemy schooner. He called to her to strike her sails at once. This was done, and the armed boat was captured, a schooner with four 6-pounders.[1] The work begun last night was continued tonight. Several traverses were made in the third parallel, and at the left wing of the left

is more probable. Von Hinrichs occasionally repeats himself, giving more details the second time.

Linie mit der feindlichen Halfmoon Batterie und denen feindl:
contre approchen voraus Sappirt bis auf 70 Gänge, und diesse
Sappe mit gehorigen Traversen versehen. Die lincke face
dersselben gab dem Jäger einen geraden Schuss in der feindlichen Front Redoute an seinem lincken Flügel. Am rechten
Flügel wurde der Weg über den Morast in der Sappe von 2–
zu 3 Parale [sic] mit Horden und Roster von Balken verbessert, indem das Wasser bey der Fluth zu hoch war.

Apr. 26. Ein Capt. Ewald etc. bessezten diessen Tag die Fronte. Das
Feüer war gemässigt, unssere Batterie N° 7 litt am meisten,
sie war leichtssinnig gemacht, 2 Canonen darinnen demon-
tirt, und fast alle Schiesscharten ausgewühlet: Der Admiral
war Tag und Nacht bemühet, eine Möglichkeit ausfindig zu
machen, seine Schiffe den Coopers river herauf zu bringen,
allein es blieb ohnmöglich ohne sicheren Verlust der Schiffe,
diesses Unternehmen zu wagen; Diese Nacht wurde im Centro
der 3ᵗ Paralele lincks (ohngefehr da wo ich die erste Traverse
hatte machen lassen) eine Bomben Batterie für 7 royals und
10 Zoll Bomben Kessel trassirt, lincks in der Paralele eine
Batterie für 2 12ˡᵇʳ, die auf die Front Redoute des Feindes
am Coopers River spielen solte, und am Ende der paralele
beym Gatterwerck eine Batterie für 4 24ˡᵇʳ, die auf die
Semi Bastion rechts der feindl: Hornworks am Thor spielen
solten, abgestochen und aufgeworfen, und Pulver Magaziene
und Sappen zu densselben ausgestochen.

Apr. 27. Ein Capt. (Hinrichs) rechts, 1 Lieut. (v. Bartholmai) lincks,
besezten heüte die Fronte. Unssere Arbeiter arbeiteten jezt die
Hälfte in der Nacht, die Hälfte bey Tage, weilen die meisten
jezt vorhabende Arbeit in der 3ᵗᵉⁿ paralele gemacht wurde.
Jch bekam 170 light Jnf. bey mir, liess sogleich mehrere
Sandsäcke aus dem Magazin holen und füllen, und von diessen
ordentliche Schiesscharten auf die feindl: richten, bessezte
jeden Posten mit 5 Jäger und 15 Engländer, wovon immer
einige mit gespannten Hahnen im Anschlag liegen musten,

section of the third parallel, in line with the enemy's half-moon battery and their counterapproaches, we advanced our sap to within seventy paces and provided it with strong traverses. The left face of it afforded the jägers a direct shot into the enemy's front redoubt on their left wing. On the right wing the road in the sap through the swamp from the second to the third parallel was improved by means of hurdles and pileworks, for it was under water at high tide.

Captain Ewald, etc., occupied the front today. The fire April 26 was moderate. Our battery No. 7 suffered most, since it had been built carelessly. Two of its guns were dismounted, and almost all embrasures were torn to pieces. The Admiral exerted himself day and night to find the safest way of bringing his ships up the Cooper River. But it was impossible to venture upon this task without certain loss of the ships. During the night we marked out a bomb battery for seven royals and 10-inch shell-throwing mortars in the center of the left section of the third parallel, approximately where I had the first traverse made. On the left of the parallel we marked out a battery for two 12-pounders that were to play on the enemy's front redoubt on the Cooper River, and at the end of the parallel, at the gate-work, we marked out and threw up a battery for four 24-pounders, which were to play on the demibastion at the right of the enemy's hornwork at the gate. We also dug some powder magazines and saps for them.

I occupied the right front today, Lieutenant von Barthol- April 27 mai the left. Half of our workmen were on duty during the day, the other half during the night, for most of the work was being done in the third parallel. My detachment was strengthened by 170 light infantry. I immediately had my men fetch some sandbags from the magazine and fill them, and with them we made strong embrasures facing those of the enemy. I stationed five jägers and fifteen Englishmen at every post, some of whom had to stand at all times with

so dass bey der geringsten Bewegung bey der feindlichen
Canone, sogleich die Kugel mit ihm sizzen muste. Capt.
Sutherland schickte mir noch 150 Arbeiter, indem ich ihm
zeigte, wie losse das parapet sey, und dass jede Kugel vom
Feind durchschlüge. Jch liess hierauf den ganz[en] Laufgraben, der 482 Schritt lang war, 4 Fus verdicken, und 3 Fus
verhöhen. Auftritte vor die Jnfanterie machen, planirte, und
fashinirte eine presch Batterie, für 1 – 24- und 1 – 12 lbr,
die auf die feindl: Front Redoute des lincken Flügels spielen
solte, liess eine Bomben Batterie aus stechen, und ganz am
rechten Flügel eine andere Canonen Batterie planiren, und
zulezt ein Canal rückwärts nach dem Morast zu graben, um
das Wasser aus der paralele und Sappe zu ziehen; Der Feind
konte nicht mehr wie eine Canone den Tag über abhauen,
indem er vor denen Büchssen nicht zum Laden kommen konte.
Er suchte durch Kuhhäuthe die Schiesscharten zu maskiren,
allein so wie die Hauth sich rührte flog[en] die Kugeln von
denen im Anschlag liegenden Jägern in die Scharte, lächerlich
genug dass er keine ordentliche manteletten machte. Jch
verlohr einen Arbeiter von 42. der mit einem Doppel Hacken
aus einem Hausse in der Stadt erschossen wurde, denn so gar
hinter ihren Sandsäcken auf dem Walle, hatten wir sie weg
gejagd.

Den Nachmittag kam Lord Cornwallis nach Habcaw
Ferry, der Feind verliesse es, mit Zurucklassung 4 Canonen,
und noch vor Abend, standt unssere Flagge auf dem Forth.
3 Ruder Galeeren, the new Vigilant (18 – 18 lbr) 1 armirter
Scooner legten sich heüte in Spencers Jnlet, und feüerten sich
mit der feindl: bridge Batterie auf Mount pleasant herum.
Diesse Nacht wurden die Batterien in der 3ᵗ paralele lincks
fertig, und die Stücke aufgefahren, und in der 3ᵗ paralele
rechts die eine Canonen batterie und Bomben batterie zu
gleich, Die Stücke waren aus Nᵒ 7. genommen worden, gegen
welche der Feind seine Stärcke gerichtet hatte und gänzlich

cocked and leveled arms, so that upon the slightest movement about the enemy's guns they would get our bullets.
Captain Sutherland sent me one hundred and fifty more workmen, since I had shown him how loose the parapet was and
that every enemy bullet was going through. Now I had the
entire trench, 482 feet long, made 4 feet thicker and 3 feet
higher. We made banquettes for the infantry, leveled the
ground, and piled up fascines for a breach battery of one 24-
pounder and one 12-pounder, which were to play on the front
redoubt of the enemy's left wing. We also threw up a bomb
battery, leveled the ground for another battery at the extreme
end of the right wing, and, lastly, dug a ditch toward the
swamp in the rear to draw the water from the parallel and the
sap. The enemy could touch off but one gun in the course of
the day, for they could not load them on account of our
rifles. They tried to mask the embrasures with cowhides;
however, as soon as a hide moved, the bullets of the jägers,
who were posted with cocked and leveled rifles, struck into
the embrasure. Ridiculous of them not to have built real
mantelets. I lost only one workman from the 42nd, who was
killed with a double-barreled blunderbuss from a house in
the city, for we had chased the enemy away even from behind
their sandbags on the rampart.

In the afternoon Lord Cornwallis arrived at Hobcaw
Ferry. The enemy deserted it, leaving behind four guns. And
before evening our flag was hoisted on the fort. Three row-
galleys, the *New Vigilant*, with eighteen 18-pounders, and one
armed schooner went to Spencer's Inlet today and exchanged
shots with the enemy's bridge battery on Mount Pleasant.
During the night the batteries in the left section of the third
parallel were completed and the pieces mounted, while in
the right section a gun battery and also a bomb battery were
built. The pieces were brought over from No. 7, against which
the enemy had been concentrating their fire and which, com-

zusammen geschossen, die jezt gänzlich abandonnirt wurde. Einige 24 lbr waren aus N°. 2 genommen.

Apr. 28. Ein Capt. (v. Bodungen) rechts, 1 Lieut (Kling) lincks, besezten die Front paralele, der Feind wurf mehrere Bumben in unssere Wercke, doch ohne grossen Schaden zu thun. Ein feindlicher Überlaufer von der Artillerie zeigte ihr Pulver Magazien an unssere Bomben Batterien an, Unssere Bomben am rechten Flügel hatten den wenigsten Schaden gethan, indem sie grösten Theils auf den common Plaz gefallen waren. Schon seyd einigen Tagen waren aus denen Schottisch[en] Rgmtrn Mineurs, an der Zahl 50 heraus gezogen worden. Diesse Nacht wurde eine 2te Sappe ganz am lincken Flügel unssers lincken Flügels, in Linie mit der feindlichen Front Redoute am Cooper River nach dem Damm zu, welcher das Wasser des feindlichen Grabens gestaudet, und von heüte an, dasselbst zur Ableitung des Wassers gearbeitet. Die Platform zu der Canon Batterie am rechten Flügel rechts, wurde heüte gelegt, und die Batterien inwendig faschienirt, und die 3t paralele rechts mehr, durch Traverse vor denen feindlichen Enfiliren aus der Front Redoute am Cooper, gedeckt. Der Feind brandte seit wir vor seinem Verhacke waren, alle Nacht zwischen dem 1t u 2t Verhack eine Menge mit Pech und combustibles gefüllete Fässer, die das approchiren von unsserer Seite hindern solten.

Apr. 29. 1 Capt. Ewald lincks, 1 Lieut, Winzingeroda rechts, waren heüte aussen Der rechte Flügel war mit light Jnf: der lincke mit Grenadiers melirt. Diesse Nacht wurden am rechten Flügel die Schiesscharten für die 2 – 24 lbr ausgeflochten, es wurden einige dabey blessirt, die Schiesschart[en] wurden hierauf maskirt. 2. 7. und 9 zöllige Haubizen kamen rechts und lincks in die avancirten Bomben Batterien. Der Damm war durchgestochen, und dass Wasser lief $\frac{3}{4}$ Zoll p. Stundte, und den andern Tag ein Zoll, so dass der berührte 10 Fus breite Graben bald möchte trocken seyn. Unssere Arbeiter

pletely shot to pieces, was now abandoned. Several 24-pounders were removed from No. 2.

Captain von Bodungen occupied the right of the front April 28 parallel, Lieutenant Kling the left. The enemy threw several shells into our works but without doing much damage. A deserter from the enemy's artillery showed our bomb batteries where their powder magazine was. Our shells from the right wing had done the least damage, for the greater part of them had fallen on the Common. Several days ago fifty sappers were taken out of the Scottish regiments.[1] Last night they dug a second sap at the extreme end of our left wing in line with the enemy's front redoubt on the Cooper River and leading toward the dam which backed the water up the enemy's ditch. During the day they worked to drain it. A platform was built today for the gun battery at the right end of the right wing, and the batteries were lined with fascines. A traverse was thrown up in the right section of the third parallel to make it safer against enfilading fire from the enemy's front redoubt on the Cooper. Since we have been in front of the enemy's abatis they have kept burning all night between their first and second abatis a number of barrels, filled with pitch and combustibles, to prevent us from advancing.

Captain Ewald was on the left front today, and Lieutenant April 29 von Winzingeroda on the right. The right wing had some light infantry, the left some grenadiers. During the night the embrasures for the two 24-pounders were lined with wickerwork (some of our men were wounded while at work), whereupon the embrasures were masked. Two 7- and 9-inch howitzers were taken into the advanced right and left bomb batteries. The dam was pierced, and the water drained three quarters of an inch an hour and the following day one inch,

[1] The Scottish regiments were the 42nd Highlanders and the 71st or Fraser's Highlanders, since disbanded.

thaten wenig, indem die Hälfte Mannschafft erst bey Tage kam, und arbeitete.

Apr. 30. 1 Capt. (Hinrichs) 30 Jäger rechts, 1 Lieut. 30 Jäger lincks. Jch bekam 200 Light Jnf: bey mir, der Feind schoss ziemlich, ich liess die Jäger blos auf die Canonen und Schiesscharten anschlagen, und die light Jnf: sich mit denen feindl: Büchssen-schüzen amusiren. die ich dann und wann durch einen case shot aus 3 royals secundirte. Muste gegen Mittag frische Batronen aus dem Magazien holen lassen, und sezte meine 2 Lossums ganz an lincken Flügel der paralele folglich im Centro des ganzen. 3. 18 lb-Kugeln brachte der Feind in unssere Paralele, und jedesmal an einen andern Flecken, indem er die Canone über die Banck feüerte woran die Jäger ihn nicht hindern konten. Den Nachmittag schickte mir Capt. Sutherland 50 Hess: Grenadiers zur Arbeit, und ich muste ein 2ᵗ Pulver Magazien mit einer doppelten Sappe aus stechen lassen. Beym Ausstechen bekam ich einen Streifschuss am rechten Bein ohne Schaden, und eine Canon Kugel begrub mich im Sande. Der Feind arbeitete den ganzen Tag an einer Lauf-graben Cummunication von seiner lincken Front Redoute zur Linie, und verpallisadirte einen trockenen Graben in Front des Laufgrabens.

Diessen Morgen landete der Admiral mit 200 Mariniers auf Lampre's Point, woselbst er 7 Canonen fand, und eine Batterie anlegte.[1] Major Ferguson recognoscirte heüte von Habcaw herunter, und glaubte es wäre Feind, und schoss sich mit den Mariniers ¼ stundte herum. Comet Galley und Re-nown men of War, wolten sich an die bridge Batterie auf Mount pleasant machen und fuhren veste, Ersteres ging ver-lohren, die Renown kam wieder los.— Diesse Nacht wurde die Batterie am rechten Flügell rechts mit 2 – 24 ˡᵇʳ bessezt, Die

---

[1] The Admiral remained on the *Roebuck* in Charleston harbor. It was Lord Cornwallis who took possession of the deserted works on Lempriere's Point.

so that the said ditch, ten feet wide, will probably be dry soon. Our workmen accomplished but little, for half of them did not come to work till after daybreak.

With thirty jägers I occupied the right, a lieutenant and thirty jägers the left. I received a detachment of two hundred light infantry. The enemy kept up a rather brisk fire. I had the jägers aim only at the guns and embrasures and let the light infantry have their fun with the enemy's musketry, supporting them now and then with case shot from three royals. Toward noon I had to get more cartridges from the magazine. I mounted my two Lawsons at the very end of the left wing, i.e. in the center of the parallel. The enemy succeeded in firing three 18-pound balls into our parallel, each one at a different spot, for they were firing the guns over the barbette, which the jägers could not prevent them from doing. In the afternoon Captain Sutherland sent me a working party of fifty Hessian grenadiers. I had my men dig out a second powder magazine with a double sap. While so engaged a shot grazed my right leg without injuring me, and a cannon ball covered me with sand. The enemy worked all day on a communicating trench between their left front redoubt and the line. They also picketed a dry ditch in front of the trench.

This morning the Admiral with two hundred sailors landed on Lempriere's Point,[1] where he found seven guns. He threw up a battery. Major Ferguson reconnoitred today down the Hobcaw and, believing them to be enemy, fired at the sailors for a quarter of an hour. The *Comet* galley and *Renown* man-of-war, intending to attack the bridge battery on Mount Pleasant, ran aground. The former was lost;[2] the latter got afloat again. During the night two 24-pounders were mounted in the battery on the right wing of the right section. This battery was given to the marines, as was the

April 30

---

[2] The editor has been unable to verify the loss of the *Comet* galley.

Marine bekam diesse, und die am Gatterwerck, welche am rechten Flügel der paralele lincks lag, zu commandiren. Und da die Auftritte bey der lossen Erde nicht halten wolten, wurden etliche 1000 Fashienen diesse Nacht in die vorderste paralele gebracht, um die Banck damit am Tage aus zu flechten, und die Auftritte vester zu machen.

Maij. 1– 1 Capt. (v. Bodungen) lincks, 1 Lieut. (v. Winzingeroda) rechts. Unssere Batterie N° 7, war abandonirt, N° 2 halb ledig, und N° 6 konte blos die Facen vom Coopers River her, bestreichen, desswegen sich der Feind bemühete unssere vorderste Batterien zu rasiren. Wir verlohren einige Jäger dabey. Den Nachmittag wurde wenig geschossen, Diesse Nacht wurde die Batterie am rechten Flügel der Paralele lincks, die vor dem feindlich: Gatterwercke lag, ausgebessert, und mit 18 Fus dicken Traversen versehen, um das enfiliren zu verhindern. Auch wurde ein Pulver Magazien bey der Bomben Batterie im Centro diesser paralele fertig.

Maij. 2. 1 Capt. (Ewald) 1 Lieut. (Schaeffer) rechts, Der Feind suchte die Batterien der Front paralele zu beschädigen, und brachte einige Bomben in Graben. Gegen Mittag kam das 64te R^{gt} wieder über den Cooperriver herüber, und brachte 22. Gefangene mit, unter welchen der Sohn des Rebel Governeurs in Charlestown war; die Gefangenen wurden auf die Schiffe gebracht. Diesse Nacht wurde die paralele lincks verstärckt und die Batterie für 2 – 12 lb mit Traversen verssehen. Die Mineurs arbeiteten mit gutem Erfolg an Ableitung des feindl: Canals.

Maij 3. Es waren verschiedliche Uberlaufer diesse Tage eingekommen, Jhre Nachrichten stimmten nicht überein. es war natürlich. indem kein Rgmt zu dem andern gelassen wurde, und jedes sein bessonderes Lager hatte. Der neülich vom General Washington geschickte französsische Jngenieur fing an, ihre Wercke alle hinten zu schliessen. Das Horn Work im centro war beynahe fertig—D. 30 Apr. hatte der Feind seinen be-

one at the gate-work on the right wing of the left parallel. Since the banquettes were not firm enough because of the loose earth, some thousand fascines were brought into the front parallel during the night in order to line the embankment the following day and so strengthen them.

Captain von Bodungen occupied the left, Lieutenant von Winzingeroda the right. Our battery No. 7 has been abandoned; No. 2 was only half occupied, and No. 6 could rake no more than the faces from the Cooper River. Therefore the enemy endeavored to raze our advanced batteries. This caused us to lose several jägers. In the afternoon there was but little firing. During the night we repaired the battery in front of the gate-work on the right wing of the left section of the parallel. To prevent the enemy from firing enfilading shot down the parallel we threw up some traverses eighteen feet thick. We also completed a powder magazine at the bomb battery in the center of this parallel. *May 1*

Captain Ewald occupied the left, Lieutenant Schaeffer the right. The enemy tried to damage the batteries of the front parallel and were successful in getting several shells into the trench. Toward noon the 64th Regiment returned from the other side of the Cooper River, bringing along twenty-two prisoners, among them the son of the rebel governor in Charleston.[1] The prisoners were taken on board the ships. During the night the left parallel was reinforced and the battery of two 12-pounders provided with traverses. The sappers worked with good results at bleeding the enemy's ditch. *May 2*

Within the last few days several deserters had come to us. Their reports did not agree. This was quite to be expected, for no regiment was permitted to have communication with any of the others, each regiment having its own encampment. The French engineer recently sent by General Washington began to close all their works in the rear. The hornwork in *May 3*

[1] See p. 79, note 1.

sten Bombardier einen Major der Artillerie, durch eine Büchs-
senkugel verlohren. Diesse Nacht wurde ein ander Pulver
Magazien fertig, und Laufgraben hinter der bresh Batterie der
Front paralele gemacht. Der von Lord Cornwallis erbeütete
Scooner hatte einen 18 [1br] bekommen, und holte diesse Nacht
ein grosses abgetackeltes 3 mastiges feindl: Schiff, welches
zwischen Habcaw und der Stadt lag, und vormals ein Gefan-
genschiff gewessen war, Es wurde nach der Ship Yard oberhalb Governors Hauss gebracht, ohne dass wir einen Mann
dabey verlohren.

Maij. 4. Diessen Morgen als das Jäger Detachement wie gewöhnlich
hinnaus marchirte, schlug eine Canon Kugel diesseits N° 3,
7 Jäger nieder, 1 verlohr das Bein, der andere wurde mit
dersselben Kugel am dicken Bein blessirt, und 5 von Splittern
eines abgeschlagenen Baums, gegen welchen die Kugel fuhr.
Den Nachmittag wurde noch ein Jäger erschossen. Diesse
Nacht wurde ganz am lincken Flügel der 2^t paralele hart am
Morast des Coopers eine Batterie für 2 Stück angelegt.

Maij. 5. 1 Capt. (Ewald) etc. gingen heüte einen andern Weg hart
am Ashly auf N° 1 zu, und längst den Laufgraben. etc etc.
Unssere Batterie in der 3^t paralele waren noch alle maskirt
und schossen nicht Der Feind enfilirte sie en Revers und zum
Theil en Flanc, und sie litten sehr.—*Der Fehler lag in der 2^t
Paralele.* Weil durch die Überlaufer von unssrer Seite dem
Feind die Ablössungen der Arbeiter um 3 Uhr des Morgens,
war bekannt worden, und er desswegen von der Zeit an, bis
zum Tage, ein immerwährendes auf der Strasse sich creüzen-
des ricochett feüer machte, so ging ich heüte Nachmittag

---

[1] The editor has been unable to ascertain the name of this major of the
artillery. In his entry for May 12 Hinrichs makes the same statement after
entering the city. Major John Gilbank, an able engineer, was accidentally
killed on the 11th of April while making experiments with shells. It is not
unlikely that he is the major in question, for Hinrichs remarks (p. 295) that
after he had been killed the Americans had "no one who could make good
fuses."

the center was almost closed. On the 30th of April the enemy lost their best bombardier, a major of the artillery, who was killed by a rifle shot.[1] During the night we completed another powder magazine and dug trenches behind the breach battery of the front parallel. The schooner captured by Lord Cornwallis, on which we had mounted an 18-pounder, took a large unrigged three-masted enemy ship during the night; it lay between Hobcaw and the city and had formerly been a prison ship.[2] It was taken to the shipyard above the Governor's house without the loss of a single man.

This morning, when the jäger detachment marched out to the front as usual, a cannon ball struck among seven jägers this side of No. 3. One of them lost a leg, a second received a wound in the thigh (from the same shot), and the other five were injured by splinters of a felled tree against which the ball struck. In the afternoon a jäger was killed. During the night a two-gun battery was thrown up at the extreme end of the left wing of the second parallel, close to the swamp on the Cooper. *May 4*

Captain Ewald, etc., took a different route today. They went along the Ashley toward No. 1 and then followed the trenches, etc., etc. All our batteries in the third parallel were still masked and did not fire. The enemy cannonaded them with enfilading reverse fire and with flanking shot, doing considerable damage to them. *The trouble lay in the second parallel.* Since the enemy had found out from deserters from our side that the working parties were relieved at three o'clock in the morning, they poured an incessant ricochet cross fire *May 5*

---

[2] De Brahm (Simms, *op. cit.*, p. 140) refers to this vessel as a hospital ship, as does McIntosh also (*ibid.*, p. 143). Captain Ewald (p. 79) states that it had sick Negroes on board, and in the manuscript journal of the Grenadier Battalion von Platte it is said that it was full of smallpox patients (Lowell, *op. cit.*, p. 249).

hinnaus, und stach mit Strohwischen einen andern Weeg rechts an der Strasse ab, auf welchen nur 3 Schiesscharten spielen konten. Diesse Nacht wurde die Batterie in der 2^t paralele, die vorige Nacht angefangen war, völlig fertig, und die auf der Strasse 160 Schritte hinter der 2^t paralele liegende Batterie en barbette, mit 3 Schiesscharten versehen, ausgeflochten und stärcker gemacht.

Maij 6.   Jch marchirte diessen Morgen mit dem Commando den neüen Weg, und nur eine Kugel kam nahe. Jch ging lincks, der Lieut. Schaefer rechts. Unssere Arbeiter waren fleissig gewessen, sie hatten vieles gemacht, aber nicht viel; Z.E. Wir stachen mitten in dem feindl:^{n} Wercke. Unssere 3^t Paralele lief nach dem centro zu mit obliquer Linie des feindlichen Durchschnittes. Keine einzige Canone von den feindl: vorliegenden Redout[en] war zum Stillschweigen gebracht wòrden.   folglich enfilrte en revers sein lincker Flügel unssern lincken, und sein rechter unssern rechten, und auch diessen Fehler hatte man nicht einmal durch gehörige *hinlängliche* Traversen, oder ein und ausspringende Winckel zu verbessern gesucht. Der Feind bemühete sich, diessen [   ] so viel möglich zu Nuze zu machen, und schoss rasch. Die Jäger hielten ihn zwar im Zaum, dass er den Tag über seine Schiesscharten nicht viel öffnen durfte, und nur verstohlner weisse einen Schuss manchmal aus einer oder andern Canone geben konte, aber desto mehr feüerte er in der Nacht, und rasirte diesse neüen so leicht gemachte Batterien, dass den andern Morgen genug aus zu bessern war. Von unsserer Seite wurden einzelne Bomben geworffen, und beständiges Jager Feüer unterhalten. Ich liess 300 Sandsäcke den Tag füllen, und ordentliche Schiesscharten auf dem parapet für die Büchssen in Richtung mit den feindlichen Schiesscharten machen, Den

¹ Hinrichs' amanuensis, it seems, slipped and unwittingly garbled this phrase. Translated less freely this sentence would read: "They had done much but not many things." This is still twisting the German con-

upon the road from that time until daybreak. Consequently, this afternoon I went out and with wisps of straw marked out a different route, which lay to the right of the causeway and on which only three embrasures could play. During the night the battery in the second parallel which had been begun last night was finished, and the battery in barbette situated 160 paces behind the second parallel was provided with three embrasures, lined with wickerwork, and reinforced.

I with my command followed the new route this morning. May 6 Only one shot came near us. I proceeded to the right, Lieutenant Schaefer to the left. Our working parties had been industrious. They had done much, but left many things undone.[1] For instance, we were right upon the center of the enemy's works; our parallel ran obliquely to the axis of the enemy's fortification, but not a single gun of their advanced redoubt had been silenced. Consequently, the enemy enfiladed with reverse fire our left wing from their left and our right from their right. Nor has any attempt been made to correct this mistake by means of substantial and *sufficient* traverses, or salient and reëntering angles. The enemy sought to take the greatest advantage of this [   ] and fired briskly. The jägers, to be sure, kept them sufficiently under control, so that they could not open their embrasures often and could fire only a furtive shot from some gun or other. But so much more did they fire at night, razing these new, so lightly built batteries that the following morning there was much to be repaired. We threw some shells, and the jägers kept up a constant fire. I had my men fill three hundred sandbags in the course of the day, and with them they made regular rifle embrasures on the parapet, opening on those of the enemy. At five o'clock in the afternoon, when we were

---

siderably, for it really says the opposite. However, the phrase is: *nicht vieles, sondern viel; non multa, sed multum.*

Nachmittag 5 Uhr, wie wir in Bauung diesser Schiesscharten begriffen waren, gab uns der Feind eine Lage von 13 Canonen, die unter die Sandsacke schlugen, diesse in die Luft nahmen, und in den Graben fielen. Glücklichr weisse wurde kein Jäger blessirt, obgleich allenthalben sie im Anschlag lagen, theils die Sandsacke zu rechte richteten. Der Wind und Sand wurf uns alle übern Haufen. Einige Gewehre wurden zerschlagen.

Diesse Nacht wurden unssere Batterien alle fertig, und mit Amunit: verssehen, der Feind feüerte so starck, wie er noch nie gethan hatte. Um 1 Uhr wurde in der Stadt Lerm geschlagen. Das Gekreische wolte kein Ende nehmen, und es schien als ob ein janisches [*sic*] Schrecken unter ihnen gekom̃en wäre.

Maij. 7- Heüte wurde noch mit Tragung der Amunition zu gebracht, und die Sailors batterie am Gatterwerck besser verstärckt. Gegen Mittag bekamen wir die Nachricht von der Einnahme des Forth Moultrie. Ferguson von der einen Seite und mariniers von der Richmond Fregatte von der andern, landeten um sich der bridge Batterie, (die hinten geschlossen war) zu bemächtigen, in welcher der feindl: Capt Williams mit etlichen und 20 Mann standt. So bald diesser die Landung der mariniers erfuhr, glaubte er, es wären einige Matrossen, die Vieh holen wolten, und ging mit seinen Leüthen hin, um sie zu verjagen. Major Ferguson war jezt auch gelandet, und beyde Partheyen zusam̃en bekam̃en jezt den Capt Williams mit allen seinen Leüthen, ohne einen Schuss zu thun, gefangen, ging mit ihnen auf die Bridge Batterie zu, es war nichts wie Artillerie in dersselben, und das Thor war offen, kamen alsso in ruhigen Bessiz diesses Wercks, ohne dass die Bessazung vom Forth Moultrie davon etwas erfuhr. Sobald als unssere Trouppen Bessiz von diessem Wercke hatten, schickten sie durch einen Trommelschläger, um 2 Uhr die Nacht eine Aufforderung an das Forth und hängten diesser

making these embrasures, the enemy gave us a volley from thirteen guns that struck beneath the sandbags, which flew up into the air and fell into the trench. Fortunately, not a single jäger was wounded, although they were either standing with leveled rifles or putting the sandbags in place. The blast and the sand knocked all of us down. Several rifles were broken to pieces.

During the night all our batteries were finished and provided with ammunition. The enemy fired more briskly than ever. At one o'clock there was a tumultuous noise in the city. It seemed as though the yelling would never end, as though a panicky fear had seized them all.

This day was spent in carrying more ammunition and in *May 7* strengthening the sailors' battery at the gate-work. Toward noon we received the news of the taking of Fort Moultrie. Ferguson had landed on one side and the marines of the *Richmond* frigate on the other in order to take the bridge battery (it was closed in the rear), which was manned by Captain Williams and some twenty men. When he heard of the landing of the marines, he supposed they were some sailors who had come to get cattle, so he went with his men to chase them away. By this time Major Ferguson, too, had landed, and the two parties now took Captain Williams and all his men prisoners without firing a shot. With the prisoners they went to the bridge battery. There were only artillery in it, and the door was open. Thus they quietly came into possession of this work without the garrison of Fort Moultrie hearing anything about it. As soon as our troops had occupied this work, they dispatched a drummer to the fort at two o'clock in the morning, with a summons to surrender. To this summons was attached a letter in which "the Admiral advised that they accept this arrangement, and that, in case the garrison should not surrender before daybreak, he would take position below the fort with six ships and play their

Aufforderung einen Brief bey, "worinnen der Admiral ihnen "diesse Verrichtung anbefohlen hatte, und dass wenn die Bes- "sazung des Forths nicht vor Tages Anbruch übergäbe, er "sich mit 6 Schiffen unter dasselbe legen wolte, und seine "Canonen spielen lassen. Der Commandant des Forths, war durch die ganz unerwartete Bessiznehmung der Bridge batterie, und diesser nächtlichen Bedrohung so sehr überrumbelt, dass er sich ergab. Die Capitulation war honorable. 1) Die Conti- nental Trouppen zu Kriegs gefangenen. 2). Die Miliz auf parole nach ihren respe Häussern zu gehen, nachdem sie die Waffen niedergelegt, 3). fur Krancke und blessirte solte Sorge getragen werden, 4). Die ganze Besazung ihre Bagage und die Offrs ihre Seiten Gewehre zu behalten, 5). mit klingendem Spiel aus zu marchiren. 6). Canonen, Amunition, Provision in dem jezigen Stand zu überliefern. etc etc

Es fand sich ein ansehnlicher Vorrath an lebendig[em] Vieh, Brodt, Mehl und Rum, Brunnen zu Wasser, waren mehrere da, aber kein Salzfleisch. 40 Canonen von 6–24^{lbr} und 1 – 10 Zoll Haubize, mit 125 Bomben und Amunition hinlänglich. Die Wichtigkeit diesses Forths in unssern Hän- den, war augenscheinlich. Unssere Schiffe konten jezt nach 5 Fathom Hole gehen, und jeden ankom̄enden Feind hintern uber die Bar zu gehen, folglich war uns der Haffen gesichert. unssere Transport-Schiffe konten jezo von Stono abgehen, und wir hatten unmittelbar Communication mit ihnen bey Forth Johnston, und konten folgl: unssere Chaine mehr concentriren.

Heüte Nachmittag bekamen wir die Nachricht von einem 2^t Uberfall der feindlichen Cavallerie, durch unssere am San- tie bey Hell Hole Swamp. Das erstemal hatte OL^t Tarleton sie kurz vor dem Ubergang über den Cooper überfallen, und jezt war der Rest aufgerieben. so dass fast kein einziger davon gekom̄en war, und eine Menge ersoffen. Oberst Washington und Oberst White (der Bailie's Light Dragoons commandirte und seyd kurzem aus Norden angekom̄en war, und täglich

guns upon it." The commandant of the fort was so dumfounded by the unexpected taking of the bridge battery and by the threat at this hour of the night that he surrendered. It was an honorable capitulation: (1) The Continental troops to be prisoners of war; (2) the militia to lay down their arms and then return home on parole; (3) the sick and wounded to be cared for; (4) the entire garrison to retain their baggage and the officers their side arms; (5) to march off with drums beating and trumpets sounding; (6) guns, ammunition, and provisions to be delivered in their present condition, etc., etc.

We found respectable stores of livestock, bread, flour, and rum. There were several good wells, but no salt meat. Furthermore, we got possession of forty guns, 6- to 24-pounders, one 10-inch howitzer with 125 shells, and considerable ammunition. The importance of having this fort in our possession is apparent. Our ships could now go to Five-Fathom Hole and prevent any arriving enemy ships from crossing the Bar. We were consequently in safe possession of the harbor. Our transports could now leave the Stono, and we had direct communication with them by way of Fort Johnson. We could, therefore, tighten our chain around the city.

This afternoon we received the news of our cavalry surprising the enemy's cavalry a second time, at the Santee near Hell-Hole Swamp. The first time Lieutenant Colonel Tarleton had surprised them shortly before crossing the Cooper, and this time the rest were annihilated. Hardly any of them got away, and many were drowned. Colonel Washington and Colonel White (who was commanding Baylor's Light Horse[1] and had a short time ago arrived from the North and was

[1] At Lenud's Ferry Colonel Anthony White's troops consisted of some dragoons he had brought from the North, of the remains of Brigadier General Huger's cavalry, and of a detachment of Colonel Horry's Light Horse. It must have been Colonel William A. Washington who commanded Baylor's Light Horse.

sein R^{gmt}, das auch unterwegs war, erwartete) retteten sich zu Fus, sprangen in Santie und schwammen durch.

Maij. 8– Da jezt unssere presch Batterien alle fertig waren, wurden in voriger Nacht die Ambrasseurs geöffnet, und mit Anbruch des Tags eine nochmalige Auforderung der Stadt und Garnison gemacht. Die ganze jensseitige Küste des Coopers war in unsserer Hand, von Cain hoi bis Forth Moultrie, folglich alle mögliche Communication dem Feind abgeschnitten, seine ganze Cavallerie aufgerieben, keine Jdee von Succurs, dessen ganze Force in der Stadt concentrirt, unssere Wercke bis vor ihren Graben, diesser Graben auf 100 Schritt lang schon trocken, und wurde jeden Augenblick mehr trocken. Forth Moultrie und der ganze Haffen in unsserer Handt. 2 Stundten Bedenck Zeit wurden ihm gewähret, diesse immer und immer prolongirt, diesses dauerte bis 6 Uhr Abends; Verschiedliche Puncte waren schon vest gessezt, und auf einmal wurde abgebrochen, (vide Beylage) Um 8 Uhr Abends war der Waffenstillstandt zu Ende, Der Feind liess auf alle Glocken in der Stadt läuten, und nach einem 3 maligen Hurray, machte er ein solches unbändiges Batterie Feüer die ganze sinckende Nacht hindurch wie noch nie geschehen war. es war ein betrunckenes Feüer, denn ich glaube es war die ganze Garnison voll.—Diesse Nacht approchirten unssere Arbeiter von dem lincken Flügel der rechten Paralele rechts, durch den feindl: Fosse und 20 Schritt hinter dem Verhack. und aus dem centro diesser paralele nach dem detachirten Front Werck des feindl: lincken Flügells.

Maij. 9. Den Morgen fingen unssere Batterien und Bomben mit mordendem Feüer an zu spielen. Die feindliche Front Redoute des lincken Flügells demolirten unsser 1 – 24^{lbr} der auf dasselbe spielte, so gleich in der ersten Salve, aber noch geschwinder war ein anderer hinnein gebracht, der in 2 Stund[en] die ganze 4 Canonen Batterie dessen lincken Flügel Front Redoute zum Stillschweigen brachte, 2 Canons davon in Stücken schoss,

expecting his regiment any day), got away on foot, jumped into the Santee, and swam to safety.

Since all our breach batteries were now completed, the embrasures were opened last night, and at daybreak, a second summons was sent to the city and the garrison. The entire opposite side of the Cooper from Cainhoy to Fort Moultrie was in our hands. Thus every possible communication of the enemy was cut off. All their cavalry was annihilated. They could not entertain the least hope of succor. Their entire force was concentrated in the city. Our works came up to their ditch. This ditch was already dry for a distance of a hundred paces and was becoming drier every moment. Fort Moultrie and the entire harbor were in our hands. They were given two hours for consideration. This time was prolonged again and again. Several points had already been agreed upon, when suddenly, at six o'clock in the evening, negotiations were broken off (*vide* enclosure). At eight o'clock the armistice was over.[1] The enemy rang all the bells in the city and after a threefold "Hurray!" opened a cannonade more furious than any before, keeping it up until it was completely dark. It was a drunken fire, for I believe that the entire garrison was intoxicated. During the night our workmen dug approaches from the left wing of the right parallel through their fosse to within twenty paces of the abatis and from the center of this parallel to the detached front work of their left wing.

In the morning our guns and howitzers opened a murderous fire. The first salvo of the enemy's front redoubt of the left wing demolished our 24-pounder which was playing upon it. Immediately another 24-pounder was mounted, which within two hours completely silenced the four-gun battery of that redoubt. Two of the guns were shot to pieces, and all four embrasures were demolished to such an extent that we could

May 8

May 9

---

[1] This was on the 9th, not on the 8th. Hinrichs probably made his entries several days after the truce.

und alle 4 Schiesscharten umwühlte, dass keine mehr zu sehen war, Der Feind hatte alle seine Schiesscharten mit Manteletten verssehen, aber eine Stangen Kugel machte die Schiesscharten rein, und gab dem Jäger einen frey[en] Schuss.

Maij. 10. Das Feüern dauerte den Tag durch, und diesse Nacht wurden eine Menge Bomben geworfen, der Feind wurf seyd 14 Tagen wenige: Es kam die im Forth Moultrie bekomene 10 Zoll Haubize diesse Nacht den Ashly River herauf, und wurde in die 3ᵗ paralele rechts gebracht.

Maij. 11- Der Feind hielte diesses Feuer ab, und erwiederte es bis gegen Mittag da eine abermalige Flagge heraus geschickt wurde. Das Feüern war so heftig dass man sie nicht kom̄en sahe, und sie musten wieder retiriren. Um 2 Uhr den Mittag steckte der Feind eine grosse weisse Fahne auf dem Hornwork aus, und schickte eine 2ᵗᵉ Flagge, in welcher er eine Ubergabe der Stadt etc etc auf die von unsserer Seite ihm angebottene Capitulation, antrug Waffenstillstandt wurde ihm gewähret, zum Admiral geschickt, der um 8 Uhr den Abend kam, und um 11 Uhr des Abends, war die Haupt-Capitulation richtig.

Maij. 12. Obgleich die Ubergabe der Stadt, so gut als vest gessezt war, musten dennoch das gewöhnliche Jäger Detachement heüte Morgen heraus. Jch kam lincks bey dem Gatterwerck, sezte meine Posten am Thor Weege, und fertigte die Flagg in Truces ab. die bis um 12 Uhr Mittags gewechsselt wurden, und blos Nebenpuncte enthielten. Nicht die Ubergabe selber, sondern die Art dersselben. Um 12 Uhr war noch keine Möglichkeit die Miliz zusam̄en und unter das Gewehr zu bring[en] und nur die Drohungen des Gr: Leslie, dass er seine Soldaten wolte in die Hausser quartieren, war fähig, sie in etwas unter die Fahne zu bringen.—Sobald alles bestimmt, die Artickeln (vide Beylage) unterschrieben und ausgewechsselt waren, so wurde das Gatterwerck durch Pioniers nieder gebrochen, und die Brücke gedeckt, um Canonen tragen zu können. Jch muss gestehen, die Empfindung, die in meiner Seele vorging, da

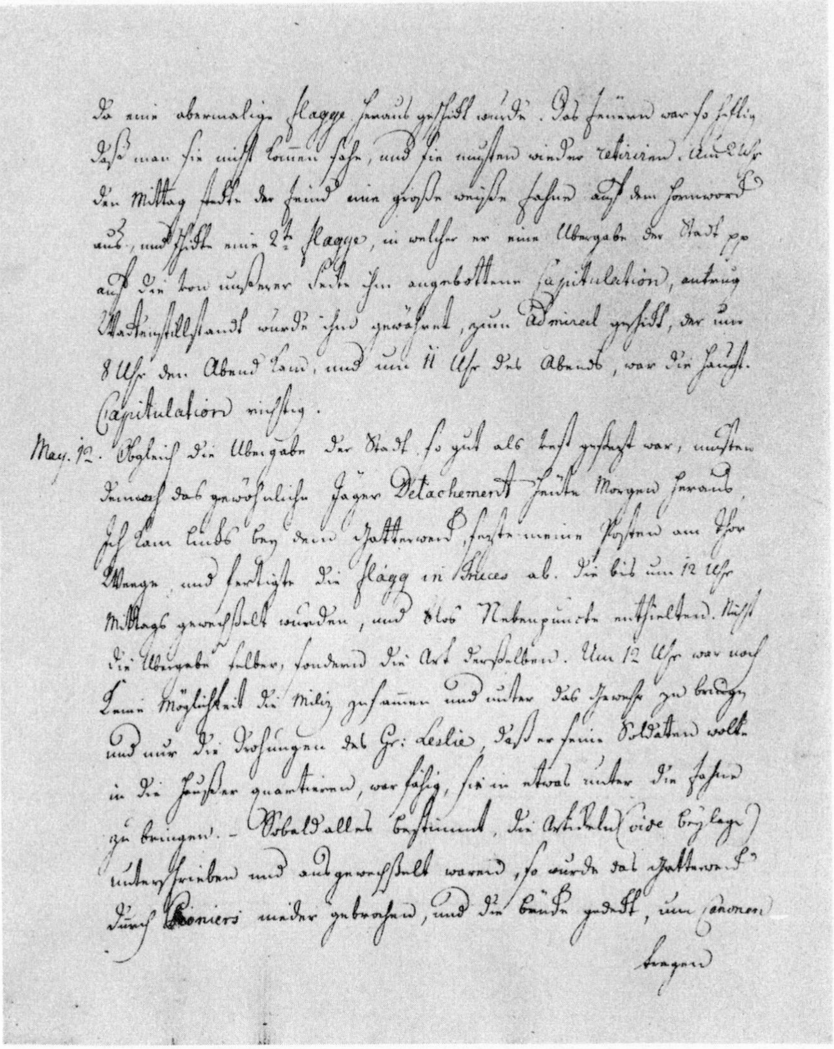

PLATE V

FACSIMILE PAGE OF HINRICHS' DIARY
(About one half of original size)

not make them out any more. The enemy had provided all their embrasures with mantelets; but our crossbar shot tore them down most effectively, giving the jägers a good target.

The cannonade lasted the entire day, and during the night *May 10* a great number of shells were thrown. The past fortnight the enemy have been throwing but few of them. The 10-inch howitzer taken at Fort Moultrie was conveyed up the Ashley River in the night and mounted in the right section of the third parallel.

The enemy stood our fire well and returned it till about *May 11* noon, when again a flag was sent out. But since our fire was so violent that we did not see them coming, they were compelled to withdraw. At two o'clock in the afternoon the enemy hoisted a large white flag on the hornwork and dispatched a second flag, offering the capitulation of the city, etc., etc., on the terms we had proposed. We granted a truce, sent for the Admiral, who arrived at eight o'clock in the evening, and at eleven o'clock at night the principal points of the capitulation had been agreed upon.

Although the surrender of the city was almost certain, *May 12* nevertheless the jäger detachment had to go out as usual. I took position at the left of the gate-work, stationed my posts at the gateway, and dispatched the flags of truce, which were exchanged until noon and which concerned only minor points, i.e. not the capitulation as such, but the manner of carrying it out. At noon the enemy had not yet succeeded in bringing together the militia and in getting them under arms. Only when General Leslie threatened to quarter his soldiers in their houses could some of them be summoned to the colors. As soon as everything had been agreed upon and the articles (*vide* enclosure) signed and exchanged, our pioneers tore down the gate-work and covered the bridge, so that we could take guns over it. When with a noncommissioned officer and two men I went over the banquettes for the

ich mit einem Soffr.—und 2 Mann zuerst über die Laufbäncke ging, die Pioniers dann mit einem Krach das zerschossene Gatterwerck umstürzten, und ich dann Posto jensseits demsselben faste und nun die feindlichen Schildwachten sich zurück ziehen musten, diesse Empfindung war geschwinder, war stärcker gefühlt, denn ausgedrückt! General Major Leslie war zum Commandant der Stadt ernannt worden, um 2. Uhr ritten diesselben mit einer starcken Suite Staabs Officiers und Adjutanten an der Spizze 2er Grenadier Compagnien, neml: der 7^t brittischen, commandirt bey ObL^t Hope und der hess: guarde grenad: Compagnie, commandirt bey OL^t v. Linsing, jede Compagnie mit ihrem Bat: feldstücke in die Stadt, hinter diessen folgte die Königliche Flagge. am Thore hielte General Major Lincoln zu Pferdte, und Gr. Maj: Moultrie zu Fus, und übergaben die Stadt. So wie die brittisch[en] Grenadiers unter das Thor kamen, bliessen die Hauboisten God bless King George etc Die Grenadiers nahmen hierauf Bessiz vom Hornwerck, und pflanzten ihre Canonen auf dem Plaçe d'armes hinter dasselbe, nach der Stadt zu. Hierauf wurde ich mit 20 Jäger und 20 Light Jnf: der 7^t Comp: commandirt, unter Befehl des OberstL^t York (welcher ältester Staabs Officier der Tranchéen war,) eine Chaine zwischen dem Verhacke und feindl: Aussenwercken zu ziehen, und die feindliche Garnison, welche dasselbst ihr Gewehr strecken solten zu empfangen. Die ganze Bessazung der Linie muste im Gewehr bleiben, und die Jäger unter Major v. Wurmb, und light Jnf: unter OL^t Abercrombie aus dem Lager in die 2te paralele rücken, und dasselbst so lange unterm Gewehr liegen, bis der Feind das Gewehr gestreckt hatte.

Sobald der OL^t York mit denen 20 Jägern und 20 light Jnf: posto gefast hatte, und die beyden Gren. Comp: vom feindl: Thor und Hauptwerck Bessiz genom̃en, so kam die feindl:^{e} Bessazung heraus, Sie hatten Erlaubniss mit klingendem Spiel (aber verdeckten Fahnen) aus zu marchiren,

first time, when the pioneers with a terrific crash demolished what was left of the gate-work, and when the enemy's posts withdrew and I took position on the other side, the resulting emotions, I must admit, followed in more rapid succession and were more intensely felt than they can be expressed. Major General Leslie was made commandant of the city. At two o'clock the commanders rode into the city accompanied by many staff officers and adjutants. They were followed by two grenadier companies, namely, the 7th British, commanded by Lieutenant Colonel Hope, and the Hessian guard grenadier company, commanded by Lieutenant Colonel von Linsing, each company bringing its battery of fieldpieces. Then followed the King's flag. At the gate the generals were received by Major General Lincoln on horseback and Major General Moultrie on foot, who surrendered the city. The moment the British grenadiers came under the gate the oboists played "God save the King." Then the grenadiers took possession of the hornwork and mounted their guns in the place of arms behind it, facing the city. Thereupon I with twenty jägers and twenty light infantry of the 7th Regiment was ordered to form a chain between the abatis and the outwork under the command of Lieutenant Colonel Yorke (who was the oldest staff officer of the trenches) and to receive the enemy garrison who were to pile arms there. All the troops of the line had to remain under arms, and the jägers under Major von Wurmb and the light infantry under Lieutenant Colonel Abercrombie had to move from their encampment into the second parallel, where they were to remain under arms until the enemy should have laid down theirs.

As soon as Lieutenant Colonel Yorke had taken post with the twenty jägers and twenty light infantry, and the two grenadier companies had taken possession of the gate and the main works, the garrison came out. They were permitted

durch [= doch] durften sie keinen engländischen Marsch spielen (spielten alsso den türckischen). Zuerst kam das Bat: artillerie, sodann 1. und 2. South Carolina continentals, dann 1. und 2. North Carolina 1. u 2. Virginier und das frey Bat: Französische und Span: Volontairs. Wie der Feind das Gewehr gestreckt hatte, wurde die Königl: Flagge auf das Thor ausgesteckt, und von unsserm Lager aus, mit 22 Canonen Schüsse salutirt, hierauf marchirte das 7te und 63te Rgmt mit klingendem Spiel und fliegender Fahne in die Stadt, und weil nur 500 Miliz den Tag in der Stadt konten in Reyhe und Glieder gebracht werden, und so zur Ablegung des Gewehrs gezwungen, eine grosse Menge dersselben noch in allen Haussern stachen, und diesse sowohl, als die Bürger der Stadt, mit Gewehr, Waffen und Amunition verssehen waren, so bate sich der General Major Leslie noch mehrere Rgtr aus, und noch vor Anbruch der Nacht, rückte 64, und 42 zur Verstärckung der Garnison in die Stadt, und campirten auf dem grossen Marcktplaz, indem 7- und 63 benebst denen Gren. Comp: die Wercke besezte. Die Gefangene wurden hierauf in öffentliche Gebaude, Baracken etc, unter gehörige Wachen gebracht, Die Offrs, welche ihre Seiten Gewehre behielten, und bey Tage Freyheit hatten, in der Stadt herum zu gehen, bis sie nach Haterals point in die Baracken konten gebracht werden.

So war denn diesser, aus mehr den einer Ursache wichtige Posten in unsser Hand,—Es war der Stapel des französisch Amerikanisch[en] Tausch-Handels, es war der einzige veste Haffen 2er Provinzen, die durch die Güte ihrer Producte nur in etwas die Balanz gegen die franzosisch, holländische Zufuhr halten konte, indem Jndigo, Baumwolle, Reiss, Producte sind, die der Kaufmann oft gerne dem baaren Geld vorzieht—es war endlich der Haffen, den England mit wenigen Schiffen, gegen die stärckste französische Macht vertheidigen kann, indem eine Sandbanck, die bey der höchsten

to march off with drums beating and trumpets sounding, but their colors had to be cased. Since they were not allowed to play an English march, they played the Turk's march. First came a battalion of artillery, then the 1st and 2nd South Carolina Continentals, the 1st and 2nd North Carolinians, the 1st and 2nd Virginians, and, lastly, a battalion of French and Spanish volunteers. As soon as the enemy had piled arms, the royal colors were hoisted on the gate and a salute was fired from our encampment with twenty-two cannon. Thereupon the 7th and 63rd Regiments marched into the city with music and flying colors. Since this day only five hundred militia could be got into rank and file and so compelled to deliver up their arms, the rest being still in the houses and, like the inhabitants of the city, provided with muskets and other weapons as well as ammunition, Major General Leslie asked for several other regiments. So the 64th and 42nd moved into the city before nightfall to strengthen the garrison. They were encamped on the large market square, while the 7th, the 63rd, and the grenadier companies occupied the works. Then the prisoners were taken into public buildings, barracks, etc., where a suitable guard was placed over them. The officers, who were permitted to retain their side arms and walk about in the city during daytime, were to stay here only until they could be taken into the barracks on Haddrell's Point.

Thus this port, important for more than one reason, was in our possession. It was the staple of the French-American trade. It was the only fortified harbor of two provinces which, because of the quality of their products, could to some extent hold a balance against the French and Dutch imports, for indigo, cotton, and rice are products which the merchant often prefers to cash. It is, lastly, a harbor which England can defend with a few ships against the strongest French

Fluth 17– bis 19¾ Fus Wasser nur trägt, die ganze Mundung desselben umgiebt, und so ein jedes Schiff, das über 40 Canonen führt, ohne vorherige Ausladung der untersten Reihe Canons, es ohnmöglich macht über die Bar zu gehen.—Amunition war haufig vorräthig, und Artillerie in Menge Es waren in der Stadt 290 Eisserne, 21 metallene Canonen, und mehrere grosse und kleine Haubizzen und Bomben Kessell. Ausser die 2 Fregatten Ranger und Providence, welche noch alle ihre Canonen inne hatten Ausserdem bekamen wir 40 Canonen im Forth Moultrie (jezt wieder Forth Sullivan genant. 7 Canonen auf Lambriers point und 4 auf Habcaw.—Was die feindl: Fortification und ihre Vertheidigung betrifft, so wie unssere Attaquen auf diesselbe, diesses verspare ich bis zur Verfertigung des Plans, an welchen mich jezt völlige Ohnmöglichkeit gehindert hat, ihn zu Standte zu bringen. Jhre Artillerie war besser den unssere, und ihr eigen Geständniss, dass blos das klein Gewehr seyd Eröffnung unsserer 3ᵗ paralele ihnen an 3–400 Todten und Blessirt[en] kostete, und dass sie nie ohne Verlust ihre Schiesscharten hatten öffnen können. Die Ursache, warum sie die lezte Zeit der Belagerung, so wenig Bumb[en] wurfen, war, dass ihr bester Bombardier, ein Major der Artillerie d: 30ᵗ Apr. war erschossen worden, und sie niemand hatten, der gute Brandröhren, an welchen es ihnen fehlte, verfertigen konte, weswegen auch die meisten Bomben crepirten.—Und so viel ist gewiss, wäre der vor 3 Wochen vom General Washington geschickte Franz: Jngenieur eher angekom̃en, so hätten wir eine noch viel saurere Arbeit bekommen—denn die Natur ist der Lage diesses Orts sehr günstig

force, since a sandbank which at high tide is seventeen to nineteen and three-quarters feet under water surrounds the entire inlet. Hence no ship carrying more than forty guns can cross the Bar without first unloading the lowest tier of cannon. We found abundant stores of ammunition and a great deal of artillery. There were in the city 290 iron and 21 brass cannon, as well as several large and small howitzers and shell mortars. Then there were two frigates, the *Ranger* and the *Providence*, which still had all their guns. In addition to these we got forty guns at Fort Moultrie, now called Fort Sullivan again, seven guns on Lempriere's Point, and four at Hobcaw. —As regards the enemy's fortifications and their defense, as well as our attack upon them, I shall wait till I have drawn my plan, which I have so far found no time to do. Their artillery was better than ours. They confessed that since the opening of the third parallel our small-arms fire alone cost them between three and four hundred killed and wounded and that they could never open their embrasures without losses. The reason why they threw so few shells during the latter part of the siege was that their best bombardier, a major of the artillery, was killed on the 30th of April and that they had no one who could make good fuses, of which they were in need. It was because of this that most of their shells failed to explode. This much is certain: had the French engineer sent by General Washington three weeks ago arrived earlier, our work would have been considerably harder, for nature has favored the situation of this town.

4ter Theil.

Von der Übergabe der Stadt bis zur Ankunft bey
dem Corps auf Philipsburgh.

Maij 13—Iunij 25—1780.

Maij 13. Da aller Drohungen des General Major Leslie ohngeachtet,
der General Lincoln die Militia gestern nicht hatte unters
Gewehr bringen können, 500 Mann ausgenommen, so wurde
heüte Morgen der ganzen Stadt proclamirt, binnen 2-mal 24
Stundten, in einem vormaligen kleinen Pulver Magazien
ohnweit die New Barracks, an denen dazu bestelten Artillerie
Officiers Capt. Collins und Lieut: Gordon, ihre Gewehre ab
zu liefern: Sowohl die Stadt als Land Miliz folgten diessem Befehl auf das genaueste, und da mehrere Gewehre geladen waren, und sie bey $\frac{1}{2}$ Duzent[en] ins Magazien hinnein
gewurfen wurden, erfolgte, was sehr wahrscheinlich zu vermuthen war—ein Gewehr schlug feüer, die Kugel schlug in
ein Pulverfass, und das Magazien flog in die Luft, Capt.
Collins, Lt Gordon, 15 Bombardiers und Canoniers und L^t
M'Klow von 42 mit 6 M: schildwachten, benebst einer Menge
Negroes, Artillerie Wagen, Pulver Karren, Pferdte, Geräthschafften, 2-3000 Gewehre, Büchssen, Patrontaschen u.s.w.
alles flog auf. Ein schrecklicher Anblick war es, Einige waren
zerschmettert, einige auf 200 Schritte an Mauren, und Thüren
geschleüdert, manchen waren die Armen, manchen die Beine
ausgerissen, und eine noch grössere Menge gequetscht, und
verbrennt, und beschädiget. 150 Schritte davon lag ein Magazien von 180 Fassern Pulver. Die Gewehre sprungen in der

Part Four

From the Capitulation of the City till our Arrival at
Phillipsburgh, where we Joined the Corps

May 13—June 25, 1780

Since, in spite of the threats of Major General Leslie, May 13
General Lincoln was unable to get the militia under arms,
five hundred men excepted, a proclamation was issued to the
entire city this morning calling on them to surrender their
arms within forty-eight hours to the artillery officers Captain
Collins and Lieutenant Gordon in a former powder magazine
near the new barracks. The town militia as well as the country militia obeyed these orders implicitly. Since several muskets were loaded and they were thrown into the magazine half
a dozen at a time, something happened that might well have
been foreseen. A musket went off; the bullet struck into a
barrel of powder and the magazine blew up. Captain Collins,
Lieutenant Gordon, fifteen bombardiers and gunners, Lieutenant M'Klow [?] of the 42nd with six guards, as well
as a number of Negroes, artillery wagons, powder carts,
horses, tools, 2,000 to 3,000 muskets, rifles, cartridge boxes,
etc.—everything blew up. It was a terrible sight. Some were
blown to bits, others thrown two hundred paces against
walls and doors; some had their legs torn off, others their
arms, and a still greater number were bruised, burnt, and
otherwise injured. One hundred and fifty paces away was a
magazine containing 180 barrels of powder. The muskets

Luft, die Lade Stöcker und Bajonette[n] stachen auf denen Dächern der Hausser, und 6 Stundten hernach ging[en] noch einige los. Das Feüer wurde gelöscht, aber der Schade, den diesse Unvorsichtigkeit angerichtet hatte, war gros, indem 1) die besten und geschicktesten Artificiers und Feüerwercker, welche ziemlich selten in englisch[en] Diensten sind, benebst dem würdigen Capt. Collins, und dem viel versprechend[en] Lieut. Gordon, auf so eine schändliche Art; dahin gerissen wurden, die ganze Belagerung kostete nicht so viel Artilleristen, und den Verlust der Gewehre misten wir, indem wir schon auf der Russian Merchand 4000 Stück verlohren hatten, und jezt wieder 2–3000. die zu Bewaffnung der back countrie Peoples, welche alle Königs Freünde waren, oder sich doch zum wenigsten dafür ausgaben, bestimmt waren.

Den Nachmittag kam R^{gmt} v. Dittfourth und v. Huyne bey Gibs's über den Ashly und rückten gegen Abend in die Stadt, 100 Mann von Huyne blieben bey Wappoo stehen, bis die Magaziene dasselbst eingeladen waren, und durch Stono inlet gehen konten, um nach Charlestown zu kommen.

Maij 14 etc etc. Diessen und die folgende Tage, waren paroles für die Miliz ausgeschrieben, und sie sodann Battalions weisse transportirt, die in Beauforth, Grenville und Colleton waren die ersten, und die nördlichen die lezten.

Maij 20. Diesse Nacht ging OL^t Clarcke nach Savannah, um das Commando dasselbst zu übernehmen, indem General Major Prevost über Charlestown nach England gehen wolte, das Regiment Angenelli wurde nach Charlestown beordert, und zu Savannah war, während der Belagerung von Charlestown, unter Aufsicht des Ingenieur Capitaine Dunmore's statt der alten Wercke eine Citadelle aufgeworfen worden   Gegen Abend marchirten unter Comando OL^t Abercrombie 1^t u 2^t Bat. light Jnf: und 42. nach Dorchester, Lord Cornwallis stand bey Nelsons Ferry am Santee River.

flew up into the air; ramrods and bayonets were blown onto the roofs of houses, and as much as six hours later some muskets went off. The fire was extinguished, but the damage caused by this act of negligence was great indeed, for the best and most skillful artificers and gunners, of whom there are not many in the English service, as well as the worthy Captain Collins and the very promising Lieutenant Gordon were carried off in a most inglorious manner. The entire siege did not cost us so many artillerymen. The loss of the muskets was an especially hard blow, for 4,000 had already been lost on the *Russia Merchant*, and now another 2,000 to 3,000 which were intended to arm the back-country people, all of whom are loyalists, or at least pretend to be.

In the afternoon von Dittfurth's and von Huyn's Regiments crossed the Ashley at Gibbes' and moved into the city toward evening. A hundred men of von Huyn's remained posted at the Wappoo until the stores should be loaded there and the ships come up through Stono Inlet to Charleston.

Today and the following days paroles were made out for the militia, whereupon they were transported by battalions. Those from Beaufort, Granville, and Colleton were the first and those from the northern counties the last. *May 14, etc., etc.*

This night Lieutenant Colonel Clarke went to Savannah in order to take over the command there, for Major General Prevost intends to go to England by way of Charleston. D'Angelelli's Regiment was ordered here. During the siege of Charleston a citadel had been built in place of the old works of Savannah under the supervision of Captain Dunmore [?] of the Engineers. Toward evening the 1st and 2nd battalions of light infantry as well as the 42nd marched to Dorchester under the command of Lieutenant Colonel Abercrombie. Lord Cornwallis was at Nelson's Ferry on the Santee River. *May 20*

Maij 21. Heüte kamen Newyork Volonteers herüber, und rückten bey
Kingsdock ins Lager, Queen's Rangers gingen nach Dorchester und Abercrombie nach Cypress. Unssere Transport-
schiffe kamen heüte unter Anführung des Jäger Schiffs Appollo
Transport aus Stono Jnlet, längst denen Küst[en] von Lighthouse und James Island, gingen über die Bar bey Ships Channel, und legten sich längst der Stadt, jensseits Shutes Folly
im Cooper river vor Ancker, Die für Jäger, light Jnf:, brittish
und hess: Grenadiers, 42. u Queen's Rangers bestimte, wurden
beordert auf 6 Wochen frisches Wasser ein zu nehmen, und
wurden auf 60 Tage mit provision verssehen, bekamen aber
statt Zwieback, gröstentheils Mehl und Reiss

Maij– Unssere Linien gegen die Stadt, waren jezt bis auf die Redoutten, benebst einem Theil des natürlichen Grabens von
Negroes zu geworfen worden, die Canonen in die Stadt, und
von da auf die Schiffe transportirt worden, Artillerie und
Provisions Magaziens, Engl: und Hess: Hospitals in die Stadt
gebracht worden. Ein Detachement Brittisch und Hessische
Grenadiers, lösseten die Marins auf Forth Sullivan ab.

Maij 22– Auf die diessen Morgen ertheilte Ordre, marchirten gegen
Abend unter Commando des Gen. Maj. v. Kosboth, Jäger,
Brittish und 3 Bat. Hess: Grenadiers nach Ashly Ferry, und
rückten dasselbst den andern Morgen ins Lager. Die Grenadiers hatten den Ashly river im Rücken, und die Strasse nach
Dorchester in Front, Jäger deckten Flanque und stundten
zwischen dem Ashly und der Strasse, Dorchester in Fronte.
Queens Ranger gingen nach Dorchester, Abercrombie nach
Moncks Corner, und Legion (welche alle beritten waren
gemacht word[en]) benebst Jrish Volontairs und 33, waren
den Santee River über Nelsons Ferry unter OberstL^t Webster
passirt; Es war diesses blos um das so lange bessezte Lager zu
verändern, und denen Truppen Gelegenheit zu geben, mit

Today the New York Volunteers came over and went into May 21
camp near King's dock; the Queen's Rangers went to Dorchester, and Abercrombie to Cypress. Our transports arrived
today under the command of the jäger ship *Apollo*. From
Stono Inlet they proceeded along the coasts of Lighthouse
and James islands, crossed the Bar through Ship Channel,
and cast anchor in the Cooper River along the city on the
other side of Shutes Folly. Those on which the jägers, the
light infantry, the British and Hessian grenadiers, the 42nd,
and the Queen's Rangers were to be embarked were ordered
to take in six weeks' supply of fresh water. They received
sixty days' provisions, but were given mostly flour and rice
instead of biscuits.

Except the redoubts, our lines in front of the city, in- May
cluding part of the natural ditch, have now been filled up by
Negroes; the guns have been transported into the city and
thence on board the ships; artillery and stores and also the
English and Hessian hospitals have been moved into the city.
A detachment of British and Hessian grenadiers have relieved the marines at Fort Sullivan.

In compliance with orders received yesterday the jägers, May 22
the British grenadiers, and the three battalions of Hessian
grenadiers, under the command of Major General von
Kospoth, marched toward evening to Ashley Ferry, where
they encamped the following morning. The grenadiers had
the Ashley River in the rear and the road to Dorchester in
front; the jägers covered the flank and stood between the
Ashley and the highway, facing Dorchester. The Queen's
Rangers went to Dorchester; Abercrombie to Moncks Corner,
and the Legion (now all mounted), together with the Irish
Volunteers and the 33rd, crossed the Santee River at Nelson's
Ferry under Lieutenant Colonel Webster. The old camp where
the troops had been so long was vacated in order to give the
men a change of environment and an opportunity to provide

frischem Gemüsse u s w. auf die bevorhabende See-Reisse sich zu verssehen, Unssere patrouill[en] gingen bis Dorchester.

Der Feind hatte Georgetown abandonirt, und sich nach Camden zurück gezogen.

Maij 27. Kam des Detachement Grenadiers und Jäger wieder zurück und bezogen ihr voriges Lager, um dem Embarquement nahe zu seyn.

Maij 28. Das Commando auf Forth Sullivan wurde heüte durch die Garnison der Stadt abgelösset. Die Light Jnf: und 42. folgten heüte, nach, und den andern Tag die Queens Rangers, und rückten in ihre respect: Lagers wieder ein, und das Corps unter Lord Cornwallis zog sich einige Tage darauf auch zurück und bezog bey Habcaw und Lambriers sein altes Lager wieder. Die Einwohner der back Countries waren in ganzen Partheyen gekoมen, und hatten frey willig ihre Gewehre abgeliefert an die differente Corps mit den Ausdrücken, dass sie des Fechtens müde wären.

Maij 30. Da unssere Schiffe fertig waren mit Provision etc verssehen, so machten die Jäger heüte den Anfang der Embarkation auf

Maij 31 Draytons Wharff. Den andern Tag, *Maij 31*, embarkirten die sämtl: Grenadiers und Artillerie, und den folgenden Tag

Junij 1– *Junij 1*. light Jnf:, 42, und Queens Rangers, benebst dem Hospital, von welchem blos diejenige schwer blessirte zurück blieben, welchen die Bewegung mercklich Schaden konte.

Vom Corps des Lord Cornwallis bekamen wir Gestern die Nachricht, dass OL^t Tarleton durch einen forcirten Marsch, indem er in 2 Tag[en] 100 Meilen (zu Pferdt) gemacht hatte, dem feindl: avancirten Posten von 200 Mann, 10 Meilen diesseits Camden auf den Halss gekommen war, und da er auf seine Auforderung sich nicht ergeben wolte, seine Jnfanterie abssizzen lassen, den Posten berennt, 170 nieder gestochen, und 30 Mann benebst 4 Canonen, und alle Bagage, Amunition, etc genoมen habe. Er nannte in seinem Brief an

¹ There is a Swift Creek in Chesterfield County (north of Camden, how-

themselves with fresh vegetables, etc., for the approaching passage. Our patrols went as far as Dorchester.

The enemy have abandoned Georgetown and have withdrawn to Camden.

The detachment of grenadiers and jägers returned and went into their former camp in order to be close to the place of embarkation. May 27

The detachment at Fort Sullivan was relieved by the garrison of the city. The light infantry and the 42nd followed on the 28th and the Queen's Rangers the next day, all returning to their respective encampments. The corps under Lord Cornwallis likewise withdrew several days later, returning to their old camp on Hobcaw and Lempriere's. The back-country people, saying they were tired of fighting, have come in parties to surrender their arms voluntarily to the different corps. May 28 [etc.]

Since our ships were ready and furnished with provisions, etc., the jägers began to embark today at Drayton's wharf. The following day, *May 31*, all the grenadiers and the artillery embarked and on the day after that, *June 1*, the light infantry, the 42nd, and the Queen's Rangers, as well as the sick and wounded, except those who would suffer decided harm from being moved. May 30

May 31
June 1

Yesterday we received news from the corps of Lord Cornwallis to the effect that Lieutenant Colonel Tarleton, after making a hundred miles on horseback in two days, had fallen in with an advanced post of two hundred men ten miles this side of Camden. Since they did not heed his demand to surrender, he had his infantry dismount, charged their post, killed and wounded one hundred and seventy, and captured thirty men, four guns, and all baggage, ammunition, etc. He did not mention the place in his dispatch to the Commanding General, but I presume it was between Town Creek and Swift Creek.[1] This young partisan has more

---

ever), very close to the Waxhaws, where this encounter took place. The editor has been unable to find any trace of a Town Creek near by.

den commandirenden General den Ort nicht, ich vermuthe es war zwischen Town creek und Swift Creek—Diesser junge Partisan hat mehr Glück in Süden, denn er in Norden hat, solte seine Kentnisse unssers Metiers so sehr in der kürzen Zeit zu genom̃en haben, oder ist etwa diesse race Volck, welche in den südlichen Theilen gegen uns stehet von furchtsamen Bauern, und unwissenden Anführern zusammen gessezt.

Junij. 2. Zur Bessazzung Charlestowns und der Provinz bleiben, Mylord Cornwallis, Brig: Gr. Patterson. 7. 23. 33. 63. 64. 71. v. Ditfourth, v. Huyne Angilelli (welches von Savannah erwartet wurde) Legion, South and [sic] North Carolina R^gt, Browns Corps, Jrish Volonteers, Newyork Volonteers and [sic] Fergusons Corps, zu welchen unter Commando des Major Ferguson und Capitaine Hangers alle Refugees and [sic] Loyalists von denen beyden Carolinas stiessen, indem diesse beyden Officiers zu Superintendent[en] der Loyalists von South und North Carolina vom commandirend[en] General ernant waren. Major Moncrief mit mehreren Jngenieurs blieb hier, um die Fortification der Stadt zu bessorgen.

Junij 3. Heüte Morgen um 8 Uhr lichteten wir die Ancker, passirten die versenckten Schiffe, und legten uns unter Forth Johnston vor Ancker, 2 Divisionen Jägers des Capt. Hinrichs u Capt. v. Bodungen unter Major v. Wurmb, waren an Bord des Appolo Transport, und 1 Division unter Capt Ewald unt: L^t v. Winzingerode auf der Dispatch brig Transport.

Junij. 4. Die Flotte fuhr diessen Morgen mit schwachem Winde bis 5 Fathom Hole. Wir passirten um 10 Uhr Forth Sullivan, welches von Cabbage Tree à flu d'eau gebauet ist. Wir hatten mehrere Sandbäncke zu passiren, kamen aber, ohne Hinderniss zu unsserer Station. Die Men of Wars lagen schon jenseits der Bar. Um 1 Uhr wurde des Konigs Geburtstag mit Canonen von denen Kriegs Schiffen und Batterien der Stadt gefeüert. Den Nachmittag kam unter Anführung der Bonnetta Fregatte

luck in the South than he had in the North. Is it likely that his knowledge of our metier has so much increased in this short time? Or, is the race of people opposing us in the southern parts made up of timid peasants and ignorant commanders?

For the occupation of Charleston and the province there June 2 remained behind Lord Cornwallis, Brigadier General Paterson, the 7th, 23rd, 33rd, 63rd, 64th, 71st, von Dittfurth's, von Huyn's, and d'Angelelli's Regiments (the latter was expected from Savannah), the Legion, the North and South Carolina Regiments, Brown's Corps, the Irish Volunteers, the New York Volunteers, Ferguson's Corps, and the refugees and loyalists of the two Carolinas under the command of Major Ferguson and Captain Hanger,[1] for the Commanding General had appointed these two officers superintendents of the loyalists of South and North Carolina. Major Moncrieff, with a number of engineers, remained here in order to look after the fortifications of the city.

At eight o'clock this morning we weighed anchor, passed June 3 the sunken ships, and anchored again below Fort Johnson. Captain Hinrichs' and Captain von Bodungen's jäger detachments were on the *Apollo* transport, under Major von Wurmb, and another detachment under Captain Ewald and Lieutenant von Winzingerode was on the brig *Dispatch*.

The fleet sailed this morning with a gentle breeze to Five- June 4 Fathom Hole. At ten o'clock we passed Fort Sullivan, which is built of palmetto *à fleur d'eau*. We had to pass several sandbanks, but arrived at our station without delay. The men-of-war already lay on the other side of the Bar. At one o'clock the King's birthday was celebrated by firing the guns of the warships and of the batteries of the city. In the afternoon a fleet came from Savannah under escort of the *Bon-*

[1] While the transport *Anna* was in tow (see p. 24, note 1) Captain Hanger must have repaired to some other vessel.

eine Flotte von Savannah, unter welchen ein Schiff kürzlich
von Westindien gekom̄[en] war, und die Nachricht eines See-
Gefechtes zwischen Admiral Parker und la Mothe Piquet mit
brachte; die Franzossen verlohren 2 Kriegs Schiffe von 74
Canonen und wäre nicht ein Sturm dazwischen gekom̄en, so
hiess es, hätte Parker die ganze franz: Flotte ruinirt.

Junij. 5. Ein sehr heisser Tag, den Morgen und gegen Mittag versuchte
die Flotte, die Bar zu passiren, allein der Wind war völlig
entgegen. Den Nachmittag musten die Schiffs Capts der
Transportschiffe auf gegebenes Signal an Board des Adjutanten
Tomkins fahren, um die verssiegelten Ordres des Rendevous
Plazzes, im Falle einer Trennung von der Flotte, zu empfangen. Der Wind blieb wie er war, die Luft war schwul.

Junij 6. Einige Schiffe kamen noch von Charlestown herunter. Diessen
Morgen gegen 10 Uhr veränderte sich der Wind, und wurde
uns günstig, wurde aber gegen Mittag so schwach, dass die
nächst an der Bank gelegene Schiffe nur passiren konten. Den
Nachmittag kam eine Sloop von Savannah. Sie passirte die
Bar durch Lawford Channel

Junij. 8. Da der Wind uns günstig blieb, so lichtete der Rest der Flotte,
nach gegebenem Signal diessen Morgen um 9 Uhr die Anckers,
und passirten die Bar durch Ship Channel, ohne den geringsten Schaden oder Hinderniss. Es waren an verschiedenen
Schiffen Lootssen an Boord, und der Canal durch Zeichen,
Fahnen, kleine Boots etc etc ausgezeichnet. So bald die Flotte
passirt war, lichtete der Admiral die Ancker, und wir stachen
mit günstigem Northwest Winde E. in die See. Den Nachmittag wurde der Wind etwas stärker. Das Transportschiff the
Earl of Darby verlohr alle Seegel und Stricke von seinem
Hauptmast, und der Roebuck towete es.

Junij 9. Gegen Abend ging der Wind nach N:E. und wurde diessen
30.° 31. Morgen so starck, dass er dem Sturm sehr ähnlich war.
Gegen Mittag kamen wir in Currant, woselbst die See noch
starcker ging. Den Nachmittag verlohr der Renown men of

netta frigate. With it was a ship lately arrived from the West Indies which brought the news of a naval engagement between Admiral Parker and La Motte-Piquet. The French lost two men-of-war of 74 guns and, we were told, if a storm had not interfered, Parker would have annihilated the entire French fleet.

A very hot day. In the morning and again toward noon June 5 the fleet attempted to pass the Bar, but there was a head wind. In the afternoon the masters of the transports, upon a given signal, repaired on board the ship of Adjutant Tonken in order to receive the sealed orders informing them of the place of rendezvous in case any of them should be separated from the fleet. The wind remained the same. The air was sultry.

Several ships were still coming down from Charleston. June 6 At ten o'clock this morning the wind changed and became favorable. Toward noon, however, it became so faint that only the ships closest to the Bar had time to pass. In the afternoon a sloop arrived from Savannah. She passed the Bar through Lawford Channel.

Since the wind remained fair, the rest of the fleet, upon a June 8 given signal, weighed anchor this morning at nine o'clock and passed the Bar through Ship Channel without the least damage or delay. Several ships had pilots on board, and the channel was marked with signs, flags, little boats, etc., etc. As soon as the fleet had passed, the Admiral weighed anchor, and we stood easterly to sea with a fair northwest wind. During the afternoon the breeze became somewhat stronger. The *Earl of Darby* transport lost all her sails and rigging from the mainmast, and the *Roebuck* took her in tow.

Toward evening the wind veered to NE. and became so June 9 strong this morning that it was little short of a storm. 30° 31′ Toward noon we got into the current, where the sea ran even higher. In the afternoon the *Renown* man-of-war lost her

war seinen öberen Mittelmast, es war, als wenn der Mast
abgehauen wurde, so kurz, und auf einmal fuhr er ab, und
blieb in den Stricken hängen, die den Vorder und Mittelmast
zusammenhalten. Die mehresten, so wie unsser Schiff, nahmen
gegen Abend ihre oberen Masten herunter

Junij 10– Die Nacht war sehr unruhig, indem die See starck gestiegen
32.° 47.   war. Ein Regen gegen Morgen brach die Grösse der Wellen,
der Wind ging mehr nach Westen, und war den Nachmittag
sehr vortheilhaft, indem wir 6–7 Meilen N.E. fuhren, die
Nacht ging er wieder mehr nördlich.

Junij. 11– Der Wind war uns den ganzen Tag sehr günstig. Gegen Mittag
33.° 24.   gab der Admiral Signal, dass Grund da wäre, wir fanden 20
Faden Wasser, und sandigten mit feinen Muscheln gedeckten
Boden, die Nacht fuhren wir mit schwachem Winde—2–3
Meilen in einer Stunde O.N.O.

Junij 12– Der Wind war sehr schwach, alle mögliche Seegel wurden
aufgessezt, und der Cours ging N.E. Unsser Schiff konte
nicht denen meisten beysegeln. Der Boden war zu faul, und
mit Ellen langem Moos bewachssen, welches die Haupt-
Ursache war, es war in 2½ J. nicht reine gemacht worden,
weilen es immer war gebraucht worden. Das Wasser in der
Flotte war sehr schlecht, wir suchten die besten Fässer aus,
und halfen es durch pumpen. Verschiedene Krancke bekamen
wir dadurch auf dem Schiff, das ganze Wasser in South Carolina taugt nicht, wenige Quellen ausgenoͤmen. und dieses
Wasser in der Flotte, war aus einem stehenden Teiche geschöpft worden. Mangel an WeinEssig war auch da; Den
Nachmittag ging der Admiral mit dem Europe, Roebuck and
[sic] Rainbow nach Newyork voraus, und die Richmond
Fregatte führte die Flotte

Junij 13. Der Wind war uns sehr günstig, wir fuhren 5–7. Meilen in
einer Stunde längst der Küste weg. Es waren Landwinde, und
eine gesunde Luft, Unssere Flotte war, wie wir aus Charlestown liefen, 99 Seegel starck. Diessen Nachmittag kamen 2

main-topgallant. It broke so clean that it looked as though
it had been chopped down. All of a sudden it gave way and
remained hanging in the rigging which holds the foremast
and mainmast together. Most of the ships, including ours,
lowered their topmasts toward evening.

The night was very rough, for the sea was running much   June 10
higher. Toward morning a rain broke the height of the   32° 47'
waves. The wind backed more to the west and was very fair
in the afternoon, permitting us to sail six to seven miles NE.
During the night it veered more to northward again.

The wind was very favorable all day. Toward noon the   June 11
Admiral signalled that we were in shallow water. We found   33° 24'
twenty fathoms and a sandy bottom covered with mussels.
During the night we made two to three miles an hour ENE.
before a gentle breeze.

The breeze was very faint. We hoisted all sails, and our   June 12
course was NE. Our ship could not keep abreast with the
greater part of the fleet. Her bottom was foul and covered
with moss a yard long, which was the greater hindrance.
She had not been cleaned for two and one-half years, since
she was always in use. The water in the fleet was very bad.
We picked out the best casks and improved it by pumping.
Because of the foul water we had several sick on board. All
the water in South Carolina is poor, with the exception of
a few springs, and the water in the fleet had been taken from
a stagnant pond. There was also shortage of vinegar.[1] In the
afternoon the Admiral started to sail ahead to New York
with the *Europe*, the *Roebuck*, and the *Rainbow*, and left the
Richmond in command of the fleet.

The wind was very favorable; we made five to seven miles   June 13
an hour, sailing coastwise. We had land breezes and healthy
air. Our fleet when leaving Charleston consisted of ninety-

[1] Vinegar was commonly used as an antiscorbutic and disinfectant on
ships.

Kaufartheyschiffe in unssere Flotte. An Kriegsschiffen hatten wir bey uns von Charlestown aus.

Europe		Richmond	34	
Rainbow		Blonde	32	
Reasonable	men of War	Jris	32	Fregatten.
Romulus		Camilla	24	
Roebuck		Delight	16	Sloop of War

Die Reasonable commandirte jezt der vormalige Prem: L^t von Europe, und Capt. Ewans war Port Capt auf der erbeüteten Fregatte Boston, jezt Charlestown 34, genant, geworden, und mit dersselben, und der Hallifax (vormals Ranger) Capt. Bowen, Providence, new Vigilant etc zu Charlestown verblieben.

Junij. 14.
37.° 22.

Den Morgen war der Wind noch günstig, gegen Mittag passirten wir die Höhen von Cheasepeak und Cape Henry. Die See war hier rauh, eine Folge war diesses des Stroms, den der Ausfluss der Cheasepeak Bay macht, welche mit dem Currant zusammen sties. Eine Heerde Turkins zog diessen Mittag durch die Flotte südlich, es mochten über 500 seyn, die alle einen Cours hielten. Gegen Nachmittag deckte sich die Luft, und der Wind ging auf einmal nach Norden. Es war ein bemerckungswürdiger Anblick zu sehen, wie der nord und Süd Wind mit einander kämpften, bald der eine, bald der andere die Oberhand hatte, bald beyde ruheten, um gleichssam neue Kräfte zum Kampfe zu samlen. Wir liessen die Seegel denen Winden gleich spielen. Gegen Abend kam ein dicker, düsterer Nebel, der Wind ging östlich, und wurde die Nacht wieder günstig.

Junij. 15–
37.° 59.

Der gestrige Calm und widrige Wind hatte uns bis heüte in der Fahrt ziemlich zuruck gehalten, die Luft klärte sich diessen Morgen vom Nebel, war aber noch bedeckt, und die

---

1 The editor has been unable to ascertain what these "turkins" are, fish or fowl. Turkeys (which one thinks of first) do not fly in large flocks, never any considerable distance, and certainly not over water. They may have

nine sail. In the afternoon two merchantmen joined us. The warships leaving Charleston with us were:

Europe	⎫	*Richmond* 34	⎫	
Rainbow	⎪	*Blonde* 32	⎪	
Raisonnable	⎬ Men-of-war	*Iris* 32	⎬ Frigates	
Romulus	⎪	*Camilla* 24	⎭	
Roebuck	⎭	*Delight* 16	Sloop-of-War	

The *Raisonnable* was now commanded by the former first lieutenant of the *Europe*. Captain Evans had been made port captain on the captured *Boston* (34), now called *Charlestown*, and remained at Charleston with his ship and the *Halifax*, formerly *Ranger* (Captain Bowen), the *Providence*, *New Vigilant*, etc.

In the morning the wind was still favorable. Toward noon we passed the heights of Chesapeake and Cape Henry. The sea was rough here, a result of the drift occasioned by the outflow of Chesapeake Bay meeting with the current. A group of *turkins* [?] passed through the fleet this noon, going southward. There were probably upward of five hundred, all holding the same course.[1] Toward afternoon the air became murky, and the wind suddenly changed to the north. It was remarkable to see how the north and the south wind fought with each other, how now one, now the other, had the upper hand, and again both lay low, gathering, as it were, new strength for the combat. We kept turning our sails with the shifting wind. Toward evening came a thick, murky fog; the wind veered eastward and became favorable again during the night.

Yesterday's calm and contrary wind held us back considerably. The fog lifted this morning, but the sky was still overcast, and the cold was so penetrating that we needed

June 14
37° 22′

June 15
37° 59′

been some kind of large fish, or even large sea turtles—the corrupted form "turkie" is given in Webster's Dictionary as late as the 1930 edition and "turkle" appears in the 1934 edition.

Kälte so scharf, dass die wärmsten Winter Kleidungen, zur Schüzung des Cörpers nötig waren. Der Currant war, da wir den Lauf der Cheasapeak hinter uns gelassen hatten, wieder starck, und trieb uns mehr, wie der Schwache Wind fort. Gegen Mittag wurde der Wind stärcker, wir fuhren 2–3. Meilen, indem ein Theil der Flotte noch weit zurück war. Den Mittag kam ein Portugiesisches Schiff von N.E. in die Flotte, und den Nachmittag eine engl: Fregatte von Süden.

Junij 16– Der Wind war die Nacht beynahe völlig stille, und diessen
38.° 45.   Tag über fuhren wir 2–4 Meilen abwechsselnd, der Wind war östlich, und wir fuhren N.b.E. Wir sahen heüte Grampen und Seegeflügel und treib Gras. Die Luft war kalt, gegen Abend ging der Wind wieder etwas südlich, und die Luft wurde wärmer.

Junij. 17   Mit schwachem S.O. Winde fuhren wir diesse Nacht fort,
39.° 59.   gegen Morgen ging der Wind nach Suden. Um 6 Uhr sahen wir die Höhe von 39.° 40.' die Küsten von Yersey zwischen great und little Eik Harbour W.b.N. um 8 Uhr ging der Wind nach S.S.W. die Luft wurde bedeckt, Ein dicker Landregen aus Süden dauerte 2 Stundten, die Luft klärte sich wieder auf, und mit blossen Augen konten wir die Küsten von Yersey erkennen, an welchen wir mit dem herrlichsten Winde und vollen Seegel vorbey stachen, den Nachmittag sahen wir Never Sink. Jeder Augenblick wurde uns günstiger, und niemand zweifelte daran, dass wir nicht noch diessen Abend, wo nicht in York, doch im Hook vor Ancker liegen würden, allein wer kennet nicht diesses betrügerische Element, um 3 Uhr stieg ein dicker Nebel und starcker Wind von S.S.W. auf, der uns zwank bey 12 Fadem Wasser längst never Sink beyzulegen, und da das Wetter jeden Augenblick bösser wurde, und zu befürchten war, dass wir möchten bey Veränderung des Windes an die Küste geworfen werden so stachen wir um 5 Uhr E.S.E. wieder in die See, Wir hielten diessen Cours bis 12 Uhr des Nachts, und da der Nebel dicker war,

our warmest winter clothing to keep warm. The current, after we had left behind the drift of the Chesapeake, was swift again and carried us more than did the faint breeze. Toward noon the breeze became stronger; we made two to three miles an hour, for part of the fleet was still far astern. At noon a Portuguese ship joined the fleet from NE., and in the afternoon an English frigate from the south.

There was hardly any breeze last night. During the day June 16 we made between two and four miles an hour. The wind was 38° 45′ eastward and we sailed N. by E. We saw *grampen* [grampuses?] and sea fowl and blades of grass floating on the water. The air was cold. Toward evening the wind veered more to southward, and the air became warmer.

We sailed before a gentle SE. breeze during the night. June 17 Toward morning the wind shifted southward. At six o'clock, 39° 59′ in latitude 39° 40′, we sighted the coast of Jersey between Great and Little Egg Harbor W. by N. Around eight o'clock the wind changed to SSW., and the air became murky. For two hours we had a heavy land rain from the south. Then the air cleared up, and with the naked eye we could make out the coast of Jersey, which we passed running before a splendid wind and with a press of sail. In the afternoon we saw Never Sink. Every moment things looked more favorable, and no one doubted but that we would be at anchor this evening, if not at New York, certainly within the Hook. But who does not know this treacherous element! At three o'clock a heavy fog and a strong gale came up from SSW., which compelled us to lie to alongside of Never Sink in twelve fathoms of water. Since the weather became fouler every moment and we feared being blown against the coast with a change of wind, we stood to sea again at five o'clock ESE. We kept to this course till midnight. Since the fog had become so thick that the ships could not see one another, the greatest caution was taken by posting lookouts and firing

dass kein Schiff das andere konte gewahr werden, so wurde durch Schildwachten und Klein-Gewehr die beste Vorsichtigkeit gebraucht. Gegen Mittag klärte sich der Himmel auf,

Junij 18 und da wir von Schiff[en] frey waren, stachen wir Nordwest und kamen mit Anbruch des Tags vor Sandyhook, passirten den light Thurm mit starckem günstigen Winde, heftigen Regen, und fanden den Admiral an Boord des Roebuck, jensseits den Narrow's vor Ancker, die ganze Flotte muste dasselbst Ancker werfen, und wir bekamen die Ordre, dass keinem Offr und Soldaten solte erlaubt seyn, nach Newyork zu gehen, und den Abend die Ordre, den andern Morgen mit Anbruch des Tages auf Staaten-island zu landen, und 2 Tage Provision mit zu nehmen.

Junij 19. Die respe: Truppen wurden heüte Morgen auf Staatenisland debarquirt und bezogen dasselbst Cantonnirungs Quartiere unter Ordre des General Major Leslie, Hess: Gren: lagen zu New- und Old Town, Jäger zu Newborough, Brittish Gren: an der Strasse zwischen Newtown und Richmond, Queens Rangers in Richmond, und Light Jnfanterie zwischen Richmond und Elizabethtown Point. Der General Lieut: v. Knyphaussen war seyd 8 Tagen zu Elizabethtown point gelandet, mit Zurücklassung einiger Rgmtr auf Kingsbridge u Newyork und unssere Jäger hatten mit dem Feind eine Affaire gehabt und darinnen einen Verlust von 1 Offr todt, 2 Capt. 1 Offr. blessirt und etliche 40 todt und blessirt; dem Feind eine ziemliche Schlappe angehängt, bey welchen Gr. Washington u Marquis de la Fayette selbst angeführt hatten.

Junij 22. Hier lagen wir bis d: 22! als an welchem Tage wir beordert
Junij 23. wurden wieder zu Schiffe zu gehen, und fuhren folgenden Tag bis Philipsburgh, den nemlichen Tag hatte unssere Armee zu Springfield einen andern Standt mit dem Feind, bey welchem die Jäger ziemlich verlohren, und OL^t v. Prueschenck, Cpt Lorey, Capt Roeder, L^t v. Diemar blessirt wurden.

musket shots. Toward noon the sky cleared up. Inasmuch as June 18
we were separated from the fleet, we stood northwest and
arrived before Sandy Hook at daybreak. We passed the
lighthouse with a strong, favorable wind and a good down-
pour, and found the Admiral on board the *Roebuck* at anchor
on the other side of the Narrows. The entire fleet cast anchor
there, and we received orders that neither officers nor men
should be permitted to repair to New York. In the evening
we were ordered to land on Staten Island at break of day
with two days' provisions.

The troops were disembarked this morning on Staten June 19
Island and went into cantonments under the orders of Major
General Leslie. The Hessian grenadiers were stationed at
New Town and Old Town, the jägers at Newborough, the
British grenadiers on the road between New Town and
Richmond, the Queen's Rangers in Richmond, and the light
infantry between Richmond and Elizabethtown Point. Lieutenant General von Knyphausen had landed a week ago at
Elizabethtown Point, having left behind several regiments
at Kings Bridge and New York. Our jägers have had an engagement with the enemy and suffered the loss of one officer
killed, two captains and one subaltern wounded, and some
forty [privates] killed and wounded. The enemy's losses were
considerable. General Washington and the Marquis de Lafayette had commanded in person.[1]

Here we remained till the 22nd, when we were ordered to June 22
embark again. The following day we went to Phillipsburgh. June 23
That same day our army had an engagement with the enemy
at Springfield, where the jägers suffered considerable losses.
Lieutenant Colonel von Prueschenck, Captain Lorey, Captain
Roeder, and Lieutenant von Diemar were wounded.

[1] Neither Washington nor Lafayette commanded in person. Brigadier
General Sterling seems to have had the command.

Junij 24. Kamen die Truppen aus den Jerseys auf Scooners den North River herauf Nachdem sie die Nacht vorher nach Staatenisland übergegangen waren und wurde d: 25ᵗ die Armee zu Philipsburgh debarquirt, als an welchem Tage wir wieder zum Corps stiessen. Von dem Verschlagenen Schiff Anna erfuhren wir jezt die sichere Bestätigung, dass dasselbe zu England angekom̄en sey.

So endigte sich das Commando.

The troops arrived from the Jerseys in schooners, coming June 24
up the North River after having gone to Staten Island the
night before. On the 25th the army was disembarked at
Phillipsburgh and we joined our corps. Concerning the missing *Anna* transport we now obtained the reliable information
that she has arrived in England.

Thus ends the command.

5ter Theil, oder Anhang.

enthaltend ein

*Beytrag von Philosophisch-Historischen-Bemerckung diesser
Provinz betreffend.*

1. Geschichte. 2 Beschreibung der Stadt Charlestown, 3 Clima.
4 Producte.

1)– Das Schicksal diesser provinz von ihrer ersten Bevölckerung
durch Europaer, bis zur Trennung Georgien von derselben, welches im Jahr 1732 geschahe, haben wir in dem ersten Theil diesser Häfte, bey der kurzen Berührung der Geschichte Georgiens, welche mit diesser Provinz und North
Carolina vor der Zeit, zusaṁen unter einem Nahmen begriffen war, gesehen. Seit die Carolinas unter der Jurisdiction
des Konigs kamen, seit dass engl: Gessezze und Gerichtbar-
keit, im Gerichtshof des Caroliners die Richtschnur war,
und brittische Freyheiten (Privilegien) und Einschränckun-
gen (restrictiones) der Maasstaab seiner Handlung, erst von
diessem Zeitpunct an, fingen diese Colonien an zu blühen: das mütterliche Auge Brittaniens, welches mit gleicher
Wachssamkeit, für alle ihre Kinder in ganz America wachte,
schiene mit bessonderem Antheil die Carolinas, hauptsächlich aber South Carolina sich an zu nehmen. Seit der kurzen
Zeit, nemlich von 1732–1774, als da diesser unglückliche
Krieg ausbrach: mehrete und vermehrete sich die Cultur,
Handlung und Reichthum diesser Provinz, welche vorher dem
in Eüropa Dürftigen, blos Unterhalt verschafft hatte, in
so einem offtmal sich verdoppelten Grade, als keine ihrer

Part Five or Appendix

Containing

A Contribution of Philosophical and Historical Remarks
Concerning South Carolina

1. History. 2. Description of the city of Charleston. 3. Climate. 4. Products.

(1) THE HISTORY of the province from the first arrival of Europeans until its separation from Georgia in 1732 I have discussed in the first part of this journal where I briefly touched upon the history of Georgia, which up to that time had constituted one province with North and South Carolina. It was not until the Carolinians became immediate subjects of the King, until English laws and English jurisdiction in the courts of judicature of the Carolinas became their rule of conduct, and British privileges and restrictions the measuring stick for their actions that the colonies began to flourish. The maternal eye of Britannia, which with the same care watched over all her children in America, seemed to be especially watchful over the Carolinas and above all over South Carolina. During the short time between 1732 and 1774, when this unfortunate war broke out, the culture, trade, and wealth of this province, which formerly had given mere subsistence to indigent Europeans, increased and multiplied more rapidly than those of any other of her sister provinces on this continent. In the years '71, '72, and '73 the export of native products to England had an annual average value of £395,000

Schwester Provinzen in diessem Welttheile sich rühmen konte. Von natürlichen producten führte sie nach England in die Jahre 71. 72. u 73 im Durchschnitte genoṁen, jedes Jahr für 395,000 lb Strl: Waaren aus, und brachte davor für 365,000 die theils zur Bequemlichkeit, theils und hauptsächlich aber zur Wollust dieneten wieder zurück. Der Resultus diesser Balance wurde alsso 30,000 lb Strl. profit dem South Carolina jährlich an England verschaffte. Allein dies ist sein geringster, der Haupthandel, der hauptsächlich Schleichhandel ist, gehet von Charlestown nach St Eustatia, wosselbst er wider die Gesseze Englands seine producte an die Hollander gegen Waaren vertauschte, die von England aus, blos solten eingeführet werden, und sie dann in den Carolinas mit dem profit des erschlichenen Jmports, und dasjenige, was der engl: Kaufmann wegen der innerlichen Taxir- und Abgaben, in England bey Uberssendung der Waaren auf diesselben aufschlagen musten, wieder verkauften. Dies machte auf einige Artikel 25, und auf verschiedene 50 p Cent.. Und die Gesseze, welche diessen Handel verbothen, und die Zoll-Hausser und Zoll-Bediente zur Aufrechthaltung diesser Gessezze, nanten der Caroliner Eingriffe in seine Freyheiten, und nothwendige Ursache das Gewehr zu ergreiffen. Und da keine Provinz durch Schleichhandel einen so überschwenglichen Vortheil erhandelt, als diesse, die durch die Lage des Haffens, den vielen kleinen Flüssen und Jnssuln um die Hauptstadt dersselben, welche der Staapel aller ihrer Handlung ist, so sehr erleichtert wird, und so war auch keine Provinz wärmer in dieser Rebellion interessiret, als der handelnde Theil von South Carolina. Ein anders ist es mit dem blossen Landmann, der unter dem Nahmen von back Countrie People, hier geht, welcher glaube ich in diessem Theil Americiens gröstentheils für den Frieden geneigt ist, *indem er keinen Vortheil von dem Krieg hat*. Der wahre Maasstaab nach welchem man einen Königsfreünd und Rebelle abmessen kann, ist sicher in Beantwortung der Frage enthal-

sterling, whereas the imported goods, satisfying partly the colonists' desire for comfort, and partly, or rather principally, their craving for luxury, amounted to £365,000 sterling, leaving an annual balance of £30,000 sterling in favor of South Carolina. But this is only a small part of her trade. Her principal commerce, which consists largely of smuggling, is carried on between Charleston and St. Eustatius,[1] where in defiance of English laws the merchants of Charleston trade their products to the Dutch in exchange for wares which should be imported only from England. These in turn, by surreptitious trade, they sell at a profit in the Carolinas, boosting their prices by as much as the merchants in England would have to add to theirs on account of internal duties and excises if they should export these commodities. This amounts to twenty-five per cent on some articles, on others to fifty. The Carolinians considered the laws which forbade this commerce and the customs officials' enforcement of these laws interference with their liberty and sufficient cause to take up arms. Since no other province besides South Carolina makes such excessive profits by contraband trade, which is facilitated by the situation of her harbor and the many small rivers and islands around the capital, the staple of all her trade, no group of people was more warmly interested in this rebellion than the merchant population of South Carolina. It is quite different with the inhabitants of the country, who here go under the name of "back-country people." The greater part of the rural population of this part of America are, I believe, favorably inclined toward peace, *for they gain nothing*

[1] St. Eustatius is a small rocky island in the Leeward Islands group. Being a free port at this time, it was an emporium of illicit trade (cf. J. F. Jameson, "St. Eustatius in the American Revolution," *American Historical Review*, 8 [1903], 683–708).

ten, ob diesser oder jener Mann wahre Vortheile in Anssehung
seines privat Jnteresses, seiner Lebens Art, Handthierung
u s.w. hat, wenn er auf unsser—oder der feindl: Seite ist.
Einige sehr wenige sind hierinnen beym Feind ausgenõmen,
welche theils Schwärmer sind, theils falsche philosophische
politische Traumer, die Hugo Grotii Völcker Rechte gelessen
haben und nicht verstanden, und an unsser Seite, möchte noch
eine geringe Anzahl seyn, von denen man mit Uberzeügung
sagen kann, dass Liebe und Treüe zu Gott und ihrem recht-
mässigen König, sie unter die Fahne ihres Herrn brächte
1736. Jm August war diesse Provinz einer der schrecklichsten
Sicilianischen Vespern die je erdacht worden, nahe. Die ganze
Negroes, oder doch der bey weitem gröste Theil dersselben,
hatten eine Verschwörung zusam̃en gemacht, in einer schon
vest gesezten Nacht, jeder auf seinen Herrn zu fallen, alle
Weissen um zu bringen, und die Weiber theils zu Sclaven zu
machen, theils zu ihrem Vergnügen zu behalten, und den Rest
auf zu opfern. Obgleich eine so grosse Anzahl Köpfe mit diessem Geheimnisse bekannt waren, blieb es dennoch ver-
schwiegen. 2 Tage vor dem Ausbruch, hatte sich eine Menge
dersselben, $2\frac{1}{2}$ Meilen von Charlestown in einem dicken
Holze versamlet, welche dazu bestimmt waren auf die Stadt
zu fallen, der Magaziene sich zu bemächtigen, und die Einwohner zu massacriren, alle Anordnungen waren gemacht, in
der ganzen Provinz jedem sein Theil, den er die 2te Nacht
hierauf zu morden hatte, angewiessen, als das Schickssal der
gerechten Sache beystandt, und diesses schreckliche Unternehmen verrieth. Sogleich flogen die Bürger von Charlestown
mit der grösten Stille zu den Waffen, umringten den Verssam-
lungs Ort, nahmen sie alle gefangen, Martern und Strafen
brachten die Anführer heraus, die Nachricht flog in wenigen
Stundten durch das Land, und alle Anführer wurden mit
Martern hingerichtet, und noch eine grössere Menge mit
schweren Leibes Strafen, belegt.

by this war. The safe rule, according to which one can always ascertain whether a man is a loyalist or a rebel, is to find out whether he profits more in his private interests, his mode of life, his way of doing things, etc., when he is on our side or on that of the enemy. There are only very few exceptions to this rule: on the side of the enemy are a few enthusiasts and some pseudophilosophical-political dreamers who have read, but did not understand, Hugo Grotius' *Law of Nations*, while on our side there may be a small number of which one can say with conviction that love and faithfulness to God and their lawful King has brought them under the colors of their sovereign.

In the month of August, 1736, this province was at the point of experiencing one of the most horrible Sicilian Vespers imaginable. The entire Negro population, at least the greater part, had conspired to assault their masters on a certain night, massacre all the [male] white population, make the women either their slaves or use them to gratify their desires, and sacrifice the rest. Although many knew of this plot, it was nevertheless kept secret. Two days before the intended uprising a large group had gathered two and one-half miles from Charleston in a dense forest. They were to attack the city, seize the magazines, and massacre the inhabitants. All arrangements had been made; everyone in the entire province had been told whom he was to kill—when fate was merciful and betrayed the horrible plot. Immediately and very quietly the inhabitants of Charleston armed themselves, surrounded the Negroes' assembly place, and overpowered them. Through torture and punishment their leaders were found out. Within a few hours the news spread through the province, and all leaders were tortured to death, while many others were subjected to severe bodily punishment.

2. CHARLESTOWN.

Wann der erste Grund von Charlestown gelegt worden ist, ist
eine bey diesser, so wie bey jeder andern Stadt in der Welt,
seit die Verschickung ganzer Colonien auf einmal aus einem
Lande, nicht mehr Gewohnheit ist, so schwer zu beantworten,
als unnüzlich an sich selber: Sie wird wahrscheinlich dasselbe
Schickssal haben, was der gröste Theil der übrigen Städte
hat. Eine fischer Hütte, wo jezt eine See Stadt, und eine Jäger
oder Waldhütte, wo jezt ein Landstädgen und Flecken liegt.
Und so lange diesse Stadt oder Ort keinen Einfluss in die Geschichte des Landes hat, und so einen Theil der Welt-Ge-
schichte mit ausmacht, so lange ist sie der Aufmerckssamkeit
des Bemerckens, eben so unnüzlich, als jede andere Fischer-
und Köhler-Hütte.

Die *Lage* der Stadt, ist an dem für Handlung vortheilhafte-
sten Flecken diesser Provinz: Sie liegt auf einer Erd-Zunge,
zwischen dem Ashly und Cooper River, die 2 vorzüglichsten
und schiffbaresten Flüsse der ganzen Provinz, und die vor-
theilhaftesten, um innen Handel und Tausch zu befördern—
Der *Hafen* ist sehr gut, nur dass er an der Mündung von Lighthouse Jsland bis Sullivans Jsland mit einer Sandbanck (the
Bar) umgeben ist, durch welche 5 Canale gehen, und von
denen der tiefste (Shiph Channel hielt 12 Fus bey der Ebbe,
und 21½. bey der höchsten Fluth) Schiffe die schwerer, als
ein engl: 40 Canonen Schiff ist, nicht ohne Leichterung des
Schiffs passiren läst. Die Banck selber ist an mehreren Stellen
so flach, dass sie nur 3–4 Fuss Wasser hält. Obgleich diesses
ein nicht zu leügnender Nachtheil für die Stadt ist, indem die
Havarey bey einem unvorsichtigen oder zu kühnen Seefahrer,
der den Canal nicht genau kennt, sehr leicht ist, so ist dennoch diesser Fehler unbeträchtlich, wenn wir den hohen Grad
der heütigen Kenntniss in der Navigation, und die Anordnung
mit Leucht Thurmen, Lootssen, und andern bekannten Merck-
malen, die zur Auszeichnung gefährlicher Orter gebraucht
werden, erwägen. Und in diessem Augenblick, da England

(2) CHARLESTON. To ascertain when the first foundation was laid for Charleston is as needless and difficult as it is for every other city in the world which has been founded since the time when colonies were no longer transplanted from one land to another. Charleston's history has probably been the same as that of the greater part of all cities—a fisherman's hut where we now have a maritime town, and a hunter's or a woodcutter's hut where now an inland town or a hamlet is situated. So long as this town does not influence the history of the country and hence plays no rôle in the history of the world, its beginnings do not deserve our attention any more than the hut of any fisherman or charcoal burner.

The city of Charleston is *situated* in that spot of the province which is most advantageous for commerce, a neck of land betwen the Ashley and the Cooper, the best and most navigable rivers of the entire province and admirably suited to promote commerce and trade. Its *harbor* is very good except for the fact that, at the inlet, from Lighthouse Island to Sullivan Island, it is surrounded by a sandbank (the Bar). There are five channels through the Bar. The deepest, the Ship Channel, has twelve feet of water at low tide and twenty-one and one-half at high tide and does not permit the passage of ships heavier than an English 40-gun ship without their being lightened. At some places the Bar is covered with only three to four feet of water. This, to be sure, is an undeniable disadvantage for the city, since a careless or a foolhardy navigator who does not know the channel very well may suffer damage and loss. Nevertheless, in view of our knowledge of navigation, the presence of pilots, lighthouses, and other well-known signs which mark dangerous places, the disadvantages accruing to the city from this bar are by no means considerable. At the present, when England is master of Charleston and is entangled in a Bourbon war, I believe everyone will agree with me when I contend that this bar is

Meister von Charlestown ist, und im Bourbonischen Kriege verwickelt, glaube ich mit jedermann gleicher Meinung zu seyn, wenn ich behaupte, dass diesse Sandbanck von dem grösten Vortheile vor uns ist, und die beste Bariere gegen jede überwiegende feindliche Flotte, denn indem 3–4 – 40–64 Canonenschiffe von uns, einmal in der Bar bey 5 Fathom Hole liegen, So können Sie mit der grösten Gewissheit, jeden Feind zur See abhalten, weil die Fregatte zu schwache Canonen führt, und das Schiff von der Linie erst seine Canonen ausladen muss, wenn es die Banck passiren will.

Die Stadt selber bestehet jezt (die abgebrenten Hausser mit gerechnet) aus 1020 Haussern, welche in breiten, recht winckelligten, aber nicht gepflasterten Gassen, jedes mit einem Garten und von dem andern 20–100 Schritte entfernt, stehen. Die Wärme des Clima, macht diesse Jntervallen nothwendig, um die kühlende See Luft durch die Stadt und Hausser Spielen zu lassen, und so die überschwengliche Hizze des Junij Julij, August u Sept. Monaths, wo nicht leidlich, doch erträglich zu machen, Die schönste Strasse ist die broad-Street, sie ist 100 Fus breit und 1120 lang, und lauft vom Cooper bis Ashly river, und schneidet die Stadt in 2 Theile; Die Hauptstrasse ist die Kingsstreet, welche vom Thorwege, bis an die Spize der Stadt östlich (the South bay) laüft, 80 Fus breit und 3730 Fus lang ist, wornach sich der Umfang der Stadt, jezt ausnehmen läst. Ohnstreitig behalt Charlestown den Rang für jeder andern Stadt Americens in Anssehung der Schönheit der Häusser und der Pracht und Geschmacke die in dersselben herschet. Das geschwinde Aufkommen einer Familie, die in weniger den 10 Jahren vom ärmsten Standte zu Herrn von 100,000 und mehrern Pfundten wurden, auf eine einfache und bequeme Art es wurden, trug wohl nicht wenig dazu bey, um Pracht, Wollust, Aufwand, Verschwendung in so kurzer Zeit, hier in seiner vollen Grösse zu zeigen: Und

[1] Cf. the statement of Josiah Quincy, who visited Charleston in 1773: "I can only say, in general, that in grandeur, splendour of buildings, deco-

of the greatest advantage to us, since it is the best barrier against any overwhelming enemy fleet. Now that three or four of our 40- to 64-gun ships lie within the Bar in Five-Fathom Hole we can have the greatest confidence in being able to keep the enemy at sea, for a frigate carries too light a gun, and a ship of the line must unload her guns before she can pass the Bar.

The *city* itself (including the burnt buildings) consists of 1,020 houses, which are built along broad unpaved streets intersecting one another at right angles, each house having a garden and standing twenty to one hundred paces from any other. The warm climate makes the open spaces necessary. They permit the cool breezes to play through the city and the houses and thus make the heat of June, July, August, and September at least tolerable. Broad Street is the most beautiful street. It is 100 feet wide and 1,120 long and extends from the Cooper to the Ashley, dividing the city into two parts. The principal street is King Street, 80 feet wide and 3,730 feet long, and running from the gateway to the eastern tip of the city (the South Bay). This gives an idea of the size of the city. No other American city can compare with Charleston in the beauty of its houses and the splendor and taste displayed therein.[1] The rapid ascendancy of families which in less than ten years have risen from the lowest rank, have acquired upward of £100,000, and have, moreover, gained this wealth in a simple and easy manner, probably contributed a good deal toward the grandiose display of splendor, debauchery, luxury, and extravagance in so short a time.[2] Furthermore, the sense of equality which all possessed during this time of increasing incomes induced the people to bid

---

rations, equipages, numbers, commerce, shipping, and indeed in almost everything, it far surpasses all I ever saw, or ever expect to see, in Amerca" (*Memoir, 1744–1775* [Boston, 1875], p. 73).

[2] "All seems at present to be trade, riches, magnificence, and great state in every thing; much gayety and dissipation" (*ibid.*).

die Gleichheit, die in diessem Steigen des Einkoṁens, bey
jedem unter Jhnen herrschte, machte dass sie dem fremden
hiessen von ihrem Uberfluss mit zu geniessen, und erwarb
ihnen den Ruhm der Gastfreyen Stadt, den sie vieleicht mehr
ihrer Eitelkeit und Stolze, als der wahren Wohlthätigkeit des
Herzens zu dancken haben. Die engl: Kirchen, von welchen
St Philips in Meetingstreet die älteste ist, sind mit Pracht
und Geschmacke. Das Staate House und die Barracks für 800
Mann, sind des Anssehens werth, ausser dem ist noch ein
teutsch Lutherische, mehrere presbyterianische Meetings, eine
Synagoge, eine öffentliche Pibliothec, u.s.w.

Die besten Hausser liegen am Cooper River und Northbay, und die mehrsten Wharfts sind an dersselben. Die baystreet, meeting und Church Street pranget mit Pallästen,
wovon jeder mit Portals, die auf Ionischen und Dorisch[en]
Saulen ruhen, umgeben ist. Mitten in der Stadt zwischen
Peter Church, der Main guard, State House und Market, da
wo die Church Street die broad Strēt durchschneidet, stehet
die Statue des fameusen Pitts, gerade in dersselben Stellung,
wie die zu Newyork, und lässt mich vermuthen, dass beyde
die Geburth eines und desselben Künstlers ist. Sie ist mit dem
Gesichte nach der Exchange und Jnsurance House gerichtet,
welches am Ende der broad-Street am cooper River liegt,
stüzt mit dem rechten Arm sich auf einen abgehauenen Stamm,
und hat in der Hand die Magna Carta, mit der andern Hand
zeigt sie vor sich, Die Statue ist 8 Fus, das piedestal 10 Fus
hoch, unten am piedestal in der Fronte der Statue stehet:

In grateful memory
Of his Service to his Country in general
and to America in particular
The Commons House of Assembly
of South Carolina
unanimously voted
this Statue
of

strangers to enjoy their abundance with them and earned the renown of hospitality for this city, which she owes, perhaps, more to vanity and pride than to true generosity of the heart. The English churches, of which St. Philip's in Meeting Street is the oldest, show wealth and good taste. The State House and the barracks, quartering eight hundred men, are worth seeing. Then there are a German Lutheran church, several Presbyterian meetinghouses, a synagogue, a public library, etc.

The best houses are situated along the Cooper River and North Bay, where are also most of the wharves. In Bay Street, Meeting and Church streets are many grand palaces, every one of which has porticoes with Ionic and Doric pillars. In the center of the city between St. Peter's,[1] the Main Guard, the State House, and the market, at the intersection of Church and Broad streets there stands the statue of the famous Pitt, in posture the same as that in New York, which makes one suspect that both are the creation of the same artist. It faces the Exchange and the Insurance House, which last is situated at the end of Broad Street on the Cooper River. The right arm is supported on a tree stump and holds the Magna Charta. The other hand points ahead. The statue is eight feet and the pedestal ten feet high. At the base of the pedestal in front is inscribed:

In Grateful Memory
of His services to His country in General
And to America in particular
The Commons House of Assembly
of South Carolina
unanimously voted
This Statue
of

[1] Hinrichs was mistaken; this church was called St. Michael's.

The right honourable William Pitt Esqr:
who
gloriously exerted himself
Jn defending the Freedom of America
The true Sons of England
By promoting a repeal
of the Stamp Act
Jn the Year 1766.

Time
Shall Sooner destroy
This Mark of their Estime
Than
Erose [*sic*] of their Minds
the just Sense
Of his patriotic Virtue.

Die Materien und der Meissel, beyde stehen in Vergleichung mit der zu Newyork aufgerichteten, weit zurück, Eine verflogene Canon-Kugel hatte in der Belagerung den rechten Arm davon abgeschlagen. Das State House ist 200 Fus lang, und hat einen Portal von Jonischen Saulen mit Corinthischen Ziera[r]then. Das Dach ist (so wie an den Haussern überhaupt, und so wie in den warmen Ländern, es gewöhnlich ist) all Mezzanino und mit mansarden gebauet. Da es ein Gefangen-Hauss war, so konte ich das innere desselben nicht sehen. St Peters Kirche, jezt ein feindlich Hospital, hat ein Portal, ganz im Jonischen Geschmacke.

Ausser der Negroe Verschwörung, die 1736 diesse Stadt hauptsächlich bedrohete, erlitte sie 2 würcklich harte Stösse, der erste war d: 18 Nov. 1740, wo durch ein ausbrechendes Feüer, bey einem starcken Winde, schlechten Anstalten, und fast alles hölzerne Hausser, kaum ein Hauss den Flam̄en entgieng, der Schade wurde auf 300,000 lb gerechnet, ein gewaltiger Stoss, wenn wir bedencken, dass diesses die Hauptstadt eines Landes war, wo 70 Jahr vorher, noch kein Eüropaer in lebte—. Das Parlament schenckte den Bürgern

The Right Hon. William Pitt, Esq.
who gloriously exerted himself
In Defending the Freedom of America
The True Sons of England
By Promoting a Repeal
of the Stamp Act
in the year 1766

Time
Will sooner Destroy
This mark of their esteem
Than
Erase from their minds
their just sense
Of His Patriotic Virtue[1]

The material and workmanship cannot compare with those of the statue in New York. During the siege a stray cannon ball knocked off the right arm. The State House is two hundred feet long. It has a portico of Ionic pillars with Corinthian decorations, and a mansard roof (like other buildings in warm countries). Since it served as a prison I could not see the inside. St. Peter's Church, now an enemy hospital, has a portico entirely in Ionic style.

Besides the Negro conspiracy of 1736, which threatened the city particularly, Charleston suffered two other severe blows. The first occurred November 18, 1740, when a conflagration, whipped by a high wind and aided by a poor [fire-fighting] organization, destroyed nearly all the houses, most of them built of wood. The damage was estimated to amount to £300,000, a terrible calamity when one considers that this was the capital of a province where seventy years

[1] The inscription as given by Hinrichs is changed in the translation to conform with that quoted from the *South Carolina Gazette* of July 5, 1770, in McCrady's *History of South Carolina under the Royal Government, 1719-1776* (New York, 1899), p. 678.

20,000 lb Strl:, sie fingen an, wieder auf zu bauen, und in wenigen Jahren, standten marmorne und steinerne Paläste, wo vor hero kleine holzerne Hausser lagen—. Das 2te Unglück verbreitete sich nicht nur über die Stadt, sondern auch über das Land, Ein Huricane am 14^{t} und 15^{t} Sept 1752, jagde alle Schiffe die im Haven lagen aufs Land, und in die Stadt; kein einziges, kein Kahn war hiervon ausgenommen, ausser der Hornet men of war, der zur rechten Zeit den Hauptmast weg hieb, und vor 4 Ancker lag. Alle Wharften, Brücken, Alle Hausser in der baystreet wurden umgestürzt oder weg getrieb[en], die ganze Hausser der Stadt abgedeckt, und eine grosse Menge Waaren verdorben, und weg gespühlet, Die See stieg 10 Fus höher, als das höchste Wasser zu steigen pflegte, viele Menschen ersoffen, oder wurden erschlagen und beschädiget bey dem Fall der Hausser, Schornsteine u dgl. Jm Lande war auf 30 Meilen um Charlestown herum kaum ein Hauss stehen geblieben, und der Verlust in Horn Vieh, Schweine, Schaafen und Feld Früchte unzählbar, dennoch erholte sich die Stadt und Land sehr bald wieder, indem jezt kaum einer mehr des facti erwähnet. Seit der Zeit ist die Stadt noch mit grössern und brillianten Haussern versehen, von denen verschiedene in denen nachherigen Feüern, wieder ein Raub der Flammen geworden sind, indem allein in den Jahren diesses Kriegs, keines verflossen ist, wo nicht 2–3 Feüre ausgebrochen sind, durch welche jezt die ganze Vorstadt Midlesex und die Hausser in bay-Church, und Meeting Street langst der Southbay und Northbay eingeäschert wurden.

3. CLIMA. Mit welchen schönen Farben auch die Geschicht-schreiber der Einbildungs Krafft des Lessers, die Vortrefflich-keit diesses Climas vor zu mahlen sich bemühet haben, wird dennoch keiner so leicht ihnen Glauben beymessen vielmehr entgegen gessezter Meinung seyn, Der nur einen Fus in diesses Land gessezt hat, oder auch nur einen einzigen unparthey-ischen Einwohner desselben gesprochen hat—. Wie bekannt,

before not a single European was living. Parliament donated £20,000 sterling to the citizens. They began to rebuild and within a few years marble and stone palaces were standing where before small wooden houses had been. The second disaster spread not only over the city but also over the country. On the 14th and 15th of September, 1752, all the craft, large and small, that were anchored in the harbor were driven ashore by a hurricane. The only ship that escaped the fury of the elements was the *Hornet* man-of-war, which cut away her mainmast in the nick of time and rode out the storm at four anchors. All the wharves, bridges, and houses in Bay Street were either demolished or carried away. The other houses of the city were unroofed, and great quantities of goods were destroyed and washed away. The sea rose ten feet above high-water mark at the highest tide. Many people were drowned; others were crushed or injured by the falling of houses, chimneys, etc. In the country for thirty miles around Charleston not a house remained standing, and the loss of cattle, hogs, sheep, and crops was incalculable. Nevertheless, the city as well as the country soon recovered from this blow, and now hardly anyone ever refers to it. Since that time even larger and more luxurious houses have been built. Several of these have fallen prey to flames in subsequent conflagrations, for during the present war not a year has passed without two or three fires breaking out, so that now the entire suburb Middle Essex and the houses in Bay, Church, and Meeting streets along the South Bay and North Bay are reduced to ashes.

(3) Climate. Notwithstanding the fact that historians have endeavored to paint in beautiful colors the excellence of this climate for the fancy of the reader, no one is likely to put much faith in their delineations. On the contrary, nearly

ist die ganze Küste von Cape Hatteras südlich, ein flaches
marschigtes Land, mehrentheils noch unbebauet, ein Wohn-
plaz von Schlangen und crocodillen, uhrbar für Reiss, mit
faulen Wasser flüssen durchschnitten, und mit undurchdring-
lichen Gehölzen bedeckt; Kann diesses ein gesundes Clima
seyn?—Der Reiss erfordert ein Land, das 9 Monath im Jahr
unter Wasser liegt, die Schlangen suchen undurchdringliche
Moräste und Sümpfe die mit faulendem Gebüsche und Mo-
rasten angefüllet sind, das flache Ufer des Landes, das sich
bis in die See hinnein erstrecket (die Ursache der Gefähr-
lichkeit der Huricanes von N.E.) vermehret die Feüchtigkeit
des Erdbodens, der unendliche Wald, der das ganze Land
bedeckt, die Erde vergräbt und den Blick und wohlthatigen
Strahl der alles belebenden Sonne enzieht, und die ganze Atmo-
sphaere mit ungesunden, vergiffteten Dünsten, welche Einfluss
auf das Keimen und vegetiren jedes lebendigen Geschöpfs haben, umgiebt—dies alles zussammen erwogen, wo bleibt denn
das reine, das schöne Clima das gelobte Land des Geschicht-
schreibers? Kein Land ist wohl so vielen und plözlichen Wetter Veränderungen ausgessezt, als diesses, kein Monath, kein
Tag, keine Stunde, ist der andern gleich, der plözlichste Ubergang, selbst im Winter im Dec. u Nov: von Kälte, zur beynahe
unausstehlich[en] Hizze, Vom Regen zur Dürre, Von Huricanes zur angenehmen Lufft! ist gewöhnlich! Der Winter
dauert von Oct. bis Apr: der Januar ist meistens heiter, Febr.
u Maerz sind regenericht, windigt, mit untergemischten
schönen Tagen. Apr. ist trocken und gut, Maij ist voller
Nebel Regen und schwüler Luft, Junij, Julij, Aug: u Sept:
sind für einen fremden, wegen der übernatürlichen Hizze, der
pressenden Gewitter, der feüchten mit stinckenden Nebel
angefülleten Nächte, gefährlich, oft tödtlich. Der Oct. Nov.
u Dec. haben Regen, Kälte, mit etwas unter gemischtem Eiss,
und einigen schönen Tagen, und Huricanes, Reg[en] und
Wind, und bey dem schönsten Wetter ist dennoch die Luft

everyone who has put his foot in the province or has talked to an unprejudiced inhabitant is of an altogether different opinion. As is well known, the entire coast from Cape Hatteras southward is flat, marshy land, for the greater part still uncultivated and suited for the growing of rice only, a habitat of snakes and crocodiles, strewn with bodies of stagnant water and covered with impenetrable woods. Can this be a healthy climate? Rice demands a soil which is under water nine months out of every year; snakes live in impenetrable marshes and swamps full of decaying brushwood. The flat shore land, which extends into the sea (the reason hurricanes from NE. are so dangerous), increases the dampness of the soil. The endless forests, which cover the entire country, deprive the soil of the beneficial rays of the life-giving sun and fill the whole atmosphere with unhealthy miasmas, which affect the germination and growth of every living organism. All this considered, what remains then of the pure, the beautiful climate of the promised land of the historian? There is probably no land which is subject to so many and such sudden changes of weather as this province. No two months, days, or hours are alike. Even in winter, in November and December, the most sudden changes are common: from cold to almost unbearable heat, from rain to drought, from hurricane to pleasant air. Winter lasts from October to April. January is usually clear; February and March are rainy and windy, with occasional beautiful days; April is a dry and good month; May brings much fog, rain, and sultry air; June, July, August, and September are unhealthy and frequently fatal to foreigners because of the excessive heat, suffocating electric storms, and damp nights pregnant with fetid fogs; October, November, and December bring rain, cold, some ice, a few beautiful days, hurricanes,

nicht rein. Der Boden, welcher mit so vielen Ungesundig-
keiten angefüllet ist, dünstet diesselbe am Tage alle aus, an
welchem die Sonne sie an sich ziehet, und des Nachts fallen
sie im Nebel und Thau wieder herunter. Summiren wir alles
diesses zusam̃en so wird das facit am Ende des Jahrs, uns 1
heiterer Tag, gegen 15 bösse zeigen, und keinen einzigen
gesunden, dem Luft Kreiss des menschlich[en] Körpers ange-
messen, Ob ich gleich gerne zu geben will, dass das innere
Land besser ist, ja lass es so schön seyn, wie es will, so past
doch die Beschreibung des Geschichtschrbrs auf das jezige
Carolina nicht, und wenn soll diesses innere Land ordentlich
bewohnt, cultiviret, und benuzt werden? Kein einziger von
allen Flüssen South Caroline[ns] ist über 50 Meilen schiffbar,
in einem unabsehbarem Walde, ohne Hülfe des Flusses, um
Handlung und Tausch zu bewerckstelligen, sich an zu bauen,
und mit Nutzen an zu bauen? Dies wäre thöricht? Canale
durch Menschen Hände zu graben,? Wann soll die Zeit
kommen? So lange allso kein *Uberfluss* von Menschen in ganz
North America ist, so lange nicht alle Handwercker und
Künste in vollem Flor sind, so lange nicht *Uberfluss* und
Armuth hier herrscht, so lange wird diesses auch blos in der
Einbildungskraft eines historisch philosophischen Traumers,
für leicht und möglich scheinen.

ANMERCKUNGEN.

1) Der innere Handel mit denen back Country Peoples, die bey
und jensseits der Apalachian Mountains sich angebauet haben, geschiehet von medio Sept—1 Jan: als in welcher Zeit
diesse Leüthe in ganzen Parthey[en] mit beladenen Wagen
als dem Uberschuss ihrer Landes producte nach Charlestown
kom̃en, und diesse gegen ausländische Waaren vertauschen,
die ganze übrige Zeit des Jahrs ist keine innere Handlung in
Charlestown, und jeder Einwohner ist desswegen genötiget,
sich diesse Zeit über, auf das ganze Jahr mit denen benötigten
Artikeln zu versehen. Gemüsse, Geflügel und Hornvieh aber,

and rain with wind. But even on the most beautiful days the air is not pure. All this insalubrity of the ground the sun causes to rise during the day, and in the night it descends again in mist and dew. Summing up all this, we shall have had by the end of the year one pleasant day for every fifteen bad ones and not a single healthy day, suitable to the needs of the human body. I gladly admit that the inland is a good deal better; let us assume that it is the most beautiful imaginable—nevertheless the description of the historian does not fit the present Carolina. And when will this inland be inhabited, cultivated, and utilized? Not one of all the rivers of South Carolina is navigable for over fifty miles. Who would be foolish enough to settle in an endless forest and expect to cultivate the soil profitably when there are no rivers to facilitate trade and barter? When will the time come when canals can be dug by human hands? So long as there is no *surplus* of man power in all of North America, so long as all the trades and arts are not in full bloom, so long as neither *luxury* nor *poverty* prevails here, profitable colonization will seem easy and probable only in the imagination of a historico-philosophical dreamer.

REMARKS

(1) Trade with the back-country people who have settled near and beyond the Appalachian Mountains is carried on from the middle of September to the first of January, during which time these people come to Charleston in throngs with loaded wagons carrying the surplus of their products, which they exchange for imported wares. The rest of the year there is no inland trade in Charleston, and every inhabitant of this city is therefore compelled to provide himself with the necessities for the entire year during the trading season. How-

ziehet jedes Individuum in der ganzen Stadt und Land sich
selber.

2) Unter denen Producten, welche von denen back Country's
nach Charlestown gebracht werden, gehören auch die Hauthe
von Thieren, Hirschen und Rehe, welches ein sehr nüzlicher
Artikel ist, weilen im Jahr 1771 von diessen 70,000 Stück
auf engl:- und Americanisch: Schiffen nach Eüropa, und St.
Eustatia verfahren wurden

4 PRODUCTE.

Nicht alle producte South Carolinens, nicht blos natürl:
producte desselben sind der Gegenstand meiner jezigen Be-
merckungen, sondern diejenige Producte, welche zur Erhaltung der ersten Einwohner dieneten, und die, welche die
Grund-Ursache des ersten Aufkoͤmens, des Reichthums sind,
und die jezige Handlung bey dem Überfluss, in welchem sie,
in Verhältniss der inneren Consummation gezogen werden,
hauptsächlich ausmachen.

1) *Indian corn or Mais.* Die wohlthätige Natur, welche mit
reichen Händen ihre Gaben über den ganzen Erdball verbreitet
hat, und mit gütigem Wohlwollen, jedem Erdstrich die ange-
messensten für das Clima, und die bedürftigsten zum noth-
1) Mais wendigen Unterhalt des Bewohners dersselben hervorbringen
lässt, hat diessem Lande, in welchem Korn und Waizen etc
ein ausländisches Gewächss ist (das aber in den back County's
jezt sehr gut gedeyhet) statt dessen eine Frucht verliehen, die
nirgend besser und für den Planzer [*sic*] vortheilhaffter gerathen kann und würcklich geräth, als hier. Jch meine das
indian Corn oder Mais, Die Natur desselben, seine Beschaf-
fenheit und Cultur ist so bekannt, indem diesses Korn auch in
Teütschland schon mit Nuzen gebauet wird, dass ich mich keinen Augenblick hierbey aufhalten will, eben so wenig bey

2) denen Cartoffeln, welche ein Segen Teütschlands sind, und ob-
2) Potatoes gleich sie ein natürliches product dieses Landes, dennoch

ever, everyone in the city and in the surrounding country raises his own vegetables, fowl, and cattle.

(2) Among the products which are brought to Charleston from the back country are the hides of [domestic] animals, stags, and deer, which are a very profitable article of trade. In 1771 seventy thousand of them were exported to Europe and to St. Eustatius on English and American ships.

(4) PRODUCTS. Not all the products of South Carolina are the subject of my discussion, nor, on the other hand, its native products only, but rather those products which furnished subsistence to the first inhabitants, those which are the main cause of their early ascendancy and wealth, and those which are of the greatest commercial importance at present because of the abundance in which they are raised in comparison with domestic consumption.

(1) *Indian corn or maize.* Benevolent Nature, who with open hands has distributed her gifts over the entire earth and in her kindness has given to every region the most suitable products for its climate and everywhere supplied those most indispensable to the livelihood of the inhabitant, has be- *1. Corn* stowed upon this country, where rye and wheat, etc., are imported grains (which now, however, do very well in the back country), a grain which nowhere else grows better and more profitably than here. I am speaking of Indian corn or maize. Since this grain is now grown with profit in Germany, its nature and cultivation are so well known that I need not enter into them. The same is true of

(2) *Potatoes*, which are a blessing to Germany and, though they are a native product of this country, nevertheless do not *2. Potatoes* grow half so well here as in Holstein, Brandenburg, Pomerania, Mecklenburg, Hesse, Holland, etc. Columbus brought

nicht halb so gut hier gerathen, als in Holssstein, Brandenburg, Pom̃ern, Mecklenburg, Hessen, Holland etc etc Columbus tauschte hier diesse wohlthätige Frucht gegen venerische
Kranckheiten aus, ein harter Tausch für den Americaner!—

3) Calawan Pease. Ein natürliches product Amerikens, und von
dem Jndianer mit eben der Sorgfalt geplanzt, als wie der

3) *Calawan*
pease

Mais, das Korn wird im März und Apr. gepflanzt, und diesse
Frucht im Maij, weilen sie geschwinde wächst, in Löcher
2–3 zussam̃en, und um das indian Corn Sie hat eine Staude
wie der Epheu und schlängelt sich manchmal 10 Fus hoch
um den Mais, und wird, wenn sie trocken ist, von August
an, gepflicket, 2– und 2 Hülssen, selten 3, wachssen herunter
wärts an einem kurzen Stängel, und jede Hülsse enthält 20–30
Körner, es ist eins der Hauptfutter für die Negroes, welche es
dem Reiss vorziehen, und wird in Wasser gekocht, gestampft,
und mit gemaltem Mais gegessen. Die Hülsse ist gerade wie
die *türkische Erbsse* und die Erbsse glatt, hat die Farbe unsserer
grauen Erbssen, ausser dass sie etwas stärcker, mehr röthlicht
ist, und mehr glänzt, Stam̃, Blatt und Hülsse sind grün, und
der Auswurf ist 3–500 fältig.

4) Cowe (ciui) Bean. Der Name einer Jndianisch[en] Nation
die zwischen Virginien, und Cawbina wohnte, hat, diesser

4) *Cowe*
bean

originellen Pflanze den Namen gegeben, Sie verlangt fetten
Boden, und wird in Garten gezogen, in medio April wird sie
gesäet, und von August an, fängt sie an zu reifen, So wie bey
Türkisch[en] Bohnen, werden in Löchern, rund um eine
Stange, 3–4 in ein Loch gelegt, und schlängelt sich 8– bis 10
Fus hoch um diesselbe, gehülsset und gekocht, wird sie als
ein Gemüsse auf des Herrns Tafel gesezt.

5) Der *Weinstock* wächst wild, und geräth mittelmässig, *Garten*

5) *Wine*

Gemüsse, verschiedene Art *Bohnen* theils einländisch, theils
eingebracht, gerathen vorzüglich, und kein Monath ist im
Jahr, der nicht im offenen Felde frisches Gemüsse und Sallat
hervorkom̃en läst.

in exchange for this very useful food venereal diseases, a deplorable bargain for the Americans!

(3) *Calavance peas*, a native product of America, planted by the Indians with the same care as corn. The latter is planted in March and April, but these more quickly growing peas are planted in May, two to three in a hole and around the Indian corn. The plant is a vine resembling ivy and winds itself around the corn, sometimes ten feet high. The pods are picked when dry, which is early in August. They hang in pairs, sometimes by threes, on short stems, and every pod contains twenty to thirty peas. These peas are one of the principal foods of the Negro, who prefers them to rice. They are cooked in water, mashed, and eaten with ground corn. The pod looks exactly like that of our *Turkey pea*. The pea is smooth and has the color of our *gray pea*, except that it is somewhat larger, a little redder, and shinier. Vine, leaf, and pod are green, and the yield is three to five hundredfold. 3. *Calavance peas*

(4) *Cow* (ciui[?]) *beans*.[1] This native plant got its name from an Indian nation which lived between Virginia and Cawbina.[2] It demands a rich soil and is raised in the garden. The beans are sown in the middle of April and begin to ripen in August. Like Turkey peas, they are sown in holes around a pole, three to four in a hole. The plants twine around the pole eight to ten feet high. When shelled and cooked they are served at the master's table. 4. *Cow beans*

(5) *Grapes* grow wild and yield a fair crop. *Garden vegetables*, such as several varieties of *beans*, partly native, partly domesticated, do very well, and there is not a month in the year when fresh vegetables and lettuce cannot be obtained from the open field. 5. *Grapes*

---

[1] Perhaps cow [peas] *sive* beans.

[2] A bit of folk etymology? What Indian nation? What is Cawbina? Did the copyist blunder? Is cow bean supposed to be derived from Cawbina?

6) Dies waren ohngefehr der Unterhalt der ersten Anbauer dies-
6) *Pinewood* ses Landes, wenn wir etwas Pulver, Bley, Geräthschafften und
Salz hinzu sezen die er mit von Hausse brachte: Er fand in
dem Holze Jagd und Geflügel genug, und im Wasser Fische
die Menge; Sobald diesser neüe Colonist, nur irgend auf eine
erträgliche Art, sich angebauet hatte, und gewahr wurde,
dass jeder Tag seine eigene Nahrung ihm brachte: und ihm Zeit
übrig war, auf Mittel zu raffiniren, sich die Bequemlich-
keiten Eüropaischer producte, Manufacturen u.s.w. durch
Vertauschung der producte seines Landes zu verschaffen, so
war sicher kein Gegenstand ihm haufiger in die Augen fallend,
kein product ihm entbehrlicher und leichter zur Verschiffung
nach fremden Orter zu zu bereiten, als das *Nadeln Holz.* The
Pine wächst hier von allem Holze am haufigsten, so dass bey
dem ersten Anblicke die ganze Gegend von der See an, bis
nahe an die Apalachische Gebürge, ein Pine Wood zu seyn
scheinet, der Boden ist sandigt und unfruchtbar, und gehet
hier unter dem Nahmen von Level Land, oder Barren land.
Nehmen wir jezt an, dass $\frac{1}{2}$ diesses Strich Landes Pine land
ist, welches doch gewiss so ist von diessem so sehr gelobten
Lande, der $\frac{1}{2}$. Theil unbrauchbar; freilich eine Menge Dun-
gung würde es uhrbar machen, allein die nothwendige Gewohnheit das Vieh den grösten Theil des Jahrs in denen
Wäldern herum laufen zu lassen, würde ohne grosse Kosten
und mit Nachtheil dem Landmann die Anschaffung der Dun-
gung verschaffen. Die mit Wasser angefülten flachen Theile der
Gehölze, sind offtmals mit Reiss-Stroh gedünget, und zum
Reissbau mit Nuzen uhrbar gemacht worden. Der Baum an
sich selber ist von grossem Werthe, es ist ein schöner schnur
gerade gewachssener Stamm, von öhlichtem Holze, zu Mast-
baumen, Plancken, und überhaupt zum Schiffsbau sehr vortheilhaft, und der Colonist fand bey Verschickung dersselben
nach England, dessen starcken Handel die Eintauschung desselben zu Unterhaltung seiner Schiffe nothwendig machte,

(6) This is what the first settlers of this province mainly
subsisted on. Of course, powder, lead, implements, and salt   6. *Pine wood*
they had brought from their old home.[1] In the woods they
found game and fowl in plenty and fish in the water. It was
not long before the new colonist lived in tolerable comfort
and realized *that every day provided him with new food*. He had
enough time to think of ways of procuring the comforts of
European products, articles of manufacture, etc., by trading
the products of his land. There was nothing that attracted
his attention more, no product was as indispensable to him,
or easier to ship to other countries than *pine wood*. The pine
is the most plentiful of all trees, so that at first sight the entire
region from the sea to the Appalachian Mountains seems to
be one large forest of pines. The soil in which they grow is
sandy and poor and is referred to as level or barren land. As
we are justified in assuming that one half of this stretch of
land is pine land, then half of this promised land is barren.
To be sure, quantities of manure would make it arable. However, the necessary custom of letting livestock graze in the
woods for the greater part of the year would make dung
costly and difficult to obtain. The marshy level parts of the
woods have in many cases been fertilized with rice straw and
now yield good crops of rice. The pine as such is a very
valuable tree. It has a beautiful trunk, growing straight as
a string. The wood is oily and therefore well suited for masts,
planks, and for shipbuilding in general. Shipping pines to
England, whose extensive commerce made them a necessary

[1] The implements and other necessities which the southern colonist
of the first part of the eighteenth century had to bring from his homeland
are enumerated in Francis Moore's *Voyage to Georgia, Begun in the Year 1735.
. . .* (London, 1744), reprinted in *Collections of the Georgia Historical Society*
(Savannah, 1840), I, 80.

einen so guten Nuzzen, dass diesser Artickel bald mit dem grösten Nuzzen und Vortheil von hier aus nach West Jndien, England etc in Menge verfahren wurde. Der raffinirende Geist des Gewinstes, blieb bey diessem nicht stehen, er fand, dass er den Baum auf eine bessere Art benuzen konte, und lernte diesses vornemlich von teütschen Emigranten, die von Salzburg, Pfalz etc mit Haufen nach diessem Lande geflogen kamen, welche aus dem Oel den der Baum in sich hält Terpentine, Theer und Pech fabricirten.

a) Turpentine wurde ihnen am leichtesten: eine Offnung von 1 Fus lang wird in den Stamm gemacht, und ein Gefäss darunter gessezt, und der Terpentine trieft in dassselbe aus dem Stamm.

b) Theer kostet schon mehr Mühe, Um diesses zu verfertigen, wird der Baum in Stücken von 10–15 Fus lang, gehauen, und jedes Stück, so offt wie möglich gespalten. Diesse Stücke werden alsdann in einem Circel über einander gelegt, so dass die Spizen gegen einander koṁen, und nach dem centro zu herunterwärts incliniren (welches leztere durch Hülfe des dazu eingerichteten planirten Bodens geschiehet,) Eine Schichte wird auf die Art auf die andere gelegt, so hoch es dem Eigenthümer dünckt, so dann der ganze Haufen rund herum und oben mit nassen Rassen belegt, damit bey dem Anzünden das ganze nicht in Flaṁen auf einmal, geräth. Jn der übersten Schichte ist an der Seite eine kleine Öffnung gelassen, wosselbst der Holz Stoss angezündet wird, und da die Rassen den Ausbruch der Flaṁen hindern, so brennt es almählich herunter, und je weiter es herunter brennt, wird der Raassen an der Seite verhältnissmässig abgenoṁen. Unter dem Holzstosse ist in der Erde im Centro desselben eine grosse Höhle gegraben, die mit Leinen ausgessezt ist, in diesser samlet sich das Theer, das almählich von oben, so wie das Feüer unter sich greift, herunter sinckt, und eine Rinne mit gehörigen Abfalle führet den Theer in Fässer, welche ausser-

import for maintaining her navy, proved so profitable to the colonists that this article was soon exported in great quantities to England, the West Indies, etc. However, the colonists' crafty spirit of gain was not satisfied with this. They found that they could use this tree to better advantage by making turpentine, tar, and pitch from its oil. This they had learned chiefly from German immigrants who had come to this country in great numbers from Salzburg, the Palatinate, etc.

(*a*) Turpentine is the easiest to extract. One makes a cut in the trunk one foot long and lets the turpentine drip into a bucket.

(*b*) The making of tar is more laborious. The pine tree is cut into pieces ten to fifteen feet long, and every log is split as often as possible. These pieces are then piled on top of one another in a circle in such a way that they are inclined toward the center, their ends touching. (This is accomplished by previously preparing the ground.) Thus one layer is placed above another as high as one pleases. Then the entire pile is covered with wet sod, so that when set on fire the whole pile does not catch fire all at once. At one side of the top layer a small opening is left to kindle the woodpile. Since the sod prevents the breaking out of flames, the wood burns down gradually. As the pile diminishes in height, the sod is slowly removed on the sides. In the center under the woodpile there is a large hole in the ground, which is lined with linen. Here the tar collects as the fire slowly eats its way down. A channel with the proper slope lets the tar flow into barrels which are set in the ground outside the woodpile. Constant care must be taken (1) that the fire does not burn too fast, (2) that the full barrels are replaced by empty ones, and (3) that the fire is extinguished as soon as it reaches the lowest

halb des Holzstosses in die Erde gegraben sind. Bey diesser Arbeit muss beständig Acht gegeben werden 1) dass das Feüer nicht zu starck in Flammen geräth, 2) dass die volle Fässer durch ledige erssezt werd[en] und dass 3) das Feüer, so bald es die unterste Schichte ergreifft, gelöscht wird, weil sonst die Asche und Rassen, den drunten stehenden Theer unssauber machen würde. Ein Hauffen 16 Fus hoch, und 30 Fus im Durchschnitt, brachte 1100 Barrel Theer ein, à 2 Sp: Dollar ᵖ Barrel.

c) Pech wird aus diessem Theer in eissernen Pötten gesiedet, und ist die Verfertigung desselben in Eüropa bekannt.

7) Der Boden worauf der Pine wächsset, ist fast durchgehends unfruchtbar und kann nur durch Cultur zum Landbaue zu bereitet werden, allein der Cabbage Tree, wächst auf einem Lande, das weder durch Natur oder Kunst zur geringsten Cultur fähig zu machen ist, Es ist ein Sandhügel mit Morästen, die von See Wasser angefüllet sind, durchschnitten. Tybee Jsland in Georgien und Simmons Jsland zum Theil, bringt fast nichts als diessen Baum hervor, desswegen war in der ersten ziemlich grossen Jnsul nur 3 plantationen, und in der lezten blos 1. Der Baum ist einer der seltsamsten Gewächsse, wächst schnur gerade; die Rinde über dem Stamm ist wie ein Schachbrett, oben in der Spizze breitet sich eine Krone aus von Zweigen und Blättern beynahe wie die Aloe, wosselbst in der Mitte der Cabage sizt, diesser schmeckt roh, wie eine Art Castanien, und wenn er geblättert und fein geschnitten ist, mag er wohl dem Kraut Sallat etwas ähnlich seyn, allein der Geschmack ist nicht der angenehmste, und man hält ihn für ungesund (welches sehr wahrscheinlich ist, indem der Safft seine Nahrung aus—mit See wasser gefülletem Boden zieht.) Das Holz ist von einer zähen, biegsamen und sehr vesten Substanz, das der Gewalt nachgiebt, aber nicht dadurch zerstöret wird, Diesse Materie war es, von welcher Forth Sullivan, the bridge Battery und alle alte Verschan-

7 Cabbage Tree

layer; otherwise, the ashes and sod will make the tar under-
neath impure. A pile sixteen feet high and thirty feet in
diameter yields as much as eleven hundred barrels of tar,
which brings two Spanish dollars a barrel.

(c) Pitch is obtained from tar by boiling it in iron pots,
a process well known in Europe.

(7) Though practically all the soil in which the pine grows
is barren, it can upon cultivation be used for agriculture. The *7. Cabbage*
cabbage tree, however, grows in a soil which cannot be made *tree*
to produce, either in a natural way or by artificial means.
It grows on sand dunes which are intersected by marshes
full of sea water. Tybee Island, Georgia, and parts of Simmons Island yield almost nothing but this tree. Hence there
are on the first-named rather large island only three plantations, and in the last-named there is only one. The cabbage
tree is one of the strangest forms of vegetation. It grows
straight as a string. The bark of the trunk looks like a
checkerboard. At the top it has a crown of branches and
leaves almost like the aloe, in the center of which grows the
cabbage. When eaten raw this cabbage tastes somewhat like
chestnuts, and after the outside leaves are removed and it is
finely cut it probably tastes somewhat like slaw. However,
the taste is not the most pleasant imaginable, and it is said
to be unhealthful, which is very likely, since it gets its
nourishment from a soil saturated with sea water. Its wood
is tough, pliable, and very strong; it yields to an impact
without splintering to pieces. This wood was used in the
construction of Fort Sullivan, the Bridge Battery, and all the
old fortifications of the city on the water side. These batteries
cannot be razed by any gun on earth, for the point-blank shot
of a 24-pounder strikes not even two inches into the wood
and does no damage other than leaving the impression of the

zungen der Stadt an der Wasser Seite construirt wurden, Eine Batterie die von keinem Geschüzze in der Welt kann rasirt werden, indem der Kernschuss eines 24^{lbrs} keine 2 Zoll einschlägt, und nichts weiter thut, als den Eindruck der Kugel zeigt, ja nicht einmal die ausserste Rinde spaltet, desswegen das Unternehmen von Sir Peter Parcker auf dem Bristol im Jahr 1776 ein so verwegenes als unglückliches Unternehmen war.

Bey der grossen Kentniss in Navigation und Schiffsbau, welche mit so glücklichem Erfolg in England cultivirt wird, wundert es mich recht sehr, dass noch keiner auf den Einfall gekom̃en ist, die Kriegsschiffe zwischen beyden Verdecken, wo die Canonen und folglich die Manschafft während der Action stehet, inwendig mit 3–4 Zoll starcken Bohlen von diessem Holze zu beschiessen, nicht um die Kugel ab zu halten, denn diesse thut den wenigsten Schaden, sondern um den *See-Mann vor denen Splittern zu decken*, die die feindl: Kugell allemal mit ins Schiff wirft, und welche nach der Aussage aller alten Mariniers, 20 mal mehr Schaden anrichten, als die Kugel selber. Der Cabage aber splittert nicht, er ist biegsam, und ist die Gewalt zu gros, als ZE. ein 24 lb. Kernschuss auf ein 3 zöllig Brett so läst er die Kugel durch, und die Öffnung des Bretts, klemt sich sogleich wieder zusammen, ohne den geringsten Splitter ab zu werfen.

8) Die Eiche und der Nussbaum sind in diessem Theile der Provinz nicht so haufig, als tiefer im Lande: Wo diesse sind, ist Anzeige eines fruchtbaren Landes, auf diessem Acker ist es, wo der Jndigo, der Waizen, Mais, Calawan pease etc gesäet wird. Das Land ist 9–10 Zoll Garten Erde, und die Düngung ist Reiss-Stroh, die Bearbeitung geschiehet mit der Schippe und Hacke (einen einzigen Pflug, der wie der marseillische gestaltet war, habe ich hier nur angetroffen) sehr wenig oder fast gar kein Waizen, wird hierum gesäet, desto mehr aber, je näher man an die Apalachische Gebürge kommt, als wosselbst das Land höher, fruchtbarer und besser wird. 5–6 bessondere Gattungen der Eiche, und noch mehrere

8 *Oak and Wallnut Tree. etc.*

ball. In truth, it does not even split the outer bark. This is the reason that the enterprise of Sir Peter Parker on the *Bristol* in 1776 was as foolhardy an undertaking as it was unfortunate.[1]

Considering England's attainments in navigation and ship-building, which she has cultivated with great success, one is surprised indeed that it has never occurred to anyone to make use of this wood in building warships. The inside between the two decks, where the pieces are mounted and where, consequently, the crew is during an action, might be lined with 3- to 4-inch planks, not so much to withstand the ball (for the shot causes the least injury) as to *guard the seamen against injury from the splinters* which the ball invariably sends flying around and which, according to the assertion of old sailors, cause twenty times more injury than the ball itself. The wood of the cabbage tree does not splinter; it is pliable. When, however, the impact is too great, like that of a point-blank shot from a 24-pounder on a 3-inch board, the ball penetrates the plank, while the wood around the hole immediately draws together without even the smallest splinters flying.

(8) The *oak* and the *walnut* are not so common in this part of the province as they are farther inland. Where they will grow the soil is fertile, and it is there that indigo, wheat, corn, calavance peas, etc. are raised, there being nine to ten inches of good top soil. Rice straw is used for fertilizer. The soil is worked with spade and hoe (I have seen only one plow, and it had the shape of a Marseilles plow). Very little,

8. *Oak and Walnut Trees, etc.*

[1] The spongy palmetto wood was only one of several reasons for the failure of this enterprise. The men in the fort were further protected by sixteen feet of sand; their well-aimed shots did considerable damage to Sir Peter's ships; and an unfavorable wind prevented him from attacking the unfinished side of the fort.

Spiel-Arten von jeder, stiessen mir auf, wenn ich im Holze ging, doch keine Gattung zog meine Aufmerckssamkeit so sehr auf sich, als die *lebendige Eiche* the life Oak, welche ein weisses vestes Holz, dornichten Busch, und ein grunes Blat hat, manchmal ein gezacktes, manchmal ein ovales etc so wie die Spielarten dersselben, von einander abwichen.

9) *The Most.* Nicht seines so bessonderen Nuzens wegen in der Handlung sondern theils des Nuzens wegen, den der Land-mann in seiner Hausshaltung von diessem Artikel zieht, und theils und hauptsächlich um seiner bessonderen Seltenheit halber, kann ich nicht umhin mit wenigen Worten von dem *Most* zu reden, der hier die Bäume deckt, hauptsächlich aber den Oak Tree, diesser Most von dunckel grauer Farbe, wächst an jedem Aste, zieht seine Nahrung aus der Rinde, und hängt 2–3 Fus an den Zweigen herunter. Ein melancholi-scher Anblick! jeder Baum scheinet zu trauren, und die ganze Natur herum durch diessen Anblick, durch den schwarzen Boden, der wie verbrandt aussiehet, halb und halb mit ab-gefallenen Nadeln bedeckt ist, und durchgehends die Farbe des Elends führt, unter Schmerz und Fluch vergraben zu liegen.—Allein so traurig der Anblick desselben, so ein wohlthätiges Geschencke ist diesses in einem Lande das wenig Gras- und Vieh Futter hervor bringt, indem diesses Most bey dem Schaaf- Pferdte- und Hornvieh die Stelle des Futters vertritt Ein drolligter Gedancke, das Vieh im Walde Heü von den Baumen fressen zu sehen.

Der Jndianer bedient es sich zur Ladung des Gewehrs, der Soldat statt der Betten, und der Artillerist macht von diessem Moost Propfen für die Batterie Stücke, reibt man es ab, bis dass es die aussere Hauth verliehret, so bleibt ein feines Hahr da, das zum Ausstopfen der Sessell etc etc besser ist, als Pferdte Haare. Jn medio März fängt es sich an almählich zu verliehren, und zwar von den aussersten Spizzen des Baums zu erst, und mit Ende April ist es beynahe verschwunden.

in fact hardly any, wheat is grown hereabouts; but the nearer
one approaches the Appalachian Mountains the more wheat
one finds, for there the land is higher and more fertile. On my
walks through the woods I have observed five or six distinct
kinds of oaks, each having several varieties. But none attracted my attention so much as the *live oak*, which has white,
solid wood, thorny branches, and green leaves, sometimes
indented, sometimes oval, etc., according to the different
varieties.

(9) *Moss*. Not because it is a valuable article of merchandise,
but rather because of its usefulness in the household of the [9. *Moss*]
farmer and especially because of its decided oddity, I cannot
help saying a few words about the *moss* which covers the trees
in this region, especially the oaks. This moss is of a dark
gray color. Drawing its nourishment from the bark, it grows
on every branch and attains a length of two to three feet. A
melancholy sight! Every tree, all nature seems to mourn for
being buried here, pining and cursed! Then the sight of the
black ground that looks burnt where it is not strewn with
fallen needles—the color of misery all over. However, sad
as is the sight thereof, it nevertheless is a charitable gift in
a land where but little grass and feed grow, since this moss
takes the place of fodder for sheep, horses, and cattle. A
peculiar spectacle—to see cattle in the woods eating hay from
the trees!

The Indian uses it to prime his rifle, the gunner to prime
his battery pieces, and the soldier for a bed. If rubbed till it
loses the outer skin, one obtains a fine hair, which is used
to upholster chairs, etc., etc., and is better than horsehair.
About the middle of March the moss slowly begins to die
away, starting on the outer branches, and by the end of
April it has almost disappeared.

Der Tobac, welcher eine Amerikanische Pflanze ist, geräth
10 *Tobacco* hier nicht so guth als in Virginien und Maryland. Die Ursache ist leicht erklärt: die Pflanze will Mit Sorgfalt gewartet
seyn, und sowohl die Zeit die zu dessen Bau und Wartung gehört, als der Boden, welcher fett seyn muss, kann der Pflanzer
mit grösserem Nuzzen zum Jndigo anwenden. Er ist jezt beynahe gröstentheils die Handlung der Negroes. Er wird hier im
März gesäet, ist im Junij und Julij zeitig geschnitten zu werden,
und im Nachjahr wieder, manchmal 2, manchmal 3 Erndten.

11 *Cotton*   11) Nur erst dann, als der Pflanzer, Vortheil in seinem
neüen Lande erworben hatte, etwas zurück gelegt, Händte
und Einkommen und Unterhalt genug hatte, um neüe Versuche
anstellen zu können, ohne Gefahr zu laufen, bey einem Miss-
wachsse etc in eine widrige Lage verssezt zu werden, erst
damals als der Pflanzer ein *wohlhabender* Mann war, fing er an
die Baumwolle zu pflanzen, Diesse Staude ist ein natürliches
product des Landes, es giebt aber noch eine andere, welche
seyd 40 Jahren von Anguilla eingeführt worden ist, und in
einem Betrachte genommen, den Vorzug vor der eingebohrnen
verdient. Die beste ist jezt *die Zwitter-Art welche die Mischung
der anguillischen mit der americanischen hervor gebracht hat.* Die
Wolle der Amerikanischen, wird von dem Landmann der
Anguillischen vorgezogen, indem diesse zwar feiner, jene aber
stärcker ist. Der Saame sizt in der Wolle, und bey der Amerikanisch[en] so feste, dass er mit der blossen Hand muss
ausgepflücket werden. Dahingegen der Saamen der Anguil-
lisch[en] mit einem dazu erfundenen Jnstrumente kann ausge-
wunden werden. Diesses leztere gehet natürlich geschwinder
von statten, kostet alsso weniger Mühe, weniger Hände und
Zeit, und ist aus diessem Grundte der Amerikanisch[en] in
einem dünne bewohnten Land, wo jede Hand mit dem grösten

---

[1] Instead of Anguilla, Anguilla cotton, etc., we must, no doubt, read
Antigua, Antigua cotton, etc. Lieutenant Colonel George Lucas, Governor

[10] *Tobacco*, which is indigenous to America, does not do so well here as in Virginia and Maryland. The reason for this is that this plant demands careful cultivation, and the time required for cultivating it, as well as the rich soil it needs can be put to more profitable use by growing indigo. The greater part of the tobacco is now raised by Negroes. It is sown in the month of March and is ready to be cut in June and July and again in the fall, sometimes yielding even a third crop.   10. *Tobacco*

(11) Not until the planter had made some profit and put something aside, not until he had sufficient hands, income, and sustenance to make new experiments without danger of being reduced to unpleasant circumstances in the event of poor crops, etc., in other words, not until the planter was a *well-to-do* man, did he begin to plant *cotton*. This plant is a native product of this land. But there is also another which was imported from Anguilla forty years ago and which, in general, deserves preference over the indigenous variety. Now the best is *a hybrid species obtained by crossing the Anguilla variety with the native plant*.[1] The farmer prefers the cotton of the American plant to Anguilla cotton because of its strong fiber. That of the other variety is finer, to be sure. The seed, which   11. *Cotton*

of Antigua, had a plantation in South Carolina which was managed by his daughter. Both father and daughter were especially interested in growing cotton and indigo, the seeds being sent from Antigua. This was just about forty years before the siege of Charleston (cf. *Charleston Yearbook*, 1880, p. 249; 1883, pp. 400–401). Hinrichs' Anguilla or Antigua cotton is what is ordinarily called "sea island cotton," the other variety being commonly known as "upland cotton" or "ordinary American cotton." The editor has failed to find any contemporary, earlier, or even later discussion on the hybridization of the two varieties and is therefore unable to vouch for Hinrichs' statements.

Geize arbeiten muss, weit vor zu ziehen, weil aber die Zwitter art diesse Tugend auch an sich hat, und dazu so starck wie die Americanische geräth, so ist diesses diejenige, welche am haufigsten gebauet wird.—Die Wolle will fetten Boden haben, der Saame wird bey kleinen Hände voll 2. 3. Zoll tief in die Erde am Ende des März gelegt, 3. 4. Wochen liegt er, ehe er hervor bricht, weilen er eine harte Schale hat, und wird reif im Sept: es werden so viele Körner zusam̃en gelegt, weil oftmals viele todt sind. Die Americanische wächst bis 3 Fus, die Anguillische bis auf 5 Fus, Stamm, Blatt, und Knospe ist grun, bis zur reife, dann wird der Stamm braun, die Knospe dunckelbraun und das Blatt verliehrt sich. So wie die Knospe reif ist, wird die Wolle im Felde herausgepflückt, oder auch mit der Knospe abgebrochen, wann diesse dann auf dem Boden, oder in der Tanne gedrocknet ist, wird der Saame herausgenom̃en, und die Wolle ist zum Spinnen und verarbeiten tauglich, 5 lb mit Saamen giebt 1 lb reine Wolle. Die, zur Auswindung des Saamens, gehörige Maschiene, war ohngefehr wie eine Schneide Lade gebauet, die aber an beyden Enden sich gleich ist, und auf 4 Füssen ruhet, in der Mitte der Banck ist ein aufrecht stehendes Bret, quer über der Banck, ohngefehr 18 Zoll hoch. Jn der Mitte ist diesses Brett, durch 2 – 1 zoll dicke Walzen von einander geteilt, und jede Walze hat einen Handgriff und passen fast dichte auf einander, den ein[en] Handgriff auf der einen, und den andern auf der andern Seite. 2 Negroes sezen sich als dann auf die Banck so, dass sie die Gesichter gegen einander, und die Walzen zwischen sich haben, der eine stopft die Baumwolle worin der Saame noch sizt zwischen der Walze mit der einen Hand, und mit der andern drehet er die untere Walze von sich, und der andere Negroe zieht die Baumwolle, so wie sie an seiner Seite zwischen denen Walzen hervor komt, mit der einen Hand heraus, und drehet die obere Walze zu gleicher Zeit mit der andern Hand, von sich, jede Walze gehet folglich

adheres to the fiber, is so firmly attached in the native plant
that it must be picked out with bare hands, whereas the seed
of the Anguilla cotton can be extricated by means of a con-
trivance invented for this purpose. This, of course, requires
less time, less trouble, and fewer hands. Therefore, in a
thinly populated country, where labor is costly, the imported
variety is much to be preferred. Since the hybrid plant pos-
sesses this quality and has, moreover, the strong fiber of the
native variety, it is the hybrid kind that is grown most.
Cotton demands a rich soil. At the end of March the seed is
planted, a little handful in one spot, two to three inches deep.
Having a hard husk it takes three to four weeks before the
plant pierces the ground. The cotton is picked in September.
The reason for planting so many seeds together is that not
all seeds are fertile. The American variety grows as high as
three feet, Anguilla cotton as high as five. Until the plant is
mature, stems, leaves, and bolls are green; then the stems
turn brown, the bolls dark brown, and the leaves drop off.
As soon as the boll is ripe, the cotton is picked in the field
or else the entire boll is broken off. After the cotton has been
dried in a loft or on a thrashing floor, it is ginned, whereupon it is ready to be spun or otherwise used. Five pounds
of unginned cotton yield one pound of pure cotton. The
machine used for ginning resembles a cooper's bench, except
that it looks the same on both ends. It is supported by four
legs and has a board about eighteen inches high across the
middle of the bench. In the center of this board are two one-
inch rollers fitted close together. Both rollers have handles,
one on the right, the other on the left. Two Negroes sit
down on the bench facing each other, the rollers between
them. One of them pushes the unginned cotton between the
rollers with one hand, while with the other he turns the lower

einen andern Weg und klemmet alsso die Wolle, dass sie durch muss, weil aber die intervalle zwischen denen beyden Walzen zu klein ist, als dass der Saame mit durchkoṁen könte, so bleibt dersselbe an der Seite liegen, wo die Baumwolle hinnein gestopft wird; Wie viel geschwinder diesses, als mit der blossen Hand gehet, ist leicht zu begreifen; Es heisst: the grining [sic] of the Cotton.

12 Rice 12. Alles Land, was keine Holzung hat, ist fast durch gehends hier morastig, oder doch so flach, dass es den grösten Theil des Jahrs unter Wasser stehet, und wo bey dem geringsten Regen das Wasser sich, wegen der niedrigen Lage, von andern Gegenden hin zieht. So ungesund diesses nun wegen der beständigen übelen Ausdünstungen ist, so nuzreich ist es doch dem Pflanzer, und nächst dem Oak Lande, das er zum Jndigo, Wolle und Garten Bau, benuzen kann, das nüzlichste: dann diesses ist das Land, welches einzig und allein zum *Reissbau* dienlich ist. der eine immerwährende Feüchtigkeit verlangt, und mehr dann ein cut, Canal und Graben ist gegraben worden, um flaches Land, mit Fleiss iṁer unter Wasser zu halten, und auf die Art zum Reissbau zu zu bereiten. Der Reiss wird medio April in kleinen Reihen wie der Cress Sallat gesäet, und so flach, dass die Erde nur eben ihn bedeckt. Jn 6 bis 8 Tagen wird er aus der Erde hervor brechen, und will, wenn das Land gut ist, 6 Fus hoch, wachssen, Seine Gestalt ist ohngefehr wie der Waizen und Rocken, nur dass der Halm etwas grösser und breiter ist, Ein Korn giebt 60–70 Halmen, an jedem Halm ist eine Ähre, die 100–200 Körner in sich hat, Welche Fruchtbarkeit! Jm Septbr wird er mit Sicheln geschnitten, bleibt denn 3 Tage auf den Stoppeln liegen, welche so hoch gelassen werden, dass sie aus dem Wasser hervor ragen, und die darauf liegende Frucht trocken erhalten, wird hierauf in Garben zusammen gebunden, nach Hausse gefahren, und gedroschen; Sodann wird die Frucht auf einem Gerüste ge-

roller in a clockwise direction. As the cotton comes through, the other Negro pulls it out from between the rollers with one hand, while with the other he turns the upper roller also clockwise. Thus the rollers turn in opposite directions and so pull the cotton through. But since the space between the two rollers is too small to allow the seeds to go through with the cotton, they come out on the side where the cotton is pushed in. It is easy to see that this goes much faster than when it is done by hand. This process is called "ginning the cotton."

(12) Almost all the woodless land around here is marshy or else so flat that it is under water the greater part of the year, for the water gathers here from the higher land after the least rain. Unhealthful as this land is because of the constant noxious effluvia, it is very profitable to the planter and, next to the oak land, which he uses for indigo, cotton, and garden produce, it is the most profitable. For this is the land, the one and only land, that can be used for the cultivation of *rice*, which demands constant moisture. More than one cut, canal, and ditch has been dug in order to keep flat land under water to prepare it for rice growing. Rice is sown in the middle of April in narrow rows like water cress and so close to the surface that it is barely covered with soil. In six to eight days it pierces the ground and in good land grows as high as six feet. It looks somewhat like wheat or rye, except that the stalk is a little taller and thicker. One seed grain will grow sixty to seventy stalks, each stalk having an ear with one to two hundred grains. What fertility! In September it is cut with sickles. It is left on the stubble for three days, the stalks having been cut so that the stubble sticks out of the water and keeps the rice dry. Then it is bound into sheaves, taken

12. *Rice*

saubert, wo der Wind durch das Herumschütten der Frucht von oben durch 4 Abssäzze die Spreü davon jagd. Die gesauberte Frucht wird hierauf in einer hölzernen Mühle von der Hülsse befreyet, und durch Stampfen mit einem hölzernen Knebel in einem hölzernen Mörsser, die aussere Schale, welche braun und bitter ist, abgetrennet, wann als dann der Reiss durch ein Sifle geläutert worden ist, wird er aufgepackt zum Verkauf. Ein Acker gutes Land, d.i. 420° Fus will product geben 4–5 barril Reiss, 500 lb ᴾ barril, und diesses wurde ᴾ 100 lb für 2 Sp: Dollars (3 lb 2sh. Charlestown altes lawfull Money) vor diessem Kriege auf dem Marckt zu Charlestown verkauft.

13 *Jndigo*

13 *Jndigo*. Der Vortheil, den der Colonist von seinem glücklichen Handel mit Holz, Theer, Reiss, Baumwolle, erhielt, war nicht allein das Geld, das er dadurch erwarb, sondern der Handel, hauptsächlich den activ: Handel (nemlich da er seine Waaren selber nach fremden und weit entfernten Märckten verführte) erwurb ihm Kentnisse, klärte seine Begriffe auf, lernte ihn raffiniren, bemercken, vergleichen, und auch die Art cultur und Wissenschafften des Ausländers in seinem Heimath an zu wenden, bekannt werden zu lassen, zu benuzen. Und sicher mögte ich behaupten, dass kein einziger Westindien, oder England etc besuchte, der nicht auser dem sicheren Vortheil welchen der Verkauf, oder Vertausch seiner Waare ihm brachte, noch ausserdem eine vorher in seinem Lande unbekannte oder unbenuzte Kentniss, Vortheil, etc mit brachte, welche in der Folge von der grösten Wichtigkeit für das Vatterland war, und offtmals vieleicht die Quelle unsäglicher Reichthümer für ganze Districte. Patriotisch war nicht die Beweg-Ursache seiner Handlung hierbey, es war kaufmännisches refinement. Er suchte blos seinen Nuzen, und—der Nuzen des Landes war damit verbunden. Auf diesse

to the barn, and thrashed. After that the grain is winnowed on a rack, the wind carrying off the chaff as the grain is poured down over four inclined boards. The winnowed grain is next husked in a wooden mill; then the outer hull, which is brown and bitter, is removed by pounding the grain with a wooden piston in a wooden mortar. Finally the rice is sifted and packed for shipping. An acre of good land, i.e. 420 feet square, will yield four to five barrels of rice, 500 pounds to a barrel. Before the war it sold at Charleston for two Spanish dollars (£3 2s. Charleston old lawful money) per hundred pounds.

(13) *Indigo*. Money was not the only advantage gained by the colonist from the profitable sale of his wood, tar, rice, and cotton. Through his trade, especially when he himself took his products to foreign and very distant markets, he gained in knowledge and enlightenment. Furthermore, he acquired cunning and the ability to observe and compare. He brought back with him the culture and attainments of foreign countries and acquainted his countrymen with them, so that all profited. It is safe to maintain that no one ever visited the West Indies, or England, etc., who, beside the sure profit obtained by the sale or barter of his goods, did not also bring back with him the knowledge of something previously unknown or unused in his homeland which in the future was to be of the greatest importance and frequently, perhaps, the source of unbelievable wealth for whole regions. It was not patriotism that was the motive of the merchant's actions, but rather his cunning spirit. He sought merely his own gain; the country derived advantage from it only incidentally. It was in this manner, undoubtedly, that indigo was introduced into Carolina. While the native country of this plant is Hindustan,

13. *Indigo*

Art war es ohnstreitig, dass der Jndigo nach Carolina ver-
pflanzt wurde. Das Mutter-Land diesser Pflanze ist Hindostan
und jezt wächst und geräth sie am besten in Mexico und die
Leeward Jslands, von welchen leztern sie nach Carolina
verführet wurde. Allein sie geräth hier nicht halb so gut, und
wird desswegen auf fremden Märckten nicht halb so gut
bezalet. Die Ursache ist, weil das Clima hier noch nicht
warm genug ist, die Sonne glaube ich, ist hoch genug, aber
die immerwährende feüchte Dünste verderben die Luft zu
sehr, dass kein brennender reiner Aether diesser Pflanze ihre
gehörige Reife geben kann.

Der Jndigo wird gesaet im April, ist reif am Ende Julij
wird dann ein Fus hoch von der Erde abgeschnitten, gegen
Ende August wird wieder geschnitten, und ist das Nachjahr
gut, so giebt es 3 Erndten; Was zum Saamen auf künftiges
Jahr bestimmt ist, bleibt unbeschnitten, bis im Nachjahr
stehen, der Saame ist so klein wie ein Senffkorn, und wird
wie der Reiss in kleinen Rillen gesäet, und wächst 5–6 Fus
hoch, der Jndigo sizt in die Blätter, jedes Korn giebt eine
Stange, an welcher mehrere Zweige sind, die jedes mit einer
grossen Menge Blätter bedeckt sind. Weil aber die Abpflik-
kung der einzelnen Blätter zu viele Zeit kosten wurde, so
werden die Stauden abgebrochen, hierauf in grosse Wasser
Behälter gelegt und dasselbst 15–20 Stundten zur Auflössung
gelassen, durch eine Röhre, die mit einem feinen Sifle gestaudet ist, welche Stauden und Blätter zurück halt, wird als
dann diesses Wasser, wenn es einen ziemlichen Grad der
Farbe bekommen hat, in einen andern grossen flachen Behälter, das mit, von Muscheln und Auster Schaalen angesez-
ten Leim Wasser angefüllet ist, gelassen; Diesse Composition
trennet den Jndigo von den wasserigten Theilen, und er sezt
sich zu Boden; wenn er sich gehörig gessezt hat, so wird das
Wasser almählich abgelassen, und der Jndigo gestampft, hier-

it is now also grown with the greatest success in Mexico and the Leeward Islands, whence it was introduced into Carolina. Here, however, it does not do half so well and, consequently, does not fetch half so much on foreign markets. The reason for this is that the climate here is not warm enough. The sun, I believe, is high enough, but the everlasting damp vapours impregnate the atmosphere to such an extent that the burning, pure ether does not reach the plant to give it full maturity.

Indigo is sown in April. It is ripe at the end of July, when it is cut one foot above the ground. Toward the end of August it is cut again and, if the fall is good, will yield a third crop. That which is to be used for seed the following year remains uncut until fall. The seed is the size of mustard seed and, like rice, is sown in narrow drills. It grows five to six feet high. The indigo is contained in the leaves. From every seed grain comes a stalk with several branches covered with numerous leaves. Since picking individual leaves would require too much time, entire stalks are broken off. They are then placed in a large basin of water, where they are left from fifteen to twenty hours to disintegrate. Then the water, which has acquired an appreciable amount of color, is allowed to pass through a fine sieve, which holds back stalks and leaves, into a large vat containing limewater made of mussel and oyster shells. This composition separates the indigo from the watery parts, the indigo settling to the bottom. When it has sufficiently settled, the water is permitted to run off slowly, whereupon the indigo is pounded. This mass is put on a rack to dry. Later it is kneaded and, when completely dried in the sun, is cut into cakes. Though these may now be shipped, they are usually still exposed to the sun as much as possible.

auf auf ein Gatterwerck gelegt, um noch mehr ab zu trock-
nen, sodann gekneten und von der Sonne ganzlich aus gedrocknet, in Tafeln geschnitten: der Jndigo ist jezt fertig,
die Tafeln werden aber noch immer der Sonne so viel möglich,
ausgesezt, und wurde zu 1 Sp. Dollar ᵖ lbr: in Charlestown
(im Jahr 1773) verkaufft, Stauden und Blatt sind, wenn sie
geschnitten worden, grün. Der Waizenboden ist gutes Land
vor dasselbe, und zu viel Regen schadet eher, denn Dürre.
Zur Bestellung 100 Acker à 420 Fus ᵖ acre, werden 30 Negroes
gerechnet, dies macht 1400° Fus ᵖ Mann—. Die Düngung ist
Reiss-Stroh.

Hinrichs

Indigo was sold at Charleston in 1773 for one Spanish dollar
a pound. Stalks and leaves are green when the plant is cut.
It does well in land where wheat will grow. Too great an
amount of rain is more harmful than drought. For the cultivation of 100 acres at 420 feet the acre, 30 Negroes are required; in other words, it is possible for one Negro to
cultivate a plot 1,400 feet square.[1] The indigo is fertilized
with rice straw.

HINRICHS

[1] Hinrichs' figures about acres and feet are entirely wrong; his calculation
as to the number of Negroes needed to cultivate a hundred acres is somewhat low. One Negro could manage about two acres.

DIARY
OF
MAJOR GENERAL
JOHANN CHRISTOPH VON HUYN

UNTERTHÄNIGSTE RELATION

Von der, unter Ordre des Commandirenden Generals Sir Henry-Clinton nach Charles-Town in Sout-Carolina unternom̄enen und ausgeführten Expedition wie folget:

1779. Den 4ᵗⁿ December Wurde die Ordre vom Commandirenden General en Chef folgenden Regimentern, Batailons und Corps, um sich Stündlich zum March und Embarquement parat zu halten, ertheilet, einsweilen aber augenblicklich die Bagage zu Schiffe bringen zu lassen: nehmlich 1ᵗᵉˢ und 2ᵗᵉˢ Batailon Leichte Infanterie, 1ᵗᵉˢ und 2ᵗᵉˢ Batailon Grenadiers, das 7ᵗᵉ und 23ᵗᵉ Regiment Welsch Füseliers, das 33ᵗᵉ, 42ᵗᵉ,* 63ᵗᵉ und 64ᵗᵉ Regiment, Lord Cathcarts Legion, bestehet aus Cavallerie und Infanterie, New York Voluntairs, Fergusons Corps, Eine Esquadron Cavallerie vom 17ᵗⁿ Dragoner Regiment, dergleichen Eine bey die Leichte Infanterie und Grenadiers gehörig nebst Einem ansehnlichen Artillerie Detachement, sämtlich Britten; Sodann die 4 Hessische Grenadier Batailons, Regiment von Huyn, 250 Jäger, unter Ordre des Major von Wurmbs, und 3 Subaltern, 10 unteroffrs und 100 Gemeine, unter Ordre des Capit: Hangers, wurden nach anliegender Ordre (N° 1.) aus denen Hochlöbl: Hessischen Regimentern gezogen. Ausser dieser Ordre würde ich vom General Lieut: von Knyphausen benachrichtiget, alles was zum Regiment gehörte mit zu nehmen, indem ich mit diesem nach geendigter Expedition, vielleicht, anderwärtig placirt und von der New-

---

* [Marginal note] in dem Augenblick, da das Corps embarquirte, wurde das 42ᵗᵉ Regt. contremandirt

HUMBLE RELATION

Of the Expedition to Charleston, South Carolina, under the Command of Sir Henry Clinton

On December 4 the Commanding General issued orders to the fol- 1779
lowing regiments, battalions, and corps to be ready to march
and embark at an hour's notice and to have their baggage
taken aboard the ships immediately, namely: the 1st and
2nd battalions of light infantry, the 1st and 2nd Battalions
of Grenadiers, the 7th, 23rd (Welsh Fusiliers), 33rd, 42nd,*
63rd, and 64th Regiments, Lord Cathcart's Legion, consisting
of cavalry and infantry, the New York Volunteers, Ferguson's
Corps, a squadron of horse of the 17th Regiment of Dragoons,
a squadron serving with the light infantry and grenadiers,
as well as a considerable detachment of artillery—all British
troops; then the four Hessian grenadier battalions, von
Huyn's Regiment, and 250 jägers under the command of
Major von Wurmb. Three subalterns, ten noncommissioned
officers, and a hundred rank and file under Captain Hanger
were, in accordance with the enclosed orders (No. 1), drawn
from the Hessian regiments. I received instructions from
Lieutenant General von Knyphausen to take along everything
belonging to my regiment, since after the expedition we
would probably be stationed away from the New York

* [Marginal note] At the moment of embarkation the 42nd Regiment
was countermanded.

Yorker Garnison getrennet Bleiben dürfte. Die Generals welche Ordre zum Embarquiren erhielten und mit zu obigem Corps bestimmet wurden, waren Lord-Cornwallis, ich, der General Major von Kospoth und der Brigade General Batterson.

Den 19^{tn} selbigen Monats December erhielte ich des Morgens 2 uhr die Ordre, gleich zu Marchiren, und so wie das gantze Corps im Yorker-Hafen zu Embarquiren, welches aber erstlich den 21^{tn} d° wegen Grimmiger Kälte und Sturmigtem Wasser geendiget würde.

Den 26^{tn} Gieng die Flotte unter Seegel und bestand aus 86 Transports und Ordonnanz-Schiffen, und wurde durch die in der Anlage (N° 2.) Bemerckte Kriegs-Schiffe convoyiret.

Vom 28^{tn} bis zum 29^{tn} war Sturm, wo das Schiff Ann 2 Maste verlohr, auf welchem das aus den[en]* Hochlöbl: Hessischen Regimentern gezogene Chasseur Detachment sämtlich, ingleichen 1 unteroffr: und 18 Hessische- und 1 unteroffr: und 10-Anspachische Jäger waren, Dieses wurde nachhero an ein

1780 Kriegs-Schiff angehängt.

Vom 2^{tn} bis zum 3^{tn} Iannuar: war wieder ein sehr continuirlicher Sturm, wo die Flotte fast gäntzlich auseinander gesprengt:— Vom 5^{tn} bis zum 6^{tn} abermals ein starcker Sturm, und wurde die Flotte nunmehro so durchaus separirt, dass nur noch etliche, Schiffe, worunter das, wo ich und der General von Kospoth auf waren noch beym Admiral sich befanden; Nachdem der Sturm nach lies versam̃lete sich die Flotte bis zu 50 Seegel, inclusive Kriegs-Schiffe, Das Schiff *Ann* aber wurde durch diesen Sturm von seinem Kriegs Schiff wieder los gerissen; Man glaubt es sey entweder nach Westindien oder New-Providenz verschlagen. Drey Transporte, welche Britten an board hatten, giengen, nach dem die Menschen davon gerettet, augenblicklich zu Grunde. Ein 4tes, welches 80

---

* The brackets in this diary, except here and in the entry for April 31—May 1, indicate material worn away in the original.

garrison.[1] The generals who received orders to embark and
partake in the expedition are Lord Cornwallis, myself, Major
General von Kospoth, and Brigadier General Paterson.

On the 19th of the same month, December, I received orders at two
o'clock in the morning to march at once and embark with
the entire corps in New York harbor. However, because of
very cold weather and rough water the embarkation was not
completed until the 21st of the month.

On the 26th the fleet set sail. It consisted of eighty-six transports
and ordnance ships and was convoyed by the men-of-war
noted in the enclosure (No. 2).

From the 28th till the 29th we had storms, during which the *Anna*
lost two masts. She had on board the entire detachment of
chasseurs drawn from the Hessian regiments, as well as a noncommissioned officer with eighteen Hessian jägers and a
noncommissioned officer with ten Anspach jägers. She was
later taken in tow by a warship.

From the 2nd till the 3rd of January we had stormy weather all the
time. The fleet was almost entirely scattered. From the 5th
till the 6th there was likewise a severe storm, and the fleet
was now dispersed so completely that only a few ships were
with the Admiral, among them that on which were myself and
General von Kospoth. After the storm had subsided the fleet
reassembled to the number of fifty sail, including the warships. The *Anna*, however, was torn away from the warship
towing her. It is believed that she has been driven either to
the West Indies or to New Providence. Three transports with
British troops on board foundered the moment the last men
were rescued. A fourth transport, which had on board eighty

[1] Von Huyn's Regiment remained at Charleston until December, 1782,
when the city was evacuated. He himself, however, returned to New York,
where he died from consumption July 25, 1780.

Brittische Constables und Artillerie ordonnancen hatte, war just so nahe zum untergehen, dass nährlich ein Brittischer Privateer, so diesem Begegnete, die Menschen davon nehmen konte und solche auf die Jnsul Permudes absetzte; ingleichen ist ein Cavallerie Schiff von denen Rebellen weggenoṁen und zu Charles Town eingebracht. Endlich kam die Flotte

Den 1ᵗⁿ Februarii zu Tybee an, woselbst etwa 16 Schiffe zur Flotte gehörig und durch die Stürṁe von solcher separirt gewesen, allbereits vorgefunden wurden. Säṁtliche Schiffe, wo die Hochlöbl: Hessische Trouppen auf waren, sind glücklich Arrivirt, ausser das vorerwehnte *Ann*.

Den 2ᵗⁿ Gieng die Flotte bis zu 20 Englische Meilen von Savannah in Georgien vor Ancker und nahm frisch-Wasser. Der Coṁandirende General en Chef avertirte mich durch ein Schreiben, dass ich nebst dem General Major von Kospoth etwa einen Tag nach der Stadt gehen könnte: welches denn auch den 4ᵗⁿ geschahe, wo ich die 2 Regimenter D'Angelleli und vacant von Wissenbach und deren Parade besahe und alles in gehöriger Ordnung vorfande: Die Krankheit daselbst hatte sich ziemlich gelegt, nur sehen die Soldaten etwas Blass aus. Nachdem die Flotte Wasser genoṁen, die zu oben erwehnten Regimentern gehörige Recroutten und Montirungsstücke, den Brigade General Batterson nebst denen Brittischen Leichten Corps debarquirt hatte, gieng solche

den 9ᵗⁿ wieder unter Seegel, und kam

den 11ᵗⁿ zu Nord Edisto nahe bey Iohns Island, ohngefehr 25 Meilen von Charles-Town in Sout Carolina an, und würde die Armeé nach der Anlage (Nº 3) Debarquirt, und in Divissions und Brigaden eingetheilt, und enbibac auf gedachtes Jsland gelagert. Sämtliche Weisse Einwohner machten sich mit ihrem Gewehr und Waffen nebst Munition, welche der Militz dahier eigen, nach der Stadt, liesen Weib und Kinder nebst ihre Mohren zurück.

Jn der Ordre vom 12ᵗⁿ recoṁandirte der Coṁandirende General en

British gunners and ordnance stores, was so near foundering when she met a British privateer that there was barely enough time to save the men. They were later landed in the Bermudas. Also, a cavalry transport was captured by the rebels and has been taken into Charleston. Finally,

on February 1, the fleet arrived at Tybee, where we found about [February] sixteen ships that had been separated from the fleet during the storms. With the exception of the said *Anna* all the ships that had Hessian troops on board arrived safely.

On the 2nd the fleet came to anchor twenty English miles from Savannah, Georgia, and began to take on fresh water. From the Commanding General I received a letter informing me that I myself and Major General von Kospoth could go to the city for a day or two, which we did on the 4th. While there I looked over the Regiments d'Angelelli and Vacant von Wissenbach and witnessed their parade, finding everything in good order. There is not much sickness now, though the men look a little pale. After the fleet had taken on water, disembarked the troops, and unloaded the uniforms for the regiments mentioned above,[1] and Brigadier General Paterson together with the British light corps had been disembarked, the fleet set sail again

on the 9th and arrived

on the 11th in the North Edisto close to Johns Island, approximately twenty-five miles from Charleston, South Carolina. The army, divided into divisions and brigades, disembarked as per enclosure (No. 3) and encamped on the said island. All the white inhabitants were on their way to the city with their guns, arms, and ammunition, leaving behind their wives and children as well as their Negroes.

On the 12th the Commanding General issued an order requesting

---

[1] See p. 106, note 2, and p. 107, note 3.

Februar: Chef, dass ein jeder Officier aufs aüsserste sich Bemühen würde die gute Disciplin die einem Rechtschaffenen Soldaten anständig zu Beobachten; damit der Ehre der Trouppen durch keine desordre Abbruch geschähe, indem die Sorge der guten Mans-Zucht niemalen entEhrte.

Den 14^{tn} Gieng der General Major Lessle, welcher mit von Savannah gekoñen, mit dem 33^{tn} Regt., 1^{tn} Batailon Leichte Jnfanterie, und denen Jägers über den Edisto Fluss Westwärts oder Stono Ferry um der Armee vermuthlich die Lincke Flanque zu decken.

Den 16^{tn} Würden die 2 Regimenter das 7te und 23te hinüber und zu obigem Corps Detachirt und das Batailon Leichte Infanterie wurde wieder zu der Divission der Lord-Cornwallis herüber gezogen, Der Oberst Lieut: Webster 33^{tn} Regiments erhielte das Coñando und der General Lessle gieng wieder zu seiner Brigade.

Den 24^{tn} Passirte Lord Cornwallis, der General Lessle nebst der Leichten Jnfanterie und Brittischen Grenadiers den Stono Fluss und faste Posto auf James-Jsland.

Den 25^{tn} folgten die 4 Hessische Grenadier Batailons unter Ordre des General Major von Kospoths.

Den 26^{tn} Der Commandirende General en Chef selbsten.

Den 27^{tn} ich mit meiner Brigade, ausser das 63te Regiment wurde einsweilen zur Deckung der Provission zurück gelassen. An diesem Tage kam der Admiral ans Landt, wo der Commandirende General verlangte, dass mein unterhabendes Regiment ausrücken, und gedachtem Admiral die Honeur machen muste, Er auch dieses zu sehen verlangte. Die Anstalten wurden bey Wasser und Lande getroffen, um die Artillerie und Munition, nunmehro auf dieses Jsland zu schaffen, und musten die Canonen, in ermangelung Pferdten, welche auf der See verlohren worden, durch Soldaten gezogen werden, und waren zu weilen 100 Man zu einer 24 pfündigen erforderlich.

Die Armee wurde Lincks Rangirt und folgender gestalt gela-

that every officer should strive to the utmost to maintain the good discipline becoming a soldier, so that the reputation of the troops should not be sullied, since attention to good discipline had never brought dishonor upon an army.

On the 14th Major General Leslie, who had come with us from Savannah, crossed either Stono Ferry or the Edisto River to the westward with the 33rd Regiment, the 1st battalion of light infantry, and the jägers, presumably in order to cover the left flank of the army.[1]

On the 16th the 7th and 23rd Regiments joined General Leslie's corps, while the battalion of light infantry was ordered back to the division of Lord Cornwallis. Lieutenant Colonel Webster of the 33rd Regiment received the command and General Leslie went back to his brigade.

On the 24th Lord Cornwallis and General Leslie with the light infantry and British grenadiers crossed the Stono River and took post on James Island.

On the 25th the four Hessian grenadier battalions followed under Major General von Kospoth and

on the 26th the Commanding General himself.

I and my brigade except the 63rd Regiment stayed behind for the time being in order to cover our stores. This day the Admiral landed and, in accordance with the wishes of the Commanding General, my regiment turned out to do him the honors, which was also in accordance with his wishes. Preparations were made on water and on land to bring artillery and munitions to this island. Since our horses had been lost at sea, the guns had to be hauled by soldiers, a 24-pounder sometimes requiring a hundred men.

The army was drawn up on the left and encamped as fol-

[1] He did not cross either river at this time. On the 16th, however, the Stono was crossed. See Hinrichs' diary and Ewald's letter under February 16.

Februar: gert: nehmlich, Lincker-Flügell gerade gegen der Stadt über, 1tes und 2tes Batailon Leicht Jnfanterie, 1tes und 2tes Batailon Brittische Grenadiers; Die Huynische Brigade in der Mitte, und die Hessische Grenadiers auf den Rechten Flügell, nahe hinter das Forth Johnston, welches hart am Aschleyfluss liegt.

Den 28^{tn} Legte sich eine Rebellen Fregatte hart vors Ufer gedachten Forths, Canonirte die Hessische Grenadiers in ihrem Lager, worbey einem Grenadier ein Bein abgeschossen, welcher dann auch verstarb, und ein anderer an einem Arm hart Blessirt wurde, waren beyde vom Batailon Graff und stunden auf der Brandtwacht, nicht weniger wurden denen Grenadiers verschiedene Gewehre entzwey Geschossen, ingleichen blieb bey dieser Gelegenheit ein Brittischer Constable Todt.

Den 29^{tn} bis zum 6^{tn} Mart: würde eine Brücke über den Wappoofluss gemacht und das Hauptquartier (Perroneaus hauss) starck befestigt, und noch 2 andere Redoutten gemacht, dieses alles ist die Gegend wo die Leichte Infanterie campirt, auch wurden hier die nöthige Verhacke angelegt und überhaupt Täglich

Martii 2000. Arbeiter gegeben.

Den 3^{tn} Langte das 2te Batailon vom 71^{tn} Regiment von Savannah hier an, wurde aber zum Oberst Lieut: Webster Detachirt und dargegen das 7te und 23te Reg^{t} anhero gezogen und conjungirten sich mit der Leichten Jnfanterie auf dem Lincken Flügell.

Den 6^{tn} Wurde das 2te Batailon 71^{tn} Regts under Ordre des Oberst Lieut: Websters weggenoṁen und auf das Leichthauss Jsland, so gegen der Charles Towner Bar über ist, postirt, um den Admiral, wenn er solche passiren würde, von daher zu decken. Die Nacht vom 6^{tn} zum 7^{tn} passirte Lord Cornwallis die über dem Wappoo Fluss gemachte Brücke, mit der Leichten Infanterie, und des Morgens früh 5 uhr folgte der Commandirende General mit dem 1^{tn} Batailon Brittischer Grenadiers. Die intention dieses schleünigen übergangs war, um die auf gedachtem Wappoo Jsland postirte Feindliche Cavallerie und Militz zu surpreniren, gelung aber nicht, indem ein Bedienter eines

lows: the left wing, directly opposite the city, was formed
by the 1st and 2nd battalions of light infantry and the 1st
and 2nd Battalions of British Grenadiers; Huyn's brigade
was in the middle; and the Hessian grenadiers were on the
right wing close behind Fort Johnson, which is situated right
against the Ashley River.

On the 28th a rebel frigate came close to this fort and cannonaded
the Hessian grenadiers in their camp. One grenadier had a
leg shot off, from which he later died; another was severely
wounded in the arm. Both were from Graff's Battalion and
were on duty as fireguards. In addition, the grenadiers had
some muskets shot to pieces, and a British gunner was killed.

Between the 29th of February and the 6th of March a bridge
was built over the Wappoo River; headquarters, Peronneau's
house, was strongly fortified, and two redoubts were thrown
up—all this in the neighborhood of the light infantry camp.
Also, the necessary abatis were put up. This took working
parties of two thousand men a day.

On March 3 the 2nd Battalion of the 71st Regiment arrived from
Savannah. It was detached to serve under the command of
Lieutenant Colonel Webster, while the 7th and 23rd Regiments left his command to join the light infantry on the left
wing.

On the 6th the 2nd Battalion of the 71st Regiment was taken from
the command of Lieutenant Colonel Webster and posted on
Lighthouse Island, opposite the Bar of Charleston, to cover
the Admiral when he should cross the Bar. In the night of
the 6–7th Lord Cornwallis with the light infantry crossed
the bridge built over the Wappoo River, and at five in the
morning the Commanding General followed with the 1st
Battalion of British Grenadiers. By crossing thus early they
had hoped to surprise the hostile cavalry and militia posted

Mart. Grenadier Capt. Desertirte und vermuthlich den March verrathen hatte; einige Gefangene wurden gemacht, welche die
unmöglichkeit des wegnehmen der Stadt Behaupteten.

Den 9^{tn} wurde der Poste jenseits Stono Ferry verlassen und der
Oberst Lieut: Webster mit dem 33^{tn} Reg^t. und den Jägers von
daher und an die Brittische Grenadiers gezogen.

Den 10^{tn} Fasste Lord Cornwallis und General Lessle auf Wappoo
mit der Brittischen Leicht-Jnfanterie und Grenadiers, 7^{tn}, 23-
und 33^{tn} Reg^t: nebst denen Hessischen Jägers Posto: und
wurden nunmehro 2 Hessische Grenadier Batailons von ihrer
Postirung abgefordert, und occupirten einen Theil von dem
Grund wo erste wegmarschiert, und das 64te Reg^t. wo die
Brittische Grenadier gestanden.

Den 12^{tn} Rückte 64. bey das Hauptquartier an die 2. Hessische Grenadier Batailons, Reg^t. Huyn occupirte den Platz den ersteres
verlies.

Den 13^{tn} Wurde 63 von Johns Jsland herüber Beordert und bey Huyn
gelagert.

Den 14^{tn} Wurden unter Ordre des Major Mecan 23^{tn} Regts:, 2
Capt:, 2 Subalterns und 150 Unteroffrs und Gemeine von 64
und Huyn in eine von denen Hessischen Grenadiers Neügc-
machte Redoutte nahe bey Forth Johnston gegeben.

Den 17^{tn} Wurde der General Major von Kospoth mit denen noch
bey sich habenden 2 Batailons Grenadier anhero und an die 2
andere Hessische Batailons gezogen.

Der Admiral legte sich mit seiner Flotte vor die sogenannte
Bar und nahm die nötigen Canonen und Wasser Fässer aus und
embarquirte solche auf etliche Transports, seine Schiffe etwas
leichter zu machen, um mehr besagte Bar passiren zu können.

Den 20^{tn} wurde solche von dem Admiral passirt, ohne von der
Feindlichen Flotte daran gehindert werden zu können, nahm
seine Canonen und Wasserfässer wieder ein, und legte sich,
doch ausser Schuss, dem Forth Moultrie, welches auf Sulivans
Jsland und sehr considerable ist, en Linie entgegen. Die Re-

on Wappoo Island. They were unsuccessful, however, since a March
servant of a grenadier captain deserted and, apparently, betrayed their march. They made several prisoners who con-
tended that it was impossible to reduce the city.

On the 9th the post on the far side of Stono Ferry was abandoned
and Lieutenant Colonel Webster with the 33rd Regiment and
the jägers joined the British grenadiers.

On the 10th Lord Cornwallis and General Leslie took post on
Wappoo [mainland] with the British light infantry and grenadiers, the 7th, 23rd, and 33rd Regiments, as well as the
Hessian jägers. Two Hessian grenadier battalions received
orders to leave their post and occupy a part of the ground
vacated by these troops, while the 64th Regiment encamped
where the British grenadiers had been stationed.

On the 12th the 64th moved to headquarters and joined the two
Hessian grenadier battalions, while Huyn's Regiment occupied the place thus vacated.

On the 13th the 63rd was ordered to come over from Johns Island
and encamp near Huyn's.

On the 14th Major Mecan of the 23rd Regiment with two captains,
two subalterns, and one hundred and fifty noncommissioned
officers and privates of the 64th and Huyn's was sent into
one of the redoubts near Fort Johnson, which had just been
thrown up by the Hessian grenadiers.

On the 17th Major General von Kospoth, with the two grenadier
battalions still under him, arrived here and joined the two
other Hessian battalions.

The Admiral and his fleet approached what is called the
Bar and loaded enough guns and water casks onto transports
to lighten his ships to cross it.

On the 20th the Admiral crossed the Bar without the enemy's being
able to hinder him, took his guns and water casks on again,

Mart. bellische und Franzoesische Fregatten, welcher 7 von unter-
schiedlichen Calibres waren, nebst noch andern dergleichen
Bewaffneten Fahrzeügen verliessen ihre Stellung und Retirirten sich in den Kopperfluss.

Den 22^{tn} Passirte der General Major von Kospoth nebst 3 Grenadier Batailons die über den Wappo Fluss gemachte Brücke,
und vereinigte sich mit dem Corps Britten, welches vorhero
erwehnt worden, und diese passirt hatte, Das 4te Batailon
folgte den andern Tag.

Die Nacht vom 22^{tn} zum 23^{tn} wurden 4 Rebellen, welche von der
Stadt aus den Aschlefluss passirt und herüber gekoṁen, vom
Capit: Haecker zu gefangene gemacht, dieser ward von mir
mit 1 unteroffr: und 8 Man, nachdem ein Schwartzer die
Anzeige that, dass 5 Rebellen ¼ stunde von meinem Q^{rtier} wären, des Nachts 11 uhr solchen in möglichster Geschwindigkeit nachgeschickt, welcher durch 1 unteroffr. und 4 Man
deren Rückgang augenblicklich besetzte, und mit de[n] übrigen nach dem Platz, wo sie seyn solten sich verfügte. Nachdem er an kam gaben solche Feüer und liefen den Weg woher
sie gekoṁen und einfolglich denen die ihre Retraite occupirt
in die Hände, der 5te aber sauvirte sich durch Morast und
Wasser.

Den 23^{tn} ward über obige Gefangene General-Kriegs-Gericht gehalten, um zu vernehmen, ob sie als Spionen, oder was Absichten
herüber gekoṁen.*

eodem. Wurde das 2te Batailon 71^{tn} Reg^{ts}. von dem Leichthauss
Jsland Beordert und zwischen Huyn und das Hauptquartier
gelagert. Auf Wappoo und zwar Fenwicks point wurden 2
starcke Redoutten nahe an dem Aschle-Fluss gemacht, und
gleich mit 9–32 pfünder augmentirt.

Den 26^{tn} Wurde der Admiral durch 5 Kriegs Schiffe verstärckt;
diese waren als convoy mit einer Provissions-Flotte von England gekommen.

* [Marginal note] ihre intent: war ein oder die andere Schildwacht auf
zu heben, um Nachricht von der Armee zu haben.

and anchored in a line with Fort Moultrie, but beyond the March range of its guns. This fort is situated on Sullivan Island and is very strong. Seven rebel and French frigates of various sizes and other armed vessels left their station and withdrew into the Cooper River.

On the 22nd Major General von Kospoth and three grenadier battalions crossed the bridge built over the Wappoo and joined the above-mentioned British corps, which had crossed over some time ago. The fourth battalion followed the next day.

In the night of the 22nd–23rd four rebels, who had crossed the Ashley River from the city, were taken prisoners by Captain Haecker. After being informed by a Negro that five rebels had advanced to within about a mile of my quarters, I dispatched the said captain with one noncommissioned officer and eight men at eleven o'clock at night to act with all possible haste. Captain Haecker immediately posted the noncommissioned officer and four men to cut off their retreat and with the rest went to the place where the little party was said to be. When he arrived, they fired their muskets and then ran back the way they had come; thus four were taken prisoners, the fifth escaping through morass and water.

On the 23rd a general court-martial was held to determine whether these prisoners had come as spies or for some other purpose.*

On this day the 2nd Battalion of the 71st was ordered from Lighthouse Island and was encamped between Huyn's and headquarters. On Wappoo [mainland], on Fenwick's Point, to be exact, two strong redoubts were thrown up close to the Ashley River and fortified immediately with nine 32-pounders.

On the 26th the Admiral's shipping was reinforced by five men-of-war that had come from England as convoys with a provision fleet.

* [Marginal note] Their intention had been to capture some sentinel or other to obtain information about the army.

Mart: Die Nacht vom 28ᵗⁿ zum 29ᵗⁿ Gieng der Commandirende General
en Chef, mit der Leichten Jnfanterie, Brittischen und Hessischen Grenadiers, 7ᵗⁿ 23, 33, 1ᵗⁿ und 2ᵗⁿ Batailon 71 Regts:
nebst denen Hessischen Jäger über den Aschlefluss auf Charles
Towns Neck und fasste posto folgender gestalt: 1ᵗᵉˢ Treffen,
Fronte nach der Stadt zu: Leichte Jnfanterie, Brittische Grenadiers und Jägers; 2ᵗᵉˢ Treffen, welches hart an die Brittische
Grenadiers angehängt, Bestund aus den Hessischen Grenadiers;
3ᵗᵉˢ Treffen Fronte rückwärts nach dem Rebellischen Corps zu
(welches ihnen nunmehro im Rücken stand) um dieses zu ob-
serviren, nehmlich das 7ᵗᵉ, 23, 33, und das 71ᵗᵉ Regiment.
Die Stadt ward nunmehro Nordwärts und von daher ebenfalss
ploquirt. Der General Batterson (welcher von Savannah mit
denen so dort von der Flotte ausgesetzten Leichten Trouppen,
dort gestandenen Leichten Jnfanterie, 1ᵗⁿ Batailon vom 71ᵗⁿ
Regᵗ. und 2 Batailons Provincial Trouppen bey Lande angekoṁen) occupirte den Grund, welchen Lord Cornwallis vom
28ᵗⁿ zum 29ᵗⁿ verlassen, und die coṁunication zwischen der
Huynischen Brigade und dem Coṁandirenden General zu unterhalten; besagter General wurde zwar verschiedene malen
von kleinen feindlichen Corps auf seinem March gehindert,
die Sache wurde aber jedes malen kurtz decedirt und der
Feind zum fliehen genöthigt.

Den 30ᵗⁿ Recognoscirte der Commandirende General en Chef die
Feindliche Linien und Wercker, bey dieser Gelegenheit wurde
der Lord Caithness, welcher mit in der Suitte war, gar hart
Blessirt; Auch wurde ein Jäger, von einem dergleichen Detachement, welches nahe bey jene Wercker postirt war, nach-
deme dieses vom Feind einen ziemlichen Anfall hatte, sehr
misshandelt und getödtet, und 2 andere blessirt, welche aber
nicht in Rebellen Hände fielen, an sonsten wurde es diesen
als erstern ergangen seyn. Bey dieser Gelegenheit wurden verschiedene Rebellen Officiers von ihren Pferdten, durch die
Jäger herunter geschossen.

In the night of the 28–29th the Commanding General with the March
light infantry, the British and Hessian grenadiers, the 7th,
23rd, and 33rd Regiments, the 1st and 2nd Battalions of the
71st, and the Hessian jägers crossed the Ashley River to
Charleston Neck and took post as follows: the first contingent, consisting of light infantry, British grenadiers, and
jägers, faced the city; the second contingent, namely, the
Hessian grenadiers, were in touch with the British grenadiers;
the third contingent, made up of the 7th, 23rd, 33rd, and 71st,
faced the rear to observe the rebel corps.

The city was now blockaded also on the north, for General Paterson, in order to maintain communication between
Huyn's brigade and the Commanding General, occupied the
ground which Lord Cornwallis had vacated in the night of
the 28–29th. General Paterson had come by land from Savannah with the light troops disembarked from the fleet, the
light infantry previously stationed there, the 1st Battalion
of the 71st Regiment, and two battalions of provincials. On
this march he was repeatedly annoyed by small enemy troops,
but each affair was quickly decided and the enemy put to
flight.

On the 30th the Commanding General reconnoitred the enemy's
lines and works. Lord Caithness, who was in his suite, was
severely wounded. In another encounter a jäger with a scouting party posted near the enemy's works was badly mal-
treated and then killed; two others were wounded but did
not fall into the rebels' hands; otherwise, their fate would
have been the same. During this skirmish several rebel officers
were shot from their horses by jägers.

From the 31st of March to the 3rd of April some sixty heavy [April]
pieces, howitzers, etc., etc., were brought over. A thousand

April Vom 31^{tn} zum 3^{tn} April wurden an die 60 stück schwehre Canonen und Haubitzen etc etc hinüber gebracht, die Schantzen bis zu N^{ro} 7, ingleichen die Lauffgraben und überhaupt die nötigen Linien waren durch 1000. Arbeiter* Tag und Nacht beschleüniget und ohngefehr 5–u. 600 Ehlen von den Feindlichen angelegt: Allnächtlich wurde Ein General nebst 1000 Man in die Linien ins Piquet comandirt.

Den 4^{tn} Fingen die Feindliche Fregatten aus dem Kopper River an, auf unssere Arbeiter zu Canoniren, ingleichen von ihren Werckern; Hier wurde ein Brittischer Officier und dergleichen 3 Gemeine blessirt und einer Todt geschossen, ingleichen wurden einige Hessische Grenadier Leicht blessirt.

Den 5^{tn} machten die 4 Brittische Galeeren, welche in der Mundung des Wappooflusses vor der Stadt lagen, ingleichen die 2 Redoutten auf Fenwicks Neck ihre erste Attaque auf die Stadt; auch kamen heüte die zu Bermudes abgesetzte Brittische Constabler Glücklich und Gesund und noch zur rechten zeit hier an.

Den 6^{tn} waren die Arbeiter, ingleichen die Galeeren sehr heftig von der Stadt Canonirt, ingleichen die Redoutten zu Fenwicks Neck, aber ohne effect.

Den 7^{tn} Ziemlich ruhig.

Den 8^{tn} Passirte nunmehro der Admiral das auf Sulivans-Jsland gelegene considerable Forth Moultrie in folgenden Manöuvres und attaque: nehml. das Schiff Roebuck, welches durch Sir Henry Hanmond commandird wird, und auf diesem sich dann auch der Admiral selbsten befande, machte die Téte, und nachdem es gerade gegen das Forth kam, und mit etlichen 100 Schüssen empfangen wurde, legte es sich gegen Wind und Gab eine gantze Lage, warff sich in diesem Augenblick herum, und gab die 2te; in diesem Zeit verlust passirte ein anderes hinter und neben ersterem weg, ohne sich hier zu engagiren, machte aber seine Attaque auf ein anderes, gleich auf erstes folgende

* [Marginal note] Diese Arbeiter wurden nachhero nur bis zu 500 gegeben.

workmen* labored day and night to finish quickly the earthworks leading to redoubt No. 7, as well as the trenches and
the necessary lines, about five or six hundred yards from the
enemy's works. A general and one thousand men were ordered
to go into the lines every night for picket duty.

On the 4th the enemy opened fire on our working parties from
several of their frigates in the Cooper River and also from
their works. A British officer and three British privates were
wounded and another private was killed; several Hessian
grenadiers were slightly wounded also.

On the 5th the four British galleys lying in the mouth of the
Wappoo River opposite the city and the two redoubts on
Fenwick's Neck opened fire on the city. Today the British
gunners who had disembarked in the Bermudas arrived hale
and hearty and in good time.

On the 6th the working parties and the galleys as well as the redoubts on Fenwick's Neck were severely bombarded from the
city, but without effect.

On the 7th rather quiet.

On the 8th the Admiral passed Fort Moultrie on Sullivan Island,
executing the following manoeuvres and attack: The *Roebuck,*
commanded by Sir Andrew Hamond, with the Admiral on
board, led the column. When she was directly in front of the
fort, having been received with some hundred shots, she lay
to and fired a broadside, then quickly put about ship and fired
another. During this time the second ship passed without
engaging Fort Moultrie and made an attack upon another
fort just beyond. In the ensuing cannonade she lost a mast.
The third ship came and relieved the first, attacking in the
same manner. The rest then followed, all executing the same

* [Marginal note] Later only five hundred workmen were furnished.

April   Forth, w[o] es den Augenblick eine Mast verlohr; Das 3te
kam und lösste, das erstere mit nehmlicher Attaque, wie
gesagt worden, ab, und so folgten die übrigen hierzu bestim̃-
ten in vorstehenden Manöuvres.* Drey Transporte waren mit
unter obigem Zuge, welche mit Canonen und Amunition etc
etc Beladen, wovon eins auf eine Sandbanck kam und da ein
ausserordentlich Feüer abhalten muste, kam aber durch Hülfe
der Fluth wieder los, und wurde, nachdem die Menschen
davon Gerettet, von unsse[r] Seite in Brand gesteckt. Den 9^{tn}
aber canonirten die Rebellen ohne effect.

Den 10^{tn}.   Der Com̃andirende General forderte nunmehro nach der Anlage (N° 1.) d[ie] Stadt auf, und machte dem General Lincoln
bekant, dass er fertig sey die Stadt zu Canoniren und zu Bombardiren: Er würde sich gefallen lassen die Stadt nebst Fe-
stungs Werckern etc und allen Schiffen Jhme einzuraumen,
und sämtliche Trouppen die Gewehre nieder zu legen und sich
zu Kriegs-Gefangene zu ergeben.

Die Antwort vom General Lincoln war folgende:

> Er habe seit 62 Tagen des General Clintons intention
> gewust, und daher die Stadt in Vertheydigungsstand ge-
> setzt. Seine Neigunge und selbsten die Pflicht, beydes
> erlaubten nicht die Stadt zu übergeben, sondern Er diese
> zum lezten Bluts-Tropfen deffentiren wolte—.

Den 12^{tn} u. 13^{tn} Wurde Fergusons Corps und 64 auf Charles Towns
Neck gezogen und in das 3te Treffen gelagert; Reg^{t}: Huyn
occupirte den Grund bey den 2 Redoutten auf Fenwicks Neck,
welchen 64 verlies, ausser 100 Man blieben bey Perroneaus und
einfolglich bey 63 stehen, weilen dieses alda nicht hinlänglich. Nunmehro wurden die Batterien auf Charles-Towns Neck
zum 1^{tn} mal eröfnet, und so folgten die von Fenwicks Neck
mit solchem effect, dass die Stadt an 2 Orthen Brandte; Die

* [Marginal note] Bey dieser Gelegenheit hatte der Admiral 7 Todte und
14 Blessirt.

manoeuvres.* [1] Among them were three transports loaded
with guns, ammunition, etc., etc., one of which ran aground
on a sandbank, where she had to withstand a terrific cannonade. With the help of the incoming tide she got afloat
again, but was set on fire by our men after the persons on
board had been rescued. On the 9th the rebels cannonaded
without effect. April

The Commanding General then summoned the city to surrender (enclosure No. 1 [4]). He informed General Lincoln
that he was prepared to cannonade and bombard the city,
but that he would be satisfied if given possession of the city,
the fortifications, and all the ships, and if the entire army
laid down its arms and surrendered as prisoners of war. The 10th

General Lincoln's answer was to this effect:

> For sixty-two days[2] he had known General Clinton's
> intentions and had therefore put the city in a state of
> defense. His inclination and his duty did not permit him
> to surrender the city. He would, on the contrary, defend
> it to the last extremity.

On the 12th and 13th Ferguson's Corps and the 64th moved to
Charleston Neck and encamped with the third contingent.
Huyn's Regiment, except for a hundred men who remained at
Peronneau's with the 63rd, since this force was not sufficiently

---

* [Marginal note] On this occasion the Admiral had seven killed and
fourteen wounded.

[1] Von Huyn seems to be drawing on his imagination. No other account,
American, British, or Hessian, makes reference to such manoeuvres.

[2] Lincoln's letter says: "Sixty days have passed . . . ." It was exactly
sixty days since the British troops had landed in the North Edisto. However, General Lincoln had certain knowledge of the impending siege long
before that. At least he wrote to General Washington, July 17, 1780: "On
ye 10 of Novem[r] following [1779], when ye enemy's designs no longer remained a doubt, they [Congress] ordered three of ye Contin[l] frigates to
Chas. Town, for ye defence of it's harbour" (printed in *Charleston Yearbook*,
1897, p. 353).

April Rebellen erwiederten dieses Feüer sehr heftig. Hier würde einem Hessischen Grenadier der Kopf weggeschossen, dergleichen ein anderer und 7 Britten blessirt. Der Oberst Lieut: Webster wurde mit Einem Corps aus dem 3ten Treffen nebst dem 33ten Regt. und der Cavallerie unter Ordre des Oberst Lieut: Tarletons an den Kopperfluss rückwärts Detachirt, wo bey noch am ende gedachten Flusses die Rebellen eine Brücke hatten, wo sie ihre Munition, Provission etc aus dem Lande hinüber und an der andern Seite herunter zur Stadt Brachten; Dieser Coup gelung mit gutem Success, Er kam der daseyenden Rebellischen Cavallerie und Militz so geheim und geschwind auf den Hals, dass sie kaum im Stande waren, einen Canonen Schuss zu thun, so ward er Meister von der Brücke, von etlichen 40 mit Provission und Munition Beladenen Wagens, Boats, Chalouppen und machte 73 Dragoner und Militz zu gefangenen, exclusive einige 100 Pferdte; Der Oberst Wassington ward mit gefangen, sein flüchtiges Pferdt ward ihme, vielleicht aus übereylung einsweilen gelassen, worauf er dann sich auch wieder sauvirte; Ein Rebellen Major nebst 12 Man dergleichen Blieben Todt. Der Oberst Lieut: setzte nunmehro seinen March an der andern Seite des Kopper Rivers herunter fort, um von daher die Stadt ebenfalls einzuschliessen.

Den 14ten 15ten u. 16ten ward stark von beyden Seiten Canonirt und Bombardirt, wo einem Officier auf denen Galeeren ein Bein Abgeschossen und das andere blessirt wurde, auch blieb ein Brittischer Grenadier Todt. Das Huynische Lager bey Fenwicks Batterie, wurde starck aber ohne effect Bombardirt.

Den 17ten u. 18ten starck canonirt, und wurden 2 Britten Blessirt, auch hatte man schon Nachricht, dass der Oberst Lieut: Webster auf der andern Seite des Kopper-Rivers und der Stadt Glück-

1 This is Biggins bridge (see p. 61, note 1).

2 The wounded officer was Mr. Jackson, master of the *Comet* galley. It is interesting to note that it was the surgeon of von Huyn's own regiment who amputated one of his legs. See letter of Lieutenant James Duncan to

strong, occupied the ground near the two redoubts on Fen- April
wick's Neck which had been vacated by the 64th. The batteries on Charleston Neck were opened for the first time and
supported by those on Fenwick's Point with such effect that
the city was set on fire at two places. The rebels answered
the cannonade with great vigor. A Hessian grenadier had his
head shot off; another grenadier and seven Englishmen were
wounded. Lieutenant Colonel Webster, with a corps from the
third contingent, the 33rd Regiment, and the cavalry under
Lieutenant Colonel Tarleton, was detached to the bridge near
the head of the Cooper River.[1] Over this the rebels bring their
ammunition, provisions, etc., from the country, taking them
down on the other side to the city. This coup was crowned
with success. He came upon the rebel cavalry and militia so
unexpectedly and quickly that they could not even fire a
cannon. Thus he got possession of the bridge and some forty
wagons, boats, and sloops, all loaded with provisions and
munitions. He made prisoners of seventy-three dragoons and
militia and captured some hundred horses. Among the prisoners was Colonel Washington, who later escaped on his
swift horse, which they had neglected to take away from
him. A rebel major and twelve rank and file were killed. The
Lieutenant Colonel now continued his march down the other
side of the Cooper River in order to invest the city from that
side also.

On the 14th, 15th, and 16th there was heavy cannonading and
bombarding on both sides. An officer on one of the galleys
had one leg shot off and the other wounded,[2] a British grenadier was killed, and Huyn's camp near Fenwick's battery
was heavily bombarded, but without effect.

On the 17th and 18th there was heavy cannonading, during which

---

Elphinstone, where von Huyn's is called "of Hinde" (*Keith Papers*, I, 168).
The services of the Hessian surgeons were in general demand, as has been
gathered from the von Jungkenn Papers.

April lich angelangt; ingleichen kam heüte die Flotte von New-
york, mit noch 2500 Trouppen, worunter Regiment von
Dittfourth, hier an. Mit approchiren war es bis ohngefehr 18
Ehlen an die Rebellische Verhacke nunmehro gekomen.

Den 19ᵗⁿ Lezte Nacht veränderte der Admiral die Position der 4 Ga-
léeren und nahm 3 bey seine Flotte, welche bey Passirung
der Stadt den Aschlefluss hinunter eine terrible Feüer abhalten musten und bekamen 3 Todt u. 7 blessirte.

Den 20–
u. 21ᵗⁿ Von Beyderseit starck Canonirt und Bombardirt, und so dass
zuweilen von 12– zu 16 Bomben in die Stadt geworffen wurden. Hier war unsser Verlust 2 Todte und 7 blessirte, sämtl.
von der Leichten Jnfanterie. Nachmittags wurde vom Feind
um einen 6 Stündigen Stillstand nachgesucht, um einige Article wegen übergabe der Stadt an Sir Henry Clinton zu über-
schicken, ward gewilliget und Weisse fahnen ausgesteckt.
Die Articles waren nach der Anlage (Nᵒ 2.)
Die Antwort (Nᵒ 3.) von Sir Henry Clinton an den General
Lincoln ward überschickt, und keiner von denen verlangten
Articles, als nur dasjenige was vorhero offerirt worden zuge-
standen, auch soll dieser nicht gehalten werden, wann sich
die Hartnäckigkeit nicht legen würde. Der Stillstand wurde
nach Verlauff einer Stunde durch Bomben wieder gebrochen,
und die Feindseeligkeit eröfnet.

Den 22ᵗⁿ wurde ein Brittischer Grenadier Todtgeschossen. 4 Batailons von denen Neü angekomenen Trouppen würden Debarquirt, und die 1ᵗᵉ Nacht bey die Division des Commandirenden
Generals gelagert;—nachhero aber, um dem Websterischen
Corps den Rücken zu decken, ohne weit der Brücke wo jener
hinüber gangen, postirt und hatte communication mit solchen, so wie mit dem 3ᵗⁿ Treffen der Armée.

Den 23ᵗⁿ Debarquirten die andern 2 Batailons, wobey Regiment v.
Dittfourth welches an 2 Orthe postirt wurde, nehml. die
halbschied, wo die 2 von Sav[an]nah gekomene Provincial
Batailons und ein Theil vom Regt: Huyn a[m] Wappoo ge-

two British soldiers were wounded. We have been informed that Lieutenant Colonel Webster has safely reached the opposite side of the Cooper River, across from the city. The fleet arrived from New York with 2,500 additional troops, among them the Regiment von Dittfurth. Our approaches had by this time been advanced to within about eighteen yards of the rebels' abatis.

Last night the Admiral changed the position of the four galleys. Three of them, while passing down the Ashley River on their way to the fleet, withstood a terrific fire from the city. Three men were killed and seven wounded.

On these days severe cannonading and bombarding on both sides. At times as many as twelve to sixteen shells were thrown into the city at once. We had two killed and seven wounded, all of the light infantry. In the afternoon the enemy requested a truce of six hours to send to Sir Henry Clinton some articles concerning the capitulation of the city. The truce was granted, and white flags were hoisted. The articles are enclosed (No. 2 [5]).

Sir Henry Clinton replied to General Lincoln (No. 3 [6]) that he would allow no terms except those previously offered and that these, too, would not be given if their obstinacy continued. After one hour the truce was broken by a bombardment, and hostilities recommenced.

On the 22nd a British grenadier was killed. Four contingents of the new reinforcements were disembarked and during the first night were encamped with the division of the Commanding General. They then were posted near the bridge over which Webster's corps had passed, so that they might cover his rear. They had communication with the said corps as well as with the third division of the army.

On the 23rd the two remaining contingents disembarked. The first, von Dittfurth's Regiment, was split up into two divisions. The first of these encamped on Wappoo [mainland], where

April   standen, und der andere Theil unter ordre des Major von
Borck bey Tills pluff ohnweit das Forth Johnston; Das 2te
Bataillon hingegen occupirte den Grund auf Fenwicks Neck
bey denen Redoutten, und Regiment Huyn wurde nunmehro
wieder zusammengezogen und bey Perroneaus, wo *63* stand nebst
den 100 Man von Huyn, postirt, dagegen *jenes* in das 3te Treffen auf Charles Towns Neck gezogen wur[de,] nicht weniger
wurden die vorher erwehnte 2 Provincial Batailons u[n]ter
Ordre des Brigade General Battersons, mit diesem bey den
The[il] der Armée des Commandirenden Generals gelagert.

Vom 23^{tn} die Nacht machten die Rebellen einen Versuch auf ein uns-
zum 24^{tn} ser Jäger Posten, würden aber von der Leichten Jnfanterie
Soutinirt und trieben die Rebellen mit Verlust wieder in ihre
Linien, liesen 16 stück Gewehre zurück, wo vermuthlich deren eigener von Todtgeschossen oder blessirt und zurück ge-
schlept worden. Die Jäger hatten bey dieser Gelegenheit 4
hart blessirte und 2 wurden gefangen.

Vom 24^{tn} die Nacht attaquirten die Rebellen die Arbeiter, wo ein Brit-
zum 25^{tn} tischer Officer Todt blieb, und 2 von nehml. 71^{tn} Reg^t. Blessirt, ingleichen hatten diese etliche Zwantzig Todt und
Blessirte an unterofficiers und Gemeine, nicht weniger blieben 2 Hessische Grenadiers Todt und 11 dergleichen wurden
leicht blessirt; Ein Jngineur L^t. wurde durch ein Missver-
ständnis, von unssern eigenen Leüten, mit einem Bajonet hart
blessirt.

Zum 23^{tn} Lord Cornwallis übernahm das Commando über das Webster-
gehörig,   ische Corps, nachdem es mit verschiedenen Batailons und
Corps verstärckt worden.

Den 26
u. 27^{tn} Beyderseits starck Canonirt und Bombardirt.

Den 28^{tn} des Nachts Desertirte ein Hessischer Grenadier (Recrut, aus-
länder und Franzose von Geburth) gab denen Feinden einige
Losungen der verschiedenen Ablössungen Arbeits Commandos
und Piquets, wegen der precisen Stunden und Minuten,* wor-

* [Marginal note] Diese Nachricht brachte ein feindl: Deserteur.

the two battalions of provincials were stationed after coming from Savannah and where also part of Huyn's Regiment had been posted. The second, under the command of Major von Borck, took post at Dill's Bluff near Fort Johnson. The second contingent occupied the ground on Fenwick's Neck near the redoubts. Huyn's Regiment was united again by being posted with the hundred men of Huyn's at Peronneau's, where the 63rd had been. The latter joined the third division on Charleston Neck, while the two battalions of provincials under Brigadier General Paterson joined the Commanding General.

This night the rebels made a sally on one of our jäger posts, which, supported by the light infantry, drove them back within their lines. They left behind sixteen muskets, the owners of which were probably carried back dead or wounded. The jägers had four men severely wounded and two taken prisoners.

This night the rebels attacked the working parties, killing one officer and wounding two of the 71st Regiment. This regiment had also some twenty noncommissioned officers and soldiers killed and wounded, and the Hessian grenadiers had two killed and eleven slightly wounded. A lieutenant of the Engineers was, through some misunderstanding, severely bayoneted by our own men.

Lord Cornwallis took over the command of Webster's division after it had been reinforced by several battalions and corps.

Severe cannonading and bombarding on both sides.

During the night a Hessian grenadier deserted (recruit, foreigner, native Frenchman). He revealed to the enemy several passwords and informed them of the precise time of relieving the working parties and pickets.* As a consequence we had

* [Marginal note] This news was brought to us by an enemy deserter.

auf dann solche wohl attentirten, 3 Britten Todtschossen, nebst dergleichen 2 andere und ein Hessen Blessirten.

Den 30ᵗⁿ und 1ᵗⁿ Maij Ein Britte Todt und etliche starck blessirt, worunter ein Jäger, welchem ein Arm Abgeschossen worden. N^B kam die Nachricht, dass die Spanier ein Forth zu Pensecola weggenoññen, die Stadt selbsten aber hart belagerten. Ohnehin sind an diesem Orth lezten Winter 2 Compagnien Waldecker Gefangen word[en].

Den 2ᵗⁿ Ein Britte und ein Jäger Todt, und von erstern 2, von leztern einer blessirt.

Den 3ᵗⁿ Zwey Britten Todt und 3 dergleichen blessirt.

Den 4ᵗⁿ Ein Jäger Todt und 3 dergleichen und etliche Britten blessirt.

[Den] 5 u. 6ᵗⁿ Des Nachts wurden die Canonen in die nächsten nach dem Feind zu Neügemachten Forths gebracht. Die Rebellen machten eine terrible Canonade, wobey ein Britte Todt und einer Blessirt wurde. Lord Cornwallis Detachirte Ein Capt. u. 12 Pferdte von Cathcarts Legion, welche ein etwas weit rückwärts im Main recognosciren solten, Diese fielen mit dem lezthin echapirten Oberst Wassington ein und wurden gefangen. Lord-Cornwallis erhielte hiervon Nachricht, coññandirte den Coññandeur Oberst Lieut: besagter Legion, nahmens Tarleton mit dem gantzen augenblicklich nach, dieser attrapirte erwehnten Wassington, welcher 200 Pferdte bey sich hatte, zu Lenuds Ferry bey Santee, 25 Meilen von George Town, attaquirte ihn sehr lebhafft Tödtete etliche und 30, nahm 40 Gefangen, worunter ein Major und ein Capt:, nebst 140 Pferden und sprengte den überrest nebst dem Wassington zum Wasser hinein, nicht weniger brachte er den vorhero Gefangenen Capitain mit seinen 12 Dragoner wieder zurück.

Den 7ᵗⁿ Wurde Fergusons Corps vom Lord Cornwallis auf Sulivans Jsland gesetzt, ingleichen vom Admiral etliche 100 Marins und Matrosen, worauf lezterer das darauf seyende considerable Forth Moultrie auffordern liess, mit dem Bedeüten, wo sie nicht das Forth übergäben und es auf eine fernere Attaque

three British soldiers killed and two others and one Hessian wounded.

One Englishman killed and several men severely wounded, amongst them a jäger, whose arm was shot off. N.B.: We received the news that the Spaniards had taken a fort at Pensacola and were laying siege to the city itself. Last winter two companies of Waldeckers were taken prisoners there. *The 30th of April and the 1st of May*

One Englishman and one jäger killed and two Englishmen and one jäger wounded. *The 2nd*

Two British soldiers killed and three wounded. *The 3rd*

A jäger killed and three others, as well as several Englishmen, wounded. *The 4th*

During the night the guns were taken into the redoubts nearest the enemy. The rebels fired fiercely, killing one Englishman and wounding one. Lord Cornwallis detached a captain and twelve horse of Cathcart's Legion to reconnoitre far back on the mainland. Falling in with Colonel Washington, who had recently escaped, they were taken prisoners. Lord Cornwallis, on receiving this news, ordered Lieutenant Colonel Tarleton to pursue the enemy immediately with his entire force. Tarleton encountered Washington with 200 horse at Lenud's Ferry on the Santee, twenty-five miles from Georgetown. Attacking him quickly he killed some thirty men, took forty prisoners, including a major and a captain, captured 140 horses, and drove Washington with the rest into the river. Furthermore, he rescued the captain and the twelve dragoons who had been taken. *The 5th and 6th*

On the 7th Lord Cornwallis sent Ferguson's Corps to Sullivan Island, and the Admiral sent some hundred marines and sailors. The Admiral then summoned the enemy to surrender Fort Moultrie, threatening that, if they did not and thus made an attack and an assault necessary, no one should leave alive.

Maij und Sturm ankoñen liessen, keiner mit dem Leben davon koñen solte, worauf sie Capitulirten, das Forth mit aller Munition, Provision und 40 Canonen dem Admiral einraümten und sich zu Kriegs-Gefangene, ihrer Capitulation gemäs ergaben. Die Anzahl Gefangene waren 120 Man, unter Ordre des Oberst Scotts.

Den 8^{tn} Morgens 5 uhr schickte der Coñandirende General eine Flag-Truce nach dem General Lincoln in die Stadt, und lies ihm nach der Anlage (N° 4.) seine fernere Meynung, ingleichen die Lage, worinnen sich nunmehro ein Lincoln befand, bekant machen. Es wurde hierauf mit einem Stillstand übereingekommen, welcher von Zeit zu Zeit bis den 9^{tn} des Abends 9 uhr prolongirt wurde; es wurde nicht übereingekoñen, sondern nach dem Gewöhnlichen Retrait-Schuss, die Feindseeligkeit aufs äusserste,* durch alle Press-Batterien eröfnet, und wurde von unsserer Seite mit Bomben werffen, welche dem Feind, nach allen Nachrichten, unendlichen Schaden gethan, bis den 11^{tn} 11 uhr continuiret, worauf der General Lincoln eine Flag Truce zu unssern Vorposten schickte, welche nicht acceptirt, sondern der Ordre gemäs, mit Feüer zurück gewiesen wurde. worauf er eine 2te schickte, welche die Vorposten mundlich Bedeütete: wie besagter General Lincoln resolvirt hätte, die Stadt Sir Henry Clinton nach denen von diesem offerirten Articuln einzuräumen, worauf sie angenoñen, und von beyden Seiten Commissairs ernannt wurden, welche des Nachts 11 uhr, wegen übergabe der Stadt, nach der Anlage (N° 5.) überein kamen.

Den 12^{tn} Nachmittags 2 uhr marchirte ein Detachement Brittisch- und Hessisch[e] Grenadiers nebst dem 7^{tn} 41^{tn} und 63^{tn} Reg^t. in die Stadt und fassten Posto, an denen Pforten und Haupt

---

* [Marginal note] Den 10^{tn} würde der Lieut: Fritsch vom Batailon Graff nebst noch einigen Grenadiers Blessirt, ingleichen 2 Britten Todt u. verschiedene verwundet.

They capitulated, surrendering the fort with all the ammu-   May
nition and provisions and forty guns to the Admiral and
giving themselves up as prisoners of war in accordance with
the terms of the capitulation. The prisoners numbered one
hundred and twenty and had been under the command of
Colonel Scott.

At five o'clock in the morning the Commanding General   The 8th
dispatched a flag of truce to General Lincoln, once more
stating his opinion and acquainting him with the situation
which now confronted him (enclosure No. 4 [7]). A truce
was agreed upon, which was repeatedly prolonged until the
9th at nine o'clock at night. No agreement was reached, and,
after the customary retreat gun, hostilities commenced again.*
All breach batteries were brought to bear, and our bombardment, which, according to information received, did infinite
damage, continued till the 11th when, at eleven o'clock,
General Lincoln sent a flag of truce to our advanced posts.
The flag was not permitted to pass, but, according to orders,
was turned back with fire. Then a second flag was sent, and
the advanced posts were told by word of mouth that General Lincoln had decided to surrender the city to Sir Henry
Clinton according to the articles offered by him. The truce
was then accepted, and both sides appointed commissioners,
who at eleven o'clock at night came to an agreement
upon the terms of the capitulation, according to the enclosure
(No. 5 [8]).

At two o'clock in the afternoon a detachment of British   The 12th
and Hessian grenadiers, and the 7th, 41st,[1] and 63rd Regi-

* [Marginal note] On the 10th Lieutenant Fritsch of Graff's Battalion
and several other grenadiers were wounded, while two Englishmen were
killed and a number injured.
[1] Should read "42nd."

Fortifications,* und sämtliche Rebellische Flaggen wurden
herunter genom̄en, und von denen Feinde[n] welche ohngefehr aus 5000. bestehen, das Gewehr Gestreckt. ingleichen
nahm der Admiral besitz von denen Feindlichen Schiffen.

*[Marginal note] General Major-Lessle führte die Trouppen in die Stadt.

ments marched into the city and took post at the gates and principal fortifications.* All rebel flags were struck, and the enemy, numbering about five thousand, piled arms, while the Admiral took possession of all enemy ships.

J. C. v. Huyn

* [Marginal note] Major General Leslie led the troops into the city.

LETTERS
TO
BARON VON JUNGKENN

LETTERS TO BARON VON JUNGKENN

FROM CAPTAIN JOHANN HINRICHS

HOCHWOHLGEBOHRNER FREYHERR,
HOCHGEBIETENDER HERR GENERAL MAJOR!

Beygehend habe ich die Ehre Euer Hochwohlgebohren, den Auszug aus meinem Hand-Journal unterthänigst zu überreichen.—Es ist der Anfang einer Winter-Expedition, die die Wegnahme Charlestown, eines durch Natur und Kunst befestigten Platzes zur Absicht hat.—Der Feind macht Minen den Ort zu behaupten, und bemühet sich, seit vorigem Herbste uns die Wegname desselben so viel möglich zu erschweren. 5000 Mann sind die Besatzung unter Gen: Maj: Lincoln, und Gen: Wayne mit der feindlich: Light Infanterie und Grenadier werden stündlich erwartet.—Jch vermuthe nicht dass Gen: Clinton zum zweitenmal wieder unverrichteter Sache zurück gehen wird.—Wir werden es also nehmen. Mein erstes Bemühen wird dann seyn, Eu: Hochwohlgebohren mit einem getreuen Plann und relation unterthänigst aufzuwarten, und mein ganzes Bemühen während dieser Expedition, wird seyn, auch hier, so wie ich allezeit gesucht habe, zu zeigen, mit welchem Eifer ich wünsche, den edlen Namen eines Hessen zu verdienen.

Mit der grössten Hochachtung empfele ich mich Euer Hoch-

¹ This letter accompanied the first part of Captain Hinrichs' diary, i.e. through February 10, 1780.

LETTERS TO BARON VON JUNGKENN

FROM CAPTAIN JOHANN HINRICHS

RIGHT HONORABLE BARON,
HIGH AND MIGHTY MAJOR GENERAL:—

Herewith I humbly present to your Lordship the extract of my private journal.[1] It covers the beginning of a winter expedition which aims at the reduction of Charleston, a town well fortified by nature and art. The enemy seem intent on defending the place and have been engaged since last fall in rendering its reduction as difficult as possible. Its garrison under Major General Lincoln amounts to 5,000 men, and General Wayne[2] with the light infantry and the grenadiers is expected any hour. I do not believe that General Clinton will have to withdraw a second time without having effected his purpose. In other words, we shall reduce the city! Then my first endeavor will be to submit to your Lordship a faithful plan and account. Through the entire expedition I shall strive with all my might, as I have always done, to show how anxiously I desire to deserve the noble name of a Hessian.

---

[2] General Wayne did not come to swell the number of prisoners. In January, 1780, he retired to his home in Chester County, Pennsylvania, where he remained until May, when Washington asked him to resume command of the Pennsylvania line.

wohlgebohren seiner Gewogenheit, und nenne mich mit Verzug

Hochwohlgebohrner Freyherr
Hochgebietender Herr General-Major.
Euer Hochwohlgebohren
unterthäniger

J. Hinrichs
Staabs Capit. im Jäger Corps

North Edisto River South Carolina
  d: 10 Febr. 1780.

FROM MAJOR PHILIP VON WURMB

Hochwohlgebohrner Frey Herr
Gnädig Hoch zu gebiethender Herr Generall!
EwEr Exellence habe die Ehre gehabt zu berichten das mit einen de Daschment Jäger von 250 Man 3 Capitaines 4 offciers, mit der Arme nach South America den 20ten December abgangen bien unser See Reise ist nicht die beste gewesen. Viele Schiffe sind verunglückt, die Menschen aber noch gerettet, auser das Schiff *Anna* worauf eine Chasseur Compagnie aus denen Hessischen Regimenter gezogen, unter den Commando des Captaein Hanger, und Worauf sich auch 1 Feldscher 2 unter offcier und 27 Jager befinden, vermüst worden es ist bies dado noch keine gewisse nachricht ein gekommen, man will aber vor gewies sagen das Sie in Westindien ein gelauffen währen, wier wollen das beste hoffen, Ew: Excellence habe nun die Gnade von unsern glücklichen Progressen auf den lande zu berichten Den 30ten Martz sind wier vor Charlstawn gekommen, und die belagerung gleich angefangen, und solche den 11ten Maij zu ende gebracht Die Garnison ist Krieges gefangen, eine schöne Artilleri haben wir hier vorfunden, es hatt uns zwar menschen genug gekostet und besonders uns Jäger, so Ew: Excellence aus den bey

With the greatest esteem I commend myself to the good will of your Lordship and remain,

Right Honorable Baron,

High and Mighty Major General,

Your Lordship's

obedient

J. Hinrichs

Staff Captain in the Jäger Corps

North Edisto River, South Carolina

Feb. 10, 1780

FROM MAJOR PHILIP VON WURMB

Right Honorable Baron,

Gracious High and Mighty General:—

I have had the honor of informing your Excellency that on the 20th of December I departed with the army for the South, commanding a detachment of jägers consisting of 250 men, 3 captains, and 4 subaltern officers. Our passage was by no means a good one. Many ships foundered. The men, however, were all saved except those on the *Anna*, which carried a company of chasseurs drawn from the Hessian regiments, Captain Hanger commanding, as well as a surgeon, two noncommissioned officers, and twenty-seven jägers. To date we have no reliable information concerning their fate, but it is said with a good deal of assurance that they have reached the West Indies. We shall hope for the best. Now I take the liberty of informing Your Excellency about our progress on land. On the 30th of March we arrived before Charleston and immediately began to lay siege to the city, which capitulated on the 11th of May. The garrison are prisoners of war. We also came into possession of considerable artillery. To be sure, it cost us a good many lives, especially jägers, as Your Excellency will see from the enclosed return which I have the

liegenden Rapport so die Gnade zu über senden ersehen werden, die Zahl der gefangenen und Canonen auch ihre Schiffe kan nicht bestim̄en, da wier ordre haben so gleich zu marschiren, und nicht wissen wan unser zu ruckkunft ist, das Schiff aber bald abgeth so wolte es nicht verfehlen, Ew: Excellence den Rapport zu über senden, und mich zu Dero gnädigen an dencken zu Recommandiern,   Mit den grösten Estiem habe die Gnade zu seyn,

Ew: Excellence
unter thaniger Diener
PHILIP VON WURMB
Major

Im Lager bey
Charlstawn
d. 13ten Maij

FROM MAJOR WILHELM VON WILMOWSKY

HOCHWOHLGEBOHRNER HERR
HÖCHSTGEEHRTESTER-HOCHGEBIETHENDER HERR GENERAL-
   LIEUTENANT!

Ew: Excellenz von der Heute mittag in besitz genommenen und wichtigen Eroberung der Stadt Charlestown, und was sich während der 40. Tägigen Belagerung merckwurdiges dabey zugetragen, davon nehme ich mir die unterthänige Freiheit einen kurzen Bericht abzustatten:

Durch die geschwinde absendung einer Fregate, um diese gluckliche ausgeführte expedition nach London zu bringen, und welche von hier morgen abseegelt, werde ich ausser stand gesetzt einen gezeigneten Dispositions-Plan beyzufügen: Ew: Excellenz wollen gnädigst dieses, und dass ich nicht ein ganz accurates Verzeichniss aller Eroberten Stücke und anzahl Gefangene melden kan, zu meiner Entschuldigung aufnehmen, zumalen ich durch eine unpässlichkeit in welche mich ein harter Fall mit dem Pferd seit 12. Tagen zu bette

honor of sending. I cannot state the exact number of prisoners, guns, and vessels, for we have orders to march immediately and do not know when we shall be back. Since a ship is to sail soon, I did not want to neglect an opportunity of sending Your Excellency this report and commending myself to your kind remembrance. With the highest esteem I have the honor of being

Your Excellency's
humble servant
PHILIP VON WURMB
Major

In camp near
Charleston
May 13

FROM MAJOR WILHELM VON WILMOWSKY

RIGHT HONORABLE LORD,
MOST ESTEEMED HIGH AND MIGHTY LIEUTENANT GENERAL:—

I take the liberty, Your Excellency, of making a brief report concerning the significant reduction of the city of Charleston, which came into our possession at noon today, and the noteworthy events that occurred during the forty days' siege.

Since a frigate which is to take the news of this successful expedition to London is to sail tomorrow, I am unable to enclose a plan of the disposition. Your Excellency will be so kind as to pardon me for this, and also for not furnishing an accurate account of all the captured pieces and the number of prisoners, especially since I have been confined to my bed for twelve days as a result of a bad fall from my horse and am not yet able to do service or to go out to obtain the necessary information.

gehalten und noch ausserstand bin Dienst zu thun oder Aus-
zugehen um die dazu nöthige nachrichten einzuziehen.

Die Anzahl der Gefangenen belauf sich über 6000. Mann
und aus denen Fortification-Wercken bey der Stadt herum
sind über 120. stück Canons erobert worden. Jngleichen Eine
Französche, und zwei rebellen-Fregaten jede von 28. Canons,
Vier Armirte-Schife von 14. bis zu 20. Canons. Dreysig kleine
Kaufmanns Schife von 2. und 3. Masten, 80 Boots. Ein grosser
vorrath von Munition, provision und Schifsgeräthschaften
sind in den Magazinen gefunden worden.

Der Anfang zur Belagerung und die erste Arbeit an unsren
Trenchéen wurde in der Nacht zwischen d: 31.^{t} Martz und 1.^{t}
april gemacht und 3. Redouten verfertigt, welches so in stiller ordnung geschahe dass der Feind nichts davon bis den andern Morgen gewahr wurde.

Der Feind fing den Morgen an mit einer heftigen Cannonade
auf diese redouten, und auf die Arbeiters welche die folgende
Nächte angestelt waren, die Erstere parallelle fertig zu bringen; welche aus 4. redouten und 3. Batterien construirt war.
Als diese sämtl: im stande, welches d: 13ten april war, so
fingen wir den ersten Canon-Schuss mit 28. st: 24. lb^{er} und 2.
Haubitz[en] auf die feindl: Werke zu spielen an. Der Feind
hatte gegen unsre front eine gleiche Anzahl Canonen die an
diesem Tage eine 4. stündige heftige Cannonade machten.

Von unsrer seite hat man des nachts nicht mit Canons gefeuer
wol aber mit Mörschels und einer menge kleiner Coehorns
Bomben geworfen; Der Feind hingegen hat wenige Nächte
verstreichen lassen in deren weniger dann 300. Canon-Schüsse
gethan worden.

D: 10^t april kamen 9. KriegsSchife unter der Anfuhrung des
Admiral Arbuthnot in den Hafen herein: Diese musten das
Forts (Sulivan genant) welches an der Mundung vom Hafen
liegt und mit 40. st: Canons, wovon die mehrsten 32. lb.
schiesen besetzt war, in einer distance von 200. Schritt passi-

The number of prisoners is over 6,000 men, and we have come into possession of over 120 guns (taken in the fortifications of the city), a French and two rebel frigates, each of 28 guns, four armed ships, 14 to 20 guns, 30 small merchantmen, two- and three-masted, and 80 boats. In the magazines we found great quantities of ammunition, provisions, and ship's furniture.

The siege began on the night of the 31st of March, when we started work on our trenches and erected three redoubts, all of which was done so quietly that the enemy knew nothing of it till the following morning.

In the morning the enemy opened a violent cannonade upon these redoubts and upon the working parties that were engaged during subsequent nights in finishing the first parallel, which consisted of four redoubts and three batteries. When all this was finished on the 13th of April, we opened fire on the enemy's works with twenty-eight 24-pounders and two howitzers. The enemy had an equal number of cannons opposing us, which that day fired violently for four hours.

Our side did not fire guns at night; but mortars and a quantity of small coehorns threw many shells. The enemy, however, let few nights pass in which they fired fewer than three hundred shots.

On the 10th of April nine warships entered the harbor under the command of Admiral Arbuthnot. They had to pass one after another within two hundred paces of a fort (called Sullivan), which is situated at the entrance of the harbor and is fortified with forty guns, mostly 32-pounders. All the ships passed the fort safely under a heavy cannonade. One ship lost half of her mainmast, and the total loss in seamen was thirteen killed and fifteen wounded.

ren, und zwar ein Schif nach dem andren: Alle Schife kamen glücklich unter einer heftigen Canonade vor diesem Forts vorbey. Ein Schif verlohre den halben mittel-mast und alle Schife zusammen verlohren an See-Leuten 13. Todte und 15. blessirte.

Die Rhede, wo man zum Hafen über fahren muss, hat nicht die Höhe dass ein Schif von 64. Canons übergehen kan, die drey grösten Schife blieben auf der Rhede in See liegen und kreuzten unsre Kusten. Ein Schif von 44. Canons und die Fregaten von 32. und 28. Canons welche über die Höhe auf der Rhede passirten, mussten zuvor durch Ausladen ihrer Canons Sich leichter machen und nach geschehener uberfahrt wieder die Canons einladen; welches einen grossen aufenthalt in der ganzen operation und den Schifen viele arbeit machte.

Den 18.ᵗ apr: kam alhier eine Verstärkung von 2600. Mann von NewYork hier an. Durch diesen renfort wurde die Stadt in eine volkommene blocade gebracht: Lord Cornwallis wurde mit 2500. Mann uber den Fluss Cooper detachirt und nahm possession von denen Schantzen auf Montplaissant von welchen der Hafen so wie vom Forts Sulivan bestrichen werden kan, auch wurde zugleich das Fort Sulivan blocquirt.

Die Stadt Charlestown liegt an der spitze einer Land-Zunge welche 1½ stunde lang ist und eine egale breite von 1500. Schritte hat, und zur lincken der Cooper River (ohngefehr 3000. Schritt breit) und zur reckten [sic] seite der Ashly River von 1800. Schritt breit.

Den 21ᵗ apr: da Unsere zweyte parallelle fertig war und Unsre Hessische Jägers dadurch im stande waren denen feindl: Artilleristen vielen schaden durch ihr accuratesse feuern in den Schisscharten zu thun, so legte sich das starke feuern mit Canons am Tage mercklich; Gegen abend 5. uhr schickte der Commandant der Rebellen General Major Lincoln und offerirte die Stadt Uns einzuräumen; seine propositiones waren aber nicht anzunehmen, weilen er just nichts als die leeren Häusser und die Stadt uns ubergeben wolte und

The channel through which one must pass to get into the harbor is not deep enough for a 64-gun ship. The three largest ships remained on the open sea and cruised before our coast. One ship of 44 guns and two frigates of 32 and 28 which came through the channel had to lighten their cargoes by unloading some guns, which later had to be taken on again. This caused considerable delay in the entire operation and gave much trouble to the ships.

On the 18th of April we received a reinforcement of 2,600 men from New York. With the help of these troops the city was completely invested. Lord Cornwallis with 2,500 men was detached across the Cooper River, and he took possession of the works on Mount Pleasant, from which the harbor can be raked. At the same time we blockaded Fort Sullivan, another harbor defense.

The city of Charleston is situated on the tip of a neck of land about five miles long and fifteen hundred paces wide, with the Cooper River, about three thousand paces wide, at the left and the Ashley River, eighteen hundred paces wide, at the right.

On the 21st of April our second parallel was finished, and our Hessian jägers, excellent marksmen that they are, fired with good results on the enemy's gunners in the embrasures. Hence the cannonading began to subside noticeably during the day. Toward five o'clock in the evening the Commander-in-Chief of the rebels, Major General Lincoln, sent out a flag offering to surrender the city. His proposals, however, were not acceptable because he would surrender nothing but a city of empty houses. Furthermore, he demanded two days to take his belongings aboard the ships and twelve days during which he could march off quietly and unpursued.

The Admiral could not pass the city and come up the

hierzu verlangte er auch noch 2. Tage Zeit die sachen in die Schife packen zu können, und auf seinen Abmarsch ruhig und ohne verfolgt 12. Tage gelassen zu werden.

Der Admiral könte nicht mit seinen Schifen bey der Stadt vorbey und den Cooper River herauf kommen, ohne die gröste gefahr zu stehen von den batterien der Stadt sowol als von den Feindlich: Schifen, alzu gross an seinen Schifen schaden zu leiten oder wol gar zuruckgeschlagen zu werden: Weshalben Er dann seine maasregeln zur attaque des Forts Sulivan so gut zunehmen gewust dass Er den 6.ten Maij in besitz des Forts und die garnison von 130. Mann sich zu Gefangen ergaben.

Den 8.^t Maij, da die 3te parallelle fertig, auch einen Canal gegraben war, der das wasser aus dem Graben ableitete und unsre avancirten batterien mit 40. st. Canons beplanzt waren: Wurde die Feindl: garnison wiedrum aufgefodert auch zugleich die Capitulations Puncten vorgelegt "dass die Continental troupen und militz ihre Bagage behalten, auch den Einwohner der Stadt (welche Sämtl: auch das Gewehr ergrifen) ihre Häuser und Güther in der Stadt gelassen werden solte"

Dieses wurde von den rebellen Abgeschlagen, die entschliesung dazu wurde aber bis den andren Tag (d: 9.^t) abends 6. uhr verzögert und da erst die abschlägl: antwort eingeschickt. Hierauf folgte sogleich eine der heftigsten Cannonade die die ganze Nacht hindurch fortdauerte und man wil rechnen dass mehr als 1000. Schüsse durch Canons vom Feind geschehen sind; wodurch nur 5. Mann von Unsrer Seite blessirt worden.

Den 11.^t Nachmittags 3. uhr offerirte der Comandant General Lincoln die Übergabe der Stadt und nach denen vor 3. Tage von Uns eingesandten Puncten zur Capitulation zu unterschreiben welche heute morgen beschlossen und von Sr Excel: dhl: General en Chef Sir Henry Clinton und Admiral Arbuthnot unterschrieben worden.

Cooper River without running the greatest danger of the batteries of the city and the enemy's ships doing considerable damage, or even repulsing him. However, he planned his attack on Fort Sullivan so well that he came into possession of the fort on the 6th of May, making prisoners of its garrison, numbering 130 men.

On the 8th of May, when the third parallel was finished and a sap had been dug to bleed the ditch, and when our advanced batteries mounted forty guns, the enemy was again summoned to surrender and at the same time presented with articles of capitulation, permitting "the Continental troops and the militia to retain their baggage and the inhabitants of the city (all of whom had been under arms) to keep their houses and other property."

This the rebels refused, though their final decision was not given us till the following day (the 9th), at six o'clock in the evening, when their refusal was dispatched to us. Then followed one of the heaviest cannonades, which lasted through the entire night. It is calculated that more than a thousand shots were fired by the enemy, which, however, wounded only five of our men.

On the 11th, at three o'clock in the afternoon, the commandant, General Lincoln, offered to surrender the city and sign the articles of capitulation which had been sent him three days before. The negotiations were completed this morning and signed by his Excellency, the Honorable Commander-in-Chief, Sir Henry Clinton, and by Admiral Arbuthnot.

The generals taken prisoners are:
Lincoln, Scott, Hogan, Woodford, Simons.[1]

[1] Simons was a colonel. The other generals were McIntosh, Moultrie, and Duportail.

Die Nahmens der 5. Gefangenen Generals sind.
Lincoln—Scott—Hozam—Woodfort—Simion.

Der ich mich zu Hohen Wohlwollen Hochdenenselben
unterthänig empfehle und mit der volkommensten Ehrfurcht
verharre

Hochgebiethender Herr General

Ew. Excellenz

ganz unterthäniger Diener

W. von Wilmowsky

bey Charlestown in South-Carolina
d: 13ᵗ. Maij 1780.

FROM CAPTAIN JOHANN EWALD

Hochwohlgebohrner Frey Herr,
Insonders Hochzugebietender Herr General!

Sᵉ Excellentz werden gnädigst erlauben, dass ich meine
unterthänige gratulation zu der neüen Beförderung gehor-
samst abstatte. Nichts in der Welt kann mir theürer seyn als
die beständige Erhaltung und hohem Wohlseyn von Dieselben, da ich Niemand anders mein Glück im Dienst zu ver-
dancken habe.

Sᵉ Excellentz habe auch unterthänigst benachrichten wol-
len, dass, nachdem die Armee in dem Nord Edisto fluss auf
Simons Eiland gelandet, die Märsche über Iohns, Iames und
Wappoo Inseln fortgesetzt, den Ashley fluss bey Draitons
landungs fluss passirt, solche die Vestung Charlestown d: 30ᵗ
Mertz berennt.

Den 3ᵗᵉⁿ April wurden die Tranchées eröfnet, und den 8ᵗ*
hatten wir die 3ᵗᵉ paralelle biss an den Rand ihres ersten
Grabens poussirt, den 11ᵗ Maij wurde dieser Graben in der
vergangenen Nacht durch eine Gallerie passirt und ein Logement unter dem heftigsten Geschütz und klein Gewehr

---

* [Marginal correction] Maij.

Humbly commending myself to your good will and with the most profound reverence, I remain,

High and Mighty General,
Your Excellency's
most humble servant
W. von Wilmowsky

Near Charleston, South Carolina
May 13, 1780

FROM CAPTAIN JOHANN EWALD

Right Honorable Baron,
Especially High and Mighty General:—

Your Excellency will kindly permit me to extend my congratulations on your new advancement.[1] Nothing in the world can be dearer to me than His Serene Highness' benevolence toward your Excellency, since I owe my good fortune in military service to no one but you.

At the same time I humbly wish to inform your Excellency that, after the army had landed on Simmons Island from the North Edisto River and proceeded over Johns, James, and Wappoo islands, then crossed the Ashley River at Drayton's landing, it began to advance upon the city on the 30th of March.

On the 3rd of April the trenches were opened, and by the 8th of May we had pushed the third parallel to the edge of the enemy's first ditch. In the night of the 10–11th this ditch was crossed by means of a gallery. A lodgment between the

---

[1] The editor was unable to ascertain to what new advancement Captain Ewald here refers. According to Fritz Herrmann, *Die Familie Jungkenn* . . . , Baron von Jungkenn became minister of state in 1780 and lieutenant general in 1781. However, if the last date is correct, why does von Wilmowsky address him in both letters as lieutenant general?

feüer, welches seit zwey Tagen von beyden Seiten anhaltend gewesen, zwischen denen beyden feindlichen Verhacken gemacht, und den 11ᵗ gegen 2 Uhr Nachmittags schlug die Garnison Chammade, und den 12ᵗ Nachmittags gegen 4 Uhr streckte selbige das Gewehr. Es synd bei dieser Gelegenheit 5,000 Mann benebst denen Generals Lincolms, Multrie und Woodfurht zu Gefangene gemacht wurden, rechnet man die Schifs Canons; so synd über 200 in unsere Hände gerahten. Drey Fregatten benebst 3 Galleeren und eine grosse Anzahl bewafneter und Transport Schiffe synd ebenfals bey dieser Gelegenheit genoṁen worden, und ich hoffe, dass dieser Streich, die Krone Engeland von Pensecola bis Iames fluss in kurtzem zum Meister machen wird, besonders ist es sehr gut vor die Bourgognsche Armee und unsere übrigen Gefangene. Die Vestungs Wercke bestanden, aus einem Hornwerck, welches im Rücken oder in der Kehle gegen die Stadt durch einen hohen Wall und pallisadirten Graben bevestigt war, das Hornwerck hatte einen breiten und tieffen bekleideten Graben, über welchen eine Zugbrücke gieng, die durch einen halben Mond gedeckt war. Unter dem kleinen Gewehr schuss von diesem Werck lag das neüe Retranchement, welches einen einwärts halben Mond en redans ausmachte, dessen Flanquen durch detachirte Wercke gedeckt und deren Seiten an die Cooper und Ashley Flüsse gesetzt waren, dieses retranchement hatte einen Graben, welcher pallisadirt und mit Spanischen Reüter und einem Verhack bordirt war. Unter dem kleinem Gewehr Schuss von diesem Retranchement lage das sogenannte Canal oder Avant Fosse, welches ebenfals mit einem Verhack bordirt war, dieses Canal war 6 fuss tief und 18 breit und war besonders vor die Flanquen derer feindlichen Wercke bey der Fluht, mit 5 fuss wasser, angefüllt, dessen beyde Uffer auch morastig synd. Nach der wasser Seite war die Stadt ebenfalls mit sehr guten batterien versehen, und in dem Cooper fluss hatte der feind zehn bis zwölff Schiffe ver-

ment as well as the light infantry has orders to be ready to march at any time. I suppose we shall proceed to Georgetown, where there is said to be a fort of four bastions occupied by 1,500 men. The most unpleasant things in these provinces are the intense heat and the innumerable sand flies, whose bites are quite painful,[1] not to mention the fact that at every step in the woods one is likely to meet with a rattlesnake or some other venomous creature. This very day a poisonous snake was shot fifty paces from my hut. However, I realize that one can get used to almost anything.

I commend myself to your further graces and am in deepest reverence

Your Excellency's
most humble
J. EWALD

Before Charleston
May 13, 1780

FROM MAJOR WILHELM VON WILMOWSKY

RIGHT HONORABLE SIR,
HIGH AND MIGHTY LIEUTENANT GENERAL:—

To inform your Excellency of the departure of a part of the army from Charleston, I take the liberty of dispatching a short report on the packet extraordinary that is to leave for England immediately.

Embarkation began day before yesterday, and this morning at four o'clock his Excellency, the Commanding General, put to sea with the following troops: the four battalions of Hessian grenadiers, the detachment of Hessian jägers, the

---

[1] The German has *unempfindlich*, which, however, must be a slip of the pen, for we expect *empfindlich* (cf. the writer's statement on p. 45).

Engländ: Grenadiers Leichte Jnfanterie, das 42te Regiment, und die Queen Ranger (ein provincial Bat^{on})
Dieses Corps wird zur Armée in NewYork stossen und S^e Exc: dhl: General en Chef das commando aldort wieder übernehmen.
Lord Cornwallis bleibt mit einem Corps von 6000. Mann in der Provinz von South-Carolina; stehet aber anjezo auf der Grenze von North-Carolina und zwar jenseits Georgetown ohnweit Cambden;
Zur Garnisons in Charlestown ist zurükgeblieben, das Reg^t v. Ditfourth und das v. Huyn, ingl: kom̄t das Reg. d'Angenelli von Savannah welches so eben unsre Flotte passirt, und gleich in den Hafen einlaufen wird. Seit dem Besitz von Charlestown haben sich mehr denn 2000. Landleute zum Dienst Sr Brittanisch: Majestät freywillig anerbothen und sind mit eignen Wafen angekom̄men, wovon die mehresten den Eyd der Treue, doch mit dem Beding abgelegt haben, dass sie nicht gezwungen seyn wollen gegen ihre eigne Landsleute zu fechten, hingegen ihr leben gerne wieder Französche und Spanische troupen aufopfern wolten. Der rest der rebellen in dieser Provinz, welcher ohngefehr aus 700. Mann bestanden, ist durch ein detachement von 300. Pferden und 200. Man Jnfanterie (welche einen March von 100. Engl: Meilen in Zeit von 48. stunden abgelegt haben) unter der anführung eines Oberst Lieut: Tarleton eingeholt und mit solcher vivacité attaquirt worden, dass 170. Rebellen niedergehauen und der ganze überrest nebst 4. Canons 3. Fahnen und sämtl: bagage eingebracht worden sind.

Ein Schif von Providence so Unsre Flotte so eben passirt, brachte eine angenehme nachricht von der Flotte des Admiral Sir George Rodney, welcher ohnweit Martinique die Französche Flotte begegnet und sie angegriefen, dabey aber nicht mehr dann 4. Seiner Schife zum Fechten anbringen können, indem die Französische Flotte mehr durch starken Wind

English grenadiers and light infantry, the 42nd Regiment, and the Queen's Rangers (a provincial battalion).

This corps will join the army in New York, and his Excellency, the Commanding General, will there resume the command of the whole army.

Lord Cornwallis with a corps of 6,000 men is remaining in the province of South Carolina. At present, however, he is stationed on the North Carolina border, beyond Georgetown, not far from Camden.

For a garrison in Charleston there remain von Dittfurth's and von Huyn's Regiments, while d'Angelelli's is coming from Savannah. This very moment d'Angelelli's is passing our fleet and will enter the harbor directly. Since Charleston has been in our possession, more than 2,000 men have come from the country who have voluntarily offered their services to His Britannic Majesty. They have brought their own arms with them, but the majority have sworn allegiance on condition that they will not be compelled to fight against their own countrymen, although they will gladly sacrifice their lives against French and Spanish troops. The rest of the rebels in this province, numbering about 700, have been surprised by a detachment of 300 horse and 200 infantry under the command of Lieutenant Colonel Tarleton, who (after a forced march of a hundred English miles in forty-eight hours) attacked them with such ferocity that he cut down 170 of them. The rest, together with four guns, three flags, and all their baggage, were taken prisoners.

A ship from [New] Providence, which has just passed our fleet, brought some pleasant news concerning the fleet of Admiral Sir George Rodney, who attacked the French fleet near Martinique. Only four of his ships, however, could engage, for the French fleet was more favored by a stiff

begünstigt gewesen Die 4. Engl: Schife haben jedoch sich von zwey Französche Schife von 80. Canons bemeistert und sind solche d: 15^t Maij, in St Kitts eingebracht worden: Der Admiral Sir George Rodney ist nach den Jnsuln Grenada und sucht die Französche Flotte zum engagement zu bringen.

Bey abstattung meines unterthänigst: raports erbitte ich von Ew: Excellenz mir Hochderoselben gnädiges Wolwollen aus; Der ich in vollkommenster Ehrfurcht verharre

Hochgebietender Herr General Lieutenant

Ew. Excellenz

ganz unterthäniger Diener

W. von Wilmowsky

Vor der Rehde bey Charlestown
auf dem Kriegs Schif Romulus
d: 4^t Junij 1780.

breeze; but these four ships captured two French ships of 80 guns, which were brought into St. Kitts on the 15th of May. Admiral Sir George Rodney then proceeded to the Island of Grenada, where he will attempt to force the French fleet to engage.

Making this humble report I ask for your Excellency's kind benevolence and remain in most profound reverence,

High and Mighty Lieutenant General,
Your Excellency's
most humble servant
W. VON WILMOWSKY

In Charleston road
On the *Romulus* man-of-war
June 4, 1780

INDEX

INDEX

(Reference is made only to the English text.)